DEMOCRATIC HOPE

Democratic Hope

PRAGMATISM AND THE
POLITICS OF TRUTH

✳ ✳ ✳

ROBERT B. WESTBROOK

CORNELL UNIVERSITY PRESS

ITHACA AND LONDON

First published 2005 by Cornell University Press

Printed in the United States of America

Library of Congress Cataloging-in-Publication Data

Westbrook, Robert B. (Robert Brett), 1950–
   Democratic hope : pragmatism and the politics of truth / Robert B. Westbrook.
     v. cm.
   Includes bibliographical references and index.
   Contents: Peircean politics — Our kinsman, William James — Pullman and the professor — On the private parts of a public philosopher — Marrying Marxism — A dream country — Democratic logic — Democratic evasions — Educating citizens.
   ISBN-13: 978-0-8014-2833-3 (cloth : alk. paper)
   ISBN-10: 0-8014-2833-5 (cloth : alk. paper)
   1. Pragmatism. 2. Democracy—Philosophy. 3. Democracy—United States. 4. United States —Intellectual life. I. Title.
   B832.W47 2005
   144′.3′0973—dc22
                                     2005012276

Cornell University Press strives to use environmentally responsible suppliers and materials to the fullest extent possible in the publishing of its books. Such materials include vegetable-based, low-VOC inks and acid-free papers that are recycled, totally chlorine-free, or partly composed of nonwood fibers. For further information, visit our website at www.cornellpress.cornell.edu.

Cloth printing   10 9 8 7 6 5 4 3 2 1

In memory of Christopher Lasch,
fellow teacher, steadfast friend, and peculiar populist

Everything has come to be; there are *no eternal facts:* just as there are no absolute truths.—From now on therefore, *historical philosophizing* will be necessary, and along with it the virtue of modesty.

—FRIEDRICH NIETZSCHE, *Human, All Too Human* (1878)

Democracy is a kind of religion, and we are bound not to admit its failure. Faiths and utopias are the noblest exercise of human reason, and no one with a spark of reason in him will sit down fatalistically before the croaker's picture. The best of us are filled with the contrary vision of a democracy stumbling through every error till its institutions glow with justice and its customs shine with beauty.

—WILLIAM JAMES, "The Social Value of the College-Bred" (1908)

It's coming to America first,
The cradle of the best and of the worst.
It's here they got the range
and the machinery for change
and it's here they got the spiritual thirst.
It's here the family's broken
and it's here the lonely say
that the heart has got to open
in a fundamental way.
Democracy is coming to the U.S.A.

—LEONARD COHEN, "Democracy" (1992)

Contents

★

Preface

✭

THIS book examines the thinking of several major proponents of pragmatism, the most significant American contribution to the history of Western philosophy. It focuses on the political implications of their pragmatism and their wider contributions to American democratic thought.

In ordinary speech, a "pragmatist" is someone (often a politician) who is willing to settle for a glass half empty when standing on principle threatens to achieve less. Pragmatists are concerned above all about practical results; they have a "can do" attitude and are impatient with those of a "should do" disposition who never seem to get anything done. Americans are often said to be a particularly pragmatic people, and many Americans pride themselves on a sensibility others are inclined to label shallowly opportunistic.

Pragmatism, some might recall, is also the name given to a way of thinking about thinking developed by several towering turn-of-the-twentieth-century figures in the history of American philosophy: Charles S. Peirce, William James, and John Dewey. In this respect, as a contemporary American pragmatist has said, pragmatism "names the chief glory of our country's intellectual tradition."[1] Here the characteristic idea of pragmatism is, as one cultural authority puts it, that "the truth of any assertion is to be evaluated from its practical consequences and its bearing on human interests."[2] True

---

1. Richard Rorty, "Pragmatism, Relativism, and Irrationalism" (1980), in Rorty, *Consequences of Pragmatism* (Minneapolis: University of Minnesota Press, 1982), 160.
2. *The New Shorter Oxford English Dictionary* (Oxford: Oxford University Press, 1993), 2:2319.

beliefs for pragmatists are serviceable beliefs. When pragmatists say a belief is true, they are paying a compliment to its usefulness. On the face of it, then, philosophical pragmatism seems to put its imprimatur on the common understanding of the term, lending the "can do" attitude epistemological credentials. The true thing to believe, it suggests, is "whatever works."

But this apparent conjunction of commonplace and philosophical pragmatism is misleading. A great deal of ambiguity in the definition of philosophical pragmatism resides in the word *works,* and pragmatists have sometimes disagreed sharply among themselves about what it means. At its most implausible—which is, of course, the meaning attributed to the formulation by many of the critics of pragmatism eager to put it in the worst light—pragmatism has been taken to mean that a proposition that serves any of our interests can be said to be true. Whatever works for us, in the sense of whatever serves our purposes as we see them, is true. William James's oft-quoted statement that "the true is the name of whatever proves itself to be good in the way of belief" is said to mean that whatever beliefs we take to be good for us may, by virtue of that fact, be said to be true.[3]

Unfortunately, this sort of "pragmatism"—pragmatism at its worst—has considerable popular currency. Consider the case of presidential paramour Monica Lewinsky. Speaking to her erstwhile friend Linda Tripp, Lewinsky offered the following bit of wisdom:

> Think about truth. Truth is synonymous with good. Truth is supposed to be good. . . . If truth is synonymous with good, then truth is good and good is God, O.K.? If all those things are synonymous, then the right thing to do is not hurt someone. That's true.[4]

The "someone" in question here was, of course, Bill Clinton, an eminently "pragmatic" politician in the eyes of many, who proved even more adept than Lewinsky at defining truth as those lies that served his purposes.

Philosophical pragmatists have spent decades trying to distance themselves from such misunderstandings (and from "pragmatists" the likes of Clinton), without distancing themselves from the core of truth in Lewinsky's

---

3. William James, *Pragmatism* (1907; Cambridge: Harvard University Press, 1975), 42. I have quoted James's statement in the manner in which it is usually quoted by his critics, which excludes the qualifying phrase—"and good, too, for definite assignable reasons"—which paved the way for James eventual attempts to counter misreadings of his notion of truth. See William James, *Meaning of Truth* (1909; Cambridge: Harvard University Press, 1975), 99–116. Unlike James's most sympathetic readers, such as Hilary Putnam, I do not find James entirely blameless for these misunderstandings. See Hilary Putnam, *Pragmatism* (Oxford: Blackwell, 1995), 8–12, 24–25. The neopragmatist remark provoking similar outrage might be Richard Rorty's assertion that truth is "what our peers will, *ceteris paribus,* let us get away with saying." The oft-overlooked qualification here is "*ceteris paribus.*" Richard Rorty, *Philosophy and the Mirror of Nature* (Princeton: Princeton University Press, 1979), 176.

4. Maureen Dowd, "Truth & Catsup," *New York Times,* 4 October 1998, 4/15.

reflections on truth: her conviction that truth—or, at least what we confidently take for truth—is a human artifact, embedded in our experience in the service of guiding and enriching that experience. Pragmatists do indeed believe that the truth of a proposition is to be judged by its consequences in experience. But not every consequence of asserting or believing a proposition to be true is relevant to its justification. A false belief may make us feel good or protect those we love, but these consequences are of no consequence in testing its veracity. We live in a world (including other human beings) that is quite often indifferent to our desires and intrudes on the testing of our beliefs. To return to my example, publicly asserting that he did not have sexual relations with Lewinsky may have "worked" politically (in the short term) for Clinton, but this sort of "working" had no bearing on the plausibility of his statement. Rather, the truth of his assertion depended (as a negative) on the absence of evidence of any of the consequences that might have followed on sexual relations between himself and Lewinsky. When such consequences turned up in the form of a dress of Lewinsky's bespattered with semen loaded with his DNA, Clinton's statement lost all credibility, and his assertion failed the pragmatic test. His assertion failed to "work" in the sense that philosophical pragmatists understand it. Clinton then, of course, tried to make his statement more "workable" by fiddling with the commonplace definition of "sexual relations" (or, one might say, by offering what Richard Rorty would term a "redescription" of sex) though even this revised assertion ("we did not have sexual relations because, while she touched my genitalia, I did not touch hers") was contradicted by the more credible testimony of Lewinsky.[5]

Pragmatist philosophers have had mixed success in deflecting misunderstandings of their arguments and in persuading skeptics of their cogency. Pragmatism has been a controversial philosophy under attack from a diverse range of critics from the moment James delivered the lecture that gave the term currency in 1898. And this criticism has taken its toll.[6]

5. For a particularly good defense of the pragmatist conception of truth from the charge of "subjectivism" of the Clinton/Lewinsky sort, see John Dewey, "What Pragmatism Means by Practical" (1908), *Middle Works*, 4:98–115. For an example of a reading of pragmatism as sheer opportunism of a Clintonian sort, see John P. Diggins, "Pragmatism: A Philosophy for Adults Only," *Partisan Review* 66 (1999): 255–62. A recent article on "pragmatist architecture" provides a nice example of the popularization of this view ("You decide that God exists or that the sky is blue simply because you like the practical consequences of thinking them true"): Sarah Boxer, "The New Face of Architecture," *New York Times*, 25 November 2000, B9. Two useful recent correctives are Christine L. McCarthy and Evelyn Sears, "Deweyan Pragmatism and the Quest for True Belief," *Educational Theory* 50 (2000): 213–27; and Eric A. MacGilvray, "Five Myths about Pragmatism, or Against a Second Pragmatic Acquiescence," *Political Theory* 28 (2000): 480–508.

6. William James, "Philosophical Conceptions and Practical Results" (1898) in James, *Pragmatism*, 257–70. An abbreviated version is William James, "The Pragmatic Method" (1904) in James, *Essays in Philosophy* (Cambridge: Harvard University Press, 1978), 123–39. For an ex-

Following its dramatic appearance in the first two decades of the twentieth century, pragmatism went into a long half-century eclipse among philosophers, even as its more vulgar formulations became more deeply embedded in American life. Battered by all manner of idealists and realists in the early years of the century, the pragmatists never established a strong institutional presence among academic philosophers, even as their impact on the wider culture grew. James and Dewey were intellectuals who attempted to make their thinking accessible to broad audiences and to bring that thinking to bear on the public debates of their time, and Dewey remained a central figure in controversies over education, domestic politics, and foreign policy for more than fifty years. Pragmatism also captured the imagination of younger intellectuals such as Randolph Bourne, Max Eastman, Sidney Hook, and Walter Lippmann, and had a substantial interdisciplinary effect, particularly in the social sciences. But after Dewey left Chicago for Columbia in 1904, thereby breaking up the "Chicago School" that he had founded there, pragmatists would never again hold sway in the philosophy department of a major American university, and within the professional organizations of American philosophers they found themselves a distinct minority by the 1920s.[7]

In the years surrounding World War II, pragmatism was further swamped by the tidal wave of "analytic philosophy" that first crashed on American shores in the person of the émigré "logical positivists" of the Vienna Circle, who were fleeing the terror and bad metaphysics of Nazism. Held in the condescending embrace of these hard-nosed logicians and philosophers of science, pragmatism, despite Dewey's best efforts, survived principally in "positivized" form in the third quarter of the century. No longer a clearly identified or distinctive school of thought, it lent its arguments to those analytic rebels such as W. V. O. Quine who were seeking to cure scientistic empiricism of its dogmas. So truncated, pragmatism was barely breathing, and observers could be forgiven if they thought that it had expired with Dewey in 1952. In retrospect, one can with Rorty see the work of some analytic philosophers such as Quine, Wilfrid Sellars, and Donald Davidson as a "pragmatizing" of analytic philosophy, but as Rorty readily admits, this is

cellent overview of the history of modern American philosophy that situates pragmatism within its confines, see David J. Depew, "Philosophy," in Stanley Kutler, ed., *Encyclopedia of the United States in the Twentieth Century* (New York: Scribner's, 1996), 4:1635–63.

7. On pragmatism's place in the wider culture, see David Hollinger, "The Problem of Pragmatism in American History: A Look Back and a Look Ahead," in Robert Hollinger and David Depew, eds., *Pragmatism: From Progressivism to Postmodernism* (Westport, Ct.: Praeger, 1995), 19–37. A somewhat different and earlier version of this important article is in David Hollinger, *In the American Province: Studies in the History and Historiography of Ideas* (Baltimore: Johns Hopkins University Press, 1985), 23–43. For a full account of the epistemological debate among idealists, realists, and pragmatists, see Robert B. Westbrook, *John Dewey and American Democracy* (Ithaca: Cornell University Press, 1991), chapter 5.

Whiggish history that depends for its force on knowing that Rorty himself lies at the end of this road.[8]

But the last twenty-five years have witnessed a dramatic revival of philosophical pragmatism, spurred above all by the "neopragmatism" of Rorty, one of the most prominent (and certainly the most famous) of American philosophers at work today.[9] Armed with respectable analytic credentials and fully capable of trading punches with the most sophisticated of philosophical opponents on their own terms, Rorty once again put pragmatism on the American intellectual map as a forceful and independent presence— not only among philosophers but across disciplinary lines and in the wider culture. Like James before him, Rorty is a provocateur given to striking (and sometimes careless) expression of his views, and Rorty's pragmatism no less than that of James and Dewey has generated heated controversy, controversy that is at the heart of a dramatic revival of a philosophical tradition over which many an obituary had been read.[10]

Not least among the signs of the persistent force of this revival and its widespread appeal is the acclaim that greeted Louis Menand's fine, award-winning narrative of pragmatism's making, *The Metaphysical Club* (2001). In a series of exceptionally well-drawn portraits of Peirce, James, Dewey, and

8. David Depew, "Introduction," and Daniel J. Wilson, "Fertile Ground: Pragmatism, Science, and Logical Positivism," in Hollinger and Depew, *Pragmatism*, 109–21, 122–41. We now have a full and superb history of analytic philosophy: Scott Soames, *Philosophical Analysis in the Twentieth Century*, 2 vols. (Princeton: Princeton University Press, 2003). John McCumber has provocatively, if not entirely persuasively, linked the eclipse of pragmatism to the intellectual timidity fostered by the Cold War: *Time in the Ditch: American Philosophy and the McCarthy Era* (Evanston: Northwestern University Press, 2001). See also the symposia on the book in *Philosophical Studies* 102 (2002): 173–211 and *Transactions of the Charles S. Peirce Society* 39 (2003): 61–86.

9. This is not to say that the pragmatism was altogether ignored until Rorty came along. As Cornel West says, one should not overlook "the contributions of those lonely laborers in the vineyard who continued to keep alive the pragmatist tradition during the age of logical positivism"—Richard Bernstein, James Gouinlock, John McDermott, John Smith, Morton White, and others—even though they were unable to foster anything approaching the current interest in pragmatism despite the fact (or perhaps because of the fact) that their work—call it perhaps "paleo-pragmatism"—rests on better historical scholarship than that of many recent converts to pragmatism. It was Rorty's willingness to borrow very selectively from Dewey's philosophy that enabled him to link pragmatism to more fashionable currents of thought and thereby earn Dewey a second look among the fashionably inclined. West, *The American Evasion of Philosophy: A Genealogy of Pragmatism* (Madison: University of Wisconsin Press, 1989), 194.

10. A fine account of the revival of pragmatism is Richard J. Bernstein, "The Resurgence of Pragmatism," *Social Research* 59 (1992): 813–40; and a substantial gathering of the returns of this revival can be found in Morris Dickstein, ed., *The Revival of Pragmatism* (Durham, N.C.: Duke University Press, 1998). For a sense of the controversy that has surrounded Rorty's neopragmatism, see Alan Malachowski, ed., *Reading Rorty* (Oxford: Blackwell, 1990); Herman J. Saatkamp, Jr., ed., *Rorty and Pragmatism: The Philosopher Responds to His Critics* (Nashville: Vanderbilt University Press, 1995); Robert B. Brandom, ed., *Rorty and His Critics* (Oxford: Blackwell, 2000); John Pettegrew, ed., *A Pragmatist's Progress: Richard Rorty and American Intellectual History* (Lanham, Md.: Rowman and Littlefield, 2000); Matthew Festenstein and Simon Thompson, eds., *Richard Rorty: Critical Dialogues* (London: Polity Press, 2001); and Charles Guignon and David Hiley, eds., *Richard Rorty* (Cambridge: Cambridge University Press, 2003).

Oliver Wendell Holmes, Jr., and a rich contextualization of their thinking, Menand told this story as one of a peculiarly American response to modernity cast within an abiding recoil from ideological warfare. Menand's skillful interweaving of biography and thought was itself exemplary of his sympathetic view of the pragmatists as engaged in an effort "to bring ideas and principles and beliefs down to a human level because they wished to avoid the violence they saw hidden in abstractions."[11] And Menand's story no doubt resonated, as well it might, with many American readers newly awakened to the devastating effects of the merger of terror and absolutism, though not, alas, with those who moved to respond to violent theologues with their own well-armed, competing certainties.

One of the distinctive features of the revival of pragmatism is the fruitful conversation it has engendered between philosophers and intellectual historians. I have myself been fortunate to participate in this conversation and to play a small part in the pragmatist revival and in the controversies it has engendered. Several of the essays collected here are occasional pieces prompted by this particular moment in American intellectual history, and all of them are reflective of it. I critically engage not only a number of my contemporaries among philosophers, but also several fellow intellectual historians who have made signal contributions to the pragmatist revival. Because they are part of this larger occasion, these essays constitute a gathering more unified than a miscellany, if not a whole as tightly structured as books of less serendipitous conception. I once heard another historian self-mockingly refer to a collection of his essays as a "book effect." If these chapters comprise something more than such a simulacrum, it is because they are all part of my efforts to insure that the genealogy of pragmatism is an honest one and to argue for a shaping of the revival of pragmatism in particular directions, both philosophical and political.[12]

I am grateful to those who have provided me with the opportunity in the last decade to play a part in debates over the meaning and implications of pragmatism by affording the forums in which several of the essays in this book first took shape. They include Philip Jackson and the Department of Education at the University of Chicago; Larry Hickman and the Center for Dewey Studies; Roger Soder and the Center for Educational Renewal; Richard Shusterman and the Greater Philadelphia Philosophy Consortium;

11. Louis Menand, *The Metaphysical Club: A Story of Ideas in America* (New York: Farrar, Straus and Giroux, 2001), 440. See the symposium on Menand's book in *Intellectual History Newsletter* 24 (2002): 84–125.

12. For my own route to the revival of pragmatism, see Robert Westbrook, "Doing Dewey: An Autobiographical Fragment," *Transactions of the Charles S. Peirce Society* 29 (1993): 493–511. On the movement generally, see Neil Gross, "Becoming a Pragmatist Philosopher: Status, Self-Concept, and Intellectual Choice," *American Sociological Review* 67 (2002): 52–76.

Hans Joas and the Werner Reimers Foundation; Morris Dickstein and the CUNY Graduate School; the Comparative Literature Symposium of the University of Tulsa; Jeff Sklansky and the American Culture and Politics Speakers Series of Oregon State University; and Thomas Haskell and the Department of History at Rice University. It has once again been a pleasure to publish a book with Cornell University Press. Roger Haydon has been generous with both patience and insight. Karen Laun skillfully guided the manuscript to publication. Readers are, as am I, indebted to the copyediting of Jack Rummel.

I have learned much from those I have met on the road to this book. Whatever our disagreements about pragmatism and democratic politics, I count myself lucky for an oft-renewed debate with Richard Rorty and Cornel West. Fortunate as well are those such as myself who can draw on rich conversations with the likes of Elizabeth Anderson, Richard Bernstein, Casey Blake, Jeffrey Brown, David Chappell, John Diggins, Owen Flanagan, James Good, Thomas Haskell, Hans Joas, James Johnson, Jordan Kleiman, James Kloppenberg, Ellen Condliffe Lagemann, Kevin Mattson, Christopher Phelps, Alan Ryan, Richard Shusterman, Marion Smiley, Peter Stone, John Wenzler, and Alan Wolfe. I am blessed with three colleagues—Celia Applegate, Daniel Borus, and Stewart Weaver—who know how to write and are ever willing to apply their know-how to my stuff. The same must be said for my old friend Robert Cummings, who has been carefully reading my work for longer than I care to remember. Lee Benson, Ernie Cortes, and especially, Bill Bradley have given me opportunities to face up to the chastening practical realities confronting contemporary American democrats, for which I am much obliged. I am particularly indebted to John Diggins, Giles Gunn, James Hoopes, James Livingston, Brian Lloyd, Christopher Phelps, and Richard Posner for provocation, and to Jean-Christophe Agnew, Richard Fox, Christopher Lasch, and especially, Shamra Westbrook for indispensable reminders of the inextricability of mind and heart.

Five of these essays have been previously published in whole or in part, but none of these stands here without revision, and I have attempted as best I could to take account in these revisions of the outpouring of literature in the last decade on pragmatism old and new. Chapter 4 appeared as "On the Private Life of a Public Philosopher: John Dewey in Love," *Teachers College Record* 96 (1994): 183–97; chapter 8 as "Democratic Evasions: Cornel West and the Politics of Pragmatism," *Praxis International* 13 (1993): 1–13; and chapter 9 as "Public Schooling and American Democracy" in Roger Soder, ed., *Democracy, Education, and the Schools* (San Francisco: Jossey-Bass, 1995) (used by permission of John Wiley & Sons, Inc.). Two earlier versions of portions of chapter 7 appeared as "Pragmatism and Democracy: Reconstructing the Logic of John Dewey's Faith," in Morris Dickstein, ed., *The Revival of Pragmatism* (Durham: Duke University Press, 1998); and "John Dewey und die Logik der Demokratie," in Hans Joas, ed., *Philosophie de Demokratie: Beiträge zum Werk von John Dewey* (Frankfurt am Main: Suhrkamp, 2000). A substantial chunk of chapter 3 appeared in "Schools for Industrial Democrats: The Social Origins of John Dewey's Philosophy of Education," *American Journal of Education* 100 (1992): 401–19, (c) 1992 by The University of Chicago.

In the case of the published writings of John Dewey, I have throughout cited the fine edition of *The Collected Works of John Dewey, 1882–1953* (Carbondale: Southern Illinois University Press, 1969–1991), 37 vols., which is divided into three series: *The Early Works, 1881–1898* (cited as *Early Works*); *The Middle Works, 1899–1924* (cited as *Middle Works*); and *The Later Works, 1925–1953* (cited as *Later Works*).

DEMOCRATIC HOPE

Introduction

✷

T HE recent revival of philosophical pragmatism is one of the signal events of American intellectual history in the last quarter century. It has been held in a big tent, and a sometimes rowdy one. And appropriately so. American pragmatism has always been less a coherent philosophical school or movement than a philosophical family—often a contentious family—of thinkers holding distinct if related positions on the "workmanlike" nature of knowledge, meaning, and truth.

Pragmatists, that is, have been as inclined to squabble among themselves as to do battle with their nonpragmatic adversaries. Almost from the moment William James first used the term *pragmatism* to refer to a philosophical creed, it was not only attacked by critics of competing philosophical schools but repudiated or qualified by those whom he sought to embrace warmly as fellow pragmatists. Charles Sanders Peirce, the difficult friend to whom he granted an honored place as father of the pragmatic method, quickly denied paternity of the child James had adopted and announced he would henceforth refer to his own doctrine as "pragmaticism," a word "ugly enough to be safe from kidnappers." John Dewey, though deeply indebted to James's thinking, nonetheless took care to distinguish his own "instrumentalism" from what he took to be James's more tender-minded efforts to use pragmatism to secure religious belief. Peirce, in turn, responded to Dewey's praise of his essay on "What Pragmatism Is" (1905) with a puzzled letter noting that Dewey's instrumental logic "forbids all such researches as those which I have been absorbed in for the last eighteen years." And when

1

one extends the term *pragmatism* to include the metaphysical, ethical, aesthetic, religious, and political arguments that Peirce, James, and Dewey attached more or less loosely to their epistemological positions, the differences among these three philosophers become even more apparent.[1]

If anything, contemporary "neopragmatism" is even more diverse than its turn-of-the-century predecessor, and Arthur Lovejoy's early estimate of "thirteen pragmatisms" is now improbably low.[2] Today we are confronted with an often bewildering array of efforts by philosophers, political theorists, legal scholars, and literary critics to reappropriate, recast, and reconstruct pragmatism. These projects not only contrast with one another but differ significantly from those of the founding pragmatists. Hence, some have reasonably come to suspect, as James Kloppenberg has nicely put it, that the pragmatism of neopragmatism is "an old name for some new ways of thinking."[3]

Nonetheless, one can identify some shared features of the philosophy of pragmatists old and new, features that put the stamp of family resemblance on diverse thinkers both within and across generations. Perhaps the best way to get at these features is to elaborate on the remark of neopragmatist Hilary Putnam that "American pragmatism (at its best) avoided both the illusions of metaphysics and the illusions of skepticism."[4]

By the "illusions of metaphysics," Putnam is referring to what is often termed "foundationalism," the belief that knowledge, if it is to be secure, must rest on certain, fixed, and incorrigible foundations. As Matthew Festenstein observes, foundationalism relies on

> the claim that there is some determinate way the world is apart from the interpretative workings of human cognitive faculties. A description of the world is true if, and only if, it corresponds to that independently existing order, false

1. Peirce, "What Pragmatism Is" (1905), in Peirce Edition Project, *The Essential Peirce*, 2 vols. (Bloomington: Indiana University Press, 1992/98), 2:331–45; John Dewey, "What Pragmatism Means by Practical" (1908), *Middle Works*, 4:98–115; Peirce to Dewey, 11 April 1905, in *The Collected Papers of Charles Sanders Peirce*, ed. Charles Hartshorne and Paul Weiss (Cambridge: Harvard University Press, 1935–1958), 8.243–44. See also Garry Brodsky, "The Pragmatic Movement," *Review of Metaphysics* 25 (1971/72): 262–91.

2. Arthur Lovejoy, "The Thirteen Pragmatisms" (1908) in Lovejoy, *The Thirteen Pragmatisms* (Baltimore: Johns Hopkins University Press, 1963), 1–29.

3. Kloppenberg's phrase is a play on the subtitle of James's *Pragmatism: A New Name for Some Old Ways of Thinking*. James Kloppenberg, "Pragmatism: An Old Name for Some New Ways of Thinking?" *Journal of American History* 83 (1996): 100–138. This article is the best guide through the thicket of contemporary pragmatism. I have myself complained about definitions of pragmatism so fuzzy that they make it difficult to determine who among us is not a pragmatist. See my exchange with Giles Gunn: Robert Westbrook, "A New Pragmatism," *American Quarterly* 45 (1993): 438–44; Giles Gunn, "Response to Robert Westbrook" and Westbrook, "Response to Giles Gunn," *American Quarterly* 46 (1994): 297–307.

4. Hilary Putnam, "A Reconsideration of Deweyan Democracy" (1990) in Putnam, *Renewing Philosophy* (Cambridge: Harvard University Press, 1992), 180.

insofar as it fails to correspond. On such a view, the way the world is, including the way human beings are, constitutes an object which is accessible from a "God's eye view," independently of actual human emotions, choices, self-understandings.[5]

Only if we attain such a view against which to measure current belief, foundationalists argue, will our knowledge have absolute, universal, and incorrigible grounds.

Pragmatists uniformly deny that human beings can secure such a God's-eye view of the world and reject the kind of "correspondence theory of truth" that requires it. For them, the attempt to find foundations for human knowledge outside of human practices is, as Dewey said, a futile, self-defeating "quest for certainty." Hence for pragmatists the world foundationalists believe truth requires is "the world well lost," since any effort to secure a view of it will be necessarily fruitless.[6]

Foundationalism has persisted despite its failures, pragmatists argue, because we fear that the only alternative to it is wholesale skepticism. Philosophers (and others) have long been in the grip of what Richard Bernstein has termed "the Cartesian anxiety," Descartes' dark view of the disaster that awaits us should we be unable to discover an Archimedean point on which to rest our knowledge. For those made anxious by this quest, Bernstein observes, "*either* there is some support for our being, a fixed foundation for our knowledge, *or* we cannot escape the forces of darkness that envelop us with madness, with intellectual and moral chaos."[7]

Pragmatists reject the Cartesian either/or. Just because we cannot attain a God's-eye view of the world, they say, does not mean we must fall into despairing skepticism. Doubt as well as belief, they argue, requires justification. "Let us not pretend to doubt in philosophy what we do not doubt in our hearts," Peirce wrote in a therapeutic remark directed explicitly at the Cartesian anxiety. Universal doubt is a philosopher's game of pretend doubt, he observed, and while we may well doubt any particular belief, we cannot doubt them all, since particular beliefs require a background of undoubted convictions if they are to be tested. As Hilary Putnam says, "One cannot summon up real doubt at will. . . . Ceasing to believe anything at all is not a real human possibility. The fact that we have sometimes been mistaken in even very fundamental beliefs cannot, by itself, make me doubt any specific belief." For example, one thing that we have no good reason to doubt and

---

5. Matthew Festenstein, *Pragmatism and Political Theory: From Dewey to Rorty* (Chicago: University of Chicago Press, 1997), 4.

6. Richard Rorty, "The World Well Lost" (1972), in Rorty, *Consequences of Pragmatism* (Minneapolis: University of Minnesota Press, 1982), 3–18.

7. Richard Bernstein, *Beyond Objectivism and Relativism: Science, Hermeneutics, and Praxis* (Philadelphia: University of Pennsylvania Press, 1983), 18.

every good reason to believe is our belief in a mind-independent reality that constrains and impinges on human experience.[8]

As pragmatists see it, the alternative to foundationalism is not skepticism but fallibilism—the conviction that belief, though never certain, is not therefore necessarily dubious. Fallibilism says we may rest content with less than certain yet confident belief. It allows us to affirm our settled convictions, as long as we do so provisionally. We may not claim absolute certainty for any belief, but neither need we doubt any belief without good reasons for doing so. "Fallibilism does not require us to doubt *everything*," Putnam observes, "it only requires us to be prepared to doubt *anything*—if good reason to do so arises."[9] Fallibilism says it is enough that we be able to put our particular doubts to rest, for the time being. As therapist Peirce advised, "Your problems would be greatly simplified if, instead of saying that you want to know the 'Truth,' you were simply to say that you want to attain a state of belief unassailable by doubt."[10]

How, then, are we to put our doubts to rest if we are denied a God's-eye view of the world? Peirce argued, and many other pragmatists have followed him in this, that there are but four ways to fix a belief: by tenaciously clinging to it and attempting to cut ourselves off from any evidence that might call it into doubt; by appealing for its protection from doubt to authorities charged with the task of regulating opinion; by deriving it from shared a priori preferences or tastes; or by participating in inquiry into its warrants by a community of competent inquirers, such as those engaged in natural scientific investigation. The last, Peirce contended, has proved the most successful route to settled belief since it is the one method that subjects belief to the determinations of a reality independent of our opinions about it—an admittedly hypothetical reality, but one we have no good reason to doubt. Science as well does not rest on the difficult suppression of doubt but on its open consideration. Moreover, scientific inquiry requires that beliefs be submitted for settlement to the scrutiny of a community of investigators committed to common methods of adjudication; no belief is secure until it has passed muster with the relevant community of inquiry. Scientific inquiry is not an Archimedean point since the knowledge it authorizes is fallible and, moreover, its methods are themselves subject to doubt and revision. Its authority rests not on the incorrigibility of its conclusions or on any metaphysical guarantees it affords, but rather on its relative success in settling our doubts. It has proved over the course of human experience to work a lot better than the alternatives.[11]

8. Peirce, "Some Consequences of Four Incapacities" (1868), in *Essential Peirce*, 1:29; Hilary Putnam, *Pragmatism: An Open Question* (Oxford: Blackwell, 1995), 68.

9. Putnam, *Pragmatism*, 21.

10. Peirce, "What Pragmatism Is," 336.

11. Peirce, "The Fixation of Belief" (1877), in *Essential Peirce*, 1:109–23.

At the core of the pragmatists' attack on what Dewey termed the "intellectual lockjaw" of insoluble epistemological conundrums willed to modern philosophy by Descartes is a rejection of a "representationalist" conception of knowledge that holds that the purpose of knowledge is to somehow represent or mirror the world as it really is, a conception that Dewey derided as a "kodak fixation."[12] In its place, pragmatists substitute a conception of knowledge that owes much to the intellectual revolution fostered by Darwin and evolutionary theory, which had a profound effect on the classical pragmatists and remains a touchstone for many neopragmatists. In this naturalized and historicized conception of the quest for knowledge, intelligence is an attribute of human beings that emerged and developed over the course of the evolution of the species in the service of its survival, adaptation, and flourishing. A belief is warranted not if it mirrors the world but if it serves to resolve what Dewey termed the doubtful "problematic situations" in human experience. As Alan Ryan has said,

> Pragmatism claims that human thinking and acting, from the least sophisticated to the most sophisticated, are driven by the need to respond to problems: all thought and action are provoked by a tension between ourselves as needy organisms on the one side and, on the other, the environment that must satisfy these needs. We think and act in order to reduce that tension. . . . What we call the truth about reality is just a way of describing successful thinking.[13]

In abandoning representationalism, pragmatists have not so much solved the conventional problems of modern philosophy as set them aside. They have not adjudicated the conflict between foundationalists and skeptics but rather told both parties to get lost.[14] Pragmatism, as Louis Menand has said, is "an effort to unhitch human beings from what pragmatists regard as a useless structure of bad abstractions about thought." As such, it "has a kind of ground-clearing sweep to it that gives many readers the sense that a pressing but vaguely understood obligation has suddenly been lifted from their shoulders, that some final examination for which they could never possibly have felt prepared has just been canceled."[15]

12. Dewey, "Does Reality Possess a Practical Character?" (1908), *Middle Works*, 4:138n, 129.

13. Alan Ryan, "The Group," *New York Review of Books* (31 May 2001): 16. For the Darwinian premises underlying pragmatism, see John Dewey, "The Influence of Darwin on Philosophy" (1909), *Middle Works*, 4:3–14. Richard Rorty has among neopragmatists been most explicit about the Darwinian underpinnings of his thinking. See, for example, Richard Rorty, "Dewey Between Hegel and Darwin" (1994), in Rorty, *Truth and Progress* (Cambridge: Cambridge University Press, 1998), 290–306; and Richard Rorty, "Cranes and Skyhooks," *Linguafranca* (July/August 1995): 62–65.

14. See Donald Davidson's comment that Rorty has convinced him that "I should not pretend that I am answering the skeptic when I am really telling him to get lost." Davidson, "A Coherence Theory of Truth and Knowledge," in Alan Malachowski, ed., *Reading Rorty* (Oxford: Blackwell, 1990), 134.

15. Louis Menand, "An Introduction to Pragmatism" in Menand, ed., *Pragmatism: A Reader* (New York: Vintage, 1997), xi–xii.

The ground-clearing sweep of pragmatism has, on the face of it, much in common with various forms of "postmodernist" skepticism, and a conjoining of pragmatism and postmodernism has been encouraged by some neo-pragmatists, above all, Rorty, who has said such things as "James and Dewey . . . are waiting at the end of the road which, for example, Foucault and Deleuze are currently traveling." He has distinguished the classical pragmatists from Nietzsche and his postmodernist progeny only by virtue of the Americans' "unjustifiable social hope and an ungroundable but vital sense of human solidarity." Rorty does say that "Deweyans are inclined to see Nietzsche as an over-reaction to the realization that we shall never fulfill Plato's demand for certainty and 'rationality' in morals. The realization that we shall never achieve such certainty makes us alternate between despair at there being nothing but power in the world, and intoxication at our own possession of power." Yet in labeling the pragmatists' moral hope unjustifiable and ungrounded, he makes it a terribly weak antidote to such despair and intoxication. Although he approvingly quotes Sidney Hook's definition of pragmatism as "the theory and practice of enlarging human freedom in a precarious and tragic world by the arts of intelligent social control," he lacks Hook's faith in these arts as the ground and justification for hope.[16]

Rorty has warmed the hearts of those few neopragmatists, most of them literature professors, who would like to see in pragmatism a kind of homespun, sunnier version of a fashionable way of thinking that usually comes equipped with a downbeat French accent. For example, Richard Poirier, perhaps the leading literary neopragmatist, has characterized pragmatism as "form of linguistic skepticism," but like many literary pragmatists, he thinks he can make the case by talking mostly about Emerson (at best, a proto-pragmatist) and ignoring Peirce and Dewey.[17] Rorty's view drives many other neopragmatists nuts, and they accuse him of abandoning the constructive project of the pragmatic tradition.

Literary pragmatist Giles Gunn may be correct as far as intellectual fashions go when he says that American pragmatism "would never have been capable of revival if it had not seemed to complement (and in some ways to confirm) rather than contest that body of critical and theoretical thought already transmitted from the Continent."[18] But many neopragmatists find less to be said for traveling with counter-Enlightenment figures such as

16. Richard Rorty, "Introduction" (1982) and "Method, Social Science, and Social Hope" (1981), in Rorty, *Consequences of Pragmatism*, xviii, 46, 69–70, 208.
17. See Richard Poirier, *Poetry and Pragmatism* (Cambridge: Harvard University Press, 1992), 4. I cannot forbear from quoting Peirce's remark in 1905 that "at present [pragmatism] begins to be met with occasionally in the literary journals, where it gets abused in the merciless way that words have to expect when they fall into literary clutches" ("What Pragmatism Is," 334).
18. Giles Gunn, *Thinking Across the American Grain: Ideology, Intellect, and the New Pragmatism* (Chicago: University of Chicago Press, 1992), 3.

Jacques Derrida and Michel Foucault than for sharing a cab with their most significant European critic, Jürgen Habermas. What joins them to Habermas is a shared unwillingness to abandon entirely the Enlightenment legacy or, to put it more positively, a willingness to stick with science while at the same time calling into question any claims that science (or any other mode of inquiry) might lead to certain truth. As Habermas says, postmodernist thinkers "believe that they have to tear philosophy away from the madness of expounding a theory that has the last word" and forget that "the fallibilist consciousness of the sciences caught up with philosophy, too, a long time ago."[19] One place where it caught up first was in the United States. Most pragmatists old and new are, as Thomas Grey puts it, "still working within the scientific empiricist tradition broadly conceived. They tend to reject both the pervasive relativism and oppositional stance toward natural science that many European philosophers and social thinkers have adopted, and they accept the spirit of scientific inquiry, in which theory is tested against experience by a reflective and critical community of inquirers."[20] Or as Bernstein puts it, "The prevailing spirit of pragmatism has been (*pace* Rorty) *not* deconstruction but reconstruction."[21]

Postmodernist skeptics and their few neopragmatist admirers turn to the old pragmatists because they (correctly) see them as potential partners in a struggle against "strong," that is, absolutist and "totalizing," conceptions of truth. But what they neglect is the old pragmatists' conviction (shared by many neopragmatists) that once they had overcome absolutism, they could then resume traveling down the road of inquiry in a more fuel-efficient vehicle than Reason toward a more modest destination than Truth. That is, they saw no need to abandon (lower-case) reason and truth or, as Dewey preferred to put it to avoid confusion, "intelligence" and "warranted assertibility." As Bernstein observes, the old pragmatists

> were not obsessed with attacking over and over again the absolutism and foundationalism that they rejected. The primary problem was how to reconstruct philosophy in a manner that was compatible with a fallibilist orientation and an appreciation of the radical plurality of experience. . . . The creative task is to learn to live *with* an irreducible contingency and ambiguity—not to ignore it and not to wallow in it. . . . Although we may abandon any claim to infallible rationality, we cannot give up on the demand for making reasonable discriminations. This is just what the pragmatists sought to do.[22]

And, for the most part, still seek to do.

19. Jürgen Habermas, *The Philosophical Discourse of Modernity* (Cambridge: MIT Press, 1987), 408n28.
20. Thomas Grey, "Holmes and Legal Pragmatism," *Stanford Law Review* 41 (1989): 790–91.
21. Richard Bernstein, "The Resurgence of Pragmatism," *Social Research* 59 (1992): 832.
22. Ibid., 837–38.

My principal concern in this book is with the political views of American pragmatists, which inevitably raises the question of what, if anything, about these views can be attributed to their pragmatism. If philosophical pragmatism is not simply a highbrow cover for mendacious politicians such as Bill Clinton, what are its political implications? Does pragmatism entail or at least point toward any particular political commitments?

Some pragmatists, most notably Rorty, have asserted that it does not. Pragmatism, he says, is "compatible with wholehearted enthusiasm and wholehearted contempt for democracy." It is "neutral between democrats and fascists."[23] On the face of it, the wide diversity of substantive political positions adopted by leading pragmatists would seem to sustain this claim. The range includes the genteel liberalism of James; the democratic progressivism of Dewey and George Herbert Mead; the revolutionary Marxism of the young Sidney Hook; the New Deal/Great Society liberalism of Rorty himself; the libertarian conservatism of Richard Posner; and the democratic socialism of Richard Bernstein, Hilary Putnam, and Cornel West. There are no fascists in this number, but if one gives credence to Benito Mussolini's embrace of pragmatism and acknowledges the pragmatic strain in onetime-Nazi Martin Heidegger's thinking, then perhaps Rorty is not exaggerating.[24] Like James, he believes that pragmatism "stands for no particular results." Pragmatism aims to be little more than the hallway in the hotel of philosophy and political theory: "Innumerable chambers open out of it." Although it was metaphysical and religious chambers James had in mind here, apparently his claim applies to political bedrooms as well.[25]

But politics is a matter of "methods" and procedures as well as substantive commitments, of hallways as well as bedrooms. And James, unlike Rorty, qualifies pragmatism's neutrality by saying that "it has no dogmas, and no doctrines *save* its method."[26] Here at least, as many pragmatists have seen it, pragmatism—by virtue of its methodological commitment to experimental inquiry—is not neutral between democrats and fascists but rather has a powerful elective affinity with democracy. That is, democracy too is (in part, at least) a set of methods, and at their best the methods of democracy and pragmatic inquiry intersect. Pragmatic inquiry shares a "discourse ethics"

23. Richard Rorty, "Pragmatism as Romantic Polytheism," in Morris Dickstein, ed., *The Revival of Pragmatism* (Durham, N.C.: Duke University Press, 1998), 25; and Richard Rorty, "The Professor and the Prophet," *Transition* 52 (1991): 75.

24. On Mussolini and pragmatism, see William Y. Elliott, *The Pragmatic Revolt in Politics: Syndicalism, Fascism, and the Constitutional State* (New York: Macmillan, 1928); and John P. Diggins, *Mussolini and Fascism: The View from America* (Princeton: Princeton University Press, 1972), 221–23, 228–31, 237–38. On Heidegger's pragmatism, see Mark Okrent, *Heidegger's Pragmatism* (Ithaca: Cornell University Press, 1988); and Richard Rorty, "Overcoming the Tradition: Heidegger and Dewey" (1976), in Rorty, *Consequences of Pragmatism*, 37–59.

25. William James, *Pragmatism* (1907; Cambridge: Harvard University Press, 1975), 32.

26. Ibid., 32, emphasis mine.

with democracy. Pragmatists who embrace Dewey's conviction that politics should be a mode of "organized intelligence" believe that the intelligence of political communities, like that of all effective communities of inquiry, should be organized democratically. "Democracy is a requirement for experimental inquiry in any area," Putnam says. "To reject democracy is to reject the idea of being experimental."[27]

Thus, if pragmatism is compatible with a wide range of political beliefs, it does offer some significant, democratic strictures about how political communities should arrive at those beliefs. In this respect, "democratic pragmatism" is redundant, and "fascist pragmatism" is an oxymoron. Of course, a political community could by such ostensibly democratic means as majority rule commit itself to oppressive practices such as discrimination against or even the enslavement or murder of a minority population. But as pragmatists see it, procedural democracy modeled on pragmatic inquiry entails much more than majority rule, including commitments to ongoing political equality and nondiscrimination that would preclude regarding such oppressive practices, even if instituted by a majority, as in any sense democratic. Communities that tried to be at once fascist and democratic, as pragmatists understand the terms, would be caught in a "performative contradiction" by simultaneously trying to act on two logically opposed commitments.[28] Hence, those pragmatists (most of them) who tightly tie pragmatism's fallibilism and antiskepticism to modes of inquiry best exemplified by (though not confined to) modern science have found in pragmatism what Putnam has called "an epistemological justification for democracy."[29] I myself once shared Rorty's view of this matter, claiming that pragmatism "has no determinate moral and political implications." I now think I was wrong, or at least think I was wrong about those versions of pragmatism (most of them) that are wedded to the conviction that inquiry in general and scientific inquiry in particular provide the best antifoundationalist, nonskeptical route to justified belief.[30]

Rorty's opposition to this justification is readily explicable. Not simply does he recoil from epistemological arguments for anything, least of all

27. Hilary Putnam, "Between the New Left and Judaism," in Giovanna Borradori, *The American Philosopher: Conversations with Quine, Davidson, Putnam, Nozick, Danto, Rorty, Cavell, MacIntyre, and Kuhn* (Chicago: University of Chicago Press, 1994), 64.

28. Cheryl Misak provides a forceful account of the performative contradiction that would afflict a Nazi pragmatist in *Truth, Politics, Morality: Pragmatism and Deliberation* (London: Routledge, 2000), 9–47, 112–17, 147–54.

29. Putnam, "A Reconsideration of Deweyan Democracy," 180.

30. For my earlier view, see Robert Westbrook, "Democratic Evasions: Cornel West and the Politics of Pragmatism," *Praxis International* 13 (1993): 1. I have revised this essay (chapter 8) to reflect this change in my thinking. No one has done more to convince me of the error of my ways than James Johnson, and I am grateful to him for it. See Jack Knight and James Johnson, "Inquiry into Democracy: What Might a Pragmatist Make of Rational Choice Theories?" *American Journal of Political Science* 43 (1999): 567–68.

democracy, but he has also called for a "pragmatism without method." Wary of falling into the "scientism" that marked the wedding of pragmatism and logical positivism, Rorty has distanced himself from the claims of positivistic pragmatists such as Sidney Hook "that there is only one reliable method of reaching the truth about the nature of things anywhere and at any time, that this reliable method comes to full fruition in the methods of science, and that a man's normal behavior in adapting means to ends belies his words whenever he denies it." Rorty responds that "if one takes the core of pragmatism to be its attempt to replace the notion of true beliefs as representations of the 'nature of things' and instead to think of them as successful rules of action, then it becomes easy to recommend an experimental, fallibilist attitude, but hard to isolate a 'method' that will embody this attitude."[31] Since it is pragmatism's method that ties it to democracy—its argument that the best route to warranted belief is cooperative inquiry such as that practiced by scientists—a pragmatism without method would indeed be bereft of political implications.

Rorty identifies the abandonment of the effort to "show that a certain procedure for justifying belief is more likely to lead to truth than some other procedure," that is, the attachment to "scientific method," as one of the two great differences between classical pragmatism and neopragmatism. (The other is that neopragmatists have made the "linguistic turn" that marks analytic philosophy and hence talk about "language" rather than "experience.") But while this position "against method" does clearly mark Rorty off from the classical pragmatists, there are many neopragmatists, led by Putnam, who still think there is something to be said for believing that some methods for justifying belief are more likely to lay doubt to rest than others.[32]

I suspect that Rorty is not as far apart from more "methodical" pragmatists as it appears; they may merely disagree about whether the "experimental, fallibilist attitude" and "good epistemic manners" he himself embraces should be termed a "method" or, as he would have it, a platitudinous set of com-

---

31. Richard Rorty, "Pragmatism Without Method" (1983), in Rorty, *Objectivity, Relativism, and Truth* (Cambridge: Cambridge University Press, 1991), 65–66 (Hook, *Quest for Being* [1963], quoted on 65). See also Rorty's introduction to volume 8 of Dewey's *Later Works*, ix–xviii.

32. Richard Rorty, "Truth without Correspondence to Reality" (1999), in Rorty, *Philosophy and Social Hope* (London: Penguin, 1999), 35. It should be said that there are also neopragmatists who think it is still worth talking about nondiscursive experience. See Richard Shusterman, *Pragmatist Aesthetics* (Cambridge: Blackwell, 1992) and "Somatic Experience: Foundation or Reconstruction?" in Shusterman, *Practicing Philosophy: Pragmatism and the Philosophical Life* (New York: Routledge, 1997), 157–77. Perhaps Rorty's closest ally among prominent neopragmatists in defining its features and denying to it any particular political valence is Stanley Fish. See, for example, Fish, "Truth and Toilets: Pragmatism and the Practices of Life," in Dickstein, ed., *Revival of Pragmatism*, 418–33; and Fish, "Truth but No Consequences: Why Philosophy Doesn't Matter," *Critical Inquiry* 29 (2003): 389–417.

mitments hardly worth bothering to argue about. He agrees that scientists are morally exemplary in their knowledge-seeking practices and commends them for putting flesh on "the idea of 'a free and open encounter'—the sort of encounter in which truth cannot fail to win."[33] If one strips statements such as Hook's of their suspiciously "foundationalist" language about the "nature of things," Rorty might have fewer objections to a pragmatist embrace of scientific "method."[34] Rorty chides Dewey for confusing "scientific method" with little more than "the virtues of curiosity, open-mindedness, and conversability." Yet even if, for the sake of argument, one agrees that there is little more to the embrace by other pragmatists of this "method" than a commitment to these and other "cognitive virtues" and "good epistemic manners," it is still hard to then imagine a "fascist pragmatist" since fascist politics fixes belief by an appeal to authority (such as "thinking with the blood") that has no place for the exercise of these virtues.[35] And when Rorty says things such as "justification gets better as the community to which justification is offered becomes more sophisticated and complex, more aware of possible sources of evidence and more capable of dreaming up imaginative new hypotheses and proposals," I am at a loss to see much significant difference between him and other pragmatists seeking to link democracy to such superior practices of justification.[36]

In any case, Rorty's disinclination to devote much energy to specifying the "ideal epistemic conditions" for inquiry and deliberation has engendered a sharp intrapragmatist debate between him and Putnam, with Putnam accusing Rorty of a debilitating relativism and Rorty venturing the suspicion that a Kantian foundation may be lurking in Putnam's pragmatism. Rorty worries that Putnam may fall prey to the illusions of metaphysics and a demand for more truth than we can secure, while Putnam charges Rorty with giving way to the illusions of skepticism and a collapse of warranted belief into mere consensual taste.[37] Putnam's worries about Rorty's version of a

33. Richard Rorty, "Method, Social Science, and Social Hope," p. 195; "Science as Solidarity" (1987) in Rorty, *Objectivity, Relativism, and Truth,* 39. See also "Solidarity or Objectivity?" (1985), "Is Natural Science a Natural Kind?" (1988), and "Texts and Lumps" (1985) in the latter volume.

34. Rorty has also said that he would go along with looking "at the normal scientific discourse of our day bifocally, both as patterns adopted for various historical reasons and as the achievement of objective truth, where 'objective truth' is no more and no less than the best idea we currently have about how to explain what is going on" (*Philosophy and the Mirror of Nature* [Princeton: Princeton University Press, 1979], 385).

35. Richard Rorty, "Introduction: Relativism: Finding and Making" (1999), in Rorty, *Philosophy and Social Hope,* xxi.

36. Richard Rorty, "Pragmatism" in Edward Craig, ed., *Routledge Encyclopedia of Philosophy* (London: Routledge, 1998), 637.

37. See Hilary Putnam, *Reason with a Human Face* (Cambridge: Harvard University Press, 1990), 19–29; Richard Rorty, "Hilary Putnam and the Relativist Menace" (1993), in Rorty, *Truth and Progress,* 43–62.

consensual conception of warranted belief, which, as Peirce observed, ultimately differs little from arguments from authority, echoes Tocqueville's
concerns about the tyranny of majority opinion in democracies. As Peirce
somewhat melodramatically put it, "If liberty of speech is to be untrammeled
from the grosser forms of constraint, then uniformity of opinion will be secured by a moral terrorism to which the respectability of society will give its
thorough approval."[38] At the least, it must be said that, as a matter of intellectual history, Putnam's concern to specify the conditions of effective inquiry is more continuous with the thinking of the classical pragmatists than
Rorty's lack of concern about such matters, and a concern widely shared by
other neopragmatists.

I examine Putnam's version of a pragmatist "epistemological justification
for democracy" at length in one of the chapters that follows.[39] So let me further illustrate this kind of argument here by attending to the view of the matter afforded by George Herbert Mead, an important pragmatist who did a
particularly good job of arguing for the link between scientific inquiry and
democratic politics.

Mead, Dewey's longtime friend and sometime colleague, was the unsur-
passed social psychologist and theorist of community among pragmatists.
Had he managed to publish more, he might well stand for historians beside
Peirce, James, and Dewey as one of the leading classical pragmatists. And a
revival of interest in his work has played an important part in fostering neopragmatism, particularly in its German precincts.[40]

In an essay on "Scientific Method and the Moral Sciences" published in
1923—a time in which Dewey was struggling against a tide of skepticism
about democracy among American intellectuals—Mead joined his friend in
linking pragmatism's embrace of the methods of modern science with a defense of democracy.[41] Like Dewey, Mead was compelled to convince critics
that the methods of science had any role to play in moral and political deliberation, beyond perhaps helping to decide on the means to otherwise
predetermined ends. Mead admitted that this role was a limited one, though
not as limited as many would have it. Scientific thinking or inquiry could

---

38. Peirce, "Fixation of Belief," 121–22.

39. See chapter 7.

40. See Gary Cook, *George Herbert Mead: The Making of a Social Pragmatist* (Urbana: University of Illinois Press, 1993); Hans Joas, *G. H. Mead* (Cambridge: Polity Press, 1985); J. David
Lewis and Richard L. Smith, *American Sociology and Pragmatism: Mead, Chicago Sociology, and Symbolic Interaction* (Chicago: University of Chicago Press, 1980); and David Miller, *George Herbert
Mead: Self, Language, and the World* (Chicago: University of Chicago Press, 1973). For examples
of Mead's impact on German social theory, see Jürgen Habermas, *The Theory of Communicative
Action* (Boston: Beacon Press, 1987), 2:2–111; and especially Hans Joas, *Pragmatism and Social
Theory* (Chicago: University of Chicago Press, 1993) and *The Creativity of Action* (Chicago: University of Chicago Press, 1996).

41. On Dewey's struggles with democracy's critics in the 1920s, see Robert B. Westbrook,
John Dewey and American Democracy (Ithaca: Cornell University Press, 1991), chapter 9.

not determine human purposes as it could arrive at conclusions about planetary motion and other extrahuman phenomena. "In our moral actions," he noted, "we control our actions in considerable degree, i.e. in proportion as we are intelligent, by our purposes, by the ideas of results not yet attained, that is, our conduct is teleological. In our comprehension of nature the result is controlled entirely by antecedent causes, that is nature proceeds mechanically, and there seems to be no kinship between such a nature and the intelligence of men seeking for a better social order."[42]

Nonetheless, if scientific inquiry could not simply determine the ends for which communities should act or step in with a moral algorithm to resolve conflicts between competing values, it could be of inestimable assistance in the formulation of social ends by virtue of its capacity to estimate systematically the consequences of the pursuit of various purposes. "It is to this task that a scientifically trained intelligence must insistently devote itself, that of stating, just as far as possible, our institutions, our social habits and customs, in terms of what they are to do, in terms of their functions." Science here as elsewhere was the exercise of fallible, practical intelligence. "We do not turn to scientific method," Mead said, "to determine what is a common good, though we have learned to avail ourselves of it in some of our common efforts and practices in pursuit of the good."[43]

A progressive reformer as well as a University of Chicago professor, Mead found one of the principal virtues of applying scientific intelligence to social concerns to be its corrosive effect on taken-for-granted assumptions that had become encrusted dogmas. For the pragmatist, all ends and purposes had to answer for the manner in which they actually functioned in social practice. "Scientific method does not undertake to say what the good is, but when it has been employed, it is uncompromising in its demand that that good is no less a good because the scientific pursuit of it brings us within the taboos of institutions that we have regarded as inviolable."[44]

Good science welcomed all interested inquirers to its deliberations, and a society that hoped to deploy scientific inquiry on behalf of its purposes would have to do the same, would have to be widely inclusive. Here, then, was a significant intersection of science and democracy. Effective inquiry required that "all the conflicting ends, the institutions and their hitherto in-

---

42. George Herbert Mead, "Scientific Method and the Moral Sciences" (1923), in Andrew J. Reck, ed., *Selected Writings of George Herbert Mead* (Chicago: University of Chicago Press, 1964), 252.

43. Ibid., 262, 255. For a masterful account of this sort of pragmatist moral inquiry and the manner in which it fosters a productive two-way traffic between facts and values, see Elizabeth Anderson, "Pragmatism, Science, and Moral Inquiry," in Richard W. Fox and Robert B. Westbrook, eds., *In Face of the Facts: Moral Inquiry in American Scholarship* (New York: Cambridge University Press, 1998), 10–39.

44. Mead, "Scientific Method and the Moral Sciences," 255.

violable values, be brought together and so restated and reconstructed that intelligent conduct may be possible, with reference to *all* of them. Scientific method requires this because it is nothing but a highly developed form of impartial intelligence."[45]

In Mead's view, a social order that was undemocratic could not hope to make the best use of scientific inquiry to achieve its purposes since it would deny some values and interests (and those wedded to them) a place at the table. As he said:

> Science does not attempt to formulate the end to which social and moral conduct ought to pursue, any more than it pretends to announce what hypothesis will be found by the research scientist to solve his problem. It only insists that the object of our conduct must take into account and do justice to all of the values that prove to be involved in the enterprise, just as it insists that every fact involved in the research problem must be taken into account in an acceptable hypothesis.[46]

As Mead saw it, then, pragmatism called for the application of free inquiry to human problems of all sorts. Moreover, effective social inquiry was unavoidably democratic because, if it was to be successful, social inquiry could not be an exclusive, strictly expert practice or a prelude to elite social engineering.[47] As two sympathetic social scientists have put it, inquiry for Mead and other "methodical" pragmatists "aims to trace the consequences of various extant and proposed social policies and political commitments." As such, it "presupposes conscious deliberation regarding social purposes" by all those subject to those consequences and serves to enhance that deliberation. Democratic deliberation is thus an essential part of social inquiry and "the results of inquiry must enter *into* social and political deliberation and debate rather than be applied *to* problems."[48]

Let me illustrate the point with a homely, local example. I live in a small town west of Rochester, New York. Recently, the town planning board received an application from a developer to build over the next two decades an enormous $100 million housing development on a large, rural parcel of land that, when completed, would increase the current population of the

45. Ibid., 256.
46. Ibid.
47. Nonetheless, as James Bohman says, the effort "not merely to apply science to social and political problems, but to bring inquiry into democratic decision making" does raise a whole host of questions about the relationship between experts and democratic publics, questions that pragmatists (and Bohman) have struggled to resolve so as to deflect the undemocratic possibilities of the "epistemic asymmetries" attendant on a necessary division of labor between experts and democratic publics. Bohman, "Democracy as Inquiry, Inquiry as Democratic: Pragmatism, Social Science, and the Cognitive Division of Labor," *American Journal of Political Science* 43 (1999): 590–607.
48. Knight and Johnson, "Inquiry into Democracy," 574–75.

town by 25 percent (population growth in the town in recent years has been near zero). In order for the development to go forward, the town board would have to rezone the property in question. Consequently, town officials in their meetings and town citizens in a series of open public hearings deliberated on the question of whether to permit this development to be built.

The manner in which this decision was made strikes me as an exemplary instance of the sort of deliberative democracy and social inquiry that Mead and other pragmatists say pragmatism requires. In public meetings, we citizens debated among ourselves the various—and sometimes conflicting—social purposes we hope the town will serve (many of us, for example, put a high premium on the semirural character of the town, while others favor more economic development and population growth), and most of these purposes are affirmed in the comprehensive town plan published a few years ago. In order to gain a grasp of the consequences for these purposes of the proposed development, the developer was required to submit an environmental impact statement. Although the state mandates that this statement consider a number of effects the project might have, the town is free to add considerations to it, and several citizens suggested additions necessary if the report was to speak to the full range of purposes the townspeople wished to pursue. Moreover, because the statement was prepared by experts hired by the developer, the town board retained its own experts to scrutinize their research. Town citizens were also free to read and respond to the report and to call for further investigation if they believed it important. Once the predicted consequences were determined, meetings were held to debate the costs and benefits of these consequences for the competing values and purposes at stake. The process was designed to be inclusively democratic throughout in that it meets Mead's requirement that "all the conflicting ends, the institutions and their hitherto inviolable values, be brought together and so restated and reconstructed that intelligent conduct may be possible, with reference to *all* of them." Although ours is not a direct democracy, it was abundantly clear that town officials would be held accountable in subsequent elections for the decision they made, and the presumption was that they would take public account of the views expressed by other citizens in the deliberations.[49]

As this practical example of democratic, pragmatic inquiry and deliberation suggests, pragmatism, especially that of a Deweyan sort, does have a political valence. To be sure, for those pragmatists such as Rorty who focus almost exclusively on the critical, antifoundationalist dimension of prag-

---

49. The developer eventually abandoned the project, shortly before the Town Planning Board was about to issue an adverse report on its environmental impact. For a host of other examples of what the ethics and politics of "applied pragmatism" looks like, see William R. Caspary, *Dewey on Democracy* (Ithaca: Cornell University Press, 2000).

matism, it has no apparent political implication. For them, it is little more than a ground-clearing philosophy, and philosophers (and others) are free to erect whatever (foundationless) political structures they wish on that vacant lot. But for those pragmatists who believe that pragmatism has a constructive dimension embedded in its commitment to effective, cooperative communities of inquiry, their philosophy imposes a democratic building code on all who would develop the property it has cleared.

Although several of the essays in this book elaborate further on this relationship between pragmatism and democracy, it must be said that the philosophers I engage here are all more than pragmatists, and I have sometimes treated them as such, resisting the too widespread practice of seeing every element of their thinking as part and parcel of their pragmatism. Many pragmatists have been quite emphatic about distinguishing their pragmatism from other elements of their thinking. Dewey, for example, complained about Benedetto Croce's effort to construe his aesthetic philosophy as "pragmatist." Dewey noted that he had "consistently treated the pragmatic theory as a theory of knowing, and as confined within the limits of the field of specifically cognitive subject matter. And in addition I have specifically rejected the idea that esthetic subject matter is a form of knowledge, and have held that a prime defect of philosophies of art has been treating subject matter as if it were (whether the creators and enjoyers of it were aware of it or not) a kind of knowledge of Reality, presumably of a higher and truer order than anything of which 'science' is capable."[50] However tightly or loosely they have believed the connection between their pragmatism and their politics to be, all these philosophers have much else besides to contribute to the efforts that we who care about such things must make to sustain the intellectual and moral possibilities of democracy. Hence, I have tried to suggest in these chapters something of what these pragmatists have to offer this project not only as epistemologists but as philosophers engaged with a wide range of ethical, political, and social questions that have preoccupied Americans for more than a century.

The first part of this book is devoted to aspects of the work of the classical pragmatists Peirce, James, and Dewey. The initial two chapters critically engage the expansive claims that have lately been made for the political implications of the philosophies of Peirce and James, who ordinarily take a back seat to Dewey in this respect. The following chapter links the origins of Dewey's conception of democratic education to late-nineteenth-century conflicts between capital and labor. I then analyze in the next chapter a pivotal moment in his private life, a love affair, which I believe puts his moral

50. Dewey, "A Comment on the Foregoing Criticisms" (1948), *Later Works of John Dewey*, 15:97–98.

and political philosophy in an intriguing light.[51] The fifth chapter examines the on-again, off-again courtship of Marxism and pragmatism.

The second part of the book takes up the thought of contemporary neo-pragmatists and their critics. It begins with a consideration of Richard Rorty's postmodernist, patriotic liberalism, which is at the center of debates about the politics of neopragmatism. I then ponder in the following two chapters the arguments for expansive democracy advanced by three of Rorty's leading critics among neopragmatists, Hilary Putnam, Cheryl Misak, and Cornel West, as well as the effort of conservative pragmatist Richard Posner to align pragmatism with a much more constricted conception of democracy. The final chapter reflects on past and present debates over public education and democratic citizenship, arguments in which Dewey figured as a key participant and continues to play a role as inspiration and whipping boy.

Disparate though these essays are, they are all animated by the conviction that pragmatists old and new have each more or less given American democracy what Dewey called an encouraging philosophical nod—a signal that experience and nature are not averse to democratic hope, even if modern philosophy is incapable of providing that hope with certain metaphysical guarantees.[52] Hope, I hasten to add, is not optimism. As Christopher Lasch said, "Hope implies a deep-seated trust in life that appears absurd to those who lack it. . . . The worst is always what the hopeful are prepared for. Their trust in life would not be worth much if it had not survived disappointments in the past, while the knowledge that the future holds further disappointments demonstrates the continuing need for hope. . . . Improvidence, a blind faith that things will somehow work out for the best, furnishes a poor substitute for the disposition to see things through even when they don't."[53] This is the disposition that American pragmatists, at their best, have nurtured with their encouraging nods. My aim here is to describe, interpret, situate, and critically assess these nods, and thereby perhaps offer one of my own.

51. Chapters 3 and 4 expand on the treatment of these subjects in Westbrook, *John Dewey and American Democracy*, 93–113, 221–22.
52. John Dewey, "Philosophy and Democracy" (1918), *Middle Works*, 11:48.
53. Christopher Lasch, *The True and Only Heaven: Progress and Its Critics* (New York: Norton, 1991), 81.

Part One

Pragmatism Old

Ours is the responsibility of conserving, transmitting,
rectifying and expanding the heritage of values we
have received that those who come after us may receive
it more solid and secure, more widely accessible and
more generously shared than we have received it.

—JOHN DEWEY, *A Common Faith* (1934)

CHAPTER 1

Peircean Politics

✳

"N<small>OBODY</small> understands me," Charles Sanders Peirce groaned to his friend William James in 1907. "America is no place for such as I am."[1] He was right on both counts. Widely celebrated in Europe for his scientific accomplishments, Peirce—who could legitimately claim eminence as a mathematician, astronomer, chemist, geodesist, philologist, lexicographer, historian of science, psychologist, logician, metaphysician, and semiotician (and much else besides)—made little headway at home. He could not find a position in the universities of his own nation, where his moral laxity weighed in the balance more heavily than his brilliance as a scholar and teacher.

Without a steady job for the last twenty-five years of his life, Peirce died in desperate poverty, leaving behind thousands of pages of unpublished manuscripts, which his friend Josiah Royce deposited in the care of the philosophy department at Harvard. Although Peirce published a good deal more in his lifetime than legend would have it, considerable important work had not found its way to readers on his death in 1914. The riches of this collection have been slow to emerge. In the 1930s, Harvard published six volumes of *The Collected Papers of Charles Sanders Peirce* and two more volumes followed twenty years later. These volumes, while invaluable, were highly selective and arranged Peirce's work in rather arbitrary topical fashion and without any concern for chronology. In 1982 the first of a projected thirty volumes of a

---

1. Charles Sanders Peirce to William James, 13 June 1907, as quoted in Joseph Brent, *Charles Sanders Peirce: A Life* (Bloomington: Indiana University Press, 1993), 306.

chronological edition entitled *Writings of Charles S. Peirce* was published under the auspices of Indiana University Press (still select—a full edition would run to perhaps a hundred fat volumes). Production of this fine edition has been fitful and to date but six handsome volumes have been published.[2] Regarded today by some as the greatest of American philosophers, Peirce's pathbreaking work in logic, metaphysics, and semiotics was little understood or appreciated by his contemporaries. Even James, who followed his thinking with care and sympathy, found much of it incomprehensible. Peirce craved a wider hearing, yet often seemed determined to do everything he could to discourage it, thereby aiding and abetting the muffling of his voice by enemies who denied him the forum of a college classroom.

Peirce, then, was the most peculiar and unpopular pragmatist, and the least overtly political in his interests. Just how peculiar he was, why he might have been so, and what significance this peculiarity has for those who would engage the difficult work of this strange genius have only been fully evident of late. Just how much it might profit those concerned with the politics of pragmatism to wrestle with Peirce has also been slow to dawn on those engaged in debates devoted almost exclusively to reappraisals and appropriations of James and, above all, Dewey. Though I do not regard this imbalance as misplaced, Peirce does deserve his due.

A Guess at the Riddle

For fresh illumination on Peirce's often tortured life, we are in the debt of Joseph Brent, whose effort to shed this light endured a torturous course of its own.[3] Brent's biography of Peirce is the first full-length account of his

2. Alert to the need for a ruthlessly select chronological anthology that would supplant earlier anthologies and meet the needs of students and nonspecialists, the editors of the Indiana edition have published a first-rate, two-volume reader, *The Essential Peirce: Selected Philosophical Writings* (Bloomington: Indiana University Press, 1992/1998), available in paperback. The first volume covers the period 1867–1893 and the second 1893–1913. Whenever possible, I will cite these volumes. The best one-volume Peirce reader currently available is James Hoopes, ed., *Peirce on Signs* (Chapel Hill: University of North Carolina Press, 1991).

3. I borrow a few paragraphs here from my review of Brent's book, "Travails and Travails," *Science* 261 (16 July 1993): 368–69. Brent's biography may be cautiously supplemented by Kenneth Laine Ketner, *His Glassy Essence: An Autobiography of Charles Sanders Peirce* (Nashville: Vanderbilt University Press, 1998). Despite its title, this is not an actual Peirce autobiography but one that Ketner has made up out of disparate Peirce manuscripts interlaced with commentary by three fictional characters: a dilettantish Boston gentleman scholar who discovers the autobiography in a chest willed to his wife by her grandfather, the Episcopal minister who befriended Peirce at the end of his life, and one of Peirce's former students and admirers, a centenarian seaman/philosopher who is a dead ringer for Ketner's Peircean friend, novelist Walker Percy. As Brent has said, it is a very weird concoction, valuable for its publication of slabs of undigested manuscript material but prone to use the cover of fiction for unwarranted speculation. See Brent's review in the *Transactions of the Charles S. Peirce Society* 35 (1999): 179–87.

tragic life and the first to make full use of the vast Peirce archive.[4] And therein lies a tale that does as little credit to Harvard as its failure to make Peirce a member of its faculty. Brent began his research nearly fifty years ago while a graduate student at UCLA and completed the dissertation that forms the foundation of his book in 1960. Yet the Harvard philosophers, who had granted him access to most of Peirce's papers, then refused for undisclosed reasons to permit him to quote further from these documents and thereby torpedoed his plans to revise his dissertation for publication. Long after Brent had set aside this project and retooled as a scholar, his work was rescued from oblivion by the good offices of semiotician Thomas Sebeok, Indiana University Press, and a fresh generation of Harvard philosophers willing to let Brent's research see the light of day. Thus this *Life* of Peirce had travails that eerily mirror those of the life it describes, though in this case the ending was a happy one.[5]

Students of the history of American philosophy and science may be glad that Brent persevered. He has given us a full and compelling account of Peirce's troubled career and a wealth of persuasive arguments and plausible inferences (what Peirce called "abductions") to help explain it.

Peirce was nothing if not ambitious. He intended, he said, "to outline a

---

The lively account of Peirce's career in Louis Menand's *Metaphysical Club* (New York: Farrar, Straus, Giroux, 2001) bears consideration as well, though it adds little new material to Brent's pioneering research.

4. I suspect that most American historians have read little of Peirce beyond the essays on "The Fixation of Belief" and "How to Make Our Ideas Clear." Important work on Peirce by American intellectual historians includes Paul Jerome Croce, *Science and Religion in the Era of William James: The Eclipse of Certainty, 1820–1880* (Chapel Hill: University of North Carolina Press, 1995), 177–224; John P. Diggins, *The Promise of Pragmatism* (Chicago: University of Chicago Press, 1994), 158–204; Thomas Haskell, "Professionalism *versus* Capitalism: R. H. Tawney, Emile Durkheim, and C. S. Peirce on the Disinterestedness of Professional Communities" in Haskell, ed., *The Authority of Experts* (Bloomington: Indiana University Press, 1984), 180–225; James Hoopes, *Consciousness in New England* (Baltimore: Johns Hopkins University Press, 1989), 190–233; Hoopes, *Community Denied: The Wrong Turn of Pragmatic Liberalism* (Ithaca: Cornell University Press, 1998); Bruce Kuklick, *The Rise of American Philosophy: Cambridge, Massachusetts, 1860–1930* (New Haven: Yale University Press, 1977), 104–26; Kuklick, *A History of Philosophy in America, 1720–2000* (New York: Oxford University Press, 2001), 129–49; Murray G. Murphey, *The Development of Peirce's Philosophy* (Cambridge: Harvard University Press, 1961); and R. Jackson Wilson, *In Quest of Community: Social Philosophy in the United States, 1860–1920* (New York: Oxford University Press, 1968), 32–59. An "intellectual biography" by a leading European scholar is more on the order of a sketch: Gérard Deledalle, *Charles S. Peirce: An Intellectual Biography* (Amsterdam: John Benjamin's, 1990). Christopher Hookway affords a lucid guide to Peirce's philosophy in his contribution to the valuable "Arguments of the Philosophers" series, *Peirce* (London: Routledge and Kegan Paul, 1985). In my estimation, the best concise account of Peirce's thought is the chapter on his philosophy in Paul Conkin's *Puritans and Pragmatists* (Bloomington: Indiana University Press, 1968), 193–265. The chapters on James and Dewey in this fine and perhaps underappreciated book are also superb.

5. See Joseph Brent, "The Singular Experience of the Peirce Biographer" in Roberta Kevelson, ed., *Spaces and Significations* (New York: Peter Lange, 1996), 26–90. See also Nathan Houser, "The Fortunes and Misfortunes of the Peirce Papers," in Gérard Deledalle, ed., *Signs of Humanity* (The Hague: Mouton de Gruyter, 1992), 3:1259–68.

theory so comprehensive that, for a long time to come, the entire work of human reason, in philosophy of every school and kind, in mathematics, in psychology, in physical science, in history, in sociology, and in whatever other department there may be, shall appear as the filling up of its details."[6] As this remark suggests, he was an extraordinarily systematic thinker—the most systematic of American philosophers—and over his career he slowly and steadily ("pedestrianism" was his own term for his thinking) built a remarkable "architectonic" that nearly matched his ambitions, while at the same time his outward career steadily collapsed. In the late 1890s as Peirce added vaulting cosmological towers to his house of theory, he could also be found stealing food on the streets of New York.

Brent's focus is on the collapsing career. He traces Peirce's downward trajectory from his birth in 1839 and a promising childhood amidst the elite world of Harvard and Cambridge, Massachusetts, as the intellectually precocious, favored son of Benjamin Peirce, the leading mathematician in the United States, to the desperate circumstances of his final years. Building on a treasure trove of unpublished correspondence and manuscripts (many of which he quotes at length), Brent opens to view many heretofore cloudy aspects of Peirce's biography: his close, loving, but eventually debilitating relationship with his father; his disastrous first marriage; the even more disastrous love affair that ended it; his brief, stormy years (1879–1884) as a lecturer at Johns Hopkins; his long, conflict-ridden career (1861–1891) as a geodesist with the U.S. Coast and Geodetic Survey; his struggles to make ends meet on book reviews, dictionary entries, translations, and handouts from friends so that he might publish the fruits of his mature philosophical labors; and the pathos of his death in 1914, "five months before the guns of August thundered abroad the beginnings of the First World War and the end of an age whose dominant values he despised."[7]

Brent leaves no doubt that many of Peirce's difficulties were self-inflicted. He was a spoiled, arrogant young man; an abusive husband; a difficult, contentious employee; and a paranoid, deceitful old man. In sum, Brent contends, Peirce was, for all his intellectual brilliance, morally blind. Brent attributes much of the philosopher's erratic, unconscionable behavior to an extraordinarily painful, chronic physical ailment, trigeminal neuralgia, from which he believes Peirce to have suffered. As he says, "when free of pain [Peirce] was often pleasant, considerate, cheerful, loving, charming, and good company, but when the pain was on him he was, at first, almost stupefied and then aloof, cold, depressed, extremely suspicious, impatient of the slightest crossing, and subject to violent outbursts of temper."[8] The pain drove Peirce to distraction, despair, and drugs.

---

6. Charles S. Peirce, "A Guess at the Riddle" (1887–88), in *Essential Peirce*, 1:247.
7. Brent, *Peirce*, 1.
8. Brent, *Peirce*, 40–41.

Brent makes a good case as a medical detective. Probably because his sources are less revealing, he has less success as an anatomist of the heart. He has difficulty explaining the public love affair that Peirce launched while still married to his first wife Harriet Melusina ("Zina") with a mysterious French woman, Juliette Pourtalai (probably not her real name), who eventually became his second wife. This scandalous behavior, more than anything else, ruined Peirce's career. It guaranteed his exile from the precincts of the American university and won him powerful enemies. Most notable of these was Simon Newcomb, the prominent astronomer, who got Peirce fired from Johns Hopkins in 1884, engineered his dismissal from the Coast Survey in 1891, and in 1903 deprived him of a grant from the Carnegie Institution that would have enabled Peirce to finish his life devoting himself full-time to philosophy rather than to writing book reviews for the *Nation*.[9]

Conservative Pragmatism

Despite his architectonic ambitions, Peirce had little to say explicitly on matters of interest to social and political theorists, leaving it to them to flesh out the implications of his thinking. In doing so, some have been inclined to push his thought in democratic directions that he himself would no doubt have resisted.

Peirce thought himself a conservative, with good reason. His political views, randomly expressed, were dyspeptic and undemocratic. And in this, as in much else, he was his revered father's son. Benjamin Peirce was a fervent anti-abolitionist and Southern sympathizer before the Civil War, though like many Northern nationalists he fell into line behind the Union once the war began. Peirce sustained his father's antipathy to egalitarianism and reform politics. "Folly in politics cannot go further than English liberalism," he told Lady Welby in 1908. "The people ought to be enslaved; only the slaveholders ought to practice the virtues that alone can maintain their rule." Describing himself late in life as an "ultra-conservative," he avowed that he was "an old-fashioned christian, a believer in the efficacy of prayer, an opponent of female suffrage and of universal male suffrage, in favor of letting business-methods develop without the interference of law, a disbeliever in democracy, etc. etc."[10]

Remarks such as these suggest we pay a greater attentiveness than usual

9. This is not to say that these reviews are without interest. See Kenneth Laine Ketner and James Edward Cook, eds., *Charles Sanders Peirce: Contributions to The Nation* (3 vols., Lubbock: Texas Tech Press, 1975, 1978). Some believe Newcomb was Sir Arthur Conan Doyle's model for the notorious villain, Professor Moriarty, who bedevils Sherlock Holmes. See David Chandler, "Sherlock Holmes Villain Unmasked," *Boston Globe*, 5 January 1993, 3.

10. C. S. Peirce to Lady Victoria Welby, 23 December 1908, in C. S. Hardwick, ed., *Semiotics and Significs: The Correspondence between Charles S. Peirce and Victoria Lady Welby* (Bloomington: In-

to the conservative implications of Peirce's famous essay on the "Fixation of Belief" (1877), the point of departure for most efforts to derive a Peircean political theory. This article was the first of six in a series of "Illustrations of the Logic of Science," published in the *Popular Science Monthly* (1877–1878), which was, as William James later claimed, the charter declaration of key features of American pragmatism, though the term *pragmatism* did not appear in any of the articles in the series.

A belief, Peirce argued in this first essay, established a habit for action, and as long as our beliefs were settled, we were disposed to act as they dictated. Doubt unsettled belief and disposed us to eliminate it in order that we might comfortably settle back into belief. Inquiry, broadly construed, was the struggle to attain a state of belief by eliminating the irritation of doubt.

As I said in the Introduction, Peirce argued that human beings had devised but four such ways to curb doubt: tenacity, authority, a priori preferences or tastes, and scientific inquiry. Inquiry was by a far measure the best. The other three methods were inevitably plagued by doubt since they lacked any method for adjudicating between competing beliefs other than the blunt and ineffective instrument of repression. Paradoxically, science was better able to fix belief in the long run by first unsettling it in the short term; science, that is, did not rest on the difficult suppression of doubt but on its embrace.[11] The effectiveness of science lay not in any particular belief it advanced but in its nonrepressive method. Scientific inquiry was authoritative without being authoritarian, since the knowledge it authorized was considered fallible and, moreover, its methods were themselves subject to doubt and revision.[12]

As this summary suggests, Peirce aimed in this essay to establish the clearly superior capacity of scientific inquiry to fix belief over the long haul. And on the face of it, his account of the other methods was uniformly disparaging—and his attack on them was couched in social and political terms. Tenacity was fit only for hermits, who cut themselves off from the divergent and doubt-inducing beliefs of other people, though tenacity, to be sure, did have the virtues of "strength, simplicity, and directness," thereby securing a resolution that was "one of the splendid qualities which generally accompany brilliant, unlasting success."[13]

The method of authority was, par excellence, the method of the despotic, authoritarian church or state:

---

diana University Press, 1977), 78; MS 645, Peirce Papers, Houghton Library, Harvard University as quoted in Hoopes, *Community Denied*, 19.

11. For an astute treatment of this tension between short-term doubt and long-term "fixation," see Robert Talisse, "On the Supposed Tension in Peirce's 'Fixation of Belief,'" *Journal of Philosophical Research* 26 (2001): 561–69.

12. Charles S. Peirce, "The Fixation of Belief" (1877) in *Essential Peirce*, 1:109–23.

13. Peirce, "Fixation of Belief," 122.

Let an institution be created which shall have for its object to keep correct doctrines before the attention of the people, to reiterate them perpetually, and to teach them to the young; having at the same time power to prevent contrary doctrines from being taught, advocated, or expressed. Let all possible causes of a change of mind be removed from men's apprehensions. Let them be kept ignorant, lest they should learn of some reason to think otherwise than they do. Let their passions be enlisted, so that they may regard private and unusual opinions with hatred and horror. Then, let all men who reject the established belief be terrified into silence. Let the people turn out and tar-and-feather such men, or let inquisitions be made into the manner of thinking of suspected persons, and when they are found guilty of forbidden beliefs, let them be subjected to some signal punishment. When complete agreement could not otherwise be reached, a general massacre of all who have not thought in a certain way has proved a very effective means of settling opinion in a country.[14]

The a priori method of following a "natural inclination" toward prevailing tastes constituted a softer coercive constraint on belief that "does not differ in a very essential way from that of authority." Echoing Tocqueville, Peirce saw in this method the rule of tyrannical majority opinion. "If liberty of speech is to be untrammeled from the grosser forms of constraint," he said, "then uniformity of opinion will be secured by a moral terrorism to which the respectability of society will give its thorough approval."[15]

There was an ironic, even comic, cast to Peirce's characterization of the three inferior methods of fixing belief. At his best, he could hold his tongue in cheek nearly as firmly as Thorstein Veblen. Yet in the end the mask of dispassionate detachment was dropped, and he indicted all three methods as not only unsuccessful but "immoral" in their suppression of doubt. The irony turned bitter: "Yes, the other methods do have their merits: a clear logical conscience does cost something—just as any virtue, just as all that we cherish, costs us dear."[16]

Peirce's own use of political language and examples in characterizing the inferior methods for fixing belief has invited commentators to identify the scientific method with a freely deliberative democratic politics, and hence to find in Peirce the rudiments of an "epistemological justification" for such a democracy. In this respect, Peirce is said to anticipate Dewey, who made such an argument more explicitly.[17]

14. Peirce, "Fixation of Belief," 117.
15. Peirce, "Fixation of Belief," 121–22. Robert Talisse, in an unpublished paper on "Peirce and the Politics of Inquiry" that he kindly shared with me, links the a priori method to aristocratic rule, but I think a better case can be made textually for the Tocquevillean argument I suggest here.
16. Peirce, "Fixation of Belief," 123.
17. Hilary Putnam, "A Reconsideration of Deweyan Democracy" (1990), in Putnam, Renewing Philosophy (Cambridge: Harvard University Press, 1992), 180–200; Talisse, "Peirce and the Politics of Inquiry." For more on this epistemological argument, see chapter 7.

But a good deal of evidence cuts against any temptation to claim that Peirce himself intended to advance such an argument for democracy. Not only do his Tocquevillean slants against the oppression of popular taste suggest a wariness of democracy, but his blunt assertion that "for the mass of mankind" the method of authority was perhaps the best evinces a haughty disdain for the intellectual capacities of ordinary men and women. "If it is their highest impulse to be intellectual slaves," Peirce remarked, "then slaves they ought to remain."[18] If anything, the essay points toward rule by an intellectual elite, an "epistocracy," alone capable of competent scientific thinking. And Peirce did occasionally suggest as much. In 1892, he intemperately envisioned a "modern Pythagorean brotherhood" of those "sincerely devoted to pure science" who would "subject the rest of mankind to the governance of these chosen best."[19]

Yet Peirce most consistently aimed not to associate scientific inquiry with either technocratic or democratic politics, but to insulate it from politics of every sort—in the interest, as he saw it, of both science and politics. That is, Peirce proved especially anxious over the course of his career to demarcate clear boundaries between "theoretical" and "practical" belief and the methods for securing them, and to wall off scientific inquiry from moral and political life. Early construction of such a wall may be implicit in "The Fixation of Belief." Although that essay clearly asserts that scientific inquiry is the best means for fixing beliefs about reality in the long term, it is suggestive that Peirce's use of political language and examples stops short when he begins his account of this method (as Dewey's, for example, never would). Perhaps, as Peirce then saw it, politics was an affair of settling belief proximately in the short term, in which steadfast tenacity, repressive authority, and above all, the natural inclinations of prevailing sentiments were preferable to the doubt-inducing methods of science. Perhaps his appreciative remarks about the appeal of the method of authority for the "peaceful and sympathetic man" were not entirely ironic.

In any case, Peirce's subsequent writings leave little doubt on this score. As Douglas Anderson says, late in his career Peirce found in the sort of pragmatic experimentalism that Dewey put at the heart of his political vision both "the tendency to over-intellectualize political practice and the tendency to enslave inquiry to practical ends."[20]

Peirce's clearest statement of this view was his 1898 lecture on "Philoso-

18. Peirce, "Fixation of Belief," 118.
19. Charles S. Peirce, "Pythagorics," *Open Court* 6 (8 September 1892): 3377.
20. Douglas R. Anderson, "A Political Dimension of Fixing Belief," in Jacqueline Brunning and Paul Forster, eds., *The Rule of Reason: The Philosophy of Charles Sanders Peirce* (Toronto: University of Toronto Press, 1997), 223.

phy and the Conduct of Life." This was the first in a series of lectures in Cambridge, Massachusetts, that James arranged for him to deliver in part to shore up his desperate finances. Urged by James to avoid the subject of formal logic and speak on "topics of a vitally important character," Peirce in typically perverse fashion took the opportunity to explain why as a philosopher and scientist he had little to say on topics with any bearing on morality, politics, "and all that relates to the conduct of life." He was bound "honestly to declare that I do not hold forth the slightest promise that I have any philosophical wares to offer you which will make you either better men or more successful men."[21]

Reversing Dewey's later formulation, Peirce argued that philosophers should stick to the problems of philosophers and leave the problems of men to others. Reasoned inquiry was of modest use at best in practical affairs, which should be governed by sentiment, and sentiment only poisoned the work of scientists and philosophers. "In matters of vital importance," he said, "it is very easy to exaggerate the importance of ratiocination." Here the more admirable qualities were not those tied to reasoning but to such "instincts" as "the maiden's delicacy, the mother's devotion, manly courage, and other inheritances that have come to us from the biped who did not yet speak." On the other hand, Peirce "would not allow to sentiment or instinct any weight whatsoever in theoretical matters, not the slightest." The minute a scientist allowed his investigations to be influenced by practical, utilitarian considerations, he betrayed the "scientific Eros" and put his soul as an inquirer in peril.[22]

At the heart of these sharp distinctions was a decided revision of Peirce's argument in "The Fixation of Belief." A *belief*, he continued to say, was a proposition upon which we are prepared to act. But, he now said, science had nothing to do with action, and hence properly speaking, scientific propositions were not beliefs. Scientists could, indeed should, hold their propositions lightly, ever prepared to abandon them, but in "vital matters" ordinary people required "full belief," that is, beliefs held "as a possession for all time." Thus, the embrace of doubt, which Peirce had once argued made scientific inquiry the best method for fixing belief generally, he now regarded as a liability outside the narrow confines of the world of a self-consciously impractical elite. The duty of a scientist was to be a "genuine, hon-

21. Charles S. Peirce, "Philosophy and the Conduct of Life" (1898), in *Essential Peirce*, 2:28, 29. See the exchange of letters between James and Peirce in *The Correspondence of William James*, ed. Ignas Skrupskelis and Elizabeth M. Berkeley (Charlottesville: University Press of Virginia, 2000), 8:323–27, 329–31, 334–35, 337–41. After James told Peirce to avoid formal logic, Peirce sent James an outline for lectures on . . . formal logic. James expressed his regret and urged Peirce to "be a good boy and think a more popular plan out" (8:326).

22. Peirce, "Philosophy and the Conduct of Life," 31, 29.

est, earnest, resolute, energetic, industrious, and accomplished doubter," while the duty of most people was to cling to instinct and sentiment.[23]

In politics and morality, Peirce was thus firmly committed not to inquiry but to instinct, which, as Anderson says, should be broadly construed as "encompassing both common sense and sentiment together with the cultural tradition that these spawned." This sort of sentimentalism, as Peirce said, "implies conservatism," and those commentators who have singled him out as the one traditionalist conservative among pragmatists are on target.[24]

This is not to say that Peirce's detachment of inquiry from practical affairs was without social consequence. If he warned scientists not to pollute their investigations with practical concerns, so too he sought to insulate science from the meddling of men of affairs. As Thomas Haskell has demonstrated, Peirce was the American thinker who most compellingly formulated the argument for professional autonomy underlying the claim of scholars to academic freedom. Nonetheless, at the same time, he severed the connection between inquiry and politics that other pragmatists would forge into an epistemic argument for democracy. These pragmatists have argued that it was precisely the provisional, fallible, yet antiskeptical features of scientific belief that made it an appealing analogue for belief (and policy) formation in a contentious democratic politics marked by a pluralism of values—a politics wary moreover of the potential for oppression of "full belief."[25]

23. Ibid., 33, 31. Christopher Hookway has carefully traced Peirce's often ambiguous treatment of the relationship between belief and science in "Belief, Confidence and the Method of Science," *Transactions of the Charles S. Peirce Society* 29 (1993): 1–32. See also Jakob Liszka, "Community in C. S. Peirce: Science as a Means and as an End," *Transactions of the Charles S. Peirce Society* 14 (1978): 305–21. Peirce's idealization of scientists as "accomplished doubters" is at odds with Thomas Kuhn's later, revisionist picture of "normal science," which rests on a good deal of suppression of doubt as well as a healthy admixture of tenacity, arguments from authority, consensual taste, and faith. Dewey, who was always trying from both directions to blur the distinctions between scientific, moral, and political communities of inquiry might well have welcomed Kuhn's picture of science, but Peirce would have been appalled by it since, by his lights, it makes corruptions of science an inextricable element of scientific practice. See Thomas Kuhn, *The Structure of Scientific Revolutions* (Third ed., Chicago: University of Chicago Press, 1996).

24. Anderson, "Political Dimension," 228; Peirce, "Philosophy and the Conduct of Life," 32. Intriguingly, the example Peirce offers of the wisdom of clinging to sentiment and convention is adherence to "the regnant system of sexual rule," rules that he himself had a hard time abiding. This might suggest that he sustained at least a bit of irony in his respect for authority. Anderson makes the best case for Peirce as a traditionalist conservative, but see also Thomas Short, "The Conservative Pragmatism of Charles Peirce," *Modern Age* 43 (2001): 295–304.

25. Thomas Haskell, *Objectivity Is not Neutrality: Explanatory Schemes in History* (Baltimore: Johns Hopkins University Press, 1998), 99–114, 191–95. Haskell perceptively contrasts Peirce with R. H. Tawney and Emile Durkheim, who sought to extend the ethos of the scholarly professions to the wider society. He also suggests that the choice between the visions of Peirce and Richard Rorty is "likely to hinge on our estimate of the feasibility and desirability of Rorty's effort to extend to everyone the essential features of a form of life thus far inhabited only by scholars" (p. 200). See also Haskell, *The Emergence of Professional Social Science: The American Social Science Association and the Nineteenth-Century Crisis of Authority* (Baltimore: Johns Hopkins University Press, 2000), pp. 237–40.

Although Peirce's conservatism is readily apparent, his was a conservatism with an anticapitalist cast, which did lend it a critical edge amidst the social turmoil of late-nineteenth-century America. Notwithstanding his claim to Lady Welby to favor laissez-faire, Peirce was among those romantic conservatives who regarded with horror the logic of market individualism guiding his society.

As Peirce saw it, chief among the sentiments that should guide the consideration of "vital interests" was love. "Growth," he argued in 1893, "comes only from love, from—I will not say self-*sacrifice*, but from the ardent impulse to fulfil another's highest impulse." But creative evolution through love was not the operative evolutionary theory of the Gilded Age. "The great attention paid to economical questions during our century has induced an exaggeration of the beneficial effects of greed and of the unfortunate results of sentiment, until there has resulted a philosophy which comes unwittingly to this, that greed is the great agent in the elevation of the human race and in the evolution of the universe."[26] Peirce's disgust with capitalism evoked this back-handed tribute to the labor movement in the 1908 letter to Lady Welby:

> Here are the labor-organizations, into whose hands we are delivering the government, clamoring today for the "right" to persecute and kill people as they please. We are making them a ruling class; and England is going to do the same thing. It will be a healthful revolution; for when the lowest class insists on enslaving the upper class, as they are insisting, and that is just what their intention is, and the upper class is so devoid of manhood as to permit it, clearly that will be a revolution by the grace of God; and I only hope that when they get the power they won't be so weak as to let it slip from their hands. Of course, it will mean going back relatively to the dark ages, and working out a new civilization, this time with some hopes that the governing class will use commonsense to maintain their rule.[27] The "Gospel of Greed" and the social Darwinian conviction that "progress takes place by virtue of every individual's striving for himself with all his might and trampling his neighbor under foot whenever he gets a chance to do so" were at odds with the gospel of Christ, which held that "progress comes from every individual merging his individuality in sympathy with his neighbors."

Unsurprisingly declaring himself an unabashed "sentimentalist," Peirce plumped for the latter, bestowing upon the doctrine of evolutionary love his highest compliment, a neologism: "agapasticism."[28] As he said, America—

26. Charles S. Peirce, "Evolutionary Love" (1893), in *Essential Peirce*, 1:354. Peirce, "Evolutionary Love," 357, 362.

27. Hardwick, ed., *Semiotics and Significs*, 78–79. It should be said that like Mark Twain, who bestowed the "Gilded Age" moniker on the era, Peirce's bitterness toward capitalist greed rested in part on the failure of his own entrepreneurial schemes. See Brent, *Peirce*, 248–54.

28. Peirce, "Evolutionary Love," 357, 362.

in which "conservatives" embraced an unbridled capitalism—was no place for a conservative the likes of him.

Logical Communitarianism

But portraying Peirce simply as a stolid conservative, however apt in many respects, underplays the utopian impulse at work in his philosophy. As the essay on "Evolutionary Love" indicates, his sentimental conservatism did forecast a slow yet steady progress of sentiments toward a beloved community of breathtaking proportions.[29] With this in mind, Paul Conkin has astutely noted that "although Peirce made no major contribution to social thought, he left a philosophical outline which, if fully grasped, pointed to the renovation of a whole society, away from greed, rampant individualism, social dislocation, individual alienation, and all varieties of cynical subjectivism and skepticism, and back to an organic community, with cooperation, common beliefs and ideals, and a dedication to seek new truth and greater achieved rationality."[30]

Nearly everyone who writes about Peirce has noted the irony that this proponent of evolutionary love proved so difficult to love, and that this uncompromising communitarian spent most of his life isolated and ostracized from the communities around him. As R. Jackson Wilson has nicely observed,

> An eerie dialogue developed between [Peirce's] career and his philosophical stance. As he was shut out of one concrete community after another, he responded by proclaiming his essential unity in love with infinite community as abstract, in the last resort, as Emerson's Nature. Failure in the short run only produced a more and more eloquent faith that in the infinitely long run *his* community would succeed. The communities in which he failed to find membership were finite, concrete, and organized. The concept of community with which he retorted to this experience was infinite, ideal, and not bound up in any institution, present or future.[31]

---

29. This commitment to a progress of sentiments is a point of convergence between Peirce and Richard Rorty. Even though Rorty has done his best to deprive Peirce of authentic pragmatist credentials, he has expressed a fondness for "Evolutionary Love." Richard Rorty, "Response to Hartshorne" in Herman J. Saatkamp, Jr., ed., *Rorty and Pragmatism* (Nashville: Vanderbilt University Press, 1995), 30. For Rorty's version of the progress of sentiments, see Richard Rorty, "Human Rights, Rationality, and Sentimentality" (1993), in Rorty, *Truth and Progress: Philosophical Papers* (Cambridge: Cambridge University Press, 1998), 167–85.

30. Conkin, *Puritans and Pragmatists*, 259. See also Elvira R. Tarr, "Roots and Ramifications: Peirce's Social Thought," in Kenneth Ketner et al., eds. *Proceedings of the C. S. Peirce Bicentennial Congress* (Lubbock: Texas Tech University Press, 1981), 239–45.

31. Wilson, *In Quest of Community*, 52.

Intellectual historian James Hoopes would have us put Peirce's metaphysical communitarian vision at the center of any effort to formulate a pragmatist politics, and he makes extravagant claims for the riches it has to offer political theory. Like many communitarian critics of liberalism who lament its individualism, Hoopes believes liberals could use less "rights talk" and more emphasis on the solidarity necessary to justify "the sacrifices entailed by responsibility to the national and even international community against such powerful but lesser claimants as myself, my ethnic group, my interest group, and other group loyalties."[32] Like others who have participated in the pragmatism revival, Hoopes thinks this philosophical tradition has much to contribute to a more communitarian liberalism. But both neopragmatist philosophers and other intellectual historians, he argues, have taken a disastrous "wrong turn" in relying on James and (especially) Dewey for inspiration. Peirce should be our pragmatist of choice because he "offered a sounder basis for the liberal dream than Dewey did or does." And that basis is metaphysical. "James and Dewey were less communitarian philosophers than Peirce because of their tendency, admittedly less strong in Dewey than in James, toward a metaphysical position that made it difficult to conceive of society as anything more than a mass of atomistic individuals" (2).

Hoopes is onto something, if not everything he hopes. Very early in his career Peirce made it apparent how crucial he thought the question of the relationship between individuals and society was:

> The question whether the *genus homo* has any existence except as individuals, is the question whether there is anything of more dignity, worth, and importance than individual happiness, individual aspirations, and individual life. Whether men really have anything in common, so that the *community* is to be considered as an end in itself, and if so, what the relative value of the two factors is, is the most fundamental practical question in regard to every public institution the constitution of which we have it in our power to influence.[33]

Peirce himself addressed this question systematically only in the case of the constitution of scientific communities of inquiry, but here he left no doubt where he stood. The very origins of individual identity, he argued, lay in error. Our sense of self rested on the idiosyncratic, mistaken judgments

---

32. Hoopes, *Community Denied*, 11. Subsequent page citations to this book are in the text. The literature of contemporary communitarian criticism of liberalism is too vast to cite at any length here. But see Ronald Beiner, *What's the Matter with Liberalism?* (Berkeley: University of California Press, 1992); Mary Ann Glendon, *Rights Talk* (New York: Free Press, 1992); and Michael Sandel, *Democracy's Discontent: America in Search of a Public Philosophy* (Cambridge: Harvard University Press, 1996).

33. Charles S. Peirce, "Review of Fraser's *The Works of George Berkeley*" (1871), *Essential Peirce*, 1:105.

we have made, and truth was to be found only within the practices of a community of other inquirers. "The opinion which is fated to be ultimately agreed to by all who investigate, is what we mean by truth, and the object represented in this opinion is the real."[34] As this suggests,

> the very origin of the conception of reality shows that this conception essentially involves the notion of a COMMUNITY, without definite limits, and capable of an indefinite increase of knowledge. And so those two series of cognitions—the real and the unreal—consist of those which, at a time sufficiently future, the community will always continue to reaffirm; and of those which, under the same conditions, will ever after be denied.[35]

The search for truth rested on those who would put no loyalty above that to the community of inquiry.

We might be confident, Peirce asserted, that we knew a great deal about reality which was true and that human knowledge and reality were steadily converging, though because human knowledge was inherently fallible, we could never be certain of the truth of any particular knowledge claims about reality (even those which, at present, we had no good reason to doubt). Certain truth awaited the infinitely postponed end of inquiry.

Hoopes would direct our attention to the prior metaphysical and logical underpinnings of this conception of scientific inquiry, for those underpinnings have much broader import for social and political theory, even if Peirce did not himself explore it. In his earliest statement of the great significance of the question of the relationship between self and society that I quoted above, Peirce explicitly tied this question to that of the metaphysical choice between nominalism and realism. And it is here too, Hoopes contends, that the choice between Peirce and James and Dewey lies, for Peirce was a realist, while James and Dewey were nominalists.[36]

Nominalists deny the real existence of abstract entities. Abstract, general terms such as "dog" mark only resemblances between particular dogs, and have no ontological standing in themselves. *Dog* is but a word we use to talk about a set of particular things that have some common features. Realists hold that dogs are dogs by virtue of sharing in the property of "dogness," which is as real as the particular dogs who share in it. The crucial abstraction for Hoopes, of course, is "society." For nominalists, "society" is but a term we use to refer to an aggregate of individuals, while for realists "soci-

---

34. Charles S. Peirce, "How to Make Our Ideas Clear" (1878), *Essential Peirce*, 1:139.

35. Charles S. Peirce, "Some Consequences of Four Incapacities" (1868), *Essential Peirce*, 1:52.

36. Hoopes is not the first to make this distinction or to see it as of great moment. See J. David Lewis and Richard L. Smith, *American Sociology and Pragmatism: Mead, Chicago Sociology, and Symbolic Interaction* (Chicago: University of Chicago Press, 1980), a book that has been subjected to some withering criticism.

ety" is a real thing—it is a constitutive property of individuals, not merely a word we use to describe their aggregation. Realists such as Peirce, Hoopes argues, have, by virtue of their realism a much more robust and analytically satisfying notion of society than nominalists such as James and Dewey, who, by virtue of their nominalism, have a devil of a time giving any real substance to human community.

Some have labeled Peirce's metaphysics "objective idealism," but Hoopes prefers "semiotic realism," which gets at the feature of it most crucial for his argument. By various means over the course of his career, Peirce derived a trifold set of metaphysical categories, which he came to label the "firstness," "secondness," and "thirdness" of being. Firstness was the sheer existence of an object. Secondness was the immediate, physical relationship between objects. Thirdness was the mediated, semiotic relationship between objects in which one object was represented to a second by a third, a sign (such as a word). Thirdness, Hoopes argues, is the crucial feature of Peirce's metaphysics for social theory. As Peirce saw it, thirdness, which accounts for thought, was a feature of reality at large, not merely of human thought. Indeed, it was the enclosure of human thought within the wider thirdness or thoughtfulness of reality that enabled knowledge. And since reality was shot through with thought, logic—the study of thought—was necessarily ontological, a science of being. It promised a vision of "that Reasonableness for the sake of which the Heavens and the Earth have been created." It was, as Hoopes says, "a form of human communication with the thought of the universe" (20).[37]

By these lights, reality was a universe of signs. Human beings were themselves signs—or, to be more exact, a semiotic process. "The individual self, soul, or mind, rather than preceding and creating thought," Hoopes says, "was itself a process of semiotic interpretation." And so too society.

> Social institutions such as government, political parties, corporations, labor unions, voluntary associations, and so on may be regarded as thought, once a thought is understood to be, not an idea known immediately within a mind, but rather, an interpretive relation. Once thought is understood as a process of sign interpretation, a great range of social phenomena too large to be comprehended within any individual mind may nevertheless be best understood as the result of a process of intelligence. Institutions and organizations are semiotic syntheses, so to speak, of the thoughts of a great many people.[38]

Self and society were thus for Peirce part and parcel of the same reality, the wider thirdness of the universe. "The same kind of relations—semiotic re-

---

37. Charles S. Peirce, "Why Study Logic?" (1902), *Collected Papers*, 2.122.
38. Hoopes, "Introduction" to Hoopes, ed., *Peirce on Signs*, 12.

lations—that create society also create the self so that there is no impassable barrier between self and society." A person was, "so to speak, a society of thoughts and feelings," and a society was a wider person. Society was not a mere name for an aggregate of atomized individuals, as nominalists would have it, but as real as the individuals it comprised. "The same sort of mental or semiotic relations that constitute a person are capable of constituting society and giving it some of the same sort of reality or spiritual unity as individual human beings" (23).

As this explication suggests, Peirce's metaphysics was governed by a religious hope, though Hoopes seems reluctant to say as much.[39] As Conkin has said, Peirce "wanted to read the cosmos aright, for he believed it to be a living symbol of a divinity that wanted to be fully comprehended." In the nineteenth century, constructing a theology of such soaring ambition posed a daunting challenge: "It had to be evolutionary and dynamic as well as logical and experimental. It had to be built on shifting and treacherous physical sciences, on new but precarious systems of logic, on a ferment of mathematical speculation, and on an input of new psychological theory." So formidable were the obstacles to such a systematic pursuit of God that, Conkin notes, "only a half-mad genius would have kept at it so long against so many odds." But, as Brent demonstrates in compelling fashion, that is precisely what Peirce was.[40]

In his religious vision, as in much else, Peirce was his father's son. Benjamin Peirce was a prominent member of Boston's antebellum Unitarian elite. He shoveled dirt on the dying embers of Calvinism and saw his own considerable mathematical genius as a dutiful plumbing of the mind of the "divine geometer." As Conkin says, "Charles would keep much of the outline, but change most of the details" of his father's natural theology and its argument from design; he clung to his father's conviction that "mathematical and scientific truth are insights into the divine plan of the world."[41] Peirce contended that "all science must be a delusion and a snare, if we cannot in some measure understand God's mind."[42] The stakes of Peirce's religious impulse were high. As Conkin says, "If he could obtain his objective then men could again believe in something common and general, in the possibility of a beloved community or kingdom of heaven, and in something of greater worth, dignity, and importance than the individual's desire for survival and happiness."[43]

39. Hoopes is, however, attentive to Peirce's religious convictions in *Consciousness in New England,* 231–33.
40. Conkin, *Puritans and Pragmatists,* 193–94.
41. Ibid., 195.
42. Charles S. Peirce, "Draft of review of J. J. Baldwin, *Dictionary of Philosophy and Psychology*" (1903), *Collected Papers,* 8.168.
43. Conkin, *Puritans and Pragmatists,* 204.

Peirce, as Conkin concludes, would have seen his philosophical system "as a complex system of theology if he could have conquered his fear of the word."[44] It was thus fitting that it was Josiah Royce alone among Peirce's American contemporaries who penetrated the complexities of his thought and made good use of it in order to articulate his own religious vision of beloved community in his great late book, *The Problem of Christianity* (1913).[45] Though Peirce is widely admired in our own time among secular scientists and philosophers, his "passionate attraction to the idea of God," as Brent says, is "likely to be disconcerting to most scientists and to many philosophers."[46]

Peirce was fully alert to the tension between his claims to have mapped God's mind in his metaphysics and his fallibilism. As Conkin says, he spent "a lifetime trying to bolster and solidify a better form of objective idealism. But all his elaborate evidence remained indicative; his best arguments enriched but did not prove the position." He wanted to demonstrate conclusively the convergence of human knowledge and reality, but he failed. "An element of hope or faith, possibly translated into metaphysical speculation, seemed inescapable. . . . His bent for finality warred constantly with his fallibilism and with his realistic estimate of human incompetence."[47]

But Hoopes appears to believe that Peirce's metaphysics offers more than uncertain faith, and hence has few qualms about pursuing the metaphysical politics such a belief portends. For example, he urges liberal communitarians to abandon the political liberalism of those such as John Rawls who seek assiduously to avoid conflict between partisans with competing foundational metaphysical faiths.[48] Instead, he invites "prochoice" proponents to join the debate over abortion armed with a Peircean foundationalism that posits the semiotic, relational selfhood of the fetus and contrasts with the "Cartesian" foundations of the "pro-life" camp, which treats the fetus as "unitary soul." Currently, prochoice advocates subscribe to this same Cartesianism, regarding the pregnant woman as a "unitary, atomistic individual" with the right to control her own body. But this argument, Hoopes observes, makes it difficult for them to justify abortion since they must deny the equally "ensouled" nature of the fetus they would doom, which is hard to do on Cartesian grounds. A Peircean pro-choice argument, he says, would stress an estimate of the richness or poverty of the relations a fetus would be likely to sustain upon birth—"the likelihood of a healthy body and the possibility of

44. Ibid., 261.

45. Josiah Royce, *The Problem of Christianity* (Chicago: University of Chicago Press, 1968), 273–405.

46. Brent, *Peirce*, 346.

47. Conkin, *Puritans and Pragmatists*, 208, 237–38.

48. I refer to the argument of Rawls's *Political Liberalism* (New York: Columbia University Press, 1993).

a fulfilled, satisfying life"—as the grounds for an abortion decision. "A Peircean approach," Hoopes concludes, "gives pro-choice advocates a foundational alternative to Cartesianism where pro-lifers have the logical upper hand" (171–72).

Even if one finds this argument persuasive, as I do not, and regards dueling abortion foundationalisms an attractive alternative to Rawlsian agnosticism, as I do not, the prospect of a liberal conversion to Peirceanism on this issue or any other is an unlikely one.[49] Those liberal Americans who would, with Hoopes, find Peirce a compelling metaphysician would likely be outnumbered by those who would, with Richard Rorty (taking note of Peirce's obsession with threefold distinctions), regard him not as the prophet of a new liberal trinitarian theology but as a "whacked-out triadomaniac."[50]

Hoopes's contention that a Peircean politics would be communitarian is unassailable. That it would be democratic, or even liberal, is not, and he offers little argument to demonstrate that it would. Hoopes takes pains to discourage the conclusion that Peirce's metaphysics might ground a power grab by scientific elites, but he is not altogether successful. Peirce's infinite deferral of certainty to a communal consensus at the end of inquiry with no end in sight might be taken as yet another way in which he sought to separate science from practical affairs, in which action in the present requires firm, full belief. As I have said, Peirce himself, apart from the occasional remark about rule by a Pythagorean brotherhood, seems to have intended it as such.

But pushing Peirce in a technocratic direction does not require much effort. Hoopes suggests that those who would do so focus ill-advisedly on Peirce's conception of scientific inquiry rather than on the semiotic realism that grounded it. But the two seem to me to work together in fostering a technocratic tropism for Peircean politics. To be sure, as Hoopes says, Peirce never identified truth with the current consensus of any particular community of inquiry. Yet Peirce's confidence that the knowledge sanctioned by scientific inquiry was tracking reality and would eventually converge truthfully with it might easily be taken as grounds for regarding the consensus of existing communities of scientific inquiry as the best approximation we have to truth at present and thereby for investing the consensus of these communities with exceptional authority.[51] How extensive that authority would

---

49. If one is "pro-choice," why *not* confine the argument to the constitution of a "soul" in "Cartesian" terms—is it as clear as Hoopes contends that this argument cannot be waged to, at least, a draw? And is the mounting of a competing "pro-choice" foundationalism, more or *less* likely to resolve or even enhance the debate, short of wholesale conversion to Peircean metaphysics or an intolerant power play by pro-choice Peirceans that makes their foundationalism the informing vision of public policy?

50. Richard Rorty, "The Pragmatist's Progress" in Stefan Collini, ed., *Interpretation and Overinterpretation* (Cambridge: Cambridge University Press, 1992), 93.

51. Haskell puts the point this way: "Identifying truth with the community, but lacking the

be would depend on the scope of matters thought to be subject to judgments of proximate truth, and how elite that authority would be would depend on the practices of the various communities of inquiry that addressed them. As we will see, a substantial measure of democracy is not inconceivable under these circumstances, but the tropism for those as contemptuous as Peirce of the capacities of most people for inquiry would be toward elite control.

Peirce himself resisted the technocratic tropism in his thought by putting up a wall between science and "vital matters," hoping as much to protect science from the public as the public from scientists. But for him, of course, science and logic were themselves vital matters, and the community of inquiry was subject not only to the constraints of reality and logic but to its own ethics of conduct. Above all, living in logic entailed an ethic of self-sacrifice. It required "a conceived identification of one's interest with those of an unlimited community."[52] More dramatically, "He who would not sacrifice his own soul to save the whole world, is illogical in all his inferences, collectively. . . . Just the revelation of the possibility of this complete self-sacrifice in man, and the belief in its saving power, will serve to redeem the logicality of all men."[53] As this suggests, Peirce walled off science not only to protect it from sentiment but also to allow it to flourish as a prefiguration of the utterly selfless community he imagined at the end of time.

Most men and women were left with the progress of sentiments rather than the progress of rationality. Here evolution was much less rapid, "a movement which is slow in the proportion in which it is vital." Nonetheless, Peirce held out hope for convergence here as well, a breaching of the wall between science and sentiment in the face of the mind of God. This hope too was grounded in the happy fatalism of his objective idealism. "The internal forms, that mathematics and philosophy and the other sciences make us acquainted with, will by slow percolation gradually reach the very core of one's being; and will come to influence our lives; and this they will do, not because they involve truths of merely vital importance, but because they are ideal and eternal verities."[54]

Hoopes would have us see Peirce as a "mild" communitarian, but he was anything but mild (11). As Wilson says, "He set an absolute choice between the individual and the community, and there was nowhere in his work any suggestion of a bargain, of a manipulated harmony."[55] Conkin's judgment

community's final opinion, we are bound to prefer its current best opinion to a chaos of indistinguishable truth claims, which is the only other alternative Peirce's line of reasoning leaves us" (*Objectivity Is not Neutrality*, 103).

52. Charles S. Peirce, "The Doctrine of Chances" (1878), *Essential Peirce*, 1:150.

53. Charles S. Pierce, "Grounds of Validity of the Laws of Logic: Further Consequences of Four Incapacities" (1869), *Essential Peirce*, 1:81.

54. Peirce, "Philosophy and the Conduct of Life," 40–41.

55. Wilson, *In Quest of Community*, 59.

on Peirce's prefigurative utopia is harsh but apt. Peirce "seemed to want to lose himself in a perfect whole," compensating for his own moral failings and those of the society around him with a fantastic, imagined community cleansed of self-interest. He "never had the personal confidence, the self–respect, or the courage to rely on either individual man, or on unredeemed groups of men. Only the possibility of selfless man, redeemed by a vision of truth, self-sacrificed on the altar to a future but coming kingdom of reason, and sustained by a living God, could give him the courage to face his own dismal world and his own dismal self. Peirce was a sinner and desperately needed the assurance of salvation."[56]

Dewey's Piecemeal Realism

If the only choice available to pragmatists in search of a communitarian dimension for social and political theory was between that provided by Peirce's realist theology and the putative nominalism of James and Dewey, which Hoopes claims can generate no thicker conception of society than that of an aggregate of individuals, Peirce's metaphysics might win a host of converts. But it is not the only choice, for Dewey was not a nominalist.

Hoopes is aware that convicting Dewey of nominalism is much more difficult than making the case against James, for Dewey explicitly disavowed nominalism.[57] Hence his nominalism is said by Hoopes to be "implicit." Failing until very late in life to appreciate Peirce's metaphysics and logic, Dewey denied himself the philosophical resources he needed to ground his commitment to democratic community. His own metaphysics was not up to the task, and kept slipping into the very nominalism and individualism that he disavowed. "Insist as he might on the importance of social experience in the formation of the individual, his conception of the individual remained biological and organic, related to but also distinct from the things of the spirit such as words and thoughts by which human beings are bound together in society" (5).

But Hoopes makes a wretched case against Dewey, not least because he fails to give Dewey's own metaphysics and logic the careful scrutiny they demand. Those who have, such as Ralph Sleeper, have found there a "piecemeal realism" that affords an alternative to Peirce for those who would prefer to uncouple their communitarianism from theological or metaphysical foundations.[58]

---

56. Conkin, *Puritans and Pragmatists*, 251, 246.

57. I will not consider Hoopes's indictment of James's nominalism, which I find more convincing. Indeed, I point up myself some of James's shortcomings as a theorist of the social self in chapter 2.

58. My argument here closely follows that of Sleeper in *The Necessity of Pragmatism: John*

As Sleeper demonstrates, Dewey was much more alert to Peirce's philosophy early in his career than is often supposed. The testy exchanges between the two philosophers at the opening of the twentieth century reflected not mutual incomprehension and misunderstanding, but a clear awareness of their differences. When Peirce complained of the "intolerance" of Dewey's genetic method in logic and metaphysics, he was fully alert to the challenge to his own thinking that it posed. And Dewey saw in Peirce's invocation of progressive evolution toward a "real potential world" of "eternal forms" and his increasingly favorable disposition toward Hegelian idealism and even New England transcendentalism evidences of the sort of metaphysics he was himself abandoning.[59] Dewey found much to admire in Peirce's philosophy, particularly his account of belief and doubt (which Dewey reconstructed into his notion of the "problematic situation," a pivotal feature of his philosophy) and his semiotic. But he had little use for much of the late Peirce, especially the theological-cum-evolutionary blend of "synechism" (pervasive continuity), "tychism" (chance), and "agapasticism."[60]

The detail of the differences between Peirce and Dewey in metaphysics and logic need not detain us here. Suffice it to say that those differences were not between realism and nominalism but between a wholesale and a piecemeal realism. As Dewey saw it, Peirce gave every evidence of not having freed himself from the commitment of classical and scholastic realism to "fixed essences" and to a logical method that imposed a priori forms on reality, the sort of "apart thought" pioneered by Kant. Peirce had, to be sure, overhauled Kant's categories and replaced them with his own, but his was still a categorical metaphysics in which logic was the royal road to Being. As Sleeper nicely sums up a critical difference between the two philosophers, "Dewey's conception of logic differed from that of Peirce less in terms of how each understood the methods of experimental science than in the ontology each thought those methods to be based on. . . . We ought to get

---

Dewey's Conception of Philosophy (New Haven: Yale University Press, 1986), and subsequent page citations to this book are in the text. But see also Thomas Burke, *Dewey's New Logic: A Reply to Russell* (Chicago: University of Chicago Press, 1994); and Larry Hickman, "Dewey's Theory of Inquiry" in Hickman, ed., *Reading Dewey: Interpretations for a Postmodern Generation* (Bloomington: Indiana University Press, 1998), pp. 166–86. The absence of any consideration by Hoopes of Sleeper's important book is curious in that it poses such a direct challenge to his reading of Dewey.

59. Charles S. Peirce to John Dewey, 11 April 1905, in Peirce, *Collected Papers*, 8.243–44; Peirce, "Philosophy and the Conduct of Life," 40–41; Charles S. Peirce, "What Pragmatism Is" (1905), *Essential Peirce*, 2:345; Charles S. Peirce, "The Law of the Mind" (1892), *Essential Peirce*, 1:312–13. See also Peirce's review of Dewey's *Studies in Logical Theory* (1903), "Logical Lights" in Peirce, *Contributions to The Nation*, 3:186. Sleeper locates the beginnings of contention between Peirce and Dewey in the early 1890s in their competing views of the logic of necessity. Compare Charles S. Peirce, "The Doctrine of Necessity Examined" (1892), *Essential Peirce* 1:298–311, with John Dewey, "The Superstition of Necessity" (1893), *Early Works*, 4:19–36.

60. As he made clear by ignoring them and fashioning a "Peirce" to his liking in John Dewey, "The Pragmatism of Peirce" (1916), *Middle Works*, 10:71–78.

our logic from our ontology, Dewey maintains, not our ontology from our logic" (47).

Peirce, as Hoopes says, was after the logic of the universe, and inquiry answered to this logic. Dewey was content with the logic of human experience, that which emerged in the course of inquiry; logic answered to inquiry. But because Dewey was an (epistemological) "naive realist," he believed that experience provided access to the "brute existences" of reality, which, "detected or laid bare by thinking but in no way constituted out of thought or any mental process, set every problem for reflection and hence serve to test its otherwise merely speculative results."[61] As Sleeper puts it, "Dewey shows how our logical norms emerge from the process of inquiry and reflect the ontological structures encountered in that process" (47). Human logic hooked onto nature not because it mirrored divine logic but because it was forged in light of what Dewey termed nature's "generic traits" ("an impressive and irresistible mixture of sufficiencies, tight completenesses, order, recurrences which make possible prediction and control, and singularities, ambiguities, uncertain possibilities, processes going on to consequences as yet indeterminate").[62]

Dewey's metaphysics, which centered on these traits and their implications, thus provided what Sleeper calls a "background theory" for his logic without underpinning it with the foundations that Peirce hoped his metaphysics would provide(6). Dewey's logic in good antinominalist fashion allowed for "universals" and "natural kinds" reflecting nature's stabilities, but these were within inquiry, though they were shaped by nature's regularities (and threatened by its precariousness). As Sleeper says,

> Dewey is arguing that kinds exist, that they are existentially real. He has worked out an empirical argument against nominalism. At the same time, he is quick to acknowledge that kinds instituted in this way are temporal. They are neither the eternal objects that philosophers sometimes invoke nor objects having necessary existence. Not modal, they are contingently real objects. That they are not *permanently* real in Dewey's ontology is not merely a consequence of the fact that they are temporally instituted as the consequent objects of cognitive inquiry; it is also the result of their being causally contingent on conditions the permanence of which cannot be taken for granted (147).

Dewey's metaphysics maintained that "nature is not that well organized, contains no rational core such as Peirce supposes. What it does possess, however, are generic traits that offer piecemeal support, temporal generic forms that allow provisional inference and regional ontologies" (126). Dewey's logic in turn offered "ontological realism, but on a piecemeal basis" (159).

61. John Dewey, "Introduction to *Essays in Experimental Logic*" (1916), *Middle Works*, 10:341.
62. John Dewey, *Experience and Nature* (1929) in Dewey, *Later Works*, 1:47.

The piecemeal realism of Dewey's metaphysics and logic underwrote his social theory, provided his philosophy of culture, as Sleeper says, with a "deep structure" (101).[63] Hoopes's most peculiar and unconvincing claim is that Dewey "had no conception of *social* life, of there being a life *among* people as well as in them" (79). As he sees it, Dewey's social philosophy was marked by a "failure to conceive society as a communicative process, a real self that resembled in some respects the individual self" (92). But it is precisely as a communicative process that Dewey conceived of human society and culture. As Sleeper points out, the centerpiece of his major metaphysical book, *Experience and Nature* (1929), was its chapters on the genesis of communication and the importance of language to the making of human society and inquiry. "When communication occurs," Dewey remarked there, "all natural events are subject to reconsideration and revision; they are readapted to meet the requirements of conversation, whether it be public discourse or that preliminary discourse termed thinking. Events turned into objects; things with a meaning."[64]

Dewey's theory of communication began as did Peirce's with a semiotic. Events and objects in nature pointed as signs to other events and objects, and most organisms had the capacity to use these signs in their environment as the basis for inference. Language, originating in initially meaningless gestures and cries, opened the way to *shared* inferences, and with human beings evolution threw up an intelligent creature whose language provided an exponential growth in the capacity for shared inference—and for inquiry and the theory of inquiry, which was logic. For Dewey as for Peirce, language, semiotic, was the antecedent—not the consequence—of thought. It was language that "changed dumb creatures—as we so significantly call them—into thinking and knowing animals and created the realm of meanings." Language did not express ideas, rather ideas were a soliloquy that was "the product and reflex of converse with others." Thinking was, so to speak, talking to ourselves, which presupposed a prior talking with our fellows. Like Peirce, Dewey held that it was not because they had minds that some creatures had language, but because they had language that they had minds.[65]

As these arguments suggest, Dewey did not, as Hoopes claims, fail to conceive of society as a communicative process, nor did he fail to construe a life *among* people as well as in them. Nor even did he lack a view of society as a real self that resembled in some respects the individual self. With language,

63. Richard Rorty has argued that there is no need for such a deep structure and criticized Dewey for trying to provide it. See Richard Rorty, "Dewey's Metaphysics" (1977), in Rorty, *The Consequences of Pragmatism* (Minneapolis: University of Minnesota Press, 1982), 72–89. My sympathies are with Dewey and Sleeper. See Robert B. Westbrook, *John Dewey and American Democracy* (Ithaca: Cornell University Press, 1992), 319–73.

64. Dewey, *Experience and Nature*, 132.

65. Ibid., 133–35.

Dewey said, "something is literally made common in at least two different centres of behavior." Hoopes observes that for Peirce "words enabled people not merely to communicate but to unite, to become literally one. The satisfaction people take in communication, in understanding and being understood, confirmed, according to Peirce, this unity of people via words and symbols" (41). Dewey could not have agreed more. "Of all affairs," he said, "communication is the most wonderful. . . . And that the fruit of communication should be participation, sharing, is a wonder by the side of which transubstantiation pales."[66]

One might well complain, as I have myself, that Dewey was better at conveying the deep structure of communication and community than at saying something equally satisfying at the level of social psychology, sociology, cultural anthropology, and political theory. But the same could be said, even more so, of Peirce. What Peirce did have on offer that Dewey did not was metaphysical foundations for human community. As Sleeper concludes, "It is here that the radical nature of Dewey's conception of philosophy stands out most clearly, for he tells us that there are no such foundations" (128). He afforded only a metaphysical "ground-map" of an uncertain, often precarious, reality in which human community would rest on the constructive intelligence and will of human beings themselves.

The important contrast between Peirce and Dewey, then, is not between realism and nominalism—they were both realists, albeit of decidedly different sorts—but between a vision of human community as a manifestation of the concrete reasonableness of God's Reality and a vision of human community as a manifestation of the work of a particularly clever, language-using animal. Hoopes, it seems, wants foundations for his communitarianism and finds them in Peirce. Dewey could only offer communitarians an "encouraging nod," and a warning of the consequences, including the political consequences, of asking for more.[67]

Low-Profile Truth

If Peirce is to prove useful to democratic political theory and practice, it would seem some fiddling with his thought is in order. And Cheryl Misak gets my vote for the most accomplished fiddler thus far.

Misak makes two crucial moves in her argument for Peircean democracy, each of which closes the gap between Peirce and Dewey and makes her perspective decidedly *neo*-Peircean. First, she brackets the metaphysical specu-

66. Ibid., 141, 132.
67. John Dewey, "Philosophy and Democracy" (1918), *Middle Works*, 11:48.

lations of the late Peirce, and focuses on the problems of doubt, belief, and inquiry that most drew Dewey to Peirce. In so doing, she reconstructs Peirce's pragmatism and his fallibilistic conception of truth, so as to avoid some of its difficulties. Second, she argues for the extension of pragmatic, truth-seeking inquiry to the domain of ethics and politics, another decidedly Deweyan move. The consequences of doing so, she contends, are democratic, even radically democratic. This train of argument, as I see it, is the most compelling "epistemological justification for democracy" advanced by any pragmatist, old or new.

Like all pragmatists, Misak targets "correspondence" theories of truth that locate it outside of human experience and that try to take the "God's-eye" view of things about which Peirce could not resist speculating. Like most pragmatists, including Peirce in his fallibilist mode, she locates truth instead within the experience of human inquiry. In this respect, pragmatism is part of a wider "deflation" of the notion of truth. The most deflationary of contemporary conceptions of truth is "disquotationalism," which holds that truth is a more or less trivial compliment that we pay to the beliefs that we assert; there is no difference between asserting a belief and saying that it is true. Or as the philosophers put it, "p" is true if and only if p (truth, that is, is a matter of removing the quotation marks, hence "disquotationalism").

Misak does not want to let all of the air out of the concept of truth in this fashion, and neither, she says, should any pragmatist. Truth requires truth conditions that disquotationalism does not allow. The "best kind of pragmatist" will argue that "there is a conception of truth to be had which captures what is important about truth, is non-metaphysical, and goes beyond the triviality expressed by the disquotational schema." What is most important about such a conception of truth, as she sees it, is that it implies that a belief "*answers* to something." To assert a belief is to believe it to be true, "but if this is right, then the belief that p must be sensitive to something—something must be able to speak for and against it." Peirce said in "The Fixation of Belief" that truth answered to reality, but he could not establish this. What we can say is that truth answers to our experience of reality, a reality whose existence and features are known by virtue of experience (as Dewey would say).[68]

68. Cheryl Misak, *Truth, Politics, Morality: Pragmatism and Deliberation* (London: Routledge, 2000), pp. 57, 107. Subsequent page citations to this book are in the text. This book builds on, and alters modestly, Misak's earlier study of Peirce's epistemology, *Truth and the End of Inquiry: A Peircean Account of Truth* (Oxford: Oxford University Press, 1991). Rorty is probably the pragmatist most drawn to disquotationalism. He has often said that "true" is a pretty empty compliment we pay to well-justified belief. But he has also admitted that a belief that is currently regarded by the community of inquiry as well-justified may later be regarded as unjustified, and we need a "cautionary" phrase such as "well-justified but perhaps not true" to cover such cases. This seems to me to close the gap between Rorty and Misak considerably, though neither would

Inquiry is the means to resolve doubt and sort out true from false beliefs. "A minimal characterisation of good inquiry" is that it "takes experience seriously" (78). And because beliefs to be adequately tested must be subject to the widest possible range of experience, inquiry to be effective must, as Peirce said, be communal. "What fits with *my* experience is not of paramount importance as far as truth is concerned. What is important is what fits with all the experience that would be available, what the community of inquirers would converge upon" (95). Inquiry is our means of subjecting belief to the challenge of reasons, argument, and evidence. A belief that fully meets this challenge is true. "The pragmatist's view of truth keeps inquiry at the centre; it refuses to sever the link between truth and inquiry" (54). Truth is the upshot of exhaustive inquiry.

> Pragmatism thus abandons the kind of metaphysics which is currently in so much disrepute—it abandons concepts which pretend to transcend experience. Truth and objectivity are matters of what is best for the community of inquirers to believe, "best" here amounting to that which best fits with the evidence and argument. On the pragmatist view of truth, when we aim at empirical adequacy, predictive power, understanding the way things work, understanding ourselves, and the like, we aim at the truth. For a true belief is the belief which best satisfies those and other particular aims in inquiry. (1)[69]

For the pragmatist, then, "a true belief is one that would withstand doubt, were we to inquire as far as we fruitfully could on the matter. A true belief is such that, no matter how much further we were to investigate and debate, that belief would not be overturned by recalcitrant experience and argument" (49). But since no inquiry can be exhaustive, we can never know for sure that any of our beliefs are true, however indubitable they may seem at present. Truth is thus a "regulative ideal," an ideal that is unrealizable and yet serves a valuable function, in this case that of keeping the road of inquiry open (98). Truth is "what inquirers must *hope* for if they are to make sense of their practices of inquiry" (69). Truth is the aim of inquiry, but the best that can be secured at any moment in its course is well-justified belief, which is not necessarily true. It is *rational* nonetheless to adopt well-justified beliefs, even if these beliefs later prove to be false. Beliefs about matters that are in doubt are always forged against a background of beliefs about matters that, for the moment at least, are not—these fallible yet undoubted beliefs provide the warrants for new belief. Hence, beliefs can be deeply embedded in

probably accept this conclusion. See Rorty, "Is Truth a Goal of Inquiry?: Donald Davidson Versus Crispin Wright" (1995), in Rorty, *Truth and Progress*, p. 21.

69. Misak, like many pragmatists, wants to distance herself here from the identification of "best" belief with consoling or comforting belief that James, at his worst, advanced.

history and established cultural practices and nonetheless be well-justified (if not necessarily true).[70]

Following Peirce, Misak insists that

> the pragmatist should not connect truth to inquiry with an indicative conditional, but rather with a subjunctive conditional. It is not that a true belief is one which *will* fit the evidence and which *will* measure up to the standards of inquiry as we now know them. Rather a true belief is one which *would* fit with the evidence and which *would* measure up to the standards of inquiry *were* inquiry to be pursued so far that no recalcitrant experience and no revisions in the standards of inquiry would be called for. (68)

Given this subjunctive formulation of pragmatist truth conditions, Misak argues it would be best to drop the talk, into which Peirce sometimes fell, of taking true beliefs as those reached at an empirical "end of inquiry." Dropping such talk avoids the logical problem of appearing to conclude that the beliefs held when, for example, a meteor destroys life on earth, are, by virtue of the "end of inquiry," true. Insisting on the subjunctive also allows pragmatists to avoid "the doomed task of saying just what is meant by the hypothetical end of inquiry, cognitively ideal conditions, or perfect evidence, whatever these might be. Any attempt at articulating such notions will have to face the objection that it is a mere glorification of what we presently take to be good" (49–50). Finally, the subjunctive formulation absolves pragmatists of the charge that they confuse any existing agreement or consensus of belief with "being the best a belief could be."

Misak's neo-Peircean pragmatism thus works with a "substantive, low profile conception of truth and objectivity, a conception which nonetheless can guide us in inquiry" (14). For the pragmatists, to assert a belief is to assert its truth, and hence "those who want true belief undertake certain commitments," such as to subject belief to inquiry (57). "If truth were to be the belief which would best fit with experience and argument, then if we want true beliefs, we should expose them to experience and argument which might overturn them" (83). Since all functioning human beings are believers, they all assert their beliefs to be true, and hence all implicitly assume an obligation to participate in inquiry. Belief is inseparable from justification. To believe is "to commit oneself to giving reasons—to be prepared, in the appropriate circumstances, to justify the claim to others, *and to oneself.* Those

70. On regulative ideals, see Dorothy Emmet, *The Role of the Unrealisable: A Study in Regulative Ideals* (New York: St. Martin's, 1994). Rorty says that to say that truth is the goal of inquiry implies to him that truth is fixed and can be reached. A goal that is ever-retreating and that we can never know ourselves to have reached "is not what common sense would call a goal." Maybe so, in which case, one should distinguish between a goal and a regulative ideal, a horizon of possibility, which it seems to me is a concept that common sense can also grasp quite easily. Rorty, "Is Truth a Goal of Inquiry?" 39.

claiming to hold a belief, something which has truth-value, commit them-selves to being open to evidence and argument" (94).

If this pragmatist conception of truth is to have a bearing on ethics and politics, then moral and political life have to be realms in which it applies. Moral and political beliefs have to be "truth-apt," as Misak says (2). But this is a claim denied by various "noncognitivists" and relativists. Noncognitivism and relativism are parasitic on high-profile, correspondence theories of truth that hold that a proposition is true "if and only if it corresponds to something like a fact in the believer-independent world." As Misak says, "Since truth and objectivity in morals and politics cannot be anything like that, realism seems to lead directly to the conclusion that moral and politi-cal judgments cannot fall within our cognitive scope—within the scope of truth and knowledge"(2).

But, Misak contends, for those who embrace pragmatism's low-profile conception of truth, moral "cognitivism" is a real possibility, for it requires only that in morals and politics we have "genuine beliefs with truth as their aim" (48). As we have seen, this is a claim that Peirce rejected, but Misak as-serts (rightly, I think) that nothing in Peirce's philosophy (as opposed to his temperament) precludes it, and it accords with Dewey's convictions.[71]

It accords as well with the phenomenology of the moral experience of most people. Misak's impassioned description of this phenomenology mer-its quoting in full:

> When we make moral judgments and when we act in the ways which we think are morally right, we take ourselves to be aiming at something objective—at the truth or at getting things right, where "right" does not mean merely "right by the lights of my group." We distinguish between thinking, on the one hand, that one (or one's culture) is right and, on the other hand, being right. We at-tribute moral beliefs to ourselves and to others, we use such beliefs in infer-ences, and we think that they can conflict and compete with each other. We think that we can discover that something is right or wrong—that we can im-prove our views. We want not the illusion that our projects, plans, ambitions, and relationships are worthwhile—we want good reason to think that they are worthwhile. We think that it is appropriate, or even required, that we give rea-sons and arguments for our beliefs, that "rational" persuasion, not browbeat-ing or force, is the appropriate means to getting someone to agree with us. Indeed, we want people to *agree* with, or at least respect, our judgments, as op-posed to merely mouthing them, or falling in line with them. And we criticize the beliefs, actions, and even the final ends and desires of others, as false, vi-cious, immoral, or irrational. The fact that our moral judgments come under such internal discipline is a mark of their objectivity. The above phenomena

71. See John Dewey, "Does Reality Possess Practical Character?" (1908), *Middle Works*, 4:131–32.

are indications that moral inquiry aims at truth. They are indications that the relativist or non-cognitivist thought is not the thought which should stand at the start of our moral theory (3).

Of course, these convictions are defeasible and subject to doubt. But as Peirce insisted, we should not cultivate fake, philosophical doubt about beliefs that we have no good reasons to doubt.

But since philosophical doubt has arisen, Misak is prepared to demonstrate that pragmatists can bring the moral and political domain within the scope of their conception of truth. Pragmatism's low-profile conception of truth does not require that a belief correspond to a mind-independent world of objects; it requires only that it answer to experience, broadly defined, and to inquiry. In order to be a candidate for truth, pragmatist empiricists require only that "every non-spurious belief must have experiential consequences. It must answer to experience of one kind or another" (88).[72]

Moral beliefs, Misak argues, do answer to experience, and hence moral inquiry is possible. We experience moral perceptions and intuitions (as when we watch pop star Michael Jackson hold his infant son over a penthouse balcony), and we subject these intuitions to scrutiny and revision. We can reasonably change our mind or discover something new about a moral matter; we can see things in a different light; we can be alerted by others to features of an act that we had overlooked; we can arrive at better interpretations of moral situations. We can, in short, "be *challenged* by new experience" in ethics as well as science (93). Moral inquiry, like scientific and mathematical inquiry, is "experience-driven, example-driven, and argument-driven" (94). Moreover, as in science, pragmatists argue, moral beliefs are forged against a background of fallible but stable background beliefs. And in both instances, "there is a constant dialectic between perception and the background theory. The theory facilitates certain observations and then those observations have to be squared with the rest of the theory. Through critical reflection, exposing oneself to more experience and perspectives, one's background beliefs can be improved and one's judgments revised, despite being able to see only what one's theory allows" (93). This is not to say there are not important differences in inquiry undertaken in different domains, but it is to say that for a pragmatist moral beliefs are no less truth-apt than scientific or mathematical beliefs.

The political implications of Misak's argument are narrow but powerful. Pragmatism, as she conceives it, points to "a kind of radical democracy in in-

72. For another forceful pragmatist argument against calling on the fact/value distinction to head off moral inquiry, see Elizabeth Anderson, "Pragmatism, Science, and Moral Inquiry," in Richard Wightman Fox and Robert B. Westbrook, eds., *In Face of the Facts: Moral Inquiry in American Scholarship* (Cambridge: Cambridge University Press, 1998), 10–39.

quiry" (94). If belief is to answer to the experience of the community of inquiry, then no one with relevant experience can be denied participation in it. "Belief involves being prepared to try to justify one's views to others and being prepared to test one's belief against the experience of others. Thus, the differences of inquirers—their different perspectives, sensibilities, and experiences—*must* be taken seriously. If they are not, reaching the best or the true belief is not in the cards" (94).

Deliberative, participatory democracy thus has for the pragmatist great cognitive significance, and insofar as the moral and political realms are for (some) pragmatists cognitive realms in which beliefs are truth-apt, democracy is essential to the success of communities of inquiry within them.

> Moral deliberation displays a kind of epistemological democracy. We are all involved in moral discussion and in experiments in living, to borrow a phrase from Mill. Moral judgment is inextricably bound up with our relations with others and anyone who stands in such relationships has plenty of engagement in moral deliberation. Truth requires us to listen to others, and anyone might be an expert. (96)

Pragmatism in this fashion takes on its democratic political valence by virtue of adhering to Peirce's thin, methodological injunction not to block the road of inquiry and the pursuit of truth. But thinly methodological though it is, this informing principle is, as Misak says, a political "workhorse" (92). Because Misak's pragmatism links deliberative, democratic inquiry to "the requirements of genuine belief," it requires that all believers be democrats simply by virtue of their desire to assert their beliefs as true. Those who refuse to take the experience of others seriously or, worse, choose to exclude that experience from consideration altogether are doing their own beliefs a disservice by not allowing them to answer to experience and thereby denying that they are truth-apt. Indeed, these beliefs can no longer be said, properly speaking, to be beliefs.

Pragmatists thus argue that "if we are to take seriously the experiences of all, we must let ways of life flourish so that they can be articulated and we must let people articulate them for themselves" (115). The practical, political implications of this argument are perhaps obvious. As Misak says, "Deliberation must be encouraged and political institutions and mechanisms for decision-making must be as inclusive as is reasonably possible. The pragmatist voices the requirement that we try, at least until such attempts fail, to include rather than exclude others" (127). For the pragmatist, to say that moral and political beliefs are truth-apt is not to say they are incontestable or to make a fetish of agreement, consensus, and convergence. Indeed, moral and political inquiry are, by their very nature, rife with contestation, dissensus, and disagreement. Moreover, fully deliberative democracy is for

pragmatists a regulative ideal much like truth, an unrealizable hope and ambition that serves "to set a direction and provide a focus of criticism for actual arrangements" (98).

Misak's argument, as I say, strikes me as the strongest argument yet offered for claiming a democratic political valence for pragmatism. It is much
stronger than Dewey's, and stronger even than Hilary Putnam's.[73] It is an
argument that would, I suspect, have delighted Dewey and troubled Peirce.
But it does expose the resources that Peirce has to offer political theory,
even if those are not resources that he himself cared to exploit.

73. See chapter 7.

CHAPTER 2

Our Kinsman,
William James

★

No pragmatist, indeed no philosopher, is more congenial than William James—"that adorable genius," as Alfred North Whitehead called him. For many Americans, critic Monroe Spears has observed, James "is the kind of person we hope that we are: modest, unpretentious, a genuine democrat, spiritually as well as politically, always warm and generous to others, candid and honest, and at the same time fearless, absolutely independent, hardworking, and productive. As admired ancestor, regarded with pride and affection, he is a true culture hero."[1]

Given this congeniality, the temptation to make James our kinsman, to slight the features of his thought and its context that distance us from him in favor of those that make him serviceable in the present, is nearly irresistible, and Jacques Barzun is far from alone in believing that James "knows better than anyone else the material and spiritual country I am traveling through." He is a rare figure among major modern philosophers, a thinker, as Barzun says, with whom we may "stroll" rather than struggle.[2]

Those intellectuals most inclined to stroll with James have been those

---

1. Whitehead as quoted in Jacques Barzun, *A Stroll with William James* (Chicago: University of Chicago Press, 1984), 1; Monroe Spears, *American Ambitions* (Baltimore: Johns Hopkins University Press, 1987), 25.

2. Barzun, *Stroll,* 4. It is, I think, no accident that James is as yet the lone philosopher to win a place (two volumes) in the canonical Library of America. See William James, *Writings, 1878–1899* (New York: Library of America, 1992) and *Writings, 1902–1910* (New York: Library of America, 1987).

who have worried over such matters as the difficulties of religious belief in the wake of the uncertain universe afforded us by modern science.[3] His terrain is, above all, the modern "crisis of the individual." As one critic has said, "We are drawn to James because he forcefully confronted the essential problems of modernity—the metaphysics of the abyss, the bewildering plurality of a world growing at the edges, the nightmare of reason, and the numbing freedom of subjectivity."[4] But for those like myself who would add the uncertain fate of democracy to this list of "essential problems of modernity," James has proved less of a draw. Generally speaking, it is John Dewey not William James who has been at the center of debates about pragmatism and politics.

But recently some students of pragmatism—led by historians George Cotkin and James Livingston and literary critic Frank Lentricchia—have suggested that James has something significant to say about politics and complained of the neglect of his virtues as a social and political theorist. Livingston has numbered me among "a new generation of young intellectuals" who "tend to treat Dewey as the central figure in the creation of the pragmatist-progressive tradition, and to be slightly embarrassed by James. At any rate they seem always to deal with him in passing—on their way to the more tough-minded Dewey—as if he were the demented uncle whose place in the family tree is still in question."[5] Since many times I have wished that Dewey could write like James, I am grateful for this incitement to engage the claims that have been made for his political thinking.

Anyone who would assert that James is underrated as a social and political theorist must contend with the truth of Bruce Kuklick's observation that, as a matter of explicit theorizing, James's "social and political philosophy was negligible." There is nothing in his work to compare with Dewey's substantial venture into abstract political theory, *The Public and Its Problems,* nor even his more topical volumes such as *Individualism Old and New, Liberalism and Social Action,* and *Freedom and Culture.* Indeed, as Kuklick says, James "did not even develop a reasoned account of moral argument," and certainly nothing to compare with the hefty *Ethics* textbook that Dewey coauthored with James Tufts—a text that not only explored moral argument in the abstract but tied its analysis to a wide range of contemporary social and political issues. James, on the other hand, authored but one weighty essay

---

3. See the fine book by Paul Jerome Croce, *Science and Religion in the Era of William James: Eclipse of Certainty, 1820–1880* (Chapel Hill: University of North Carolina Press, 1995), the first of what is to be a two-volume study of these issues.

4. George Cotkin, *William James, Public Philosopher* (Baltimore: Johns Hopkins University Press, 1990), 1.

5. James Livingston, *Pragmatism and the Political Economy of Cultural Revolution, 1850–1940* (Chapel Hill: University of North Carolina Press, 1994), 227–28, 372n5. Much as I might wish I was still a *young* intellectual, I am afraid the designation is misleading.

devoted to a political theme, "The Moral Equivalent of War" (1910), an essay published the year of his death.[6]

James's career as a political activist also pales in comparison to that of
Dewey, though it was more substantial than his work as a political and social
theorist. Beginning in 1895 James was a prominent voice in debates over
American imperialism, and allusions not only to these debates but to other
social and political controversies at home and abroad creep with some reg-
ularity into his philosophical writing and popular lectures. Yet this activism
was confined mostly to the last decade of his life, and the only cause to which
James devoted sustained energy was anti-imperialism. In his final years,
James was oft-given to expressions of sympathy with anarchism, but even
Deborah Coon, the historian who has done the most to expose these sympathies, acknowledges that they were, for the most part, communicated privately and must be "pieced together" before venturing a view of just what
sort of anarchism ("a pacifist, communitarian anarchism," she says) James
had in mind.[7]

In sum, James's virtues as a social and political theorist are not obvious. If
they are to be found, they must lie less in the realm of explication than of
implication.[8]

A Singular Mugwump

The best account we have of James's social and political thought is George
Cotkin's perceptive book, *William James, Public Philosopher.* Cotkin is less eager
to stroll with James than to temper the strolling of others. "In claiming
[James] as one of our own," he says, "we often wrench him from his own historicity. We reduce, in the process, this historically grounded and complex figure into a document to be quoted and thereby contained for our purposes. . . .
What we gain for our present purposes on the one side, we perhaps lose on
the other in terms of fully comprehending James as a historical figure."[9]

I think a good way to characterize Cotkin's view of James is to see it as one
that (in effect) takes Cornel West's throwaway line that James was a "bour-

---

6. Bruce Kuklick, *The Rise of American Philosophy: Cambridge, Massachusetts, 1860–1930*
(New Haven: Yale University Press, 1977), 309.

7. Deborah Coon, "'One Moment in the World's Salvation': Anarchism and the Radicalization of William James," *Journal of American History* 83 (1996): 86.

8. The sort of indirection required to derive much of a yield for political theory from
James's thinking requires is perhaps most obvious in Joshua Miller, *Democratic Temperament: The
Legacy of William James* (Lawrence: University Press of Kansas, 1997), in which Miller struggles
mightily (and, to my mind, too often vainly) to use James as a launching pad for his own
thoughts on a wide range of contemporary issues. See my review in the *American Historical Review* 103 (1998): 1337–38.

9. Cotkin, *William James*, 2. Subsequent page citations to this book are in the text.

geois individualist" and thoroughly unpacks it.[10] That is, Cotkin places James within the context of the culture of the late-nineteenth-century American bourgeoisie, particularly its college-educated elite, and emerges with a compelling portrait that explains a great deal about the nature and development of his philosophy.

This class, of course, was James's own class, and Cotkin demonstrates that the vocational uncertainty and psychological enervation through which James suffered in the 1860s and 1870s, which has attracted so much attention from his biographers, was, for all the idiosyncrasies attributable to his extraordinary family, characteristic of others in the "generation of the 1840s"—young, college-educated men of the Northeastern, urban, upper class. Like James, many of those in his generational cohort suffered from a Hamletlike inability to make up their minds about what to do with their lives, wrestled with religious uncertainty, and endured physical and nervous ailments that sometimes brought them to the edge of despair. For some of James's friends, such as Oliver Wendell Holmes, Jr., service in the Civil War brought an end to their youthful debilities, and they marched without doubt into successful careers in the new bureaucratic civilization that took shape in the wake of the war. James, who—thanks to his father—missed the war, fell among those judged by veterans like Holmes "not to have lived," and struggled for years to find a place in the world. This struggle was made all the more difficult by Darwinism and other scientific theories that shattered long-held assumptions about free will and autonomy, theories that held, as James moaned in 1869, that "we are wholly conditioned, that not a wiggle of our will happens save as the result of physical laws." At the same time, James was haunted by an opposing metaphysical suspicion that the world might be utterly without order, merely an "abyss of horrors" (8–9).

When James finally emerged from his depression in the mid-1870s, he found himself part of a cultured bourgeoisie wracked by anxieties similar to his own. The "crisis of individual autonomy" that plagued him had become, as Cotkin says, "the common social and economic, as well as intellectual, property of *fin-de-siècle* Americans" (9). Terms such as "neurasthenic, hysterical, melancholic, powerless, doubting, and Hamletian" were the common coin of bourgeois self-description, and "images of the sickly woman, the nervous intellectual, and the sadly peripatetic businessman" dotted the cultural landscape. The rise of the modern corporation supplanted the autonomous entrepreneur with the salaried manager, "who became little more than a cog in the vast machinery of ordered, rational business progress. The

---

10. Cornel West, *The American Evasion of Philosophy: A Genealogy of Pragmatism* (Madison: University of Wisconsin Press, 1989), 67.

control and rationalization exercised by the trust in the period from 1880 to 1910 within the economic sphere of existence came to serve as an analogue to the psychic economy of the individual: control replaced chaos but also inhibited excitement and spontaneity" (74–77). The iron cage of the intellectual determinisms that distressed James distressed others in his class, and the liberal Protestant clergy that ministered to their needs found itself uncomfortably wedged between a scientific positivism that denied belief and fundamentalisms that merely asserted it.[11]

This cultural crisis and the efforts of others to address it, Cotkin says, "riveted James's attention," and "he designed the passions and specifics of his philosophy to battle those who, in philosophical and cultural texts, would forever banish religion and individual autonomy from modern life" (77). Reading the essays in *The Will to Believe* and popular lectures such as "Is Life Worth Living?" as James's response to what he called the "*tedium vitae*" of the American bourgeoisie, Cotkin finds James again and again sallying forth to slay the dragons of determinism and weightlessness that haunted the nightmares of his class.

In his war on the *tedium vitae*, Cotkin demonstrates, James developed a "discourse of heroism" designed to reenergize his bourgeois audience, a "passionate vision and espousal of life *in extremis*" that promised to recapture the intense experience that modern life had stifled. To tired businessmen, bedridden women, and doubt-plagued students, he offered the examples of soldiers, saints, and workers as models of lives worth living. He urged his audiences to exercise their right to believe in a God powerful enough to be on their side in life's struggles, offering them, if not a muscular Christianity, at least a well-fortified theism (or polytheism). "The familiar Jamesian imperatives of the will to believe, the strenuous life, and the pragmatic attitude," Cotkin argues, "became the anodynes that he prescribed to the next generation of neurasthenic and disgruntled Americans" (11).

In prescribing a discourse of heroism to a debilitated bourgeoisie, James was once again in good company. His attack on the *tedium vitae* was part of a wider moment of bourgeois "revitalization" in the last decades of the century. Others were not only feeling the enervation of bourgeois life but responding to it. By the 1880s, as Cotkin notes,

> ennui wrestled with strenuosity, and the latter was increasingly the victor—in both every day life and cultural expressiveness. Physical exercise suddenly became *de rigueur* and bicycling, rowing, and mountain climbing gained prominence. For those who preferred to experience heroic strivings in vicarious fashion, the birth of intercollegiate sports, the organization of professional

11. See James, "Vacations" (1873) in James, *Essays, Comments, and Reviews* (Cambridge: Harvard University Press, 1987), 3–7.

sports, and even the "taming" of bare-knuckle brawling into an acceptable spectator sport all vied to supply excitement to the public. (96–98)

And, of course, in the person of Theodore Roosevelt, James found a fellow advocate of the "strenuous life" of uncommon vigor and authority. They were together engaged in the project that Christopher Lasch termed the "moral and intellectual rehabilitation of the ruling class."[12]

When he turns explicitly to James's politics, Cotkin puts some meat on the bones of Robert Beisner's characterization of James as a "singular mugwump."[13] Like other mugwumps—those independent reformers who bolted the Republican party in 1884 to protest the presidential nomination of the corrupt James G. Blaine and later figured so prominently in the anti-imperialist movement—James pursued a politics of, by, and for the "best men." As a New Englander of substantial means and a superior college education, James shared all the social characteristics of most other mugwumps, as well as many of their views. He attributed his political education to the *Nation*, the flagship journal of the mugwumps, and as he told his brother Henry, he often did his best to work "some mugwumpery" into his public lectures and speeches.[14]

Mugwumps saw themselves as men of superior education, culture, character, and moral sensibility, and they believed they were entitled by virtue of these credentials to political leadership. James was a democrat of sorts, but for him the central problem of democracy was the difficulty of securing the leadership of "our better men." The "social-value of the college bred," he argued, was "to divine the worthier and better leaders," for "in our democracy, where everything else is so shifting, we alumni and alumnae of the colleges are the only permanent presence that corresponds to the aristocracy in older countries. We have continuous traditions, as they have; our motto too is *noblesse oblige;* and, unlike them, we stand for ideal interests solely, for we have no corporate selfishness and wield no powers of corruption."[15]

On the other hand, James lacked many of the prejudices and the cranky self-righteousness that make the mugwumps such an unattractive bunch. Although he characterized the Haymarket Massacre as the "work of a lot of pathological Germans and Poles," James was much more favorably disposed to both workers and immigrants than most mugwumps, usually reserving

12. Christopher Lasch, "The Moral and Intellectual Rehabilitation of the Ruling Class" in Lasch, *World of Nations* (New York: Knopf, 1973), 80–99.

13. Robert L. Beisner, *Twelve against Empire* (New York: McGraw Hill, 1968), 35–52.

14. William James to Henry James, 5 June 1897, *The Correspondence of William James*, ed. Ignas K. Skrupskelis and Elizabeth M. Berkeley, 12 vols. (Charlottesville: University Press of Virginia, 1992–2004), 3:9. Hereafter cited as *Correspondence*.

15. William James, "The Social Value of the College-Bred" (1907), in James, *Essays, Comments, and Reviews*, 110.

the occasional note of ethnic prejudice and class condescension for his correspondence with his novelist brother, whom one suspects brought out the worst in him in that respect. Most important, perhaps, James's anti-imperialism was marred by none of the racism so prominent in that movement. "Although his ideas were clearly nurtured within the Mugwump milieu," Cotkin judiciously concludes, "James was always a party of one" (129).[16]

Cotkin's contextualization of James's life and thought is brilliant and persuasive. Not the least of its virtues is that it helps explain—if only by implication—why it was the issue of imperialism that finally moved James to political activism and argument and why it was anti-imperialism that remained at the center of his politics for the remainder of his life. American imperialism sought legitimation in the very "discourse of heroism" in which James participated, and he was moved to public protest by what he saw as a perversion of this discourse. There is about James's anti-imperialism, that is, something of a troubled conscience. Hence, it is not surprising that James's most forceful and polemical assaults on the imperialist camp were reserved for Theodore Roosevelt, who turned their shared ideal of the strenuous life into a justification for laying waste to the Filipino people. James had not counted on the transformation of heroism into a will to power and domination, and when Roosevelt showed him how easily this might be accomplished, James started to read the newspaper. James's troubled conscience is on full display in "The Moral Equivalent of War," in which he preached the persistent virtues of the soldier's life to his fellow pacifists yet struggled to figure out an alternative arena (a war against nature) within which they might manifest themselves.

Cotkin's success in contextualizing James's politics weakens any impulse we might have to put him in the service of our own. Accomplished historian that he is, Cotkin has brought a certain strangeness to James's social and political thought and thereby put further distance between him and us. The elite for which James wrote no longer exists, and mugwumpery is an unlikely politics for an age of presidents named "Jimmy," "Bill," and "Dubya."

The "discourse of heroism" at the heart of James's pragmatic politics was conceived within such narrow class boundaries that it lacks much general appeal, as even critical observers at the time recognized. His plea for soldiers in a war on nature, for example, was strictly a petition to the "gilded

16. Livingston objects to my earlier characterization of James as a mugwump. I regret the dismissive tone of that remark, for it neglected the idiosyncrasies of James's views. Yet I still believe he is best seen as a mugwump, if a complicated one of the sort Cotkin describes. See Robert B. Westbrook, "Lewis Mumford, John Dewey, and the 'Pragmatic Acquiescence,'" in Thomas Hughes and Agatha Hughes, eds., *Lewis Mumford: Public Intellectual* (New York: Oxford University Press, 1990), 420n4; and Livingston, *Pragmatism*, 372n5.

youths" of the "luxurious classes." It is hard to see what is in the proposal for those already consigned for life to coal and iron mines, foundries and stokeholes. Women are excluded as well. Their role is to value more highly the bourgeois males who have for a time abandoned "unmanly ease" and thereby become "better fathers and teachers of the following generation." As Dewey remarked, "The idea that most people need any substitute for fighting for life, or that they have to have life made artificially hard for them in order to keep up their battling nerve could have come only from a man who was brought up an aristocrat and who had lived a sheltered existence. I think [James] had no real intimation that the 'labor problem' has always been for the great mass of people a much harder fight than any war; in fact one reason people are so ready to fight [in wars] is the fact that it is so much easier than their ordinary existence."[17]

Cotkin rightly calls "The Moral Equivalent of War" James's "fullest entry into the realm of social theory," and rightly labels it "weak" (150). James's "politics of pragmatism remains vague and unimpressive in various ways," he concludes, leaving us with little more than the modest harvest of a warm respect for James's tolerant sensibility (177). This sensibility was perhaps most evident in his moving essay "On a Certain Blindness in Human Beings" (1897), which concludes with a forceful admonition to "tolerate, respect, and indulge those whom we see harmlessly interested and happy in their own ways, however unintelligible these may be to us." Sentiments such as these, conveyed to students such as W. E. B. DuBois, Horace Kallen, Alain Locke, and Gertrude Stein, would inspire their efforts to incorporate a full measure of cultural pluralism into American democratic life. Yet, however apt, deeply felt, and influential, James's sentiments remained just that, leaving it to others to work out the political theory and practice they implied.[18]

---

17. William James, "The Moral Equivalent of War" (1910) in James, *Essays in Religion and Morality* (Cambridge: Harvard University Press, 1982), 171–72; John Dewey to Scudder Klyce, 29 May 1915, Scudder Klyce Papers, Library of Congress. For a more appreciative account of James's thinking about modern work see James B. Gilbert, *Work without Salvation: America's Intellectuals and Industrial Alienation, 1880–1910* (Baltimore: Johns Hopkins University Press, 1977), 180–211.

18. William James, "On a Certain Blindness in Human Beings" (1899), in James, *Talks to Teachers on Psychology and to Students on Some of Life's Ideals* (Cambridge: Harvard University Press, 1983), 149. As the title—*Democratic Temperament*—suggests, an appreciation of James's temperament—one comprised of "the inclination to action in the service of an ideal and mutual respect for all citizens and people in foreign countries, including those with different aims" (112)—is the principal yield of Joshua Miller's book as well. See also two fine studies of modern African-American intellectuals that consider the impact of James's sensibility, and that of pragmatism generally, on DuBois, Locke, and others: George Hutchinson, *The Harlem Renaissance in Black and White* (Cambridge: Harvard University Press, 1995); and Ross Posnock, *Color and Culture: Black Writers and the Making of the Modern Intellectual* (Cambridge: Harvard University Press, 1998).

Postmodern Prophet

James Livingston does not traffic in modest claims for James as a social and political theorist. Rather, he argues, in one of the most extraordinary volumes in recent American cultural history, that pragmatism, and James's pragmatism in particular, originated as a powerful legitimating "narrative of the transition from proprietary to corporate capitalism." In this pragmatist narrative, "the decline of proprietary capitalism loses its pathos," as the triumph of corporate capitalism takes on a more smiling disposition than we have any reason to expect, especially if we have been reading the work of American social and cultural historians lately. Unlike these historians, Livingston promises, William James can help us embrace our fate.[19]

Livingston takes this narrative he claims to find in pragmatism—the "comic" narrative of the transition from proprietary to corporate capitalism—and makes it his own.[20] He encloses his study of James's philosophy within an ambitious reconstruction of the history of the American political economy that deploys the economic theories of Karl Marx, Martin Sklar, and others to locate the emergence of consumer culture in the context of the corporate reconstruction of American capitalism at the end of the nineteenth century in the face of a crisis of overproduction and declining profits. He stresses that this reconstruction was not inevitable and that its success rested to a significant degree on a cultural revolution that legitimated the proletarianization of American workers by supplanting the notions of productive and unproductive labor that had fueled their opposition to corporate capital. This cultural revolution also undermined the dominant conception of selfhood, which tied the moral personality tightly to the ownership of productive property by virtuous farmers and artisans. Marginalist economics led the fight against subaltern "producerism" by discrediting the labor theory of value and relocating value in the desires of consumers, while at the same time establishing the credentials of capital as a factor essential to the satisfaction of these desires. Pragmatism, in turn, led the battle against the "modern self" of petty-producers, which posited a fixed location for selfhood in propertied space and a rigid dualism between subjects and objects that echoed artisanal labor. In its stead, pragmatists forecast a postmodern self—a more fluid "social self" located in time rather than space, a self not bound by rigid distinctions between subject and object and thereby well suited to a credit economy of floating signifiers in which the distinction between thoughts and things was often difficult to discern.

19. Livingston, *Pragmatism*, xvi. Subsequent page citations to this book are in the text.
20. As will become evident, I believe that the transaction would be more accurately described as one in which Livingston has tried to transfer the ownership of his narrative to the pragmatists.

Livingston offers this putatively pragmatist narrative as an alternative to the unhappy tale that has taken shape among the "new social historians" and critics of consumer culture in the last generation, a story in which

> the "democratic promise" of the populist moment was betrayed and the house of labor was demolished by corporate capital, the "popular politics" of the nineteenth century declined with the rise of professional expertise and the bureaucratization of the bourgeoisie, and the self-mastering citizens characteristic of proprietary capitalism gave way to the rootless, hedonistic, political, and artificial personalities—the "other-directed" individuals—sanctioned by consumer culture.[21]

Livingston conducts a running polemic against this narrative, and in endeavoring to supplant it with his own, he aims to help us to "appreciate the evidence of progress in the Progressive Era, and to comprehend the remainder of the twentieth century—our own time—as something more than the nonheroic and unintelligible residue of tragedy."[22]

I do not have the credentials to interrogate the whole of Livingston's remarkable narrative. I will confine myself here only to the place he attempts to establish within it for William James.

Livingston's treatment of pragmatism can be read as an ironic embrace of the characterization of James by one of his sharpest critics, Lewis Mumford, who in turn is a principal whipping boy for Livingston. In *The Golden Day,* Mumford contended that industrialism in the Gilded Age ruled the American mind as well as the political economy. The "guts of idealism" went out of late-nineteenth-century writers and intellectuals, he said. Having lost their idealism, these intellectuals were paralyzed, and they bowed to the inevitable, idealized the real, and drifted with the prevailing currents of their culture. William James was among the most important of these intellectuals, Mumford argued, because he named this acquiescence: "he called it pragmatism: and the name stands not merely for his own philosophy, but for something in which that philosophy was deeply if unconsciously entan-

---

21. James Livingston, "The Politics of Pragmatism," *Social Text* 14 (1996): 156. This article, reprinted in Livingston's *Pragmatism, Feminism, and Democracy: Rethinking the Politics of American History* (New York: Routledge, 2001), 35–56, focuses on Dewey rather than James. I consider Livingston's treatment of Dewey in chapter 5.

22. Livingston, "Politics of Pragmatism," 156. Among those American historians that Livingston singles out as tragedians are Lawrence Goodwyn, David Montgomery, Michael McGerr, Burton Bledstein, Jackson Lears, and William Leach ("Politics of Pragmatism," 169n17), though the *locus classicus* of the tragic narrative is Christopher Lasch, *The True and Only Heaven: Progress and Its Critics* (New York: Norton, 1991). Damned once for slighting James, here I am myself twice-damned, this time as a contributor to Richard Fox and Jackson Lears, eds., *The Culture of Consumption* (New York: Pantheon, 1983), and thereby a party to the tragic "Fox, Lears" criticism of consumer culture that Livingston rejects. See Livingston, *Pragmatism,* 62–65.

gled, the spirit of a whole age." James was less a creative philosopher than a "reporter," for he offered no weltanschauung that challenged the premises of his industrializing culture; in his philosophy one got "an excellent view of America." Mumford acknowledged that James's philosophy had been caricatured by many into "a belief in the supremacy of cash-values and practical results" and admitted that "there is an enormous distance between William James and the modern professors who become employees in advertising agencies, or bond salesmen, or publicity experts, without any sense of degradation." Nevertheless, James's thought was "permeated by the smell of the Gilded Age," and Mumford felt that he had to bear a substantial measure of responsibility for the reinforcement his work provided for those whose eye was on the main chance. James, Mumford concluded, "built much worse than he knew."[23]

Livingston does not so much dispute Mumford's characterization of James as reverse its valence. James's philosophy *is* permeated by the smell of the Gilded Age, he contends, but it is not, as Mumford would have it, the stench of declension but the fresh odor of progress. James's pragmatism is not exactly an "acquiescence" to the corporate reconstruction of American capitalism and consumer culture, but it is a "frame of acceptance" for it. That is, James's philosophy is not, strictly speaking, "an apology for modern capitalism," but it does have little use for futile romantic protests against it, such as Mumford's. Like a good Marxist, James did not contest the progress of capitalism into its corporate stage, but rather saw it as opening unexplored possibilities for self and society. As Livingston puts it, "Pragmatists dispense with the moral polemic against proletarianization. They accept the social consequences of that historic process as the premise of their thinking about the meaning and the moral stability of the human personality" (279). In so doing, they set the stage for an "ethos of historicist socialism" that would "recognize in the development of capitalism the necessary condition of a passage beyond class society" (274–75).[24]

Livingston is not altogether clear about whether he believes James knew that he was thinking what Livingston says he was thinking. The contention that James was among those writers "looking for a way to specify the relation between the 'economic revolution' residing in the 'trust movement' and the cultural revolution residing in the redefinition of subjectivity" implies intention, but Livingston never provides any compelling evidence of such intention (68). Instead, he offers imaginatively tendentious readings

23. Lewis Mumford, *The Golden Day* (New York: Dover, 1968), 83, 92–98.

24. Here I am thrice-damned, this time for my reading of Mumford's quarrel with pragmatism, in which I argued that Mumford was wrong about pragmatism's acquiescence to industrial capitalism. See Westbrook, "Mumford, Dewey, and the 'Pragmatic Acquiescence,'" and for Livingston's criticisms, see Livingston, *Pragmatism*, 228–29 and Livingston, "Politics of Pragmatism," 157–58.

of James's work that substitute his own clever wordplay for the more obvious meanings of the texts. For example, he tries to convince us that James's appreciative account in "On a Certain Blindness in Human Beings" of the "unproductive" loafing of Walt Whitman is evidence that James appreciated the distinction between productive laborers and parasitic unproductive capitalists that guided the protest politics of populists and other subaltern groups in the late nineteenth century, yet rejected that distinction because he believed that "the course of nineteenth-century events had abolished the customary distinction between productive and unproductive labor" (171). None of this is explicit in the lecture, in which James merely celebrates the manner in which a tramp like Whitman is freed from the preoccupation with worldly success that blinds most people from "any perception of life's meaning on a large objective scale."[25] That is to say, James was indeed trying to call into question the assumptions his harried bourgeois audience held about what constituted a "productive" way of being in the world, but to work this nice bit of edifying wisdom up into an antipopulist treatise in political economy and then attribute it to James is itself a tough piece of hard labor—and not, I would say, terribly productive.

The suspicion that James could not have known he was thinking what Livingston says he was thinking—and indeed believed he was thinking something quite close to the opposite—is enhanced by a great deal of evidence inconvenient for Livingston's thesis that he simply ignores. For example, again and again at the turn of the century James railed against the triumph of "bigness" in American life, hardly the stance one would expect of one who had adopted a "frame of acceptance" for the corporate reconstruction of the political economy. The most oft-quoted of these remarks came in a letter to Sarah Wyman Whitman in 1899:

> I am against bigness and greatness in all their forms. . . . The bigger the unit you deal with, the hollower, the more brutal, the more mendacious is the life displayed. So I am against all big organizations as such, national ones first and foremost, against all big successes and big results, and in favor of the eternal forces of truth which always work in the individual and immediately unsuccessful way, underdogs always, till history comes after they are long dead and puts them on top.[26]

Elsewhere, James bitterly complained about the individual who "*acquiesces silently* to the organization of great machines for 'slick' success"—noting

25. James, "On a Certain Blindness," 141.
26. William James to Sarah Wyman Whitman, 7 June 1899, *Correspondence*, 8:546. It is perhaps worth noting that another student of the corporate reconstruction of American capitalism, Oliver Zunz, uses a long quotation from this letter as the epigraph to a chapter describing the resistance of proprietary capitalists to incorporation—a chapter entitled "Lost Autonomy." See Zunz, *Making America Corporate, 1870–1920* (Chicago: University of Chicago Press, 1990), 11.

the manner in which such "acquiescence becomes active partnership." For his part, James declared himself a "believer in small systems of things exclusively." "Through small systems, kept pure," he said, "lies the most promising line of betterment."[27]

But perhaps the single most telling piece of evidence against Livingston's claim that James accepted the new corporate order is James's use as a metaphor of the very transformation from proprietary to corporate capitalism that Livingston says he embraced in order to damn American imperialism in the Philippines. American policymakers, James told readers of the Boston *Transcript*, approached Filipino rebel leader Emilio Aguinaldo, as if he were "a dangerous rival with whom all compromising entanglement was sedulously to be avoided by the great Yankee business concern." They tried quietly to discourage him and freeze him out of negotiations, a policy that "reeked of the infernal adroitness of the great department store, which has reached perfect expertness in the art of killing silently and with no public squealing or commotion the neighboring small concern." But this policy was unavailing since "that small concern, Aguinaldo, apparently not having the proper American business education, and being uninstructed on the irresistible character of our Republican party combine, neither offered to sell out nor to give up." So the McKinley administration, much like John D. Rockefeller, took off the gloves and was "now openly engaged in crushing out the sacredest thing in this great human world—the attempt of a people long enslaved to attain to the possession of itself, to organize its laws and government, to be free to follow its internal destinies according to its own ideals."[28] This, I would submit, was a man who regarded the incorporation of America as a tragedy.

Occasionally, Livingston himself provides the evidence that subverts his own interpretation. He quotes James's unambiguously hostile sentiments toward the "stupefying regime" of a feminized "pacific cosmopolitan industrialism"—"a world of clerks and teachers, of co-education and zo-ophily, of 'consumer's leagues' and associated charities,' of industrialism unlimited, and feminism unabashed"—and then tries to claim for James an (ambiguous) appreciation of the promise of a new subjectivity represented above all by the New Woman (71).[29] He also claims for James a "postrepublican"

27. William James to Josephine Shaw Lowell, 6 December 1903, *Correspondence*, 10:339; William James to William Dean Howells, 16 November 1900, *Correspondence*, 9:362; William James to Ernest Howard Crosby, 23 October 1901, *Correspondence*, 9:551. Among those who have commented on James's aversion to "bigness" are Cotkin, *William James*, 174–75; Coon, "Anarchism and James," 79–80; Beisner, *Twelve Against Empire*, 46–47; and Daniel B. Schirmer, "William James and the New Age," *Science and Society* 33 (1969): 434–45.

28. William James, "The Philippine Tangle" (1899), in James, *Essays, Comments, and Reviews*, 154–58.

29. On the milieu in which James's "manly" ideals developed, see Kim Townsend, *Manhood at Harvard: William James and Others* (New York: Norton, 1996).

ethos that "gives up the ghost of the freeholder, the yeoman, and the citizen-soldier," yet admits that what James was attempting to do in "The Moral Equivalent of War" was to reinscribe a republican ethic of civic virtue within "pacific cosmopolitan industrialism" by means of citizen-soldiers mobilized against nature (278, 213).[30]

If James cannot be said to have intentionally embraced the "pragmatist narrative" with which Livingston burdens him, perhaps—whatever his intentions—he built better than he knew, by Livingston's lights. Maybe he left us a postmodern self without knowing that he had done so. Here the reading of James's essays on radical empiricism toward which Livingston's account builds is crucial, for it is in these essays, particularly the earth-shaking article in which James denied the existence of consciousness, that Livingston claims that we see James plump for the social self and dislocated subjectivity that form the basis for the moral personality in the new world of consumer culture.

Livingston echoes Whitehead's characterization of the essays on radical empiricism—especially "Does Consciousness Exist?" (1904)—as a revolutionary break with the long epoch of philosophical meditation on selfhood that began with Descartes' *Discourse on Method*.[31] And there is no doubting James's decisive departure there from the extended reign of the Cartesian self and its offspring.

Consciousness—the Cartesian "I"—does not exist, James argued, at least as a distinct *entity*. On the other hand, knowing—the experience that long occasioned the positing of such an entity ("I think therefore I am")—does most certainly exist. But it exists not as the activity of a discrete soul or self apart from experience but rather as a *function* within "pure experience," which is the "only one primal stuff or material in the world."[32] Knowing or thinking was but a functional relationship obtaining between one bit of pure experience (which we may call the "subject") and another (which we may call the "object"), James contended. Experience had no "inner duplicity." It

30. I would argue that the "Moral Equivalent of War" suggests that what James—and Dewey and a number of other early-twentieth-century American intellectuals—were up to was an effort to *re-place* the moral personality of the yeoman, artisan, and citizen-soldier, that is, a search for new sites in which it could flourish in the wake of proletarianization. For a good example of a clear statement of this project of re-placement, see Herbert Croly, *Progressive Democracy* (New York: Macmillan, 1914), 384–85.

31. It is no accident, Livingston would no doubt say (though surprisingly he does not), that this revolutionary moment coincides with the transformation of the forms of proprietary capitalism traceable to the seventeenth century as well.

32. Although pure experience was the only "primal stuff" in the world, James argued, this did not mean that it was a "general" stuff, that is, it was not something to which the obvious variety in the things experienced could be reduced. "There are as many stuffs as there are 'natures' in the things experienced. . . . Experience is only a collective name for all these sensible natures" (William James, "Does Consciousness Exist?" [1904], in James, *Essays in Radical Empiricism* [1912, Cambridge: Harvard University Press, 1976], 4, 14–15).

took on such doubleness only when one concrete piece of experience was related to another, which meant that the same piece of experience could at one and the same time be both the knower and the known.[33] James's empiricism was "radical" in that it posited that the connections that hold bits of experience together are themselves in experience and are not worked up by an entity (either putatively empirical or ideal) called "consciousness" residing apart from experience. "The relations that connect experiences must themselves be experienced relations, and any kind of relation experienced must be accounted as 'real' as anything else in the system."[34]

The self, by these lights, was a set of connected experiences, indeed, the most tightly connected set of experiences conceivable. "The Self as a system of memories, purposes, strivings, fulfillments or disappointments, is incidental to this most intimate of all relations, the terms of which seem in many cases actually to compenetrate and suffuse each other's being." These relations, and hence the self, "unroll themselves in time." Radical empiricism held that there was no "bedding" holding the pieces of experience together, only the (equally real) conjunctive transitions binding them (and the equally real disjunctions keeping them apart). "Life is in the transitions as much as in the terms connected," James said,

> often, indeed, it seems to be there more emphatically, as if our spurts and sallies forward were the real firing-line of the battle, were like the thin line of flame advancing across the dry autumnal field which the farmer proceeds to burn. In this line we live prospectively as well as retrospectively. It is "of" the past, inasmuch as it comes expressly as the past's continuation; it is "of" the future in so far as the future, when it comes, will have continued it.[35]

Livingston claims that the self that James describes here replaces the modern, dualistic self, firmly fixed in propertied space, with a postmodern self in which the self is not a cause but an effect "of entanglement in externality"—a social, historicized, discursive, displaced self: a self free, like Theodore Dreiser's Sister Carrie, to find itself in the consumer marketplace (150–51). Such a self need not cry over the passage of petty-proprietorship, nor worry like the critics of consumer culture whether or not such a culture can sustain a "genuine" self. Once again James's therapeutic genius is on full display.

Even though in his reading of James's radical empiricism we again find Livingston, not James, doing most of the heavy lifting, this reading is a good deal less fanciful than others he offers us. James does shatter dualism. His

33. James, "Does Consciousness Exist?" 6.

34. William James, "A World of Pure Experience" (1904), in James, *Essays in Radical Empiricism*, 22.

35. James, "World of Pure Experience," 23–24, 29, 42.

self does unroll in time and lives out a narrative, and hence can generously be termed a historicized and discursive self, even though it is not much of a "social self." James held that the connection between selves was mere "withness," the weakest connective tissue in experience, and in his radical empiricism he held firm to a stubborn individualism. In this respect, the self Livingston is looking for might have better been found in the work of another pragmatist and radical empiricist, George Herbert Mead.[36]

Nonetheless, if James's thinking about the self at the turn of the century was confined to that evident in his essays on radical empiricism, then we might grant that Livingston had found at least the bare bones of the postmodern self he is seeking. But James's reflections on selfhood are a good deal more complicated than Livingston would allow, and, as Gerald Myers has demonstrated, it is difficult to confine him to a consistent position.[37] In the chapter on the self in *The Principles of Psychology*, James advances (among others) the very conception of the self as the "propertied" self that Livingston would have him repudiate:

> In its widest possible sense . . . *a man's Self is the sum total of all that he CAN call his*, not only his body and his psychic powers, but his clothes and his house, his wife and children, his ancestors and friends, his reputation and works, his lands and horses, and yacht and bank-account. All these things give him the same emotions. If they wax and prosper, he feels triumphant; if they dwindle and die away, he feels cast down,—not necessarily in the same degree for each thing, but in much the same way for all.

In good petty-producer fashion, James tied this propertied self to a labor theory of value. "The parts of our wealth most intimately ours," he said, "are those which are saturated with our labor." Loss of such property, he concluded, brings "a sense of the shrinkage of our personality, a partial conversion of ourselves to nothingness."[38] Frank Lentricchia offers a particularly compelling reading of this passage and others on the self in the *Principles*. He contends that James's subject/object dualism in that text is, for heuris-

36. Or, James Hoopes would argue, Charles S. Peirce. See Hoopes, *Community Denied: The Wrong Turn of Pragmatic Liberalism* (Ithaca: Cornell University Press, 1998) and my evaluation of this argument in chapter 1. For Livingston's consideration of some clearer proponents of the "social self," see *Pragmatism, Feminism, and Democracy*, 57–83. Ross Posnock has argued that the better proponent in the James family of the sort of self Livingston describes was Henry James. Ross Posnock, *The Trial of Curiosity: Henry James, William James, and the Challenge of Modernity* (New York: Oxford University Press, 1991). See also, Jean-Christophe Agnew, "The Consuming Vision of Henry James," in Richard Wightman Fox and T. J. Jackson Lears, eds., *The Culture of Consumption* (New York: Pantheon, 1983), 65–100.

37. Gerald E. Myers, *William James: His Life and Thought* (New Haven: Yale University Press, 1986), 344–86.

38. William James, *Principles of Psychology* (1890; Cambridge: Harvard University Press, 1983), 1:279–81.

tic purposes, transferred onto his politics for "instrumental" reasons as well. That is, the argument for tolerance that James advances in "On a Certain Blindness in Human Beings," an argument that forecasts his pleas to Americans to leave the Filipinos alone ("Hands off," James said, is the message of the lecture), is an argument for respecting the insular selfhood, the property, of others. As Lentricchia puts it,

> James employs the language of private property in order to describe the spiritual nature of persons and in an effort to turn the discourse of capitalism against itself by making that discourse literal in just one instance: so as to preserve a human space of freedom, however interiorized, from the vicissitudes and coercions of the marketplace. James's anti-imperialism is American anti-imperialism: his major effort is to combat the hegemonic discourse of a capitalism rooted in a democratic political context by appropriating the cornerstone economic principle of capitalism to the advantage of a counterdiscourse and a vision of human sanctity central not only to pragmatism but also to the originating myth of American political history.[39]

But this propertied self is but one of several selves that James assays in the *Principles,* and he admitted that in the end his introspective search for the "Self of selves" was not terribly productive. And, as Livingston says, by the time of the essays on radical empiricism a decade later he appears to have abandoned this quest and repudiated this propertied self in particular. Here, it would indeed seem, is the transition from proprietary to corporate capitalism nicely inscribed in James's psychology. But, as Myers shows, James could never bring himself to rest content with the terribly insubstantial self that his radical empiricism imagined. What Dewey called the "vanishing subject" in James's psychology reappears in a variety of guises in James's later work.

Above all, Livingston ignores what philosopher Richard Gale has nicely termed the "spooky side" of James's latter-day search for the self.[40] For some-

---

39. See Lentricchia "On the Ideologies of Poetic Modernism," in Sacvan Bercovitch, ed., *Reconstructing American Literary History* (Cambridge: Harvard University Press, 1986), 246.

40. Richard M. Gale, "John Dewey's Usurpation of William James's Philosophy," unpublished ms. As the title suggests, Gale's paper is a litany of what he takes to be Dewey's misinterpretations of James, including his obscuring of James's spookiness. Insofar as Livingston seems to read James's radical empiricism through the lens of Dewey's 1940 article on "The Vanishing Subject in the Psychology of James" (*Later Works,* 14:155–67), we can hold Dewey accountable in part for Livingston's partial reading of James's thinking about selfhood. See Livingston, *Pragmatism,* 259–60. A briefer version of Gale's argument can be found as an appendix to his *The Divided Self of William James* (Cambridge: Cambridge University Press, 1999), which stresses the competing, often contradictory, conceptions of selfhood in James's thinking. See also Eugene Taylor, *William James: On Consciousness Beyond the Margin* (Princeton: Princeton University Press, 1996), 40–81; and Marcus Ford, "William James's Psychical Research and Its Philosophical Implications," *Transactions of the Charles S. Peirce Society* 34 (1998): 605–26. The most important investigations of the spooky James are collected in James, *Essays in Psychical Research* (Cambridge: Harvard University Press, 1986).

times Livingston's "modern," propertied subject vanishes in James's thinking not into the postmodern, historically contingent, discursive self Livingston would have us appreciate but into a wider, panpsychic "mother sea" of consciousness. Here one finds a "social self" of quite a different sort than Livingston imagines, a social self in which even selves thought long dead participate. In James's spooky self, that is, one finds ghostly connections between selves that are well beyond "historicity," let alone mere "withness." Here one finds intersubjectivity with a vengeance.

Perhaps no one of late has better captured James's spookiness than novelist Rebecca Goldstein. In her wonderfully inventive novel, *The Dark Sister*, Goldstein tells the story of writer Hedda Dunkele, a moderately successful, reclusive, and unconventionally ugly writer of man-hating potboilers featuring a cast of JAWs—Jewish Angry Women. But when the novel opens Hedda's work has taken a peculiar turn. She is working on a very different sort of novel in which William James is one of the principal protagonists, and her style has fallen into curious proximity to that of Henry James. (The latter development appalls her editor, a lesbian feminist, who rails at her Jamesian circumlocutions: "People don't have all that much *time* nowadays! You think they can be bothered trying to figure out what the fuck some sentence *means*?").[41] In the novel within a novel, William James is inquiring into the case of what eventually is revealed to be the occupation of a single female body by the consciousness of two sisters. In the course of the story, James himself is invaded at a séance by a visitor from the spirit world. At the end of the novel, having failed to prevent the "two" sisters from committing suicide, James meditates on the failure of his panpsychism to catch on among psychologists—a remarkable passage that weaves together James's own words with Goldstein's invention and demonstrates her lucid grasp of James's spookiness:

> He lived a decade into the new century with that injured heart—lived long enough to know it was not to be his century. The tide of psychological thinking went all in one direction, and he went in another. . . . The world *ab extra* went unheard, the new jargon alone would jam all reception. . . . How would the unhoused voices find chinks through which to speak? His own thought went all another way. Personal identity seemed to him more and more a naught, a poor pale flimsy thing, its "hiddenness"—which was realer than itself—lying bathed within the sea of extrapersonal mind—as the ocean of ether bathes the physical world. There is a buried place in the psyche where the boundaries between us all dissolve. It is not the facts of personal history that lie here, not repressed records of infantile trauma, but all of earth's memories are here—and its anguish and its glory—else mediums and artists would

41. Rebecca Goldstein, *The Dark Sister* (New York: Viking, 1991), 217–18.

not get at them as they do. It is from this place that the messages of such ex-
quisite description are sent up to our poor grasping normal minds, making
the blood in our veins go ice with inhuman thoughts of terror and beauty. We
with our lives are like islands in the sea, or like trees in the forest. The maple
and the pine may whisper to each other with their leaves, and Conanicut and
Newport hear each other's foghorns. But the trees also commingle their roots
in the darkness underground, and the islands also hang together through the
ocean's bottom.[42]

Here again we find ourselves rendered distant from James, though in the
end Goldstein makes us wonder. Throughout the novel Hedda has heard
voices, which we assume to be the writer's muse. But after finishing her
"ghost story," she receives a phone call from her dead mother, the "Saint of
West End Avenue" who had made her daughter's life a living hell. She collapses into a corner of her study, crouching there for weeks until rescued at
the novel's end by her sister, Stella, who finds her appearing very much like
the green-skinned youth in the asylum who had occasioned one of James's
nervous collapses in the late 1860s. Whatever we make of Goldstein's apparent sympathies for James's spookiness, of this, at least, we should have no
doubt: were James alive today, he would like many Americans be spending
hours in front of his TV watching re-runs of *The X-Files,* and Fox Mulder is a
man with whom he would dearly love to stroll.[43]

In sum, then, James's unsettled conception of selfhood is pretty shaky
ground on which to establish him as even the unintentional prophet of
"postcapitalist" society. And it may be said more generally of Livingston's efforts to fashion James into the philosophical godfather of consumer culture
what that well-known philosopher/politician, Bill Clinton, said of the efforts
of his Republican opponents to portray him as a liberal: That dog won't
hunt. George Cotkin's dog hunts just fine, but it is unclear how he might
hunt in our time as well as his own. To find a Jamesean dog that will hunt
for us, we could do worse than turn to Frank Lentricchia.

Against Theory

Like many commentators trying to forge a connection between James's
anti-imperialist politics and his pragmatism, Lentricchia takes careful note of
the manner in which, on the one hand, James indicted American imperial-
ists (and Theodore Roosevelt, above all) for their penchant for "abstract" and

42. Ibid., pp. 264–65.
43. What this suggests is that, as uncomfortable as intellectuals in quest of James's legacy
are with his spooky self, his thinking does resonate (in his time as in ours) with some of the
realms of popular belief that intellectuals are inclined (alas) to dismiss out-of-hand.

"absolute" ideological formulations of their civilizing mission, and on the other hand, he wove references to the politics of imperialism into his criticism in *Pragmatism* and elsewhere of the abstractions of rationalist, absolutist philosophical systems. For example, in 1899 James charged Roosevelt with leading an imperial party of "arch abstractionists," guilty of the "crime" of "treating an intensely living and concrete situation by a set of bald and hollow abstractions."[44] Then, eight years later in *Pragmatism*, James described the debate between pragmatists and rationalists as one between those who saw human beings as making the truths of the universe, and those who thought them unfit for such a task. To the rationalists, he said, reversing the earlier analogy, "We're no more fit for such a part than the Filipinos are 'fit for self-government.'"[45] In this manner, James suggested that pragmatism was a philosophy drawn to an anti-imperialist politics and vice versa.[46]

But if this observation has become commonplace in the literature on James's politics, no one has worked out its implications more forcefully than Lentricchia. As he sees it, James's intimation of the disastrous politics bound up with "rationalism" and "abstraction," which emerged in the twin contexts of anti-imperialism and the blossoming of pragmatism, pointed to a wider indictment of the dark side of "theory" generally. James's assault on rationalism, Lentricchia argues, is of a piece with the concerns that others have advanced over a politics that is "totalizing" or "foundational."[47] For James, he says, "there may be nothing more ugly than theoretical consciousness in the practices it authorizes." Rationalism or theory, which appears on the face of it to be a withdrawal from the messy world of contingency, is in reality a way of being in that world with generally nasty consequences; it is, all appearances to the contrary, a practice and a politics. What theory seeks is "purity in action." Rationalism, in stripping the world (and people) of their particularity, is after a "refined object," and hence it gets expressed in "the *will* to refine," which, Lentricchia observes, was "a chilling process when considered in the existential and political contexts within which James writes."[48] Refinement of its objects was the white man's burden. Imperialism bespoke a politics drawn to rationalism and vice versa.

In this context, James's pragmatism was not, as Bertrand Russell claimed, an expression of the will to power but a warning against it. Pragmatism, Rus-

44. "Governor Roosevelt's Oration" (1899), in *Essays, Comments, and Reviews* (Cambridge: Harvard University Press, 1987), 162, 164.

45. William James, *Pragmatism* (1907; Cambridge: Harvard University Press, 1975), 125.

46. See Cotkin, *William James*, pp. 155, 157; and Coon, "Anarchism and James," 95–99.

47. These concerns have cut across the political spectrum. For example, from the right, see Michael Oakeshott, *Rationalism in Politics* (Indianapolis: Liberty Press, 1991) and from the left, Joseph Schwartz, *The Permanence of the Political: A Democratic Critique of the Radical Impulse to Transcend Politics* (Princeton: Princeton University Press, 1995), and James Scott, *Seeing Like a State* (New Haven: Yale University Press, 1998).

48. Lentricchia, "On the Ideologies of Poetic Modernism," 224, 226.

sell said, ignoring James's own claims for the anti-imperial credentials of pragmatism, "develops, by inherent necessity, into the appeal to force and the arbitrament of the big battalions. By this development it becomes equally adapted to democracy at home and to imperialism abroad." In this disagreement between James and Russell, we have, in a nutshell, a dispute that is a constant in debates between pragmatists and many of their critics over its political implications, a disagreement that boils down to a difference between those who believe that moral and epistemological relativism is the surest route to authoritarianism (Russell, Robert Hutchins, John Diggins) and those who believe that the more likely route to oppression is paved with claims to moral and epistemological certainty (James, Dewey, Richard Rorty).[49] Not the relativism that Russell lamented, but the Platonism that Russell espoused (at the time), posed the greater danger for James. For James, Lentricchia demonstrates, the will to unity of all forms of rationalism and absolutism was an "expression of impulses that would control by making uniform the variegated world of autonomous individuals, that would destroy individuality, personal and national, by trimming, fitting, and normalizing autonomous individuality, making the world safe for structure (mine, not yours; ours, not theirs)."[50] James spoke against a politics that "masked itself in rationalist certitude and self-righteousness," and articulated "a vision of heterogeneity and contentiousness—a vision always strong for criticism and self-scrutiny that never claims knowledge of a single unfolding human narrative because it refuses the often repressive conduct resulting from the belief in a single human narrative."[51]

But James's anti-rationalist politics was no easy politics, for the impulse to theory, he argued, was unavoidable. As Lentricchia says, "We are all beset by . . . the need to make the place clean and well-ordered."[52] Theory—the will to refine, the will to unity, the will to dominate—cannot be eliminated or transcended; it can only be caged. James's pragmatism proposes a politics on guard—a politics of vigilance—against the politics of theory. As Lentricchia concludes, "James has no vision of a future social arrangement that would insure the safety of the self, no vision of the good collective. His pragmatism is emancipatory—it would lead us out of suffocating and tyrannous theorizations; it has nothing to say about where we should be, only about where we do not want to be."[53]

49. See Bertrand Russell, "Pragmatism," in Russell, *Philosophical Essays* (New York: Simon and Schuster, 1966), 108–11.

50. Frank Lentricchia, "Philosophers of Modernism at Harvard, circa 1900," *South Atlantic Quarterly* 89 (1990): 802.

51. Frank Lentricchia, "On the Ideologies of Poetic Modernism," 228, 230.

52. Frank Lentricchia, "The Return of William James," in Lentricchia, *Ariel and the Police* (Madison: University of Wisconsin Press, 1988), 124.

53. Lentricchia, "Philosophers of Modernism," 817.

It seems to me that Lentricchia has gone to the heart of what is most valuable for us in James's political thought. He has exposed to view in a manner clearer and more compelling than James himself that dimension of James's political theory that travels well.

I would still contend that Dewey's democratic theory is the richest resource in pragmatist political and social thought on which we might profitably draw, in part because it runs the risk of saying something about where we should be. But James, like Reinhold Niebuhr after him, adds something to a pragmatist politics all too often missing in Dewey's formulation of it. If James's ethics warned—as Dewey's often failed to do—that the really tough moral decisions in life often eventuate in tragic choices that call on us to "butcher the ideal," so his political thinking warns of the manner in which the ideal may butcher us.[54] In practice, Dewey was not blind to this danger, but his theory, as theory must be, was insufficiently vigilant. Because Dewey was a democrat, his hunger for wholeness (always provisional, in any case) can appear benign at best and naive at worst. But the "Hegelian bacillus of reconciliation," which Dewey admitted haunted his thinking long after he abandoned absolute idealism, does have its more virulent strains.[55] James provides an antidote to this bacillus and inoculates us against its fevers.

But here we may also put ourselves in the debt of a contextualizing historian such as George Cotkin. For effective as James's political message is in the abstract—dare I say "in theory"—it is all the more powerful when we understand that it was cast within the particular context of death-dealing imperialism in the Philippines, an American project that foreshadowed the century of slaughter—much of it authorized by a rationalizing will to refine—that began in earnest hard on William James's death in 1910.

54. William James, "The Moral Philosopher and the Moral Life" (1891), in James, *The Will to Believe* (1897; Cambridge: Harvard University Press, 1979), 154–55. On this difference between James and Dewey, see James Kloppenberg, *Uncertain Victory: Social Democracy and Progressivism in European and American Thought, 1870–1920* (New York: Oxford, 1986), 132–44; and Robert B. Westbrook, *John Dewey and American Democracy* (Ithaca: Cornell University Press, 1991), 163, 416–17—as well as chapter 4 of this volume.

55. See John Dewey to William James, 27 March 1903, *Correspondence*, 10:220.

CHAPTER 3

Pullman and
the Professor

★

IF political implications and democratic possibilities must be dug out of the thinking of Charles Peirce and William James, they lay very much closer to the surface of the philosophy of John Dewey. In part, this was a matter of context.

The early years of Dewey's career in the 1880s give some hints of how deeply invested he would become in tying his work as a philosopher to the fate of American democracy. But although there were suggestions of such wider concerns in these years, he was more decidedly focused on his professional academic career, one much more successful than Peirce's and much more conventional than James's. But in the summer of 1894 Dewey moved from the University of Michigan and the college town of Ann Arbor to the city of Chicago to assume the chair of both the philosophy department and a new department of pedagogy at the recently founded University of Chicago. Thereafter, while Peirce and James observed from afar the bitter social and political conflicts that shook the country in the late nineteenth century, Dewey found himself immersed in them and felt compelled to address them, if at first only obliquely.

The tonic effect of Chicago on Dewey was nearly instantaneous. In Chicago, he told his wife Alice shortly after arriving in the city,

> every conceivable thing solicits you; the town seems filled with problems holding out their hands and asking somebody to please solve them—or else dump them in the lake. I had no conception that things could be so much more phe-

nomenal and objective than they are in a country village, and simply stick themselves at you, instead of leaving you to think about them. The first effect is pretty paralyzing, the after effect is stimulating—at least, subjectively so, and maybe that is all chaos is in the world for, and not really to be dealt with. But after all you can't really get rid feeling here that there is a 'method' and if you could only get hold of it things could be tremendously straightened out.

He advised Alice to think of the city as "hell turned loose, and yet not hell any longer, but simply material for a new creation."[1]

In November 1894, Dewey wrote another remarkable letter to Alice, who was then vacationing in Europe with two of the couple's three young children. Taking special satisfaction in his new role as a professor of pedagogy, Dewey forecast the central place that he expected the philosophy of education would assume in his thinking during the decade he spent in Chicago. "I sometimes think I will drop teaching philosophy directly," he told Alice, "and teach it via *pedagogy*."

Such a project, Dewey observed, would require a laboratory, a working school in which his philosophical arguments could be tested in practice, and he had a clear idea of what this school would be like:

> There is an image of a school growing up in my mind all the time; a school where some actual and literal constructive activity shall be the centre and source of the whole thing, and from which the work should be always growing out in two directions—one the social bearings of that constructive industry, the other the contact with nature which supplies it with its materials. I can see, theoretically, how the carpentry etc. in building a model house shall be the centre of a social training on the one side and a scientific on the other, all held within the grasp of a positive concrete physical habit of eye and hand.

In offering this prescient vision to his wife, Dewey made it clear that whatever virtues such a school might have as a laboratory for an experimental philosophy, the need for it was above all a *social* one, and the urgency with which he pressed this vision on her was that of a reformer who had been gripped by the same hopes for industrial democracy that animated his friends and fellow Chicagoans Jane Addams and Henry Demarest Lloyd. "When you think of the thousands and thousands of young ones who are practically ruined negatively if not positively in the Chicago schools every year," he remarked, "it is enough to make you go out and howl on the street corners like the Salvation Army." Alice need not worry about pulling their own children out of school for the European trip, he advised, for they were

1. John Dewey to Alice Dewey, 25 August 1894, Dewey Papers, Morris Library, Southern Illinois University, Carbondale, Illinois. Hereafter cited as Dewey Papers. The Dewey Center at Southern Illinois is near completion of a fine CD-ROM edition of Dewey's correspondence.

far better off than they would be in the classrooms of their new hometown: "at least they are still themselves with their own intelligences and their own responses—and that is more than can be said for most children of their age." With this letter, Dewey announced his intention to carve out a niche for himself and his ideas about democracy and education (and for Alice and hers as well) in the turbulent reform politics of Chicago in the 1890s.[2]

Although Dewey's arrival in Chicago was of enormous import for his subsequent career, it was by all counts not the most important event in this city in the mid-summer of 1894. Pride of place in this regard would go to the Pullman strike. Dewey himself would no doubt have insisted on it. He observed this dramatic confrontation between railroad corporations and workers with great interest, not only because he was trying to get from Ann Arbor to Chicago by train shortly after the strike began, but also because the strike enlivened a concern with the "labor question" that he had begun to develop in Michigan and deepened a perspective on that question that he shared with the leader of the strike, Eugene Debs. It is this shared perspective of Dewey and Debs—a view historians have labeled "producerism" or "producer-republicanism"—and its impact on his philosophy of education that I would like to explore in this chapter.

Strike

Let me first sketch the circumstances of the strike and describe Dewey's response to it. The Pullman strike began in the spring of 1894 following a severe wage cut at the Pullman Car Works, a cut unaccompanied by any reduction in the rents, food prices, and service rates George Pullman charged his workers in the model company town he had built for them just south of Chicago in the 1880s. After the company refused to respond to the workers' grievances and fired those who presented them, Pullman's labor force went on strike on 11 May. A month later the strikers won the support of Debs's recently formed American Railway Union, which was fresh from a signal victory in a strike against James J. Hill's Great Northern Railroad. Following Pullman's refusal to submit the dispute to arbitration, the union launched a boycott on 25 June against Pullman sleeping cars, refusing to work on any railroad that did not detach them from its trains. Pullman received support from the powerful General Managers Association of the twenty-four railroads with Chicago terminals, and by early July—when Dewey departed for the city—the strike had escalated from a local dispute

2. John Dewey to Alice Dewey, 1 November 1894, Dewey Papers.

to an effort by these powerful corporate managers to break the union and assert the superior power of capital.

They were soon successful in this effort. Enlisting the support of the national state, the managers succeeded in securing a federal injunction against Debs and the ARU on the grounds that they had interfered with the mails and interstate commerce, and President Grover Cleveland dispatched federal troops to Chicago to enforce the injunction. Up to this time the strike had been marked by little violence, but in the week that followed the arrival of the troops, riots broke out and substantial railroad property was destroyed. On 10 July Debs and other union officers were arrested on charges of violating the injunction and of conspiracy, and the strike effectively collapsed.[3]

Dewey followed the progress of the strike closely and conveyed his impressions of it in letters to Europe to Alice. In one of the first of these letters, he wrote of a moving encounter he had had on his way to Chicago with a union organizer in Durand, Michigan:

> I only talked with him 10 or 15 minutes but when I got through my nerves were more thrilled than they had been for years; I felt as if I had better resign my job teaching and follow him around till I got into life. One lost all sense of the right or wrong of things in admiration of his absolute almost fanatic, sincerity and earnestness, and in admiration of the magnificent combination that was going on. Simply as an aesthetic matter, I don't believe the world has seen but a few times such a spectacle of magnificent, widespread union of men about a common interest as this strike business.[4]

Dewey was particularly troubled throughout the strike by the hostility to the strikers expressed by intellectuals and academics, including some of his new colleagues at the University of Chicago. "I think professional people are probably worse than the capitalists themselves," he said. Appalled by attacks on the union in journals such as the *Nation* and *Harper's Weekly*, Dewey told Alice he did not know when he had seen anything that seemed "so hopeless and discouraging." It was, he said, "hard to keep one's balance. The only

---

3. For a good, brief account of the strike and its aftermath, see David Papke, *The Pullman Case: The Clash of Labor and Capital in Industrial America* (Lawrence: University Press of Kansas, 1999). Richard Schneirov, Shelton Stromquist, and Nick Salvatore, eds., *The Pullman Strike and the Crisis of the 1890s* (Urbana: University of Illinois Press, 1999) is an excellent collection of essays on the strike and its implications. Dewey's brother Davis, an eminent MIT economist, who was touring the country in 1893–1894 investigating the effects of the deep depression that afflicted the nation, visited his brother in Chicago in the summer of 1894. Davis, a talented economic historian, later contributed a book on this period to the important American Nation series, which included an even-handed account of the Pullman strike and its aftermath. See Davis Rich Dewey, *National Problems, 1885–1897* (New York: Harper, 1907).

4. John Dewey to Alice Dewey, 2 July 1894, Dewey Papers.

wonder is that when the 'higher classes'—damn them—take such views there aren't more downright socialists. . . . That a representative journal of the upper classes—damn them again—can take the attitude of that Harper's Weekly and in common with all other journals, think Debs is a simple lunatic or else doing all this to show his criminal control over criminal 'lower classes'—well it shows what it is to become a higher class." Touched by an account of the European poor that his son Fred had sent him, Dewey contrasted the boy's feelings with the insensitivity of upper-class opinion to the issues involved in the strike. "Maybe," he remarked, "[Fred will] be a social agitator—and maybe he'll get to belong to the higher classes and be strong on law and order and very weak on justice and liberty." Disgusted by the capitulation to capital by genteel liberals, Dewey's sympathies were with the populist coalition of urban workers, farmers, socialists, and reform intellectuals that Lloyd and other Chicago radicals were attempting to organize.[5]

Social Christianity

To those who had followed the development of Dewey's social thought in the early years of his career, his response to the strike would not have been particularly surprising, for it followed from the religious social gospel to which he adhered. Dewey is best placed in this period among the middle-class "social Christians" who were profoundly concerned about what they termed the "labor question": the implications of the creation of a permanent wage-earning proletariat for American ideals of liberty, equality, and democracy—ideals that had heretofore been tightly linked to a widespread distribution of the ownership and control of productive property. The most prominent of these social Christians were the "ethical economists"—Richard T. Ely, John Bates Clark, Henry Carter Adams, and Edmund J. James—but the group also included such clergymen as Washington Gladden, R. Heber Newton, and George Herron and novelists William Dean Howells and Albion W. Tourgee.[6]

5. John Dewey to Alice Dewey, 5 July 1894; John Dewey to Alice Dewey, 16 July 1894; John Dewey to Alice Dewey, 20 July 1894; John Dewey to Alice Dewey, 6 November 1894, Dewey Papers. On Lloyd's populist coalition, see Chester M. Destler, *American Radicalism, 1865–1901* (Chicago: Quadrangle, 1966), 175–211; Lawrence Goodwyn, *The Democratic Promise: The Populist Moment in America* (New York: Oxford University Press, 1976), 411–21; John L. Thomas, *Alternative America: Henry George, Edward Bellamy, Henry Demarest Lloyd and the Adversary Tradition* (Cambridge: Harvard University Press, 1983), 212–13; and Richard Schneirov, "Labor and the New Liberalism in the Wake of the Pullman Strike," in Schneirov et al., *Pullman Strike*, 212–18.

6. George M. Fredrickson, "Intellectuals and the Labor Question in Late Nineteenth-Century America" (Paper delivered at the Annual Meeting of the American Historical Association, New York, December 1985), 12–13. See also Dorothy Ross, "Socialism and American Liberal-

Most of the social Christians came from pious, often evangelical backgrounds, and from middle-class families in small Midwestern towns or the rural Northeast. Their lives had been shaped profoundly by the Civil War, and they, or their parents, were firm supporters of the Union. Many came from antislavery households, though seldom of the most radical sort. Building on the redemptive nationalism that sanctified the northern cause and the work of writers such as Elisha Mulford, who gave such nationalism a gloss of philosophical idealism, these intellectuals began their careers as advocates of a Christian commonwealth bound together by ethical and religious solidarity. Although not all social Christians were ministers, most conceived of their role in clerical terms and remained active in religious organizations. Believing with Mulford that "the only completion of the state is in the Christian state," they saw their task as nothing less than the salvation of their nation.[7]

By the mid-1880s the social Christians had made it clear that they believed the Christian state could not arrive with an unregulated corporate capitalist political economy, and they accepted much of the socialist denunciation of capitalism while carefully distancing themselves from all calls for government ownership of the means of production. In a characteristic appreciation of the socialist point of view, Washington Gladden remarked in 1886 that

> The tendencies to which [socialists] point,—the tendency of wages to sink to the starvation point, the tendency of woman's share of the national wealth to grow constantly smaller, the tendency of commercial crises and depressions to become more frequent and disastrous, the tendency of all business operations and enterprises to become more concentrated in fewer hands, and the consequent tendency to confine the wage laborers more and more rigorously to their present condition, with the steady growth of a plutocracy on the one side and the proletariat on the other,—all these are, as I believe, the natural issues of an industrial system whose sole motive power is self-interest and whose regulative principle is competition.[8]

---

ism: Academic Social Thought in the 1880s," *Perspectives in American History* 11 (1977/78): 5–79; Dorothy Ross, *The Origins of American Social Science* (New York: Cambridge University Press, 1991), 98–140; Peter J. Frederick, *Knights of the Golden Rule: The Intellectual as Christian Social Reformer in the 1890s* (Lexington: University of Kentucky Press, 1976); and Paul T. Phillips, *A Kingdom on Earth: Anglo-American Social Christianity, 1880–1940* (University Park: Pennsylvania State University Press, 1996).

7. Fredrickson, "Intellectuals and the Labor Question," 6–8; Elisha Mulford, *The Nation* (New York: Hurd and Houghton, 1870), 368. On Mulford and his influence, see Mark E. Neely, Jr., "Romanticism, Nationalism, and the New Economics: Elisha Mulford and the Organic Theory of the State," *American Quarterly* 29 (1977): 404–21.

8. Washington Gladden, *Applied Christianity* (1886), as quoted in Fredrickson, "Intellectuals and the Labor Question," 16.

Social Christians were most distressed about the way in which corporate capitalism threatened petty-proprietorship and in the process undermined the autonomy and dignity of labor that accompanied property ownership. Consequently, while rejecting state ownership of the means of production, they pressed for various forms of "cooperative" ownership and control of productive resources, and they were especially enamored of those elements of the labor movement that shared this cooperative vision. Such cooperation might range—depending on the faith a particular social Christian had in the capacities of the working class—from employee-owned workers' co-operatives to collaborative arrangements in which capital, labor, and professional managers shared the control and profits of an enterprise. While social Christians rested their hopes for the cooperative commonwealth principally on moral suasion and voluntary arrangements, they were not unwilling to advocate a significant exercise of state power to secure social justice. Given this program, it is not surprising that the social Christians gravitated toward the Knights of Labor, which admitted middle-class professionals (and even some employers) to membership and whose platform eschewed class conflict and called for workers' cooperatives and the preservation of a democracy of citizen-producers.[9]

During his years at Michigan, Dewey was a decidedly minor figure among social Christians, though he clearly belonged among them by virtue of his background and his thinking on the labor question. Dewey's father, a Burlington, Vermont, storeowner, was devoted to the Republican platform of "free soil, free labor, and free men," and at the advanced age of fifty-one, he enlisted (and then reenlisted) as a quartermaster in the Union army. Dewey's mother, who followed her husband with their children to the battlefields of Virginia, was a fervid evangelical Protestant, who did everything she could to make sure her sons were "right with Jesus" and extended her benevolence to the less fortunate citizens of Burlington as well. Dewey himself remained an active Congregationalist through his years at the University of Michigan (1884–1894), where he and his mentor and colleague George Sylvester Morris ensured that the philosophy department was "pervaded with a spirit of religious belief, unaffected, pure and independent." He lectured regularly to the Student Christian Association on such topics as "Christianity and Democracy" and taught Bible classes at his local church. Though he never apparently considered a career in the ministry, he was eager to emulate one of his intellectual heroes, British idealist T. H. Green, and make his conscience "a public and political force as well as a private and 'moral' monitor." Though it was Green rather than Mulford who was

9. On the ideology of the Knights, see Leon Fink, *Workingmen's Democracy: The Knights of Labor and American Politics* (Urbana: University of Illinois Press, 1983), esp. 3–17.

Dewey's philosophical idealist of choice in the 1880s, he later told Herbert Schneider that "in my youth" Mulford's *The Nation* was "a great book" that he took "very seriously."[10]

The ethical economist who exercised the greatest influence on Dewey was his Michigan colleague and friend Henry Carter Adams. Adams studied political economy at Johns Hopkins and was awarded the university's first Ph.D. in 1876, and he subsequently returned from a year's study in Germany determined to apply the critical insights of the socialist tradition to the American political economy. In an essay entitled "Democracy" (1881), he called for the establishment of a cooperative commonwealth of owner-workers that would "realize socialistic aims by individualistic means." He argued that "the practical plan through which that liberty promised by democracy is to be realized is the abandonment of the wages system and the establishment of industries upon the cooperative basis." These sentiments did not do Adams a lot of good on the job market. In the early 1880s he held half-time appointments at Michigan and Cornell, and, burdened with suspicions about his social views, he struggled to gain a full-time appointment. In 1886 his public support of the Knights of Labor and assertions that "there can be no permanent solution to the labor problem so long as the wage system is maintained" outraged Cornell trustee Russell Sage, who demanded that Adams be fired. He was able to obtain a permanent appointment at Michigan only after submitting himself to an interrogation on his political beliefs by the university's president, James B. Angell, in which Adams was forced to admit that his defense of the Knights had been "unwise."[11]

Dewey himself addressed the labor question briefly both in his earliest published efforts at democratic theory and in his lectures to Michigan stu-

10. George Dykhuizen, *The Life and Mind of John Dewey* (Carbondale: Southern Illinois University Press, 1973), 6–7, 47; Willinda Savage, "The Evolution of John Dewey's Philosophy of Experimentalism as Developed at the University of Michigan," Ph.D. Diss., University of Michigan, 1950, 26–27, 121–39; Dewey, "Christianity and Democracy" (1892), *Early Works*, 4:3–10; Dewey, "The Philosophy of Thomas Hill Green" (1889), *Early Works*, 3:15–16; Corliss Lamont, *Dialogue on John Dewey* (New York: Horizon Press, 1959), 100. On Dewey's appropriation of British idealism, see Robert B. Westbrook, *John Dewey and American Democracy* (Ithaca: Cornell University Press, 1991), 13–51; and Alan Ryan, *John Dewey and the High Tide of American Liberalism* (New York: Norton, 1995), 85–99. On Dewey as a secular preacher, see Robert Crunden, *Ministers of Reform* (New York: Basic Books, 1982), 52–63. The two fullest and best accounts of Dewey's early career and thought are Neil Coughlan, *Young John Dewey* (Chicago: University of Chicago Press, 1975), and Steven C. Rockefeller, *John Dewey: Religious Faith and Democratic Humanism* (New York: Columbia University Press, 1991), 27–217.

11. Henry Carter Adams, "Democracy," *New Englander* 40 (1881): 771–72; Adams in William E. Barnes, *The Labor Problem: Plain Questions and Practical Answers* (1886), as quoted in Fredrickson, "Intellectuals and the Labor Question," 24. Two excellent studies of Adams's life and thought are Ross, "Socialism and American Liberalism" and A. W. Coats, "Henry Carter Adams: A Case Study in the Emergence of the Social Sciences in the United States, 1850–1900," *Journal of American Studies* 2 (1968): 177–97. See also Mary O. Furner, *Advocacy and Objectivity: A Crisis in the Professionalization of American Social Science, 1865–1905* (Lexington: University of Kentucky Press, 1975), 127–42.

dents. In concluding his most important early essay on the democratic ideal, "The Ethics of Democracy" (1888), he declared that "there is no need to beat around the bush in saying that democracy is not in reality what it is in name until it is industrial, as well as civil and political." Although he did not beat around the bush in saying this, Dewey did not say with any precision what he meant by industrial democracy. He made it clear that he did not mean a simple egalitarian distribution of wealth, nor did he intend the term to imply the sort of socialism that could be "interpreted to mean that in some way society, as a whole, to the abolition of all individual initiative and result, is to take charge of all those undertakings which we call economic," that is, state socialism. Industrial democracy rather meant that "all industrial relations are to be regarded as subordinate to human relations, to the law of personality. . . . They are to become the material of an ethical realization; the form and substance of a community of good (though not necessarily of goods) wider than any now known." Though it is difficult to know what sort of political economy Dewey envisioned here, his call for industrial relations that manifested a "community of good" echoed the language of social Christian cooperation.[12]

In the classroom, Dewey was more precise about what he meant by industrial democracy. He told his students that the class divisions of industrial capitalism were incompatible with the ethics of democracy. The division of labor in industrial capitalism, he argued, fell far short of an ideal division of labor, that is, a division of labor that would permit every individual to achieve self-realization by means of the development of his peculiar capacities and powers. The division of labor, Dewey told his class in political philosophy, "is never complete until the laborer gets his full expression":

> The kind we now have in factories,—one-sided, mechanical—is a case of class interest; i.e. his activity is made a means to benefit others. It can't be complete till he does that for which he is best fitted,—in which he finds the most complete expression of himself.

Self-realization entailed the conscious control by the individual worker of his own labor for ends that he had chosen for himself. Industrial capitalism was a system in which "the value of an individual as an organ of activity is appropriated by others," and, as such, it blocked not only the self-realization of the individual but also the perfection of the social organism. "The imperfect realization of the individual means the imperfect realization of the whole and *vice versa*. Class interests not only put a limitation on the individual but also a limitation on the whole." Unlike Adams, Dewey expressed no open sympathies for the Knights of Labor, but the moral philosophy he

---

12. Dewey, "The Ethics of Democracy" (1888), *Early Works*, 1:246–47.

wrote in this period often made use of examples drawn from the conflict of capital and labor and left no doubt that Dewey's sympathies lay with the working class.[13]

Debs

Social Christian thinking intersected with and drew on a nineteenth-century American strain of thought that, as I say, historians have termed producer-republicanism or simply "producerism."[14] Producerism emerged in late-eighteenth-century America as an agrarian and artisanal variant of the civic republicanism that played such an important role in the ideology of the American Revolution. Producer-republicanism celebrated the dignity of productive labor as the source of civic virtue and independent citizenship, and yeoman farmers and skilled artisans formed the backbone of the ideal producerist commonwealth.[15]

"Independence"—embodied in the freehold farm or the family-run shop—was a crucial virtue for producerists. Hence, wage labor in which a worker was dependent on, even subservient to, an employer was problematic, and the prospect of permanent "wage slavery" occasioned widespread concern by the mid nineteenth century. But these anxieties were eased by the faith that for diligent workers, wage labor would be but a temporary stage of the working life, one through which they moved on their way to eventual petty-proprietorship.[16] The crucial social division for producerists was thus not between employers and employees, capital and labor, but between productive and unproductive labor. Producerists worried most over

13. Dewey, "Lecture Notes: Political Philosophy, 1892," 44–45, Dewey Papers; Dewey, "Moral Theory and Practice" (1891), *Early Works*, 3:105–6; Dewey, *Outlines of a Critical Theory of Ethics* (1891), *Early Works*, 3:351–52, 360–61.

14. Catherine McNicol Stock has supplied a superb, compact overview of the producerist tradition in *Rural Radicals: Righteous Rage in the American Grain* (Ithaca: Cornell University Press, 1996), 15–86.

15. Sean Wilentz, *Chants Democratic: New York City and the Rise of the American Working Class, 1788–1850* (New York: Oxford University Press, 1984), is the best study of early-nineteenth-century producer-republicanism. See also Tony A. Freyer, *Producers Versus Capitalists: Constitutional Conflict in Antebellum America* (Charlottesville: University of Virginia Press, 1994); Jonathan Glickstein, *Concepts of Free Labor in Antebellum America* (New Haven: Yale University Press, 1991); James L. Huston, *Securing the Fruits of Labor: The American Concept of Wealth Distribution, 1765–1900* (Baton Rouge: Louisiana State University Press, 1998); David Montgomery, *Citizen Worker* (New York: Cambridge University Press, 1993); Robert Steinfeld, *The Invention of Free Labor* (Chapel Hill: University of North Carolina Press, 1991).

16. For a classic statement of this view, see Abraham Lincoln's address to the Wisconsin State Agricultural Society (1859): Abraham Lincoln, *Speeches and Writings, 1859–1865* (New York: Library of America, 1989), 90–101. See also Christopher Lasch, "Opportunity in the Promised Land: Social Mobility or the Democratization of Competence?" in Lasch, *The Revolt of the Elites and the Betrayal of Democracy* (New York: Norton, 1995), 50–79.

the social and political power of social "parasites," such as bankers and other "nonproducers," whose "unearned" wealth was the product less of labor than of speculation and government favoritism. Employers in productive industries were generally thought to be members of the producing classes, and producerists saw no necessary conflict between the interests of workers and those of the owners and managers of the small firms in which most of the American working class labored for much of the century.

But the growth of the factory system and the corporate organization of production—which gathered workers into large firms, intensified the division of labor, degraded craft skills, and thereby threatened the dignity of labor—lent producerism an increasingly critical edge in the late nineteenth century as its adherents began to articulate a defense of the independence of working people at odds with the dynamics of industrial capitalism. Thus by the 1880s producerism pointed in both conservative and radical directions. On the one hand, it posited no necessary conflict between the class interests of employers and those of employees, but on other hand, it produced a deeply troubled response to the conflictual way those interests were shaping up in the emerging industrial regime.[17]

Producerism was the ideology that Eugene Debs brought with him to the Pullman strike. As a consequence, his view of industrial capitalism coincided in significant respects with that of Dewey and other social Christians, who were among middle-class professionals the most prominent producerist critics of the emerging corporate order.[18]

Born four years before Dewey, Debs was, like Dewey, the son of a storekeeper. Like Dewey's Burlington, Vermont, Debs's beloved hometown, Terre Haute, Indiana, was a small city undergoing the social and economic transformations of industrialization as he grew up. The producerist belief in the common interests of employers and workers was gospel in Terre Haute, and Debs, who moved rapidly up the ranks of the Brotherhood of Locomotive Firemen as a young man, was one of its firmest adherents. He formed a mutually rewarding alliance with the city's leading businessman,

17. On the increasingly critical view of capitalism afforded by late-nineteenth-century producerism, see Fink, *Workingmen's Democracy;* Victoria Hattam, *Labor Visions and State Power: The Origins of Business Unionism in the United States* (Princeton: Princeton University Press, 1993); Gretchen Ritter, *Goldbugs and Greenbacks: The Antimonopoly Tradition and the Politics of Finance in America, 1865–1896* (Cambridge: Cambridge University Press, 1997); and Kim Voss, *The Making of American Exceptionalism: The Knights of Labor and Class Formation in the Nineteenth Century* (Ithaca: Cornell University Press, 1993).

18. This is not to discount the Christian elements in Debs's worldview as well. It would not be too much of a stretch to include him among American social Christians, though the thought would have troubled the more conservative among them. Addressing the question "What is Socialism?" Debs responded, "Merely Christianity in action." Quoted in Nick Salvatore, *Eugene V. Debs: Citizen and Socialist* (Urbana: University of Illinois Press, 1982), 165. For an acute discussion of Debs's Christianity, see Richard Wightman Fox, *Jesus in America: Personal Savior, Cultural Hero, National Obsession* (San Francisco: HarperCollins, 2004), 259–94.

railroad entrepreneur William Riley McKeen. He opposed the great railroad strikes of 1877, and was elected first to the position of city clerk in 1879 and then to the state assembly in 1884 with the support of a broad, cross-class coalition of voters.[19]

Beginning in the mid-1880s Debs's producerism took an increasingly critical turn, though his criticism was focused less on corporate capitalism as a system than on the machinations of a few corporate capitalists who he believed had subverted the common interests of labor and capital. Speaking in Sedalia, Missouri, in the midst of the 1886 strike of the Knights of Labor against Jay Gould's southwestern railroads, Debs expressed the hope that the strike would teach workers and employers to respect one another and establish "an honorable alliance of capital and labor, to the end that justice would be done to both."[20]

By the end of the decade, Debs had grown more critical of corporate power and frustrated by the divisions among workers that thwarted opposition to the threat of this power to the autonomy of labor. In the wake of a bitter, year-long strike against the Chicago, Burlington, and Quincy Railroad in 1888–1889 that divided the railroad craft unions, Debs emerged convinced of the need for an industrial union of all railroad workers and set about organizing the American Railway Union. Yet on the eve of the Pullman strike, Debs had not lost his conviction that the interests of capital and labor could be harmonized under the banner of producer-republicanism. Following the ARU victory against the Great Northern, he declared that

> [The American Railway Union] believes and will work to the end of bringing the employer and employee in closer touch. An era of close relationship between capital and labor, I believe, is dawning, one which I feel will place organized labor on a higher standard. When employer and employee can thoroughly respect each other, I believe, will strikes be a thing of the past. . . . It is said the chasm between capital and labor is widening, but I do not believe it. If anything, it is narrowing and I hope to see the day when there will be none.[21]

For Debs in the spring of 1894, as his biographer Nick Salvatore has said, "the basic problem was not a system of economic organization but rather specific difficulties that might arise with a given corporate employer."[22] In this, he was even less alert at this time to the threat that industrial capital-

---

19. My reading of Debs's ideology and its context is thoroughly indebted to Salvatore, *Debs*, yet Ray Ginger's *The Bending Cross: A Biography of Eugene Victor Debs* (New Brunswick: Rutgers University Press, 1949) also remains a superb biography.

20. Debs, as quoted in Salvatore, *Debs*, 69.

21. Ibid., 124.

22. Salvatore, *Debs*, 124.

ism posed to producerist ideals than Dewey. Yet, as Andrew Feffer observes, both social Christians and labor reformers—both Dewey and Debs—were seeking a way other than divisive class conflict to restore the dignity of labor by "reasserting the autonomy workers supposedly enjoyed as artisans and farmers, thereby building an 'industrial democracy' on the ruins of the preindustrial republic."[23]

Schooling for Industrial Democracy

Shortly after the Pullman strike was crushed, Dewey argued that it may well have been an unintended success because it had made a "tremendous impression" that would ultimately benefit the union cause. "I think the few freight cars burned up a pretty cheap price to pay," he wrote Alice. "It was the stimulus necessary to direct attention, and it might easily have taken more to get the social organism thinking."[24]

But most of the social organism was thinking along quite different lines than Dewey, including many of his fellow social Christians. The strike horrified many of these intellectuals, who argued that it marked an abandonment by trade unions of cooperative strategies in favor of unlawful, even violent, coercion. Above all, it was Debs's apparent defiance of a federal injunction that disturbed them. "We must remember," Richard Ely advised, "that Christ and his apostles always recognized the authority of the State as divine in character even under the most trying and perplexing circumstances."[25]

Dewey was shaken by this retreat and by the concerted crackdown on labor supporters by college and university trustees and administrators. In the wake of the firing of his colleague, economics professor Edward Bemis, who had publicly supported the strikers, he told Alice that he had concluded that "Chicago Univ. is a capitalistic institution—that is, it too belongs to the higher classes." He was, he said, quickly realizing "how 'anarchistic' (to use the current term here) our ideas and especially feelings are."[26]

Although his social and political criticism became decidedly circumspect

23. Andrew Feffer, *The Chicago Pragmatists and American Progressivism* (Ithaca: Cornell University Press, 1993), 12.

24. John Dewey to Alice Dewey, 14 July 1894, Dewey Papers.

25. Richard Ely, "Fundamental Beliefs in My Social Philosophy" (1895), and *The Social Law of Service* (1896), as quoted in Fredrickson, "Intellectuals and the Labor Question," 29.

26. John Dewey to Alice Dewey, 5 July 1894; John Dewey to Alice Dewey, 16 July 1894; John Dewey to Alice Dewey, 20 July 1894; and John Dewey to Alice Dewey, 25 September 1894, Dewey Papers. On the Bemis case, see Harold E. Bergquist, Jr., "The Edward Bemis Controversy at the University of Chicago," *American Association of University Professors Bulletin* 58 (1972): 383–93; Walter P. Metzger, *Academic Freedom in the Age of the University* (New York: Columbia University Press, 1961), 151–62; and Furner, *Advocacy and Objectivity*, 163–204.

in the 1890s in the face of these considerations, Dewey nonetheless clung tenaciously to many elements of the producerist critique of industrial capitalism and to his hopes for industrial democracy. This persistent producerism is most apparent in his blossoming philosophy of education and in the curriculum of his Laboratory School.

A little over a year after Dewey told his wife of the sort of school he envisioned starting, the Deweys would have just such a school—the Laboratory School of the University of Chicago. It would soon become one of the most talked-about elementary schools in the United States, and a quick tour of its philosophy and pedagogy has become a staple of the history of education in this country. In shaping the curriculum of his laboratory, Dewey never lost sight of the concern he expressed in his letter to Alice for the social bearings of "constructive industry." In the wake of the Pullman strike, Dewey began immediately to wrestle intellectually with the problems of forging a pedagogy that might advance the cause of workplace democracy, and in his own school he sought with his students and fellow teachers to build a community that would, as a practical matter, prefigure the reconstructed industrial society he, Addams, Lloyd, and other Chicago democrats envisioned.

Perhaps because much of the overt evidence is largely unpublished, few students of the development of Dewey's philosophy of education have been alert to the way it was shaped by his observation of the fierce struggles between capital and labor in the last two decades of the nineteenth century. Nor have they been sufficiently attentive to the commitment to industrial democracy that peeked out between the lines of *The School and Society* and found everyday expression in the life of the Dewey school.

"Men will long dispute about material socialism," Dewey observed at the turn of the century, ". . . but there is a socialism regarding which there can be no such dispute." All members of a democratic society were equally entitled to an education that would enable them to make the best of themselves as active participants in the life of their community. Every child must have "training in science, in art, in history; command of the fundamental methods of inquiry and the fundamental tools of intercourse and communication," as well as "a trained and sound body, skillful eye and hand; habits of industry, perseverance, and, above all, habits of serviceableness." In a democratic community children had to learn to be leaders as well as followers, possessed of "power of self-direction and power of directing others, powers of administration, ability to assume positions of responsibility" as citizens and workers. Because the world was a rapidly changing one, a child could not, moreover, be educated for any "fixed station in life," but schools had to provide him with training that would "give him such possession of himself that he may take charge of himself; may not only adapt himself to the changes which are going on, but have power to shape and direct those changes." It was this sort of "socialist" education for which Dewey began a life-long defense in the 1890s.[27]

There were several reasons for the rapid growth of Dewey's interest in the philosophy and practice of schooling in his ten years at the University of Chicago. First of all, he quickly saw the educational implications of the functional psychology that he, William James, and others were developing and of the new logic of inquiry that he was beginning to articulate as he abandoned absolute idealism for pragmatism. These ideas might not only be tested in the classroom but also, if they proved fruitful, help reconstruct the dreary schools to which Americans sent their children. One should not, as well, gainsay the more personal motives that turned Dewey's attention to the schools and to a school of his own. The Laboratory School provided an outlet for the considerable reform energies of his wife (who served as its principal) and a setting in which his children could, as he said, remain themselves. But, without diminishing the significance of these explanations, I would also suggest that the Laboratory School provided a relatively safe haven in which Dewey could sustain his hope for a cooperative commonwealth and fashion a curriculum that might foster its realization. Important as the school was as a testing ground for his psychology and philosophy, it was even more important as an expression of his ethics and democratic theory. "The social phase of education," as he later said, "was put first." The Dewey School was above all an experiment in education for industrial democracy.[28]

If the school was to foster the social spirit in children and develop democratic character, Dewey argued, it had itself to be organized as a cooperative community. "I believe," he said, "that the best and deepest moral training is precisely that which one gets through having to enter into proper relations with others in a unity of work and thought." In order to educate for democracy the school had to become "an institution in which the child is, for the time, to live—to be a member of a community life in which he feels that he participates, and to which he contributes." Such a school

> must have a *community* of spirit and end realized through *diversity* of powers and acts. Only in this way can the cooperative spirit involved in the division of labor be substituted for the competitive spirit inevitably developed when a

27. Dewey, "The School as a Social Centre" (1902), *Middle Works*, 2:93; Dewey, "Ethical Principles Underlying Education" (1897), *Early Works*, 5:59–60.

28. Katherine Camp Mayhew and Anna Camp Edwards, *The Dewey School* (New York: Atherton, 1966), 467. For a thoughtful consideration of the shortcomings of Dewey's effort to conceive of his school as a literal laboratory for testing his psychology, see Philip W. Jackson's introduction to a recent edition of *The School and Society* (Chicago: University of Chicago Press, 1991), ix–xli.

number of persons of the same presumed attainments are working to secure exactly the same result.[29]

It was this sort of community—a democratic workshop—that Dewey set out to create in the Laboratory School, and by all available accounts, he was fairly successful. Those who worked in the school, Dewey said, were "animated by a desire to discover in administration, selection of subject-matter, methods of learning, teaching, and discipline, how a school could become a cooperative community while developing in individuals their own capacities and satisfying their own needs." Children shared in the planning of their projects, and the execution of these projects was marked by a cooperative division of labor in which leadership roles were frequently rotated. "The process of mental development," Dewey contended, "is essentially a social process, a process of participation," and the children in his school learned not only skills and facts but also how to work as members of a community of cooperative inquiry.[30]

Democratic community was fostered not only among the children in the Laboratory School but also (for a time) among the adults who worked there. Dewey was highly critical of the failure of schools to allow teachers to participate in the decisions affecting the conduct of public education. He was particularly disturbed by reformers who wrested control of the schools from corrupt politicians only to invest school superintendents with enormous, autocratic power. The remedy for the evils of the control of schools by politicians, he said, "is not to have one expert dictating educational methods and subject-matter to a body of passive, recipient teachers, but the adoption of intellectual initiative, discussion, and decision throughout the entire school corps."[31]

This criticism reflected Dewey's commitment to extending democracy beyond the polity to the workplace. "What does democracy mean," he asked, "save that the individual is to have a share in determining the conditions and the aims of his own work; and that, upon the whole, through the free and mutual harmonizing of different individuals, the work of the world is better done than when planned, arranged, and directed by a few, no matter how wise or of how good intent that few?" In the Laboratory School Dewey tried to implement this sort of workplace democracy. The work of teachers was organized much like that of the children: "cooperative social organization

---

29. Dewey, "My Pedagogic Creed" (1897), *Early Works,* 5:88; Dewey, "Plan of Organization of the University Primary School" (1895), *Early Works,* 5:224, 225.

30. Mayhew and Edwards, *Dewey School,* xiii–xiv, 376–77, 80–81, 467. See also Laura L. Runyon, "A Day with the New Education," *Chautauquan* 30 (1900): 589–92.

31. Dewey, "Democracy in Education" (1903), *Middle Works,* 3:232.

applied to the teaching body of the school as well as to the pupils. Association and exchange among teachers was our substitute for what is called supervision, critic teaching, and technical training." Teachers met weekly to discuss their work and, though no doubt constrained in their criticism by Dewey's commanding presence, they played an active role in shaping the school curriculum.[32]

Creating workplace democracy in the classroom and in the school was no easy task, and Dewey realized he was placing extraordinary demands on teachers. Perhaps because his philosophy of education called on teachers to perform such difficult tasks and placed such a heavy burden of responsibility on them, Dewey was given to unusual flights of rhetoric when he spoke of their social role in the 1890s. Occasionally he evoked the language of the social gospel from which he was otherwise weaning himself by the mid-1890s. Summing up his pedagogic creed in 1897, he declared:

> I believe . . . that the teacher is engaged, not simply in the training of individuals, but in the formation of the proper social life. I believe that every teacher should realize the dignity of his calling; that he is a social servant set apart for the maintenance of proper social order and the securing of the right social growth. I believe that in this way the teacher always is the prophet of the true God and the usherer in of the true kingdom of God.

As this testament suggests, Dewey's educational theory was far less child-centered and more teacher-centered than is often supposed. His confidence that children would develop a democratic character in the schools he envisioned was rooted less in a faith in the "spontaneous and crude capacities of the child" than in the ability of teachers to create an environment in the classroom in which they possessed the means to "mediate" these capacities "over into habits of social intelligence and responsiveness." As he witnessed the crushing of the labor movement in the streets of Chicago, Dewey called on teachers to pick up the banner of industrial democracy, hoping naively that they might make an end run around the power of capital to shape social life.[33]

At the center of the curriculum of the Dewey School was what Dewey termed the "occupation," that is, "a mode of activity on the part of the child which reproduces, or runs parallel to, some of work carried on in social life." Divided into eleven age groups, the students pursued a variety of projects centered on particular historical or contemporary occupations. Because occupational activities pointed on the one hand toward the scientific study of

32. Dewey, "Democracy in Education," 233; Mayhew and Edwards, *Dewey School*, 371.
33. Dewey, "My Pedagogic Creed," 94–95.

the materials and processes involved in their practice and on the other toward their role in society and culture, the thematic focus on occupations provided the occasion not only for manual training and historical inquiry but also for work in mathematics, geology, physics, biology, chemistry, reading, art, music, and languages. In the Laboratory School, Dewey reported, "the child comes to school to *do;* to cook, to sew, to work with wood and tools in simple constructive acts; within and about these acts cluster the studies— writing, reading, arithmetic, etc." Skills such as reading were developed when children came to recognize their usefulness in solving the problems that confronted them in their occupational activities. Occasionally, children of mixed age groups would cooperate. The search of the debating club formed by the thirteen-year-old students for a place to meet resulted in the building of a substantial clubhouse, which enlisted children of all ages in a cooperative project that was for many the emblematic moment in the school's history and one anticipated in Dewey's 1894 letter to his wife.[34]

Although one of the purposes of the "occupations" was to connect the school to the larger social life of the society around it, Dewey's intention was clearly not to reproduce the occupational life of industrial capitalism in the Laboratory School but rather to create a workplace that reflected his criticism of wage labor. Thus he self-consciously "purified" the occupations in his school of one of their most essential features as they were conducted in the world outside by removing them from the social relations of capitalist production and putting them in a cooperative context in which they would have been virtually unrecognizable to those who performed them in the larger society. In the school, he said, "the typical occupations followed are freed from all economic stress. The aim is not the economic value of the products, but the development of social power and insight." Freed from "narrow utilities," occupations in the school were organized so that "method, purpose, understanding shall exist in the consciousness of the one who does the work, that his activity shall have meaning to himself." The children's work was unalienated labor in which the separation of hand and brain that was proceeding apace in the nation's factories and offices was nowhere in evidence. Dewey sometimes referred to the Laboratory School as an "embryonic society," but it was far from an embryo of the society that lay outside its walls. It did not promise the reproduction of industrial America but rather prefigured its radical reconstruction along producerist lines.[35]

34. Dewey, *The School and Society* (1899), *Middle Works,* 1:92; Dewey, "A Pedagogical Experiment" (1896), *Early Works,* 5:245; Mayhew and Edwards, *Dewey School,* 26.
35. Dewey, "Educational Ethics: Syllabus" (1895), *Early Works,* 5:292; Dewey, *School and Society,* 12, 16, 19.

Reconstructing the Producer Republic

Ironically, it was a struggle over workers' control of the Laboratory School that led to Dewey's departure from the University of Chicago. Dewey and his teachers, after all, did not own their workshop; the University of Chicago did. And in 1904 the university president, William Rainey Harper, sided with disgruntled teachers and administrators from the school founded by Colonel Francis Parker (which had been merged with the Dewey School in 1903) who resented incorporation into the "Mr. and Mrs. Dewey School" and feared that Alice Dewey in particular would see no need to retain their services. When Harper fired Alice, Dewey resigned from the university and almost immediately accepted a position at Columbia, where he remained for the rest of his long career.[36]

But Dewey's commitment to industrial democracy and to schools that would foster it persisted and, indeed, became more thoroughgoing and radical. He shared the view of *New Republic* editor Herbert Croly, who remarked in 1914 that "the wage-system itself will have to be transformed in the interest of an industrial self-governing democracy. . . . The emancipation of the wage-earner demands that the same legal security and dignity and the same comparative control over his own destiny shall be attached to his position as to that of the property owner." And, like Croly, Dewey believed by World War I that the future lay with syndicalism, guild-socialism, or some other nonstatist socialism. He called for a politics that would, as he put it in 1933, "forward the formation of a genuinely cooperative society where workers are in control of industry and finance as directly as possible through the economic organization of society itself rather than through any superimposed state socialism."[37]

Dreams such as this required new schools and, more broadly speaking, a radical program of worker education. As Croly said, workers (adults as well as children) must learn the skills to become "a group of self-governing communities for the proper organization and execution of the proper work of society."[38]

Though Dewey eventually abandoned his naive hope that radical teachers could circumvent the power organized against industrial democracy, school reform remained a necessary if not a sufficient element in his politics of social reconstruction. In the years before World War I, he was a leading voice opposing schemes of vocational education that he believed would

36. Robert McCaul, "Dewey and the University of Chicago," in William W. Brickman and Stanley Lehrer, eds., *John Dewey: Master Educator,* 2d ed. (New York: Atherton, 1966), 31–74.
37. Herbert Croly, *Progressive Democracy* (New York: Macmillan, 1914), 384–85; Dewey, "Unity and Progress" (1933), *Later Works,* 9:72.
38. Croly, *Progressive Democracy,* 390.

make schools little more than agencies for the reproduction of a capitalist division of labor. In the twenties and thirties he criticized not only conventional educators but also "child-centered" progressive educators (many who spoke in his name) for doing more to develop the aesthetic sensibilities of the upper middle class than to provide children with "insight into the basic forces of industrial and urban civilization," which would be the aim of any school that claimed to be "progressive in any socially significant sense." In the midst of the Depression he urged teachers to recognize that they were as much "workers" as farmers and factory laborers and as such were subject to the control of "the small and powerful class that is economically privileged." He encouraged teachers to struggle to gain control over their work and to ally themselves with other workers and "in the alliance develop the character, skill, and intelligence that are necessary to make a democratic social order a fact." Thus, if in the later years of his life Dewey believed it was unrealistic "to suppose that the schools can be a *main* agency in producing the intellectual and moral changes, the changes in attitudes and disposition of thought and purpose, which are necessary for the creation of a new social order," he remained well aware that "in every school-building in the land a struggle is being waged against all that hems in and distorts human life."[39]

But such socialism was not a part of Dewey's thinking in Chicago, for in the 1890s he remained wedded to the conservative as well as the radical impulses of producerism. Dewey—and such other Chicago pragmatists as Jane Addams and George Herbert Mead—tended to "psychologize" the conflict between capital and labor, regarding it as the consequence of misplaced attitudes and dispositions rather than as the result of a clash of objective interests rooted in the structure of industrial capitalism. Although aspects of Dewey's educational theory and practice pointed to a radical restructuring of the work process, he did, at times, talk as if the failure of industrial capitalism lay not in its undemocratic organization of work but in the inability of managers and workers to grasp their shared interest in a common project.

"The world in which most of us live," he wrote in *The School and Society*, "is a world in which everyone has a calling and occupation, something to do. Some are managers and others are subordinates. But the great thing for one as for the other is that each shall have had the education which enables him to see within his daily work all there is in it of large and human significance."[40] Here Dewey seemed to suggest that all that was required to enable industrial workers to find self-realization in work was to educate employers

39. Dewey, "How Much Freedom in the New Schools?" (1930), *Later Works*, 5:325; Dewey, "Need for Orientation" (1935), *Later Works*, 11:165; Dewey, "The Teacher and the Public" (1935), *Later Works*, 11:161; Dewey, "Philosophy and Education" (1930), *Later Works*, 5:297–98. On these various moments in Dewey's career, see Westbrook, *John Dewey and American Democracy*, 173–82, 500–510, and the literature cited therein.

40. Dewey, *School and Society*, 16.

and employees in such a way as to give each a full sense of how the work they did fit into the larger productive and social relations of their society. Addams even went so far as to suggest that "a man who makes, year after year, but one small wheel in a modern watch factory, may if his education has properly prepared him, have a fuller life than did the old watchmaker who made a watch from beginning to end."[41]

Given this perspective, it is not surprising that the Chicago pragmatists were so enamored of arbitration by therapeutic middle-class reformers like themselves as the best way to settle labor disputes. Addams herself attempted to mediate the Pullman strike on behalf of the Civic Federation, an alliance of concerned Chicago elites led by banker Lyman Gage. She elicited a sympathetic response from the workers, but was rudely rebuffed by Pullman and his executives. She then wrote "A Modern Lear," an indictment of the strike built around an analogy between Pullman and his workers and King Lear and his daughter Cordelia and a call for class harmony. Although the essay was decidedly more critical of Pullman than of the strikers, Addams concluded with a warning to workers that "the emancipation of working people will have to be inclusive of the employer from the first or it will encounter many failures, cruelties, and reactions."[42]

Although Dewey was critical of the conservative impulses behind the activities of some in the Civic Federation, he supported Addams's efforts at mediation and applauded "A Modern Lear" as "one of the greatest things I ever read both as to its form and its ethical philosophy."[43] A few months after the strike was over, Dewey and Addams had a revealing exchange that he conveyed to his wife. With the bitter class conflict the strike had engendered clearly in mind, Addams told Dewey that

> she had always believed, still believed, that antagonism was not only useless and harmful, but entirely unnecessary; that it lay never in the objective differences, which would always grow into unity if left alone, but from a person's mixing in his own personal reactions. . . . That historically also only evil had come from antagonisms—she kept asking me what I tho't, and I agreed up to this, but then as to past history I dissented; then she went on that if Jesus drove the money changers out of the temple that accounted for the apparent difference between the later years of his ministry and the earlier, and for much

41. Jane Addams, *The Spirit of Youth and the City Street* (1909; Urbana: University of Illinois Press, 1972), 126–27.

42. Jane Addams, "A Modern Lear" (1894), in Christopher Lasch, ed., *The Social Thought of Jane Addams* (Indianapolis: Bobbs-Merrill, 1965), 120–23. On Addams's role in the strike, see Victoria Brown, "Advocate for Democracy: Jane Addams and the Pullman Strike," in Schneirov et al., *Pullman Strike*, 130–58. The most recent study of Addams's social thought is Jean Bethke Elshtain, *Jane Addams and the Dream of Democracy* (New York: Basic Books, 2002).

43. John Dewey to Alice Dewey, 14 July 1894, Dewey Papers; John Dewey to Jane Addams, 19 January 1896, Jane Addams Papers, Swarthmore College Peace Collection, Swarthmore College.

of the falsity of Christianity since *if* he did it, he lost his faith and reacted; that we freed the slaves by war and had now to free them all over again individually and pay the costs of the war and reckon with the added bitterness of the Southerner besides, etc., etc. I asked her if she didn't think that besides the personal antagonisms, there was that of ideas and institutions, as Christianity and Judaism, and Labor and Capital, the Church and Democracy now and realization of that antagonism was necessary to an appreciation of the truth and to a consciousness of growth and she said no. The antagonisms of institutions were always unreal; it was simply due to the injection of the personal attitude and reaction; and then instead of adding to the recognition of meaning, it delayed and distorted it.

Addams, Dewey told Alice, had led him to suspect that "I have always been interpreting the dialectic wrong end up—the unity as the reconciliation of opposites, instead of the opposites as the unity in its growth." Even so, Addams "converted me internally, but not really, I fear. At least I can't see what all this conflict and passing of history means if it's perfectly meaningless; my pride of intellect, I suppose it is, revolts at thinking it's all merely negative, and has no functional value."[44] Yet shortly thereafter, Dewey wrote to Addams, telling her that "I wish to take back what I said the other night. Not only is actual antagonism bad, but the assumption that there is or may be antagonism is bad. . . . I'm glad I found this out before I began to talk on social psychology as otherwise I fear I should have made a mess of it." He admitted that "this is rather a suspiciously sudden conversion, but then it's only a beginning."[45]

It was indeed a suspiciously sudden conversion, one that did not entirely hold. One can see Dewey here wrestling with the tension between the conservative and the radical implications of his amalgam of Hegelian idealism, social Christianity, and producer-republicanism. This struggle was never entirely resolved. On the one hand, his thought would always bear the marks of what he lightly called the "Hegelian bacillus of reconciliation."[46] On the other hand, he continued, despite his apparent concession to Addams, to regard antagonism and conflict as often more than mere subjective misunderstanding and sometimes productive of satisfying outcomes.[47]

One might usefully see this as a struggle in Dewey's mind between the directions for middle-class reform pointed up by Addams and Lloyd. Addams, with her adamant refusal to consider the possibility of objective conflicts and

44. John Dewey to Alice Dewey, 10 October 1894, Dewey Papers.
45. John Dewey to Jane Addams, 12 October 1894, Jane Addams Papers.
46. John Dewey to William James, 27 March 1903, in Ralph Barton Perry, *The Thought and Character of William James* (Boston: Little Brown, 1935), 2:522.
47. One can, I think, see in this exchange between Addams and Dewey an anticipation of their later competing positions on American entry into World War I, which Addams vigorously opposed and Dewey supported as a means to democratic reform.

productive antagonisms to resolve them, forecast a reconstruction of producer-republicanism into the "new liberalism" that guided much of progressive reform in subsequent decades. This new liberalism accepted the
transformation of proprietary capitalism into new corporate forms—most
notably large business corporations and trade-unions—and argued for the
reconciliation of the interests of these functional groups through mediation
by organizations such as the Civic Federation or by the state. Here the conservative producerist conviction of no necessary, intractable opposition between labor and capital was updated for a new collectivist age. As Mary
Furner has demonstrated, new liberals divided into "corporate liberals" and
"democratic collectivists," depending on the degree of state action that they
thought necessary to secure the public interest in controlling class conflict.
Corporate liberals urged voluntarism, while democratic collectivists envisioned an aggressively interventionist state. Addams fell decidedly in the latter camp.[48]

As did Dewey to a considerable degree. His former colleague and friend
Henry Carter Adams emerged as one of the most articulate spokesmen for
democratic collectivism, and Dewey shared Adams's frank recognition of
the need to reconstruct producerism along collectivist lines. And Dewey was
by no means averse to using a more powerful, regulative state to do so.[49]

But as Dewey saw it, many of his fellow democratic collectivists were too
quick to sacrifice the producerist commitment to the autonomy of free labor, even if it now had for most workers to mean not petty-proprietorship
but shared control of a democratized workplace. Hence, as I say, he was
drawn to various forms of decentralized socialism. And he invested his reform energies, particularly after World War I, less in the forging of the liberal administrative state than in a democratic (often third-party) politics
built on alliances among workers, farmers, and middle-class proprietors and
professionals that aimed at such a socialism. In this, Dewey was not only a
democratic collectivist but also a persistent populist who carried forward
into the twentieth century a good deal of the radical impulses in producer-
republicanism that guided Lloyd, perhaps the most radical of middle-class
Chicago social Christians, in the 1890s.

48. Mary Furner, "The Republican Tradition and the New Liberalism: Social Investigation,
State Building, and Social Learning in the Gilded Age," in Michael J. Lacey and Mary O. Furner,
eds., *The State and Social Investigation in Britain and the United States* (Cambridge: Cambridge University Press, 1993), 171–241. On the emergence of this "new liberalism" in Chicago, see the
essays by Victoria Brown, Shelton Stromquist, and Richard Schneirov in Schneirov et al., *Pullman Strike*. And at greater length, Richard Schneirov, *Labor and Urban Politics: Class Conflict and
the Origins of Modern Liberalism in Chicago, 1864–97* (Urbana: University of Illinois Press, 1998).

49. Furner, "Republican Tradition," 187–88, 193, 216–17. For an effort to render Dewey
a "corporate liberal," which I (and Furner) judge unconvincing, see R. Jeffrey Lustig, *Corporate
Liberalism: The Origins of Modern American Political Theory, 1890–1920* (Berkeley: University of
California Press, 1982), esp. 120–48, 155–75.

Andrew Feffer has acutely analyzed the conservative element in the producerism of Chicago pragmatism, and although he and I disagree about whether or not it remained a limitation of Dewey's social thought and politics after the turn of the century, I find his dissection of Dewey's social Christianity and producerism in the 1890s to be largely compelling.[50] But I do not believe he is sufficiently sensitive to how difficult it was for Dewey and others to shake the conservative side of producerism in this decade.

Implicit in Feffer's argument is the contention that events such as the Pullman strike should have done more to radicalize Dewey. On occasion, Feffer alludes to Debs as a counterexample to Dewey. Pullman, he argues, made Debs a "class conscious" socialist; it should have done the same for Dewey. That it did not is evidence of the strict limits Dewey and other Chicago pragmatists put on social reconstruction, limits that "belied the democratic principles they simultaneously espoused."[51]

But as it happens, Debs found it almost as difficult as Dewey to overcome the conservative dimensions of producer-republicanism. He, like Dewey, did not begin to do so until after the turn of the century. Debs did not, as myth has it, leave his Woodstock, Illinois, jail cell a socialist in 1895, though he would become one within a few years. As Salvatore says, "The Pullman and Woodstock experiences do indicate a growing radicalization, but Debs took his inspiration from Jefferson and Lincoln and not from orthodox Socialist writers."[52] In the mid-1890s Debs's politics were, like Dewey's, populist, and the most radical producerists in the People's party urged him to challenge William Jennings Bryan for the party's presidential nomination in 1896. Even in the late 1890s when Debs had assumed a leading role in ostensibly socialist political organizations, he remained wary of the narrow class consciousness and Marxism of allies such as Victor Berger (and adversaries such as Samuel Gompers). As Salvatore demonstrates, Debs "remained rooted in an older, classless vision of society" and "continued to interpret political action within an older American moral tradition that placed ultimate hope in 'the people' as citizen producers."[53]

Producerism left a deep imprint on Dewey's thinking. But the same is true of Debs. Both brought the ideals of producer-republicanism with them to the streets of Chicago in the summer of 1894, and both—though chastened by the events of those weeks—tried to sustain those ideals thereafter. Both

50. Feffer, *Chicago Pragmatists*, 166–71. See also Jeffrey Sklansky's provocative study of the wider "psychologization" of class conflict in American social theory in the late nineteenth century, *The Soul's Economy: Market Society and Selfhood in American Thought, 1820–1920* (Chapel Hill: University of North Carolina Press, 2002). Sklansky's treatment of Dewey's early social thought is similar to that of Feffer.

51. Feffer, *Chicago Pragmatists*, 180.

52. Salvatore, *Debs*, 153.

53. Ibid., 165, 167.

would eventually recognize the structural oppositions that industrial capitalism fostered, and both would speak the language of class conflict—though Dewey would take longer to do so and then in a more muted tone. But neither Dewey nor Debs would ever lose touch with the essential promise of producerism. This promise—as Salvatore nicely sums it up—was that "all who produce value within and for the community could regard themselves as citizen-producers—respected in each other's eyes, concerned with the economic and political welfare of the community, and opposed to those monopolists and financiers who desire only to extract their wealth."[54]

The persistence of producerist ideals helps explain why Dewey, when he did become a socialist, was such a peculiar socialist—one who would give fits to his more orthodox and more Marxist comrades. But in this, too, he had much in common with Eugene Debs, the greatest—and most thoroughly American—of American socialists.

54. Ibid., 25.

CHAPTER 4

On the Private Parts
of a Public Philosopher

★

W<small>E</small> have heard much of late of the "transgressive" private lives of modern philosophers, and in the company of philosophers such as Nietzsche, Wittgenstein, and Foucault, John Dewey is, on the face of it, an odd man out—or to be more precise, a conventional man out. If Dewey was not, as Allan Bloom charged, one of the best examples of Nietzsche's "last men"— who "have discovered happiness"—neither did he attempt to live beyond the goods and evils of his culture. And, indeed, he was impatient with philosophers who imagined themselves to do so. Philosophy, for Dewey, was "not a special road to something alien to ordinary beliefs, knowledge, action, enjoyment, and suffering," and one might well read much of his work as an effort to talk his fellow philosophers out of the heroic pretensions that led so many of them to side against common experience and ordinary people and to live lives that would not play at all well in Peoria.[1]

Yet if Dewey's life was not particularly heroic (in this sense), neither was it uneventful or placid—nor without its transgressions. As befit a philosopher who urged others to turn from the problems of philosophy to the "problems of men," Dewey was in the midst of public controversies throughout his career, and many of those who have written about his philosophy have sought to tie this philosophy to his activism and to the disputes and debates in which he was embroiled. But few students of Dewey's work have ven-

---

1. Allan Bloom, *The Closing of the American Mind* (New York: Simon and Schuster, 1987), 194–95; John Dewey, "Construction and Criticism" (1930), *Later Works*, 5:141.

tured into his private life and forged compelling connections between his thinking and the life he lived outside of the public sphere. To a considerable degree this shortcoming of Dewey scholarship is attributable to the limited evidence available about Dewey's private life, and I doubt there will ever be a "philosophical life" of Dewey to compare with James Miller's Foucault or Ray Monk's Wittgenstein. But as I hope to suggest here, more eye-opening things can perhaps be done in this regard than I once thought.[2]

"A Sense for the Better Kind of Life to Be Led"

For those like myself who not only write about Dewey but find much that he had to say as a philosopher convincing, lack of insight into his private life is particularly unsettling. For Dewey argued that human beings were thinkers only in the second instance. In the first instance, he said, the self was "an agent-patient, doer, sufferer, and enjoyer." Thinking emerged out of noncognitive, "primary" experience and was in the service of such experience. For Dewey, the path of reflection in both science and philosophy should be from primary experience and then back to it, not only for purposes of verification but also because the whole point of reflection was to enlarge and enrich the meaning of such experience. "To be a man," he argued, "is to be thinking desire." Hence if one is attempting to understand, interpret, and explain Dewey's thinking in light of the view of human experience he offered us, it is distressing to know so little about his own desires, enjoyments, and sufferings. Unless and until we know more about Dewey's primary experience we will not have a fully satisfying Deweyan life of Dewey.[3]

On the other hand, Dewey offered ready encouragement to those who would seek out the ethos that governed his life, both public and private, in his work. Strictly speaking, he said, philosophy was not "in any sense whatever a form of knowledge" but rather "wisdom," which he defined as "a conviction about moral values, a sense for the better kind of life to be led."

2. James Miller, *The Passion of Michel Foucault* (New York: Simon and Schuster, 1993); Ray Monk, *Wittgenstein: The Duty of Genius* (New York: Free Press, 1990). Steven Rockefeller has made the best effort thus far to make the most of the evidence available surrounding Dewey's private life and connect it to aspects of his thought. See his *John Dewey: Religious Faith and Democratic Humanism* (New York: Columbia University Press, 1991). Since the publication of the original version of this essay, Jay Martin has published *The Education of John Dewey* (New York: Columbia University Press, 2002), which aspires to convey "the continuous activity of Dewey's strong emotions" (3). Martin's biography provides as much detail as one would probably want on the minutiae of Dewey's life, but it is less successful as a psychological portrait. And it has nothing fresh to say about Dewey's philosophy or about the intersection of life and work.

3. John Dewey, "Brief Studies in Realism" (1911), *Middle Works*, 6:120; *Experience and Nature* (1929), *Later Works*, 1:15–18; "Beliefs and Existences" (1906), *Middle Works*, 3:100.

Philosophies "embodied not colorless intellectual readings of reality, but men's most passionate desires and hopes, their basic beliefs about the sort of life to be lived." Different philosophical visions reflected "incompatibilities of temperament and expectation. They are different ways of construing life."[4]

In the only sustained bit of autobiography he ever published, Dewey dropped a most helpful hint of the impulse that was crucial to the shaping of his own temperament and expectation. There he spoke guardedly of a youth marked by "an inward laceration" produced by an alienating sense of "isolation of self from the world, of soul from body, of nature from God." One can without much difficulty see the whole of Dewey's philosophy as an effort to heal this laceration, a wound that he came to perceive in the broadest possible terms. As a young academic, he found temporary relief in the higher unities and synthetic resolutions promised by the neo-Hegelian idealism he learned from his teacher George S. Morris, who had himself suffered from the same sort of alienation to which Dewey alluded. And when he abandoned absolute idealism for an original and compelling pragmatic naturalism in the 1890s, Dewey remained infected with what he characterized to William James as the "Hegelian bacillus of reconciliation." This animus against all that divided human experience and a bug for reconciliation are evident in every aspect of Dewey's philosophy, from his functional psychology to his logic of the problematic situation and its resolution to his antidualistic metaphysics to the consummatory ideal of his aesthetics to his latter-day conception of God as the uniting of the actual and the ideal.[5]

For my purposes here it is especially worth noting the persistence of the Hegelian bacillus in Dewey's ethics and social theory. Dewey's ethics began as an ethics of self-realization and remained so throughout his career. Although by the turn of the century he had stopped thinking of self-realization in neo-Hegelian terms as the human approximation of the divine self, the more or less aesthetic criteria of self-realization characteristic of what Charles Taylor has termed Hegelian "expressivism" were still very much in evidence. Self-unification, harmony, wholeness, plentitude, richness, and organic growth remained the key normative terms for Dewey. Human powers and capacities, he continued to argue, were full and free in their realization only when they worked together in a complex, diverse, expansive, yet unified whole. Dewey's social ideal—"moral democracy"—was a macrocosm of the norms guiding individual action. The good society was, like the

4. John Dewey, "Philosophy and Democracy" (1918), *Middle Works*, 11:43–44.

5. John Dewey, "From Absolutism to Experimentalism" (1930), *Later Works*, 5:153; Dewey to William James, 27 March 1903, in Ralph Barton Perry, *The Thought and Character of William James* (Boston: Little, Brown, 1935), 2:522. James Good has thoroughly analyzed the "Hegelian deposit" in Dewey's work in "A Search for Unity in Diversity: The 'Permanent Hegelian Deposit' in the Philosophy of John Dewey" (Diss., Rice University, 2001).

good self, a diverse yet harmonious, growing yet unified whole—a fully participatory democracy in which the powers and capacities of the individuals who comprised it were harmonized by their cooperative activities into a community that permitted the full and free expression of individuality.[6]

The presence of what Steven Rockefeller has called Dewey's "quest for unity" in his philosophy and public life has become something of a commonplace, which is often the destiny of an important truth. I suspect that if we knew more of Dewey's private life it could be well-integrated into this theme, which would continue to form the backbone of Dewey's biography. But something new and important would be gained as well, for knowing more about the private Dewey would put some flesh and blood on a life story that has never taken on much life. It would also put the temperamental disposition to reconciliation that so defined his particular philosophical wisdom into some unattended contexts and enhance our sense of its virtues and shortcomings. I would like to suggest some of these possibilities here by offering a reading of one episode in Dewey's private life about which we do know a great deal: his love affair with writer Anzia Yezierska.[7]

"There Stirred within Me"

The only extant documents of this love affair are the poems Dewey wrote about and to Yezierska in 1918. This poetry can be supplemented, with due caution, by the accounts later offered by Yezierska, particularly that in her novel, *All I Could Never Be* (1932), and in her autobiography, *Red Ribbon on a White Horse* (1950).[8] My consideration of these documents leads me to believe that the most reliable narrative of the romance is that offered in Louise Levitas Henriksen's biography of her mother, *Anzia Yezierska: A Writer's Life* (1988), which is superior in this regard to the error-plagued account in the most extended treatment of the affair, Mary V. Dearborn's *Love in the Promised Land* (1988). It is Dearborn's interpretation of these events that I will be at greatest pains to contest.[9]

6. On Hegelian expressivism, see Charles Taylor, *Hegel* (Cambridge: Cambridge University Press, 1975), chap. 1.

7. Rockefeller, *John Dewey,* 74–75.

8. On the advice of a friend, Yezierska thinly disguised Dewey's identity in her autobiography. He appears as "John Morrow."

9. The story of this relationship was first told in Jo Ann Boydston's introduction to *The Poems of John Dewey* (Carbondale: Southern Illinois University Press, 1977) and to Boydston goes the credit for the clever detective work that uncovered what details there are of the affair. The two later, extended accounts build on Boydston's research: Louise Levitas Henriksen, *Anzia Yezierska: A Writer's Life* (New Brunswick, N.J.: Rutgers University Press, 1988, and Mary V. Dearborn, *Love in the Promised Land: The Story of Anzia Yezierska and John Dewey* (New York: Free Press, 1988). The romance also forms the foundation of Norma Rosen's novel, *John and Anzia: An*

When Dewey first met Yezierska late in the fall of 1917 he was fifty-eight, and both his public life and private life were in turmoil. His support for American intervention in World War I had divided him from former friends and associates such as Randolph Bourne, with whom Dewey engaged in a bitter feud that would end only with Bourne's untimely death in the influenza epidemic at the end of 1918. At home, his marriage continued the steady deterioration that began with the family's move from Chicago to New York in 1904 and the tragic death from typhoid fever of his young son, Gordon, that same year. The Chicago years had been the happiest of Dewey's marriage, which had by the turn of the century produced six children. At the University of Chicago, Dewey and his wife Alice had worked closely together at their Laboratory School; indeed, it was a bitter dispute with President William Rainey Harper over Alice's role in the school that had precipitated Dewey's departure from that university. But no such formal working arrangement developed for the couple at Columbia, and following Gordon's death, Alice's health deteriorated and her zeal for reform and perfectionism degenerated into resentment and insistent nagging.[10]

Distressed by the political divisions occasioned by the war, Dewey also agonized over the fresh division of soul from body occasioned by his troubled marriage, a division he cast in strikingly sexual terms in a poem he wrote sometime between 1911 and 1916. The map of his mind, he wrote, was divided by a "livid equator" that encircled "the bulging girth / Of my hot swollen earth" where "fire after fire doth ceaseless follow." Meanwhile, his soul had flown to a "frozen pole," and he saw little chance that this divided self would ever be made whole. "So let it be," the poem concluded, "till judgment day shall roll / The spread out heavens as a scroll, / And fervent heat dissolve away / The loins of fire and head of grey."[11]

American Romance (New York: Dutton, 1989). See also Rockefeller, *John Dewey*, 344–54, and my own brief prior account of the affair in *John Dewey and American Democracy* (Ithaca: Cornell University Press, 1991), 221–22. The serendipity of the survival of Dewey's poems, the documents most essential to accounts of this love affair, suggests the challenges that await anyone who would offer a full account of Dewey's private life. Dewey never intended his poems to see the light of day, and they survived only by virtue of some questionable archival acquisition practices by Columbia librarian Milton Thomas, who rescued some of them from Dewey's wastebasket and kept them, unbeknownst to Dewey, and philosopher Herbert Schneider, who found others in Dewey's desk when he inherited his office and turned them over to Thomas without informing Dewey. Boydston gives a detailed account of this and other matters relating to the provenance of the poems in her introduction.

10. Max Eastman, "John Dewey," *Atlantic* (December 1941): 680–81. See also Philip Jackson's astute diagnosis of Dewey's marriage in "John Dewey's Poetry," *American Journal of Education* 91 (1982): 69–72.

11. *Poems of John Dewey*, 18. Dearborn misreads the last lines of this poem as a statement that the "fervent heat" of passion will dissolve away his old age ("head of grey"), though it seems to me clear that the fervent heat in question is that of "judgment day," which will dissolve both "loins of fire and head of grey" (*Love in the Promised Land*, 113). She reads Dewey as welcoming

Yezierska was in her late thirties when she met Dewey, and her life was also in disarray. The daughter of Polish-Russian Jews who immigrated to New York in 1893, she worked her way out of the Lower East Side ghetto and through Teachers College, where she earned a degree in domestic science in 1904. For the next dozen years, she lived on the fringes of bohemian Greenwich Village and clung to a precarious middle-class existence by means of a series of part-time teaching jobs. She suffered through two disastrous marriages and left her one child, a daughter, in the care of her second husband. Determined by 1917 to make a career as a writer, she nonetheless sought the security of a permanent teaching position in the New York schools and despaired when she was unable to secure one. Reading of a speech Dewey had given in early December 1917 denouncing the administrative practices of the New York City Board of Education, she traveled uptown to Columbia and burst into his office with a passionate appeal for his assistance.[12]

Dewey was immediately taken with this striking woman, and he agreed to visit the class in which she was teaching as a substitute in order to evaluate her teaching. He also read two of her stories that she brought with her. After observing Yezierska's cooking class, he advised her to devote herself to writing and invited her to audit his seminar in social and political philosophy—a class also audited by wealthy Philadelphia businessman and art collector Albert Barnes.

Yezierska said nary a word in the class, but she and Dewey spent considerable time together and grew steadily closer over the course of the semester. He read her work appreciatively, brought it to the attention of others, and gave her a typewriter. At his request, she led him on tours of the Lower East Side, and this world she had fled took on fresh meaning and new life when seen through his eyes. Eventually, the two shared a passionate intimacy, though there is no evidence that the relationship ever reached much of a sexual consummation.[13]

---

a sexual passion that would heat up his soul, while I think he was despairing of ever uniting soul and body before his death. Levitas Henriksen treats this poem as one written during the Dewey-Yezierska love affair (*Anzia Yezierska*, 100), but according to Boydston it was typed on a machine Dewey had ceased using by the time he met Yezierska.

12. There is some ambiguity about when Dewey and Yezierska first met. Boydston first dated the meeting in the late summer or early fall of 1917 (and Rockefeller repeats this dating). Dearborn says they met in November (and invests Dewey with the title of Dean of Teachers College, a position he never held). Levitas Henriksen dates the meeting in mid-December, and this seems to me to be the most reliable estimate since it is the only one that singles out a precipitating event—Yezierska's reading about Dewey's speech—to account for her visit. Since Boydston assisted Levitas Henriksen with her book, one may assume that she has revised her own estimate of the date of the first meeting. Much of the confusion, I think, arises from the fact of Dewey's invitation to Yezierska to join his seminar, which began in the fall of 1917. But as Levitas Henriksen observes, this was a two-semester course, and Yezierska probably joined the course at the beginning of the second semester in January 1918.

13. In her novel, *John and Anzia*, Norma Rosen renders the affair much more conventional

Both Dewey and Yezierska invested their relationship with enormous symbolic cultural freight. On the eve of the war, Dewey had published a number of essays attacking the melting pot idea and calling—along with Bourne and Horace Kallen—for a cultural pluralism that would instead harmonize the ethnic cultures of the United States into a symphonic, "trans-national" American culture. He saw the potential for the embodiment of this ideal in his relationship with Yezierska. In one of the two poems we know him to have given to her, he wrote:

> Generations of stifled words reaching out
> Through you,
> Aching for utt'rance, dying on lips
> That have died of hunger,
> Hunger not to have, but to be.
>
> Generations as yet unuttered, dumb, smothered,
> Inchoate, unutterable by me and mine,
> In you I see them coming to be,
> Luminous, slow revolving, ordered in rhythm.
>
> You shall not utter them; you shall be them,
> And from out the pain
> A great song shall fill the world.
> And I from afar shall see,
> As one watching sees the star
> Rise in the waiting heavens,
> And from the distance my hand shall clasp yours,
> And an old world be content to go,
> Beholding the horizons
> Tremulous with the generations
> Of the dawn.

For her part, Yezierska believed that she and Dewey were

drawn to each other by something even more compelling than the love of man for woman, and woman for man. It's that irresistible force as terrible as birth

---

than it was by getting the two lovers in bed together within weeks of their first meeting, and then turning up the sexual heat as the story moves along. At one point she has Dewey, besotted with thoughts of an absent Anzia, kissing the nipples of the Renoir nudes in Barnes's gallery. She brings the affair to an end in predictable fashion as well: Anzia gets pregnant, Alice Dewey discovers what has been going on, and Dewey chooses his wife and respectability, which disappoints not only Anzia but Rosen. On the other hand, Jay Martin offers the most chaste account of the affair, denying that there was anything sexual to it at all. He does not address the evidence to the contrary (*Education of John Dewey*, 287–93). By the nature of the case, such evidence is spotty, but the erotic charge between Dewey and Yezierska seems to me undeniable, even though, beyond allusions to kisses and light petting, there is no reliable evidence of a physically sexual encounter.

and death that sometimes flares up between Jew and Gentile. . . . Since Christ was crucified, a black chasm of hate yawned between his people and mine. But now and then threads of gold have spun through the darkness—links of understanding woven by fearless souls—Gentiles and Jews—men and women who were not afraid to trust their love.[14]

Dewey also saw in Yezierska the possibility for a revitalization of his emotional and sexual experience. According to her, he told her something along these lines:

> You can free me from the bondage of age-long repressions. You can lift me out of the dead grooves of sterile intellectuality. Without you I am the dry dust of hopes unrealized. You are fire and sunshine and desire. You make life changeable and beautiful and full of daily wonder.[15]

Throughout the winter and spring of 1918 Dewey appears to have wrestled with the possibilities and pitfalls of investing himself fully in his feelings for Anzia. In the other poem we know that he gave her, he wrote of the routines of his life as "a silken web" of "unillumined duties" that he discharged with his eyes cast earthward lest he catch a glimpse of an untrammeled life that would tempt him to break his "pact with my possessions." He feared that "the wrath of stern-eyed freedom" would break the chains that kept him from "the wilderness of tears" and "th'untracked wild of untamed desire." Yet the equally unhappy alternative seemed to be to "creep to a cooped-in grave smothered by the treasure piled." He concludes by appealing to Yezierska to take his hand "along the lonely steep."[16] In a second poem, which Yezierska may not have seen, Dewey feels the ghosts of stillborn past loves stirring in the "sepulcher" of his heart, warning him that because their "sister" Anzia is "all we might have been" they will not allow her "to stifle in this sepulcher / Where from dumb death we now murmur."[17]

As the seminar drew to a close, Barnes proposed to Dewey that the class test the efficacy of some of the ideas they had been discussing by conduct-

14. *Poems of John Dewey,* 4–5; Anzia Yezierska, "Wild Winter Love," *Century* (February 1927): 489–90. On Dewey's cultural pluralism, see Westbrook, *John Dewey and American Democracy,* 212–14. In "The Principle of Nationality" (1917), he had written: "No matter how loudly any one proclaims his Americanism, if he assumes that any one racial strain, any one component culture, no matter how early settled it was in our territory, or how effective it has proved in its own land, is to furnish a pattern to which all other strains and cultures are to conform, he is a traitor to an American nationalism. Our unity cannot be a homogeneous thing like that of the separate states of Europe from which our population is drawn; it must be a unity created by drawing out and composing into a harmonious whole the best, the most characteristic which each contributing race and people has to offer" (*Middle Works,* 10:288–89).
15. Anzia Yezierska, "Miracle Love," in Yezierska, *Hungry Hearts* (1920; New York: Arno Press, 1975), 141.
16. *Poems of John Dewey,* 5–6.
17. Ibid., 5–6.

ing an investigation in the summer of 1918 into the social life of the Philadelphia Polish community.[18] Yezierska joined the group as a translator, and she also engaged in research on the conditions of Polish women and the family. As soon as the semester ended, Dewey left for California for a month to deliver lectures at Stanford, but he returned to the east coast in early July. Meeting Yezierska in Philadelphia, he conveyed to her his deep ambivalence about their love and appeared ready to break with her. But she dissuaded him. "Maybe you know best," he tells her in *All I Could Never Be*. "Your instinct may be surer than all my reasoning."[19]

But Dewey's ambivalence was far from resolved. He left Philadelphia for two weeks at his family's summer home on Long Island, and there wrote the longest of his "Anzia" poems, laying out his persistent two-mindedness ("the harsh divisions of my mind"). Here we can see Dewey attempting to formulate his doubts about the love affair as forcefully as he can in order to meet the protests Yezierska had apparently made against the "death" of playing it "safe"—putting in poetic form arguments she had found difficult to grasp ("You said my logic you could never grasp, / While my poetic words —thus you blessed them— / Would fall like manna on a hung'ring soul"). Dewey tried to impress on Yezierska that it was not "riches, possessions" that kept him from fully embracing his love for her. He was tied to his wife and to his family not by propriety and convention (which he and Alice had repeatedly, sometimes publicly, scorned) but by the fact that Alice had done so much to make him what he was, creating with him ties into which he had "slowly grown / By which I am possest. / For I do not own":

> Who makes, has. Such the old old law.
> Owned then am I by what I felt and saw
> But most by them with whom I've loved, and fought,
> Till within me has been wrought
> My power to reach, to see and understand.
> Such is the tie, such the iron band.
> What I am to any one is but a loan
> From those who made, and own.

Relationships such as this fostered profound obligations and a reciprocity of gifts and gratitude: "I have a garden of flowers and bees? / But others built the wall and kept the flowers / Through the long and suffocating hours / That I might rest myself in pleasant ease."

Yezierska, Dewey wrote, was disposed to see their situation through the

---

18. For an account of the Polish study see Westbrook, *John Dewey and American Democracy*, 214–23.

19. Anzia Yezierska, *All I Could Never Be* (New York: Brewer, Warren, and Putnam, 1932), 65.

eyes of youth, which raged against living long years of "bare existence" until one was left with little but memories of what might have been and the "stains" of unhappy choices: "The choked up fountain and th'uneffaced scar." But he was by virtue of his age and experience less captured by the "passions few and deep" of youth and more aware of an "unnumbered diversity" of considerations that counseled renunciation. Dewey also worried that he had construed his feelings for Yezierska through a distorting lens of romantic fiction ("Damn fiction, damn romance"), and he could never know "Whether in an ancient mirror I see prance / Before me mimic passions in a row, / Or if they are authentic heaven and hell." Here again his self was not his own but the product of the influences (in this case, reading) that had shaped him ("Romantic relics of the feudal age / Stored in today's trim realistic cage").

But Dewey could not deny the powerful pull he felt toward Yezierska:

> Yet would I have you know
> How utterly my thoughts go
> With you to and fro
> In a ceaseless quest,
> Half annoy
> And all a blessed joy.
> Does she now think or write or rest?
> What at this minute—it's just eight—
> Has she written or shall I wait
> In sweet trouble of expectancy
> For some fresh wonder yet to be?
> Whate'er, howe'er you move or rest
> I see your body's breathing
> The curving of your breast
> And hear the warm thoughts seething.
> I watch the lovely eyes that visions hold
> Even in the tortured tangles of the tenement
> Of a life that's free and bold.
> I feel the hand that for a brief moment
> Has been in mine, and dream that you are near
> To talk with, and that I can hear
> Your crystalled speech
> As we converse, each to each.

When he thought of Yezierska in this fashion, Dewey wrote, "I am overcome as by thunder / Of my blood that surges / From my cold heart to my clear head— / So at least she said— / Till my body sinks and merges / In communion with the wine and bread." This, then, was where Dewey stood in mid-summer 1918, and his characterization of himself as a "mixed up mess of bad and good" also described his view of the love affair.[20]

For Dewey, his ambivalence was resolved in September 1918 by a decisive incident. The Polish project concluded its work in August, and he and Yezierska met again in New York the following month. Apparently, he had decided to risk "untamed desire," for he finally made an overtly sexual overture to her on a pier under the Williamsburg Bridge. Here is Yezierska's description of that moment in her autobiography:

> For a long moment we stood silent. Then I was in his arms and he was kissing me. His hand touched my breast. The natural delight of his touch was checked by a wild alarm that stiffened me with fear. I had the same fear of drowning in his arms that I had of drowning in the river. His overwhelming nearness, the tense body closing in on me was pushing us apart instead of fusing us. A dark river of distrust rose between us. I had not dreamed that God could become flesh. Sensing my unyielding body, he released me.[21]

Apparently, Yezierska was racked by considerable sexual ambivalence herself, something Dewey had not imagined was part of the equation.[22] They parted gloomily, and as far as Dewey was concerned, the affair was over; Yezierska was not, he discovered, the healing rain for his loins of fire. Yezierska said she almost immediately regretted her actions, but when they met a short time later in Dewey's office, he told her there was no point in trying to sustain an intimate relationship. According to Yezierska, he told her "You want love, but you do not want me. You do not love me. You only dramatize your want of love."[23]

Yezierska continued to hope that the romance might be rekindled.[24] In 1921, after her writing career had taken off and she was being hailed in Hollywood as the "sweatshop Cinderella," she sent Dewey—who was nearing the end of an extended stay in China that began soon after they parted—a two-edged, coded, public message in the form of a story, "The Miracle," in her first published collection, *Hungry Hearts* (1920), and a review of his *Democ-*

20. *Poems of John Dewey*, 14–17.

21. Anzia Yezierska, *Red Ribbon on a White Horse* (1950; New York: Persea Books, 1987), 113. Yezierska offered a nearly equivalent account in *All I Could Never Be*, 99–101.

22. Dewey was obviously unaware that Yezierska was "Hattie Mayer" (the name given her by her parents upon their immigration to America) whose effort in 1911 to annul her first marriage to Jacob Gordon on the grounds that she had not expected him to demand a sexual relationship with her was widely publicized in the New York press. See Levitas Henriksen, *Anzia Yezierska*, 36–39; and Dearborn, *Love in the Promised Land*, 76–77.

23. Yezierska, *Red Ribbon*, 116.

24. Apparently, Dewey continued to take an interest in Yezierska's career from a distance. He undoubtedly paved the way for the publication of her story, "Soap and Water and the Immigrant," in the *New Republic* (22 February 1919): 117–19.

racy and Education. In the story, the passionate kisses of the Dewey character are met not with stiff rejection but with a loving embrace freighted with the cultural significance Dewey and Yezierska had imparted to their affair. The Yezierska character "could only weep and tremble with joy at his touch. 'The miracle!' cried my heart; 'the miracle of America come true!' "[25] In the review (of a book Dewey published five years previously), Yezierska upbraided Dewey for lacking "that warm personal touch that would enable his readers to get close to him":

> Can it be that this giant of the intellect—this pioneer in the realm of philosophy—has so suppressed the personal life in himself that his book is devoid of the intimate, self-revealing touches that make writing human? Can it be that Professor Dewey, for all his large, social vision, has so choked the feelings in his own heart that he has killed in himself the power to reach the masses of people who think with the heart rather than with the head?[26]

But Dewey was now steeled against such entreaties. He and Anzia had one further frigid meeting in his office in 1927, but for all intents and purposes their love affair died under the Williamsburg Bridge in September 1918.

Butchering the Ideal

What might we make of this story? The temptation is to see the unhappy denouement of the love affair as of a piece with those other instances over the course of his career in which Dewey failed to live up to the principles of his philosophy. This, more or less, is the line of argument pursued by the most imaginative student of the Yezierska-Dewey story, Mary Dearborn. Dearborn places the burden of the failure of the romance on Dewey, attributing it to his "emotional cowardice" and a "failure of nerve" that for her render him contemptible and pathetic. Dewey, she says, "failed to live up to his own precepts and principles." Although he held out the promise of a harmonizing of ethnic cultures, his rejection of Yezierska shows that he was as filled with the patronizing, objectifying attitudes toward immigrant women as the Americanizers he criticized. Although he seemed to yearn for the kind of rich emotional life that Yezierska promised, he lacked the courage necessary to resolve the dualism of soul and body that afflicted him. As novelist Norma Rosen, who shares Dearborn's perspective, puts it, "By the end it seems that only one of them allowed experience to sink in deep enough to effect change. Which one would you expect that to be, the prophet of

---

25. Yezierska, *Hungry Hearts,* 141.
26. Anzia Yezierska, "Prophets of Democracy," *Bookman* (February 1921): 496–97.

change and growth or the immigrant ghetto girl? In matters of change and growth, the answer is always: Not what you expect!"[27]

This argument is enticing. It would enable us to find Dewey guilty of simultaneously violating his own best insights publicly and privately, for his conduct in the debate with Bourne in these same months was indeed cowardly, contemptible, and pathetic.[28] Unfortunately, this is not a persuasive reading of the love affair, for Yezierska was at least as responsible as Dewey for its collapse. As Dearborn admits, Yezierska's cold response to Dewey's sexual advances was the "crux of the matter." She "believed in sexual freedom, but—in Deweyan terms—she believed with the head rather than the heart. Her ambivalence was profound, and her sexuality extremely complicated." As Levitas Henriksen, whose treatment of the love affair is much blander yet more evenhanded than that of Dearborn, says, "Dewey had a right to expect, from Anzia's volatile, emotionally direct temperament, her seeming honesty (and the fact that she was not 23 but 33 [more likely 37], married and a mother as well), that she would virtually burst into flame at a touch. It was he who had always been reserved, disciplined, unwilling, or afraid to act on emotional impulse. He discovered like a harsh blow that Anzia had been playing a role." This was a blow from which their love could not recover.[29]

Rather than seeing this romance as revealing a failure by Dewey to live up to the virtues of his philosophy, I believe it can be better seen as a revelation of one of the signal weaknesses of his philosophy. In early 1918 Dewey found himself confronted with one of the most difficult of moral dilemmas: a choice of competing goods in which the values at stake were incompatible and incommensurable. Over the course of that spring and summer we can see him, in his poetry, agonizing over the choices that confront him—playing out the "dramatic rehearsals" of each choice and its consequences that his ethics argued were called for in such situations.

Dearborn fails to see this dilemma because she apparently does not feel the compelling force of what one might call the "Alice option," though Dewey clearly did. This blindness is the only way I can account for her charge that Dewey refused "to accept the consequences of his action." By her lights all that Alice held in store for Dewey was the dead hand of routine and the repression of his emotional and sexual longings. She fails to see the moral and emotional weight of Alice's claim on Dewey and the deep ties of obligation that bound him to her despite the difficulties of their marriage. Nonetheless, Dewey seems, by the evidence Yezierska left us, to have made

27. Dearborn, *Love in the Promised Land,* 119–21, 174; Rosen, *John and Anzia,* 14. Note that Rosen's empathetic partisanship for Anzia extends even to the effusive use of the exclamation point.

28. For this story, see Westbrook, *John Dewey and American Democracy,* 202–12, 233–35.

29. Dearborn, *Love in the Promised Land,* 130; Levitas Henriksen to Jo Ann Boydston, 9 July 1975, as quoted in *Poems of John Dewey,* xlv.

the choice Dearborn would have had him make in September 1918, but when Yezierska turned out not to be what she had led Dewey to believe she was, he quickly initiated another dramatic rehearsal of his possible actions, and in the face of a much less fraught decision, chose to remain with Alice. One can, of course, argue alongside Yezierska that Dewey took the less desirable path, but I do not see how one can charge him with cowardice. And one might reasonably guess that Dewey, like most who confront a tragic choice, was well aware of the goods he had forgone.[30]

But Dewey's own moral philosophy offered little guidance to tragic decisions. For it is precisely the sort of moral conflict that his love affair presented—choices between incompatible and incommensurable values—that Dewey's "quest for unity" obscured. Dewey's ethics, at its worst, suggested that one could always find a synthetic resolution that harmonized competing values. William James, who shared Dewey's view that such a resolution was always the ideal for which one should hope in morally troubling situations, nonetheless observed that more often than not we must settle for something less: "those ideals must be written highest which *prevail at the least cost,* or by whose realization the least possible number of other ideals are destroyed." Often, that is, "some part of the ideal must be butchered." Many of the complexities of the moral life, James said, would remain even if the universe was reduced to "one rock with two loving souls upon it." And when three loving souls find themselves on the rock, butchered ideals are all the more likely.[31]

James and Sidney Hook, among others, argued that there was nothing inherent in pragmatism that precluded a tragic sensibility, and one can find an occasional hint of such a sensibility in Dewey's later work, an awareness that often the most an agent could do in a moral situation was to "make the best adjustment he can among forces which are genuinely disparate." But such awareness was always fighting against "the bacillus of reconciliation," which afflicted Dewey's ethics (and, not incidentally as we have seen, his politics) until the end of his life.[32]

30. It is tempting to read some of Dewey's poems as meditations on what he had lost in losing Yezierska. Rockefeller does so with a poem that Boydston indicates was written before the two met (*John Dewey,* 351–52). But a good candidate that does postdate their meeting is "Round of Passion," which concludes: "The flame soared high; / To ground th'ashes fell. / The scatt'ring winds did blow. / Gone ash and flame and wood; / Bare earth sleeps cold; / Sun moves remote— / All as before. / The weary way is trod" (*Poems of John Dewey,* 10).

31. William James, "The Moral Philosopher and the Moral Life" (1891), in James, *The Will to Believe* (1897; Cambridge: Harvard University Press, 1979), 154–55.

32. John Dewey, "Three Independent Factors in Morals" (1930), *Later Works,* 5:288. See Sidney Hook, *Pragmatism and the Tragic Sense of Life* (New York: Basic Books, 1974), 3–25. Cornel West has also made a plea for a pragmatism armed with a tragic sensibility in his *The American Evasion of Philosophy: A Genealogy of Pragmatism* (Madison: University of Wisconsin Press, 1989), as has Cheryl Misak in *Truth, Politics, and Morality: Pragmatism and Deliberation* (London: Routledge, 2000), 141–44. I consider West's argument for a pragmatism tinged with tragedy in chapter 8.

I would conclude, then, that what we are left with from this rare instance in which we have been able to gain access to John Dewey's private life is a perplexing portrait of a thinker who knew full well in his own experience the messiness of the moral life as most of us live it (and who wrote poetry that, whatever its shortcomings, powerfully conveyed this messiness), and yet who—even in the face of this experience—was unable to make this messiness, this butchering of the ideal, essential to his philosophy. Perhaps it is here—and not in the decisions he made—that Dewey most failed to accept the gifts that his love for Anzia Yezierska held out for him. This failing makes Dewey a more interesting philosopher and human being than any of those of us who have contended with his life and work have made him out to be, and finds us regretting once more that he was so successful in sealing off the sepulcher of his heart.

CHAPTER 5

Marrying Marxism

★

Taking William James's talk of the "cash value" of ideas all too literally, some critics have continued to regard pragmatism in much the same way Bertrand Russell did at its origins: as the epistemological fruit of American capitalism, an expedient confusion of truth with whatever it takes to make a buck. Not surprisingly, given this characterization, Marxists of all sorts have been among the most hostile critics of pragmatism. In the midst of the Cold War, the *Large Soviet Encyclopedia* identified John Dewey as "the mouth-piece of modern imperialistic reaction," while the much less orthodox Max Horkheimer of the Frankfurt School pitched in with a haughty—and influential—dismissal of pragmatism as little more than a brief for the amoral, technical rationality of a soulless modernity.[1]

Such hostilities have often obscured the affinities between Marxism and pragmatism, particularly its Deweyan variety. As young men, both Marx and Dewey fell under the spell of the spirit—the Absolute Spirit—of Hegel. But each eventually directed withering scorn at Hegelian idealism and all other brands of philosophy detached from practical concerns; neither believed with Hegel that we must await dusk for the owl of Minerva to spread its wings. "The philosophers have only *interpreted* the world, in various ways," Marx famously griped. "The point, however, is to *change* it." Only slightly less famously, Dewey contended seventy years later that philosophy was doomed

---

1. *Large Soviet Encyclopedia* (1952 edition), as quoted in Martin Levit, "Soviet Version of John Dewey and Pragmatism," *History of Education Journal* 4 (1953): 138–39; Max Horkheimer, *The Eclipse of Reason* (New York: Oxford University Press, 1947), 41–57, 74–91.

to terminal irrelevance unless "it ceases to be a device for dealing with the problems of philosophers and becomes a method, cultivated by philosophers, for dealing with the problems of men." Beyond this common complaint, both Marx and Dewey worked out a philosophy that held, as Marx put it, that "life is not determined by consciousness, but consciousness by life." Dewey, like Marx, regarded ideas as tools, if not always weapons. For Dewey, as for Marx, "to be a man is to be thinking desire." For Dewey, as for Marx, truth was a human artifact, and truth-making was inextricable from the Enlightenment project of bettering the human estate.[2]

Given these affinities, the courtship of Marxism and pragmatism in the United States in the early decades of the twentieth century is perhaps less surprising than it might first appear. To be sure, Dewey himself was not disposed to give the match serious consideration, for, as far as he could see, most of the Marxists he encountered had been far less successful than he had in freeing themselves from Hegel's grasp. The "dialectics" of these Marxists seemed to him to be little more than Hegelian metaphysics in pseudoscientific, materialist drag.[3] But others have seen considerable virtues in a marriage of Marxism and pragmatism, and therein lies a story that has yet to be fully told.

Left Out

Brian Lloyd has told part of that story in illuminating detail and with unremitting enmity in his provocative book, *Left Out*. Addressing himself to the venerable question of why socialism has been such a miserable flop in the United States, Lloyd argues that this failure is, at least in part, a theoretical failure, a failure of American socialists to be true to "the Marxism of Marx," by which he means a Marxism like his own, one that "reflects a sympathetic engagement with the works of Marx and Engels, Lenin, György Lukács, and Mao Tse-tung."[4] Although Lloyd does not mean to say that theoretical im-

2. Karl Marx, "Theses on Feuerbach" (1845), in Robert C. Tucker, ed., *The Marx-Engels Reader* (New York: Norton, 1978), 145; John Dewey, "The Need for a Recovery of Philosophy" (1917), *Middle Works*, 10:46; Dewey, "Introduction to *Essays in Experimental Logic*" (1916), *Middle Works*, 10:331. For an early, but still perceptive, treatment of these similarities, see Sidney Hook, "The Philosophy of Dialectial Materialism," *Journal of Philosophy* 25 (1928): esp. 118, 124.

3. See Dewey, *Freedom and Culture* (1939), *Later Works*, 13:120, and Peter Manicas, "Dewey and the Class Struggle," in Murray G. Murphey and Ivan Berg, eds., *Values and Value Theory in Twentieth-Century America* (Philadelphia: Temple University Press, 1988), 67–81.

4. *Left Out: Pragmatism, Exceptionalism, and the Poverty of American Marxism, 1890–1922* (Baltimore: Johns Hopkins University Press, 1997), 457. Subsequent page citations to this book are in the text. My concern here is with accounts of the relationship between pragmatism and Marxism by historians who are themselves Marxists, but I do not mean to discount the important work on the matter by non-Marxist historians from which I have learned a great deal. See

poverishment is a sufficient explanation of the weaknesses of American socialism or that the coupling of pragmatism and Marxism is the only theoretical disaster that has afflicted the American left, he does regard it as
among the most debilitating, and he is determined to annul it.

Focusing on the heyday of the American Socialist party in the first two
decades of the twentieth century and on the party intellectuals who contributed to radical journals such as the *International Socialist Review* and the
New Review, Lloyd contends that these theorists demonstrated little understanding of what Marx had to say and as a result surrendered "the ideological ground upon which a genuinely anticapitalist campaign could even be
visualized, let alone actually fought" (14). In 1900, American socialists, like
many of their European counterparts, were plagued by the mechanical, de-
terminist Marxism that supplanted the "Marxism of Marx" in the late nineteenth century and established itself as the theoretical signature of the
Second International. Although party intellectuals such as Robert Rives La
Monte, Austin Lewis, and Ernest Untermann wrote learned tomes on Marxism, they took their theoretical cues less from Marx than from bourgeois
thinkers such as Herbert Spencer and Thorstein Veblen. Long after others
had consigned Spencer to oblivion, "radical Darwinists" in the SP spun out
sunny, cosmic Spencerian scenarios of an inevitable social evolution toward
socialism. After 1905 La Monte and Lewis abandoned Spencer for Veblen,
who offered them a less biological and more cultural evolutionary perspective and a "machine metaphysics" that envisioned the happy prospect that
the working class would develop a revolutionary consciousness simply by
virtue of its day-to-day encounter with modern industrial technology.

In 1912, the SP split apart, following a bitter dispute over the legitimacy
of the extralegal, direct-action tactics advocated by the Industrial Workers
of the World. The parliamentarian "constructivists" who controlled the
party expelled IWW leader "Big Bill" Haywood, and a host of left-wing syn-
dicalists left with him. At the same time, socialist intellectuals soured on "any
idea that walked the streets in Darwinian attire" (165). Party leaders such as
Morris Hillquit clung to evolutionary positivism but exempted the bourgeois democratic state from change and settled into a politics that was hard
to distinguish from liberal reform. Left-wingers "in search of less faint-
hearted ways of conceptualizing scientific socialism" abandoned mechanical determinism altogether and put a premium on human will (165). This
voluntarism led some of them—most notably Max Eastman and William English Walling—to pragmatism. Yet, despite their talk of class struggle, no

---

John P. Diggins, *Up from Communism: Conservative Odysseys in American Intellectual History* (New
York: Harper, 1977), 17–73; James T. Kloppenberg, *Uncertain Victory* (New York: Oxford,
1986), 145–415; and Richard Pells, *Radical Visions and American Dreams: Culture and Social
Thought in the Depression Years,* 3rd ed. (Urbana: University of Illinois Press, 1998), 125–40.

American socialist intellectual found a way back to the "Marxism of Marx." For all their militant rhetoric, they were thereby led down the path of a decidedly unrevolutionary politics that came to full flower in their enthusiastic support for, or lame opposition to, the imperialist bloodbath of World War I. Unable to grasp the essentials of Marx's anatomy of capitalism, the socialist right settled into the complacent practice of electoral politics, while the socialist left, even "American Bolsheviks" such as Louis Fraina, mistook combative trade-unionism for revolution. All were thus blind to the theoretical wisdom of the one true disciple of Marx in their time: Lenin.

As this brief summary of Lloyd's argument suggests, he is a true believer, undeterred by recent history. "I presume," he says, "that we are witnessing, not the death of Marxism, but the end of the first period during which Marxists managed to seize and, for a time, wield state power. That it has fewer adherents at the end than during other phases of this period, and that as many of them can be found in universities as in factories or fields, is neither as disheartening as is imagined by some of its proponents nor as amusing as is supposed by all of its detractors" (3). Notably silent on the sort of things that Marxists did while wielding state power, Lloyd is confident that at least some of the oppressed of the earth will still see their way clear to "turn to Marxism as the only trustworthy weapon for analyzing and transforming complex, and seemingly well defended, systems of oppression" (2).

Arguing from this perspective, Lloyd not only offers an account of the debates among American socialists but also intervenes in these debates on behalf of the Marxism of Marx and Lenin. The result is a book that crackles with polemical energy and wit. No opponent is spared a put-down, and Lloyd can be very funny in a "Moe-jabs-his-fingers-in-Curly's-eyes" kind of way. Lloyd is not as clear as one would hope about what constitutes the "Marxism of Marx" against which he unfavorably measures his subjects, and not until the appreciative account of the Marxism of Lenin with which he closes his book is he at all expansive on the subject. Nonetheless, one grasps early on that his Marx was, with Lenin, a firm believer that "without revolutionary theory, there can be no revolutionary movement" (409). Marx held that "a truly socialist consciousness had to include the concepts that make it possible to comprehend and revolutionize bourgeois society, a body of theory he believed he had worked out in *Capital*" (169).

Comprehending capitalism was no easy task; it required all those long days Marx spent in the British Museum unmasking the social relations of production hidden in the commodity form. Again and again Lloyd complains not only that American socialists failed to grasp the abstractions and dialectical reasoning that Marx deployed in his political economy, but also that they failed to appreciate how essential theory must be to the making of a socialist revolution. Unlike the Marxism of Marx, Spencerian, Veblenian, and pragmatist versions of Marxism were not themselves instrumental to the revolution they imagined; they blindly promised "revolutionary consciousness without revolutionary theory." Lenin alone understood the errors of such antitheoretical theory. As a result,

> he criticized every notion advanced by American leftists—from the notion that workers were driven by material interest to a spontaneously generated revolutionary consciousness to the "economist" conceit that trade unionism constituted the most promising form of anticapitalist struggle. Instead of casting about for some historical agent that needed only await the ripening of conditions to become revolutionary, Lenin made the defense and development of Marxist theory a precondition for revolution. Class consciousness, for Lenin, was a *cognitive* category. No meaningful change was possible unless revolutionaries understood—in the historical, many-sided way Lenin identified with Marxist science—the specific social formation they were trying to change (410).

Although they routinely dressed up their arguments in Marxist language, American socialists, unlike Lenin, made Marxism and, ironically, Marxist intellectuals irrelevant to socialist politics.

At the root of the theoretical impoverishment of American socialism, Lloyd argues, was what he sneeringly terms its "hayseed empiricism" (158). By hayseed empiricism he means a conception of knowledge wary of abstraction and theory, a "naive" empiricism that rested on "the belief that the givens of experience were as readily available as corn on the stalk or credit at a kinsman's grocery" (158).[5] This was the epistemology of the rapidly disappearing rural and small-town society, the world of the petty-bourgeoisie. To Lloyd it comes as no surprise that American socialist theory was infested with hayseed empiricism, for, as he sees it, American socialism was thoroughly petty-bourgeois. The Socialist party and its leader at the turn of the century, Eugene Debs, were heirs to the tradition of nineteenth-century "producer republicanism"—a "petty-bourgeois radicalism" that had brought small farmers, skilled workers, and small businessmen together in the Knights of Labor and the People's Party in order to defend their independence from the encroachments of industrial capitalism. Updating but never abandoning this tradition, socialists promised to use a combination of trade union organizing and electoral politics to defeat the plutocrats threatening the republic and to establish the same sort of "cooperative commonwealth" envisioned by the Populists before them—"a society that preserved, in the new industrial world, the fundamental American values of dignified, well-renumerated labor, equal opportunity, and democratic citi-

---

5. Perhaps not surprisingly, Lloyd says nothing of Lenin's *Materialism and Empirio-Criticism* (1909), an argument on behalf of hayseed empiricism if ever there was one.

zenship" (93). Hayseed empiricism was the epistemological reflex of this petty-bourgeois ideal, and hence for most American socialists it was "the philosophical touchstone for the faith that the transparent social relations and commonsense ideals proper to a society of small producers might be reesetablished—after a socialist revolution—in a near, industrial future" (158).

Some socialists, Lloyd acknowledges, were capable of a more "sophisticated empiricism," which was friendly to abstraction and theory, and he is relatively sympathetic to those such as Louis Boudin who proved capable of such sophistication. But with the exception of Boudin, all the leading socialist intellectuals of the period were, he insists, hayseeds. These included the pragmatist radicals, whose pragmatism made them hayseeds.

In order to render pragmatism complicit in the shortcomings of hayseed empiricism, Lloyd distinguishes sharply between the "two pragmatisms" of James and Dewey. James, loyal to the tradition of British empiricism, was given to a psychology that favored immediate, personal, concrete experience, while Dewey, who cut his teeth on Hegel, was more favorably disposed to abstraction. James found it difficult to abandon a dualism between the self and the world, while Dewey arrived at a fully social and cultural conception of the individual. James's commitments "to instinct, sensation, and feeling overpowered the efforts he made, as a pragmatist, to accord intelligence some practical role in human affairs" (54). Dewey could often talk of little else than intelligence. James's pragmatism centered on individual belief, while Dewey's instrumentalism (his preferred term) celebrated cooperative inquiry. Unlike James, who deplored "bigness" of any sort, Dewey "welcomed, rather than suspected, the impersonal, cooperative, large-scale, linked-with-production science deployed with such success by the modern corporation" (50). James was an old liberal and Dewey a new one, and hence "Dewey sided in the realm of ideology with the real-life despoilers of all that James held dear" (24). James, the hayseed empiricist, developed a pragmatism amenable to those still wedded to the world of the petty-bourgeoisie, while Dewey, the sophisticated empiricist, forged a pragmatism better suited to "the collective interests of a national, corporate bourgeoisie" (50). Hence James, not Dewey, supplied the philosophical foundation for the petty-bourgeois socialism of pragmatist radicals.

This is an ingenious argument, but not a convincing one. Although most of the contrasts Lloyd draws between James and Dewey are accurate, those that are most crucial to his scheme are not. James was not a hayseed empiricist, if by that term one means a philosopher who believes that our knowledge of the world can be the product simply of immediate experience. Both James and Dewey were, to be sure, what Dewey termed "immediate empiricists," that is, both believed that things "are what they are experienced as." And James was sometimes inclined, as Dewey was not, to treat sheer perception or feeling as a kind of "knowledge." But both argued that things are never, in the first instance, experienced as the objects of thought. Indeed, at the heart of the pragmatists' position in the epistemological controversies that preoccupied American philosophers in the early twentieth century was an attack on what James and Dewey called "intellectualism," the assumption that experience was pervasively a matter of thinking about the world. This assumption had guided philosophers—including such truly hayseed empiricists as Locke, Hume, and Mill, as well as their rationalist and idealist opponents—since the seventeenth century and was, Dewey said, "if not the root of all philosophic evil, at least one of its main roots."[6]

In the first instance, James and Dewey held, man was not a thinker but an "agent-patient, doer, sufferer, and enjoyer." Thinking was a mediate kind of experience that evolved in order to solve the problems that arose in immediate experience and to enrich immediate experience; it was necessarily conceptual and abstract. Both pragmatists did indeed believe that "the givens of experience were as readily available as corn on the stalk," but neither held that we could *know* that a particular given was in fact "corn on the stalk" in any immediate way. James spoke of the difference between our "acquaintance with" reality and our "knowledge about" it, and Dewey distinguished between experience that was simply "had" and that which was "known."[7]

Lloyd works James up into a hayseed empiricist by focusing on his analysis of the former kind of experience, principally the discussion of mysticism in *The Varieties of Religious Experience,* and by treating such discussions as if they were an account of "knowledge about" rather than "acquaintance with" reality. But as every disappointed reader knows who has turned to that text in search of a confirmation of a belief in God, James derives almost no truth claims from his rich investigations of immediate religious experience. That James shared with Dewey a conception of thinking as mediate is fully evident in properly epistemological books such as *Pragmatism* itself and *The Meaning of Truth,* neither of which Lloyd examines. James and Dewey both would have found as laughable as Lloyd does such hayseed empiricist pronouncements as this choice item from Veblenian socialist Austin Lewis: "Without knowing why, [the modern proletarian] arrives, by dint of the experience of his daily toil, at the same conclusions as Engels attained as the result of philosophic training and much erudition" (148).

Insofar as James shaped the thinking of young radicals such as Randolph

6. Dewey, "The Postulate of Immediate Empiricism" (1905), *Middle Works,* 3:158–60.
7. Dewey, "Postulate of Immediate Empiricism"; Dewey, "Brief Studies in Realism" (1911), *Middle Works,* 6:103–8; Dewey, *Experience and Nature* (1929), *Later Works,* 1:27–28; William James, *Psychology: Briefer Course* (1892; Cambridge: Harvard University Press, 1984), 19.

Bourne, Max Eastman, and Walter Lippmann, it was less as a pragmatic empiricist than as a romantic vitalist, a homegrown counterpart to Nietzsche
or Bergson, who alerted them to the significance of those realms of experience that eluded thought. In this sense, he may well have fostered an antitheoretical impulse among some socialists. If, Bourne said, it was Dewey who
provided "creative intelligence," it was James who offered "creative desire."
While Dewey occupied himself in the early twentieth century hammering
out a pragmatist logic, James focused on those domains of experience that
escaped logic and attempted to authorize beliefs that lacked the warrant of
truth. James came perilously close in *Pragmatism* to arguing that any of the
happy consequences of holding a belief might be taken as evidence of its
truth, but in the face of stern criticism from Dewey and others, he carefully
restored the boundaries between the claims of truth and those of faith. Insofar as socialism was for young radicals a moral faith, a "poetic vision"
(Bourne) as well as a science of society, they welcomed James's arguments
for a will to believe in, and to act upon, propositions that were live, forced,
and (as yet) unwarranted.[8]

If Lloyd covers James with too many hayseeds, he also fails to perceive the
straw that stuck to Dewey. Dewey's ties to nineteenth-century petty-bourgeois radicalism were as strong as, if not stronger than, those of James.[9] He
was sympathetic to the Populist coalition that radical journalist Henry Demarest Lloyd sought to create in Chicago in the early 1890s and to the railway workers that Debs led in the Pullman strike of 1894. There was no social
philosopher whom Dewey venerated more than Henry George, the para-
digmatic petty-bourgeois radical, and he continued to insist on the perti-
nence of George's economics to radical reform well into the 1930s. Dewey
was drawn to British guild socialism during and after World War I precisely
because it seemed to him to promise, as he later said, to be the sort of "socialism that is not state socialism" that would sustain the petty-bourgeois values toward which Brian Lloyd is so contemptuous.

Lloyd's attempt to render Dewey the philosopher of the corporate bourgeoisie and the presiding presence behind Walter Lippmann's celebration
in *Drift and Mastery* of corporate managers and professionals as the elite
bearers of a scientific, Deweyan pragmatism ignores not only Dewey's
explicit attacks on corporate capitalism but also his commitment to the democratization of scientific intelligence. Unlike Lippmann, Dewey empha-
sized the continuity between the thinking of the common man and that of

8. Randolph Bourne, "Twilight of Idols" (1917), in Olaf Hansen, ed., *The Radical Will: Randolph Bourne, Selected Writings* (New York: Urizen, 1977), 347. On James's crucial role in the philosophy, psychology, and politics of early-twentieth-century American vitalism, see Jeffrey
Brown, "Vitalism and the Modernist Search for Meaning: Subjectivity, Social Order, and the
Philosophy of Life in the Progressive Era," Ph.D. Diss., University of Rochester, 2001.
    9. As I have suggested in chapter 3.

the scientist. This claim was at the heart of his most widely read work of epistemology, *How We Think*. Dewey, unlike Lippmann, was committed to the widespread distribution of pragmatic intelligence. This effort was at the heart of his work as an educational reformer, for which he was best known before the war. As Walling perceptively observed, "If Dewey expects science to guide us, this does not mean that he expects the scientists to guide us."[10] Lippmann did expect scientists and other experts to guide us, and in the contrast between *Drift and Mastery* and Dewey's *Democracy and Education* one can see the seeds of the sharp debate the two men waged in the 1920s over the merits of expansive (Dewey) and constricted (Lippmann) conceptions of democracy.[11]

Lloyd also gets Walling wrong. This is no small error since Walling is the most significant of the prewar pragmatist socialists. Unlike the others Lloyd includes in this camp—Bourne, Eastman, and Lippmann (of *Preface to Politics* if not *Drift and Mastery*)—Walling made an extended effort to weld Marxism and pragmatism into an innovative socialism. The three books he published in rapid succession between 1912 and 1914—*Socialism as It Is, The Larger Aspects of Socialism,* and *Progressivism—and After*—are the most important works of pragmatist socialism Lloyd considers. The difficulty that Walling's socialism presents for Lloyd is that it was both petty-bourgeois and explicitly Deweyan, apparently shattering the tight connection Lloyd wants to sustain between petty-bourgeois values and hayseed (Jamesian) empiricism. Rather than abandon his scheme, Lloyd dismisses Walling's claim to be a Deweyan pragmatist and tries to sever the link between Walling's socialism and Dewey's philosophy. His key move here is to attack Walling's call for a democratization of scientific knowledge as un-Deweyan since, as Lloyd would have it, for Dewey "the community of practicing scientists modeled and safeguarded scientific inquiry" (203). But, as I say, Walling's advocacy of the democratization of scientific thinking was one of the most Deweyan things about his socialism, and he was one of the few prewar socialists to grasp the radical implications of Dewey's philosophy of education.[12]

Despite Walling's efforts to fashion Marx and Engels as proto-pragmatists, his socialism bore few of the marks of the Marxism of Marx. His class struggle was one between the "privileged" and the "nonprivileged," and his social ideal was equality of opportunity. His principal concern was to preserve and extend "bourgeois democracy," and consequently he was as hard, if not harder, on authoritarian socialists as he was on predatory capitalists. The so-

10. William English Walling, *The Larger Aspects of Socialism* (New York: Macmillan, 1913), 37–38.

11. For an account of the Lippmann-Dewey debate, see Robert B. Westbrook, *John Dewey and American Democracy* (Ithaca: Cornell University Press, 1991), 293–318.

12. Westbrook, *John Dewey,* 190–92.

cialism he envisioned was decentralized, egalitarian, and radically democratic. Petty-bourgeois though it may have been, it was quite close to that
which Dewey himself advanced. When Lippmann derided Walling for
proposing a socialism "much nearer to Henry George" than to "the organized Socialist movement," he might just as well have been calling Dewey to
task.[13] Walling demonstrated that one could be a petty-bourgeois socialist
and a "sophisticated empiricist," as did Dewey himself.

Comrade Hook

Because Lloyd concludes his account in 1920, he does not engage the single most important proponent of a pragmatist Marxism, Sidney Hook, who
was but a schoolboy radical during the war. This is too bad, since Hook and
his masterpiece, *Towards the Understanding of Karl Marx* (1933), would pose
even more interesting problems for Lloyd's attack on pragmatism than does
Walling. For as Christopher Phelps demonstrates in his study of Hook's early
career, Hook was for most of the 1930s simultaneously a Deweyan pragmatist and a Leninist.[14] Indeed, the early chapters of Hook's remarkable book,
in which he laid waste to prewar European socialists of the right and left
alike, nicely mirror Lloyd's own indictment of American socialists who
shared their infirmities. And, as in Lloyd's account, it is Lenin who emerges
for Hook as the one true heir to the Marxism of Marx. For Hook, as one re-
viewer said, "it is Lenin who is the greatest Marxian revolutionary, not
merely tactically but also dialectically."[15] If the example of Walling indicates
that Deweyan pragmatism may be as compatible with petty-bourgeois socialism as its Jamesian varieties, then the example of Hook suggests that socialists might be everything that Lloyd thinks they should be—that is,
Leninists—and pragmatists as well.

This is the case that Phelps would make, and he lucidly lays out the elements of Hook's merger of pragmatism and Leninism. Phelps does not see
pragmatism as an obstacle to Hook's Leninism but as its enabler. "Pragmatism helped him arrive at the particular *type* of Marxism that he espoused."
It "imbued him with an appreciation of democracy, flexibility, and action, a

13. Lippmann, as quoted in Lloyd, *Left Out*, 278.
14. Christopher Phelps, *Young Sidney Hook: Marxist and Pragmatist* (Ithaca: Cornell University Press, 1997). This book originated as a doctoral dissertation under my direction. But as will
be evident, Phelps and I are far from one in our views on Marxism, Leninism, and Hook. I have
nonetheless found our disagreements most illuminating and am grateful to him for his un-
daunted if unavailing efforts to convince me of the virtues of revolutionary socialism.
15. Benjamin Stolberg, "The Americanization of Karl Marx," *Nation* (12 April 1933): 414.
Towards the Understanding of Karl Marx: A Revolutionary Interpretation (Buffalo: Prometheus
Books, 2002) is finally back in print, with a fine introduction by Phelps.

disposition that enabled him to break through ossified varieties of Marxism and deliver one of the most substantial contributions to Marxist philosophy in American history."[16] And throughout much of the 1930s, Hook's Marxism—his own account of his career to the contrary notwithstanding—was at once Leninist and pragmatist.[17]

As Phelps's account makes clear, this merger rested on Hook's conviction that Deweyan pragmatism and Leninist Marxism were both radically democratic. In the case of pragmatism, Hook was, like many pragmatists, deeply invested in what Hilary Putnam has called Dewey's "epistemological justification of democracy." For Dewey, as Putnam says, democracy "is the precondition for the application of intelligence to the solution of social problems" because egalitarian inclusiveness and democratic practices such as free speech were essential to effective inquiry. Democracy has a "cognitive value" insofar as it is "a requirement for experimental inquiry in any area. To reject democracy is to reject the idea of being experimental."[18] For Hook as for Dewey, Robert Talisse has observed, pragmatist epistemology and politics are "mutually edifying. . . . the relationship between democracy and inquiry is symbiotic: the breakdown of democratic institutions obstructs or renders meaningless public inquiry, and the inability or unwillingness of citizens to participate in inquiry cripples democratic politics."[19]

Any Marxism that would also be pragmatist is, then, likely to be expansively democratic. This, I take it, is what Jürgen Habermas meant when he remarked that American pragmatism should be seen as the "radical-democratic branch of Young Hegelianism," useful in shoring up the democratic deficiencies of its other branches, not least of all Marxism.[20] Under the influence of pragmatism, Hook therefore tried for a time to make the case for the philosophical affinities between Marx and Dewey and for Leninism as a radically democratic variant of the Marxism of Marx. And under the influence of Marx and Lenin, he urged Dewey and other pragmatists to view revolutionary socialism as the obvious politics for pragmatists confronted with the inequities of bourgeois, capitalist society. For Hook, as Phelps says, "social experimentation, to take place unfettered, would require the abolition of class rule and its hierarchy of private gain over public interest" (58).

---

16. Phelps, *Young Sidney Hook*, 8–9. Subsequent page citations to this book are in the text.

17. See Hook, *Out of Step: An Unquiet Life in the 20th Century* (New York: Harper and Row, 1987), 198.

18. Hilary Putnam, "A Reconsideration of Deweyan Democracy" (1990), in Putnam, *Renewing Philosophy* (Cambridge: Harvard University Press, 1992), 180–200. For a full account of the pragmatist epistemological argument for democracy, see chapter 7.

19. Robert Talisse, "Hook's Basic Ideals: Politics without Dogmas," Unpublished paper (2002), 4. See also Robert Talisse and Robert Tempio, "Editors' Introduction," *Sidney Hook on Pragmatism, Democracy, and Freedom* (Amherst, N.Y.: Prometheus Books, 2002), 12–19.

20. Jürgen Habermas, "A Philosophico-Political Profile," in Peter Dews, ed., *Autonomy and Solidarity: Interviews with Jürgen Habermas* (New York: Verso, 1986), 151.

Phelps admits that Hook's view of Lenin as a radical democrat made him an unorthodox Leninist in the 1930s, not only to the Stalinists in the American Communist party, whom he bitterly opposed after 1932, but also to the Trotskyists with whom he worked until well into the decade. He urged his comrades in the anti-Stalinist left to abandon talk of the "dictatorship of the proletariat" in favor of "workers' democracy," a term he felt better captured the rule of democratic soviets and competitive party politics that he believed Lenin had promised if not delivered to the Russian people after 1917. Hook, Phelps says, "admired the Russian Revolution because of its original promise of a more expansive, workplace-centered democracy expressed through soviets (councils) of deputies elected freely by working people, peasants, and soldiers." After Lenin's death "the rule of the soviets had become improperly identified with the rule of the Communist Party, itself dominated by an unaccountable bureaucracy." Stalinism was a betrayal of Lenin's revolution (115n39, 116).

But even Hook's unorthodox and relatively democratic Leninism of the early 1930s was not without its shortcomings from a democratic pragmatist point of view. Most notable here was his treatment of the fate of the minority of bourgeois citizens who remained part of a communist society after the revolution. Steadfastly setting himself against the seizure of power by a revolutionary elite lacking the support of a majority of a population and carefully distinguishing between the rule of a working-class majority through its representative councils from the domination of a minority Communist party presuming to rule in its name, Hook nonetheless was insistent that in the "transition" to full-fledged socialism, the working-class would wield open dictatorial power against those bourgeois elements of the population who had yet to become "voluntary and trusted participants in the collective work of society." Though he condemned the loose use of the term, "dictatorship of the proletariat," he acknowledged that such a dictatorship would indeed be a part of "workers' democracy" until the bourgeoisie abandoned any opposition to the regime:

> A dictatorship is a rule over any class or group in which conflicts of interest are resolved ultimately by *force*. The dictatorship of the proletariat—which is presumably a democracy for workers—is a dictatorship in the eyes of the bourgeoisie because it uses the state power, directly or indirectly, forcibly or peacefully, *against* them. It deprives them of political rights, denies them freedom of press, assembly and agitation, and like the dictatorship of capital over the working-class, does not hesitate to imprison or shoot as the ultimate measure of social defence.[21]

21. Sidney Hook, "On Workers' Democracy," *Modern Monthly* 8 (October 1934): 532, 535. I am indebted to Robert Cummings for bringing such passages in Hook's essays on "workers' democracy" to my attention.

Most democrats agreed, as did Dewey, that a majoritarian revolution had every right to protect itself from armed insurrection by defeated counter-revolutionaries.[22] But most would also join Dewey in rejecting the repression of the civil and political rights of nonrevolutionary, even antirevolutionary, classes. Hook's assurance that "all measures of repression and force even against the bourgeoisie are judiciously applied" was cold comfort to such democrats. It might have been arguments such as Hook's that Dewey had in mind when he told James Farrell that "I read considerable talk about 'the democratic' as applying to the process of getting socialism; damn little about it as an adjective applying to socialism when you get it."[23]

For a pragmatist democrat, Hook's argument for a repressive workers' dictatorship over the bourgeoisie was troubling because it flew in the face of the epistemological justification for democracy that pragmatism offered. The policies of the sort of democratic, experimental polity toward which pragmatism pointed were provisional and always subject to criticism, revision, reevaluation, and repudiation. To protect a revolution by repressing the civil and political liberties of any citizens, however "counterrevolutionary" their views might be, was to violate the democratic discourse ethics of a pragmatist politics. A democratic, pragmatist revolution was one that was not only waged democratically (as Hook prescribed) but also sustained democratically (as he did not).

By the late 1930s, Hook had begun steadily distancing himself from Leninism. Initially, he continued to defend the democratic character of the Bolshevik Revolution but faulted Lenin for a woeful postrevolutionary performance in fostering Soviet democracy.[24] But by the end of the decade, Hook had turned against the revolution itself, arguing that the Bolsheviks' commitment to a "vanguard party" (which he had once vigorously defended) held within it the seeds of the antidemocratic regime that followed upon their seizure of power.[25] Unlike many anticommunist critics, Hook never read Marx out of the democratic canon. He left the door open for a revision of his pragmatist Marxism, but never pursued it himself. "It would appear," he commented in 1947, "that if I were justified in my interpretation of Marx's meaning, I would perhaps be the only true Marxist left in the world."[26]

"One cannot be a socialist or a Marxist without being a democrat," Hook

22. See John Dewey, *Liberalism and Social Action* (1935), *Later Works* 11:61.

23. Hook, "On Workers' Democracy," 536; John Dewey to James Farrell, 8 November 1948, Dewey Papers, Southern Illinois University.

24. Hook, "As a (Marxist) Professor Sees It," *Common Sense* 7 (January 1938): 22–23.

25. Hook, "Reflections on the Russian Revolution," *Southern Review* 4 (1939): 450–58.

26. Hook, "The Future of Socialism," *Partisan Review* 14 (January-February 1947): 25. Near the end of his life, Hook wrote me that "I am no longer a Marxist since I am convinced that by Marx's own tests of validity, his major views have been falsified by events. But I still regard Marx as a great figure in the calendar of human freedom. Arguing that Stalin was Lenin's heir, I do not agree that Lenin was Marx's heir." Sidney Hook to Robert Westbrook [July 1987].

wrote in the late 1940s.[27] On this understanding, Lenin, whom Hook had once, like Lloyd, believed to be the principal inheritor of the Marxism of Marx, was now for Hook no longer a Marxist of any sort. He was, like Stalin, a totalitarian. Himself no longer a revolutionary, Hook argued after World War II that the future of socialism lay in the sort of social democratic politics of elections, piecemeal reform, and class collaboration for which he had once expressed nothing but contempt.

Phelps, whose own politics lie close to those of Hook's Leninism of the early thirties, condemns Hook for abandoning revolutionary socialism. In the name of "workers' democracy," he says, Hook might still have attacked not only Stalinism but authoritarian interpretations of Lenin's legacy. He might even have rightly criticized Lenin and Trotsky for failures of democratic leadership after the Bolshevik Revolution. But he should have drawn the line at repudiating the revolution itself and the democratic theory that guided Lenin. In doing so, Phelps argues, Hook also betrayed his pragmatism, for he was once correct to believe that revolutionary socialism of a Leninist variety was the necessary basis of the sort of "experimental democracy" that Dewey's pragmatism prescribed.

Phelps says nothing about Hook's justifications for a postrevolutionary dictatorship over the remnants of the bourgeoisie and contends that democrats who worry that Bolshevik revolution by means of a vanguard party "is inevitably (if not intentionally) an elitist notion" are guilty of a "lazy argument, which closes the book on Lenin for many who think it's all they need to know about him."[28] But I think he is mistaken. Even if we grant Lenin the best of democratic intentions, it remains the case that the Bolshevik Revolution (unlike, say, the revolutionary transformation of much of central and eastern Europe in 1989) was not the work of a democratic, popular movement, as Hook well knew. Phelps says that "the Marxist method, Hook underscored, was for a majoritarian revolution of the workers and their allies to abolish all class distinctions," yet he later acknowledges that the Russian Revolution was not such a "majoritarian revolution" (102, 184).[29] At best, Lenin pursued democratic ends by undemocratic means. In

27. Hook, "Future of Socialism," 25.

28. Phelps, "Lenin and American Radicalism," *Science and Society* 60 (1996): 82.

29. Like many who defend Lenin from the claim that he set the stage for Stalin, Phelps gives great weight to Lenin's most democratic text, *State and Revolution* (1917). For a challenge to this defense, see A. J. Polan, *Lenin and the End of Politics* (Berkeley: University of California Press, 1984). In later correspondence with me, Phelps has suggested that he might consider abandoning dispute over the legacy of Lenin in particular and rest content with a defense of a minority Bolshevism, the better of the "two souls of Bolshevism," that (with or without Lenin) embodied radical democratic impulses (Christopher Phelps to Robert Westbrook, 11 November 2002). As he does in his book, Phelps recommends Samuel Farber, *Before Stalinism: The Rise and Fall of Soviet Democracy* (New York: Verso, 1990) as a corrective. See also Hal Draper, *Socialism from Below* (New York: Humanities Press, 1992).

Dewey's ethics, which focused intently on the mutually enhancing (or debilitating) relationship between means and ends, this (as Dewey said) made Bolshevism suspect. Hook's pragmatism might well, then, have put his Leninism in jeopardy from the outset—much depended on his confidence in his claims for the democratic bona fides of the Bolsheviks. Once this confidence waned, and he came to believe that "the fundamental error of Lenin and Trotsky was the underestimation of the importance of *democratic processes* even in the period of revolution and civil war," Hook had broken the bond between his pragmatism and his Leninism. Far from seeing the two as one, he was back to square one, recommending anew that Marxism "must assimilate in its present day formulation, particularly in the American here and now, the experimental philosophy as expressed in the major works of John Dewey."[30] And insofar as democratic processes include what Phelps contemptuously terms "bourgeois electoral and legal norms," Hook was on his way, as Trotsky warned, to little more than "radical bourgeois democracy" (173, 189).

So maybe even the career of a Leninist such as Sidney Hook confirms Lloyd's conviction that pragmatism will inevitably infect any socialism it touches with the values of petty-bourgeois radicalism, not because of its empiricism—hayseed or otherwise—but because those values are essential to the shared experimental life that pragmatism authorizes. Perhaps a pragmatic socialism will indeed find it difficult to press beyond dignified, well-renumerated labor, equal opportunity, and democratic citizenship. I myself do not find this a great source of disappointment, but then I am not particularly taken with the wisdom of Lenin and am among those historians whom Lloyd chides for their sympathies for those "who fought, as radical democrats and aggrieved patriots, to redeem a corrupted or endangered republic" (416). The limitations of this sort of petty-bourgeois radicalism seem to me to pale before the crimes of those who have marched under the banner that Lloyd so defiantly unfurls.

Social Democracy

Orthodox Leninists such as Lloyd, and even "democratic Bolsheviks" such as Phelps, cannot bring themselves to speak of "social democracy" without a sneer. For them, this sort of weak-kneed, tepid, and painfully "evolutionary" socialism does not deserve the name. "American social democracy's chief contribution to American life," Lloyd taunts, "has been ideological rather than political: by characterizing any strategy that does not slavishly

---

30. Hook, "As a (Marxist) Professor Sees It," 23.

kowtow to bourgeois democratic prejudices as slavish kowtowing to some foreign model, it makes national chauvinism and reformism look like necessary components of any socialist reckoning with American reality" (391). Phelps recoils in dismay as Hook moves steadily in the 1940s toward an identification of socialism with "the gradual expansion of the welfare state" and a naive embrace of an expansion of the liberties of bourgeois democracy (226). Hook "still called himself a democratic socialist, but he was in retreat from revolution and increasingly aligned with social democracy, barely distinguished from liberal reformism in the degree of compromise with capitalist institutions he was willing to accept" (199). If Lloyd and Phelps stand as representatives of what Phelps has called the competing "two souls of Bolshevism," they are one in their contempt for social democracy.[31]

As James Livingston—a proudly weak-kneed, tepid, and painfully evolutionary socialist—sees it, this contempt is itself contemptible, and an affront to the pragmatism that he shares with Phelps (if not Lloyd). Livingston pinpoints a crucial moment in Phelps's argument in which he does seem to blame Hook's pragmatism for betraying his revolutionary socialism. In an eightieth birthday tribute to Dewey in 1939, Hook applauded Dewey's refusal "to be bound in his thinking by easy oppositions like capitalism *or* socialism, socialism *or* fascism, totalitarianism *or* democracy. Once these terms are given empirical content, we can see that their presence or absence is a matter of degree." Here, Phelps complains, Hook was advancing an argument that in his better Leninist days he would have denounced as "muddleheaded." He was guilty here of treating "social systems and political ideologies in the same way that pragmatists treat philosophical dualisms. Historical conflicts between such incompatible modes of production as socialism and capitalism, and irreconcilable conflicts between such ideologies as socialism and fascism, he treated like the sort of conceptual opposition— such as existence and being—that pragmatism sought to transcend" (212).

Pragmatists, Livingston suggests, should accept this indictment and happily plead guilty. For him, to treat socialism pragmatically as "an order of *events*" that includes (but is not limited to) the extension of the welfare state, a regulated political economy, and bourgeois liberties and not merely as "an order of *ideas* forever untainted by implication in worldly realities" would be to ally with the Hook of 1939 or even 1947, rather than the Hook of 1933. Precisely the virtue of pragmatism is that it challenges us "to refuse the either/or choice between ethical principles and historical circumstances" that Phelps claims would lead a true revolutionary to choose the former and renounce any compromise with capitalist institutions.[32]

31. See note 26 above.
32. James Livingston, "Marxism, Pragmatism, and the American Political Tradition," *Intellectual History Newsletter* 20 (1998): 64–65.

Pragmatism, Livingston argues, calls for a rethinking of the meaning of "revolution," one that leads to the conclusion that social democrats such as the later Hook are the true revolutionaries, and that Leninists such as the young Hook are merely "radicals." Phelps "assumes that revolution amounts to the evacuation, not the transformation, of 'capitalist institutions,' thus erasing any differences between radicals, who typically want to escape the past, and revolutionaries, who want to recuperate it; that class struggle is the medium as well as the cause of revolution, thus making it difficult to understand how and why modern revolutionary movements are, without exception, cross-class coalitions; that socialism is the exclusive property of 'the' working class rather than a variegated movement for democracy in which every social stratum has participated; and finally that socialism must repudiate, not fulfill, the promise of modern liberalism."[33]

Pragmatism interrogates these assumptions and finds them wanting. Social democracy, what Phelps terms "gradualism and reformism, the implied alternative in Dewey's model" (190), will for Livingston "inevitably surface as the political sensibility of pragmatists," who insist that "capitalism and socialism cannot continue to appear as the terms of an either/or choice, as if one mode of production somehow excludes the other." Leninism, a "science of insurrection," sought merely to abort the "emergence of corporate–imperial capitalism" rather than pursue a social-democratic strategy of developing the socialist possibilities that lie within it. For Livingston, better to ally with those in the latter camp who "could not even hear Lenin's voice until it was too late, largely because they tried to see something more than imperial atrocities waiting on the other side of proprietary capitalism."[34]

Livingston's response to Lloyd and Phelps is unsurprising in light of his wider, remarkable historiographical and political project. As I have already said, his recent work aims to displace what he sees as the hegemonic "tragic" narrative of twentieth-century American life that finds its pivotal moment in the 1890s with the defeat of the Populist movement and the eclipse of the antimonopoly tradition. For tragedians—among whom Livingston includes many of the most influential American historians of the period—the central drama is "proletarianization," the passing of the "producers' republic" of independent farmers, artisans, and professionals and its replacement by a society of industrial workers and white-collar employees who had been denied ownership and control of the means of production. At the center of this drama is the emergence of the modern corporation and a consumer culture, which tragic historians regard with loathing. "We can see," Livingston says, "that the imagined community from which the critique of cor-

33. Ibid., 65.
34. Ibid., 65, 67.

porate capitalism and consumer culture plainly derives is a simple market society composed of those 'natural individuals' we usually designate free-holders, small producers, skilled craftsmen, or artisans—these are inde-pendent men, rugged individuals, because they retain control over their own labor-time, their capacity to produce value through work."[35]

Livingston wants to replace this tragic narrative with a "comic" one. This narrative is not a funny story but a story that, unlike tragedy, adopts a "frame of acceptance" toward the corporate order of what he calls the "third Amer-ican republic" that took shape between 1890 and 1930. American histori-ans need to wipe away their tears, stop grieving for the producers' republic, and get into the new game made possible by the very corporate society they abhor. What we need, Livingston says, is "some way of appreciating the comic potential and redeeming value of the *post*-artisanal market society that entails proletarianization, corporate bureaucracies, scientific management, and consumer culture" (33).

Livingston makes this argument not as an apologist for corporate capi-talism but as a social democrat. He would have us "understand corporate capitalism as the necessary but not sufficient condition of progress toward social democracy" (14). Several key features describe the political economy, society, and culture of corporate capitalism—and point toward the socialist possibilities embedded within it. First, consumer goods replace capital goods as the engine of the economy. Second, the social relations of pro-duction lose their overpowering role in the structuring of social relations generally. Productivity gains decrease the amount of labor-time devoted to goods production, and social relations in other realms of life become more important in shaping social organization. Third, the value of commodities comes to be determined less by the quantity of the labor power of workers required to produce them than by the subjective evaluations of those who consume them—a reconceptualization of value signaled by the develop-ment of marginalist economics. Finally, "with the completion of proletari-anization under the auspices of corporate management, the commodity form penetrates and reshapes dimensions of social life hitherto exempt from its logic, to the point where subjectivity itself seemingly becomes a com-modity to be bought and sold in the market as beauty, cleanliness, sincerity, even autonomy" (20).

Livington's account of the late-nineteenth-century transformation of cap-italism and its culture, which I can only sketch in the briefest terms here, is brilliant—among the best we have.[36] Tragedians might well accept this ac-

35. Livingston, *Pragmatism, Feminism, and Democracy: Rethinking the Politics of American History* (New York: Routledge, 2001), 47. Subsequent page citations to this book are in the text.

36. For its full explication, see Livingston, *Pragmatism and the Political Economy of Cultural Revolution, 1850–1940* (Chapel Hill: University of North Carolina Press, 1994), 3–118. Liv-

count, but besotted with petty-bourgeois nostalgia (here Livingston is one with Lloyd), they cannot reconcile themselves to the society it describes. If Leninists are radicals who try to escape the past, these tragedians are, as Lloyd says, hayseeds who refuse to look to the future. A future that just might be socialist, if Leninist radicals and populist hayseeds could be supplanted by revolutionary comics who are aware that, with the corporate transformation of 1890–1930, socialism became tightly imbricated with capitalism.

As the language of Livingston's history of capitalism suggests, he is a Marxist of sorts. But the Marxism of Marx that he favors is quite different from that of Lloyd. The passages from the socialist canon that he most often quotes are those in the third volume of *Capital,* in which Marx reflected on the implications of the modern corporation for his analysis of capitalism. The formation of "joint-stock companies," he said, meant that capital "now receives the form of social capital (capital of directly associated individuals) in contrast to private capital, and its enterprises appear as social enterprises as opposed to private ones. This is the abolition of capital as private property within the confines of the capitalist mode of production itself."[37] For Marx (and Livingston), this was good news for socialists, for it meant that "modern corporations were the conditions, not the negation, of socialism" (107). They opened the way to the socialization of capital *outside* the confines of the capitalist mode of production, that is, socialism. "We will want to argue," Livingston concludes, "that the triumph of corporate capitalism represents a kind of progress" (160).

As astute a student of the socialization of capital as Livingston is, his greater energies have been devoted to making the case that the emergence of corporate capitalism witnessed a parallel transformation of the self, the socialization of subjectivity. Selfhood, he argues, is not ahistorical but like capital can undergo change, sometimes radical change. "Individuality or subjectivity is an achievement, a *result* of historical development" (155). Here, as we have seen, pragmatism enters his account as one of two key con-

---

ingston draws on and extends the arguments of Martin Sklar, who might be said to be the founder of the "why there *is* socialism in the United States" school of thought. See Martin Sklar, *The Corporate Reconstruction of American Capitalism, 1890–1916: The Market, Law, and Politics* (Cambridge: Cambridge University Press, 1988); Sklar, *The United States as a Developing Country: Studies in U.S. History in the Progressive Era and the 1920s* (Cambridge: Cambridge University Press, 1992); Sklar, "Capitalism and Socialism in the Emergence of Modern America: The Formative Era, 1890–1916," in Elizabeth Fox-Genovese and Elisabeth Lasch-Quinn, eds., *Reconstructing History* (New York: 1999), 304–21; Sklar, "Thoughts on Capitalism and Socialism: Utopian and Realistic," *Journal of the Gilded Age and Progressive Era* 2 (2003): 361–76; Livingston, "How to Succeed in Business without Really Trying: Remarks on Martin J. Sklar's *Corporate Reconstruction of American Capitalism,*" *Business and Economic History* 21 (1992): 30–35; and Livingston, "Why Is There Still Socialism in the United States?" *Reviews in American History* 22 (1994): 577–83.

37. Karl Marx, *Capital* (London: Penguin, 1991), 3:567.

tributors (the other is feminism) to an effort to overturn philosophically the "modern subjectivity" of the producers' republic, one which posited a fixed location for selfhood in propertied space and a rigid dualism between subjects and objects that echoed artisanal labor. In its stead, pragmatists (and feminists) argued for a thoroughly "social self" of the sort they saw reflected back to them in the windows of the modern department store.

One of Livingston's heroines, Jesse Taft (at once a pragmatist and a feminist), articulated this conception of the "social self" quite nicely:

> Our age is witnessing the disappearance of the isolated individual and the growth of an internal control based on the recognition of the dependence of the individual on social relations and his actual interest in social goods and in the discovery that thought is social in origin and can be used to the advantage in the social as well as the physical world. The freedom that was supposed to reside in the individual is seen to be realized only through society. The individual is not economically or morally free except when he is able to express himself, to realize his ends through the common life (76).

The prospect of this twentieth-century, "postmodern," social self overtaking the nineteenth-century, individualistic, "modern self" disturbed William James, and as I have said, I am unconvinced by Livingston's imaginative effort to put James in the vanguard of a pragmatist embrace of modern American life.[38] But his case for Dewey's role in this story is much stronger.

Here again we arrive at some of the differences Lloyd observes between the thought of James and that of Dewey, and here they are important. Unlike James, Dewey was both an observer and a proponent of social selfhood, though his treatment of it often left much to be desired.[39] As Livingston suggests, Dewey's *Individualism Old and New* (1930)—as the title hints—was a kind of manifesto on behalf of a frame of acceptance of the "corporateness" of the new corporate order, if not its particular configuration. "The United States," Dewey said, "has steadily moved from an earlier pioneer individualism to a condition of dominant corporateness. The influence business corporations exercise in determining present industrial and economic activities is both a cause and a symbol of the tendency to combination in all phases of life. Associations tightly or loosely organized more and more define the opportunities, the choices and actions of individuals." Individuals wedded to the "old individualism" of modern subjectivity found themselves with beliefs and ideals that "are not relevant to the society in which they outwardly act and which constantly reacts upon them. Their conscious ideals and standards are inherited from an age that has passed away; their minds,

38. See chapter 2.
39. See my complaints about Dewey's insufficiently "socialized" moral philosophy and political theory in chapter 7.

as far as consciously entertained principles and methods of interpretation are concerned, are at odds with actual conditions. This profound split is the cause of distraction and bewilderment."[40]

As Livingston says, Dewey struggled to heal this split by recasting "individualism" into a form adapted to these new circumstances. "Individuals will refind themselves," he insisted, "only as their ideas and ideals are brought into harmony with the realities of the age in which they act." Hence, "the only means by which the possibilities of individuality can be realized" was by an immersion in the "moving and multiple associations" of the life one shared with others. This immersion, Dewey was careful to say, did not mean conformity to the existing capitalist order, though it did mean individuals must refind themselves as social selves. By 1930 Dewey was indeed a socialist of Livingston's sort in this at least: he grasped that "corporateness" was "the terrain on which socialism would be defined" (82). Echoing Marx, he declared that the choice was between a socialization of capital and the self inside the confines of capitalism and one that broke free of these confines. In this sense, he said, "we are in for some kind of socialism, call it by whatever name we please, and no matter what it will be called when it is realized."[41]

Livingston repeatedly stresses that the comic revolution he proposes is one that would not "repudiate" the virtues of the producers' republic and modern subjectivity but rather "annul *and* preserve" them amidst the new consumers' republic and postmodern subjectivity (58). I am not sure how one can both annul and preserve something—a marriage that has been annulled cannot at the same time be preserved. But at times he uses a different term to suggest this Hegelian strategy of synthetic remaking, "reconstruction," which was a favorite term of Dewey's (66). Yet unlike Dewey, Livingston does not indicate what it is about this past that for him remains usable and reconstructable. He engages in a great deal of enthusiastic annulling, but no preserving that I can discern. His blithe "acceptance" of "proletarianization, corporate bureaucracies, scientific management, and consumer culture" suggests that a more expansive democracy is among the ideals of the producers' republic that he would rather annul than recuperate.[42]

Reconstructing the democratic ideals of the producers' republic in a new age of "corporateness" was more clearly part of Dewey's project than it is of

40. Dewey, *Individualism Old and New* (1930), *Later Works*, 5:58, 75.

41. Ibid., 75, 98, 122.

42. As does his embrace of the sort of stringent constitutional restraints on popular rule favored by James Madison and other founding fathers. See James Livingston, "'Marxism' and the Politics of History: Reflections on the Work of Eugene D. Genovese," *Radical History Review* 88 (winter 2004): 38–41. For a more democratic, much less enthusiastic, view of Madisonian constitutionalism, see Robert A. Dahl, *How Democratic Is the American Constitution?* (New Haven: Yale University Press, 2001).

Livingston's. Dewey was not blind to the significance of the sort of "cultural politics" in the realm of civil society and consumer culture that Livingston most recommends. "If one could control the songs of a nation," he wrote, "one need not care who made its laws."[43] Yet Dewey also continued to worry over "proletarianization" and made it the target of his work as a philosopher of education and school reformer.[44] He continued to worry as well over the decay of democratic citizenship and made it the subject of his one sustained work of political theory, *The Public and Its Problems* (1927), and of his activism in cross-class, third-party politics.[45] He retained an abiding respect for artisanal labor, and in *Art as Experience* (1934) called for preserving its rewards in modern work. He directed readers to the persistent relevance of the thought of many of the heroes of the producers' republic, not only Henry George but also Thomas Jefferson.[46]

In every instance, Dewey cautioned against nostalgia, while at the same time he tried to figure out ways to make sure that individuality, autonomy, and self-government were not eclipsed in the sort of socialism he envisioned—a decentralized, fully democratic "planning" society rather than a centralized, bureaucratic "planned" society.[47] His conception of "workers' democracy" was more democratic than Hook's, and his insistence on securing it democratically more consistent than that of his favorite pupil. Even as a socialist, that is, Dewey remained a populist in important respects.

Like Dewey, I think there is at least as much worth preserving as there is in need of annulling in populism and the wider tradition of petty-bourgeois

43. Dewey, *Freedom and Culture,* 70.

44. See chapter 3. In *The Soul's Economy: Market Society and Selfhood in American Thought, 1820–1920* (Chapel Hill: University of North Carolina Press, 2002). Jeffrey Sklansky traces the emergence of the "social self" as an ideal in American social thought along much the same lines as Livingston, although across a wider spectrum of thinkers. Yet Sklansky, unlike Livingston, is troubled by the concessions that social-self thinkers made to proletarianization and corporate capitalism, depriving themselves of the critical perspective on market society that the "self-possessive" ideals of classical political economy, for all their shortcomings, had provided. Although I think (with Livingston) that Dewey's philosophy had more critical resources to bring to bear on corporate capitalism than Sklansky allows, his concerns about a "frame of acceptance" that is too accepting and a "social self" that rests content with psychological compensations for a loss of autonomy are not misplaced. On the intertwining of cultural politics with a politics of work, see Michael Denning, "Work and Culture in American Studies," in Donald Pease and Robyn Wiegman, eds., *The Futures of American Studies* (Durham, N.C.: Duke University Press, 2002), 419–40.

45. On Livingston's reading, *The Public and Its Problems* is really about creating "publics" in civil society apart from citizenship and the state, and he minimizes the significance of Walter Lippmann's powerful portrait of an eclipsed democratic citizenship to which I and others have seen Dewey trying to respond (*Pragmatism, Feminism, and Democracy,* 51–56). But as Dewey defined it, an inchoate "public" in civil society was not organized until it had taken shape as a "state" that comprised a public and its political representatives (including citizens) acting as a "government." *The Public and Its Problems* (1927), *Later Works,* 2:245–53, 277, 256.

46. Dewey, "Presenting Thomas Jefferson" (1940), *Later Works,* 14: 201–23.

47. Dewey, "Economic Basis of the New Society" (1939), *Later Works,* 13:321–22.

radicalism. If marrying Marxism precludes this preserving for pragmatists, then I say call off the wedding.[48] Livingston's warnings against a hopeless, tragic populism are well-taken, but as Robert Johnston has said, they should not preclude a hopeful, comic one.[49] There are worse things that might cling to one's politics than a few hayseeds.

48. I am not sure it does, since I am inclined to agree with Habermas and Hook that Marx is a thinker, like Dewey, with whom pragmatist democrats can continue to stroll. But an alliance between pragmatism and the Leninist varieties of Marxism would be a shotgun wedding.

49. Robert Johnston, *The Radical Middle Class: Populist Democracy and the Question of Capitalism in Progressive Era Portland, Oregon* (Princeton: Princeton University Press, 2003), 295n2. Johnston's book is not only a superb local study of the persistence of petty-bourgeois radicalism in the early twentieth century but also a deeply learned and passionate plea for its ongoing relevance. Other studies that suggest that we might take a closer look at the merits of the antimonopoly tradition include Gretchen Ritter, *Goldbugs and Greenbacks: The Anti-Monopoly Tradition and the Politics of Finance in America* (Cambridge: Cambridge University Press, 1997); and Elizabeth Sanders, *Roots of Reform: Farmers, Workers, and the American State, 1877–1917* (Chicago: University of Chicago Press, 1999). For a good example of an effort to think about the implications of preserving some of the ideal of the producers' republic for contemporary labor politics, see William E. Forbath, "The Presence of the Past: Voluntarism, Producerism, and the Fate of Economic Democracy," *Law and Social Inquiry* 19 (1994): 201–15.

Part Two

Pragmatism New

You cannot urge national political renewal on the basis of descriptions of fact. You have to describe the country in terms of what you passionately hope it will become, as well as in terms of what you know it to be now. You have to be loyal to a dream country rather than to the one to which you wake up every morning. Unless such loyalty exists, the ideal has no chance of becoming actual.

—RICHARD RORTY, *Achieving Our Country* (1998)

CHAPTER 6

A Dream Country

★

THE fate of pragmatism has long been tied to that of its native land. Since the turn of the twentieth century, one of the favored ploys of critics of the work of pragmatist philosophers has been to try to reduce it to a reflex expression of American culture, counting thereby on distaste for that culture to carry the burden of argument.

Perhaps the most relentless criticism of this sort came from Bertrand Russell, who remarked in 1909 that pragmatism was a philosophy perfectly suited to the male protagonists of an American imperium: "the inventor, the financier, the advertiser, the successful men of action generally." Russell was in this fashion forever treating the pragmatism of William James and John Dewey as so much philosophical window dressing for a ruthless American capitalism—a view later echoed by Stalinists who shared little else with Russell. From quite another political quarter, Martin Heidegger similarly characterized pragmatism as the "American interpretation of Americanism," a culture of "dreary technological frenzy" and the "unrestricted organization of the average man." Although foreign critics have long pursued this sort of argument, it is not without its domestic counterparts. Indeed, few have equaled the acid portraits of James and Dewey offered in 1926 by Lewis Mumford, who characterized pragmatism as a philosophy of "acquiescence" to the crude utilitarianism of American culture, a way of thinking "permeated by the smell of the Gilded Age."[1]

---

1. Bertrand Russell, "Pragmatism" (1909), in Russell, *Philosophical Essays* (New York: Si-

The pragmatists' response to the claim that theirs is a deeply American philosophy has been less to challenge the claim than to attempt to embrace it on their own terms. Dewey took offense at Russell's efforts to link pragmatism with the most "obnoxious aspects of American industrialism," but he did not deny pragmatism's American pedigree. He himself had argued that because philosophy was not a species of knowledge but of moral imagination, "a sense for the better kind of life to be led," philosophies would necessarily take on the coloration of particular and plural moral communities. One could speak of a national philosophy as one could not speak of a national chemistry or physics.[2]

But national cultures were complicated and often conflicted. Hence the relationship between a philosophy and a national culture could be at once close and fraught with tension. To say that a philosophy was "American," Dewey wrote in response to Mumford, was not necessarily to say that it was "merely a formulated acquiescence in the immediately predominating traits" of American life. Often the national values that a philosophy idealized were those opposed to "the ones most in evidence, the most clamorous, the most insistent," and such oppositional values furnished a set of immanent moral possibilities "upon which criticism rests and from which creative effort springs."[3] As Dewey saw it, pragmatism was the philosophy not of the ad man but of the democratic citizen. And like James, who denounced American imperialism in the Philippines as a betrayal of the best in American life, Dewey often found himself pitting America against itself.

American intellectuals—those on the left, at least—are much less inclined today than they once were to speak unironically of the promise of American life. Appropriately enough, it is the leading neopragmatist, Richard Rorty, who is perhaps the most notable exception. "National pride," Rorty has said, "is to countries what self-respect is to individuals: a necessary condition for self-improvement. . . . Those who hope to persuade a nation to exert itself need to remind their country of what it can take pride in as well as what it should be ashamed of. They must tell inspiring stories about episodes and figures in the nation's past—episodes and figures to which the country

---

mon and Schuster, 1966), 108; Russell, "As a European Radical Sees It," *Freeman* 4 (1922): 608–10; Martin Heidegger, *The Question Concerning Technology and Other Essays* (New York: Harper and Row, 1977), 153; Heidegger, *An Introduction to Metaphysics* (New Haven: Yale University Press, 1959), 37; Lewis Mumford, *The Golden Day* (1926; New York: Dover, 1968), 97.

2. John Dewey, "Pragmatic America" (1922), *Middle Works,* 13:307; "Philosophy and Democracy" (1918), *Middle Works,* 11:43–44.

3. John Dewey, "The Pragmatic Acquiescence" (1927), *Later Works,* 3:147. For a full discussion of the debate between Dewey and Mumford, see Robert Westbrook, "Lewis Mumford, John Dewey, and the 'Pragmatic Acquiescence,'" in Agatha and Thomas Hughes, eds., *Lewis Mumford: Public Intellectual* (New York: Oxford, 1990), 301–22.

should remain true."[4] Rorty's call to intellectuals to help Americans "achieve our country" binds him to James and Dewey as tightly as any other element of his peculiar pragmatism. Rorty's hope, like that of James and Dewey, is American hope.

American hope is not, of course, unique to the pragmatists. It is at least as old as John Winthrop's injunction to his fellow Puritans to make their Massachusetts community a "Citty upon a Hill." What most distinguishes the American hope of the pragmatists from that of others—and makes it so intriguing—is that it is hope without transcendent foundations. It is underwritten by neither God, nor nature, nor providential history. It is, like pragmatic truth, wholly a human artifact. The pragmatists thus offer an investment in American hope with peculiar rewards and risks. And, more so than James or Dewey, Rorty has made those rewards and risks fully evident.

Like the Americanism of James and Dewey, Rorty's American loyalties are not to the culture's most insistent aspects. Indeed, his loyalty is less to the country as it is than to the "dream country" he imagines it might be, the loyalty, one might say, of the loyal opposition.[5] What makes this dream a domestic vision rather than a foreign import is that it is fashioned largely out of American materials.

In casting his hopes in an American idiom, Rorty has assumed the mantle of what Michael Walzer has termed the "connected critic." Such critics eschew an Olympian, transcendent perch from which to criticize their own particular culture, in favor of an immanent stance within the moral life of that culture. Their criticism finds its purchase not in a moral philosophy they have discovered, invented, or found elsewhere, but in the tensions, contradictions, and incoherence of the moral world in which they find themselves at home, however uncomfortably. They offer not a view from nowhere or somewhere else, but from inside the cave they share with their cultural fellows. Connected critics are not "Kantians" but "Hegelians," practitioners of what Hegel called *Sittlichkeit*, a concrete ethics that turns on the "oughts" evident in the "is" of the prevailing practices of their community.[6]

Connected critics may well find themselves on the margins of their cul-

---

4. Richard Rorty, *Achieving Our Country: Leftist Thought in Twentieth-Century America* (Cambridge: Harvard University Press, 1998), 3–4.

5. Ibid., 101.

6. For such Hegelians, as Dewey said when he literally was one, "Reflective conscience must be *based* on the moral consciousness expressed in existing institutions, manners, and beliefs. Otherwise it is empty and arbitrary. But the existing moral status is never wholly self-consistent. It realizes ideals in one relation which it does not in another; it gives rights to 'aristocrats' which it denies to low-born; to men, which it refuses to women; it exempts the rich from obligations which it imposes on the poor. Its institutions embody a common good which turns out to be good only to a privileged few, and thus existing in self-contradiction." *Outlines of a Critical Theory of Ethics* (1891), *Early Works*, 3:358.

ture, but they are not detached or alienated from it. As Walzer says, the connected critic is one

> who earns his authority, or fails to do so, by arguing with his fellows—who, angrily and insistently, sometimes at considerable personal risk (he can be a hero too), objects, protests, and remonstrates. This critic is one of us. Perhaps he has traveled and studied abroad, but his appeal is to local or localized principles; if he has picked up new ideas on his travels, he tries to connect them to the local culture, building on his own intimate knowledge; he is not intellectually detached. Nor is he emotionally detached; he does not wish the natives well, he seeks the success of their common enterprise.

Connected critics, in short, "work mostly out of a Home Office."[7]

Rorty's American hope is expansive, at times breathtaking. He asks, as a connected critic, that his fellow Americans radically reconceive the prevailing wisdom about the national project. He proposes a new, pragmatic vocabulary for American self-understanding, a successor to the "foundational" self-understandings that have long guided the nation. He asks Americans to pioneer a "postmodernist bourgeois liberalism," a social democracy in which they "take pride in what America might, all by itself and by its own lights, make of itself, rather than in America's obedience to any authority—even the authority of God."[8] He faces tough sledding, some of it of his own making.

Pragmatism as Antiauthoritarianism

In order to understand the pragmatist dimension of Rorty's American hope, something must be said about his philosophical work generally. This work—the hard labor of careful argument for which Rorty receives too little credit—provides a charter for his embrace of connected social criticism and for his peculiar vision of American possibilities.[9]

7. Michael Walzer, *Interpretation and Social Criticism* (Cambridge: Harvard University Press, 1987), 39; Walzer, *Thick and Thin: Moral Argument at Home and Abroad* (Notre Dame: University of Notre Dame Press, 1994), 49. See also Walzer, *The Company of Critics: Social Criticism and Political Commitment in the Twentieth Century* (New York: Basic Books, 1988). For Rorty's endorsement of Walzer's appreciative view of the connected critic, see Richard Rorty, "Justice as a Larger Loyalty," in Ron Bontekoe and Marietta Stepaniants, eds., *Justice and Democracy: Cross-Cultural Perspectives* (Honolulu: University of Hawaii Press, 1997), 9–22.

8. Rorty, *Achieving Our Country*, 16.

9. See Rorty's justifiable bridling at Casey Blake's assertion that he has "largely turned his back on academic philosophy" since 1979. Richard Rorty, "Afterword: Intellectual Historians and Pragmatist Philosophy," in John Pettegrew, ed., *A Pragmatist's Progress?: Richard Rorty and American Intellectual History* (Lanham, Md.: Rowman and Littlefield, 2000), 210. As he says, three substantial volumes of philosophical papers published over the succeeding twenty years prove otherwise. I think one reason Rorty is dismissed as unserious by so many is that they skip over the difficult bits of his work, the bits that come bearing names such as Quine, Sellars,

The animating impulse of Rorty's pragmatism is a radical antiauthoritarianism that targets, above all, the quest for objective, ahistorical, transcendental constraints on human knowledge and moral judgment. He has described his inconclusive debates with those who would continue this quest as "the reciprocal unintelligibility to one another of two very different types of people. . . . These two types of people are conveniently describable in Freudian terms: they are the people who think subjection to an authority-figure is necessary to lead a properly human life and those who see such a life as requiring freedom from any such subjection." Rorty's opponents are the partisans of the superego, hawking a metaphysics that looks to him like "an attempt to snuggle up to something so pure and good as to be not really human, while still being enough like a loving parent so that it can be loved with all one's heart and soul and strength." Rorty's pragmatism, on the other hand, offers as its ego ideal a liberation from this depersonalized primal father.[10]

Given the language here of the Freudian family romance, it is worth sketching briefly the course of Rorty's own oedipal revolt against this metaphysical father, a revolt that has ironically resulted in a return to the philosophical household of his parents. Rorty was born into a family with a disposition for antiauthoritarianism. His maternal grandfather was Walter Rauschenbusch, the most significant Social Gospel theologian and a leading critic of industrial capitalism in the early twentieth century. His mother, Winifred Rauschenbusch, while sharing her father's social democratic politics, proved a willful and rebellious daughter when it came to his Victorian conception of familial responsibilities and sexual morality. Rorty's father, James Rorty, was an important American radical and a stalwart of the anti-Stalinist left during Rorty's childhood. Under the tutelage of such parents, he learned that "the point of being human was to spend one's life fighting social injustice." John Dewey was "a hero to all the people among whom I had grown up," and pragmatism was their "unofficial philosophy." The report of the Dewey Commission exonerating Leon Trotsky in the late 1930s of the charges made against him in the Moscow Trials was the family bible, and as a young man, Rorty recalls, "the Russian Revolution and its betrayal by Stalin were, for me, what the Incarnation and its betrayal by the Catholics had been to precocious little Lutherans 400 years before."[11]

As the son of antiauthoritarian parents, Rorty's youthful rebellion against

Davidson, and Brandom. Blake's remark is in his "Private Life and Public Commitment: From Walter Rauschenbusch to Richard Rorty," in the same volume, 86.

10. Richard Rorty, "Pragmatism as Anti-Authoritarianism," *Revue Internationale de Philosophie* 207 (1999): 15, 17.

11. Richard Rorty, "Trotsky and the Wild Orchids" (1993), in Rorty, *Philosophy and Social Hope* (London: Penguin, 1999), 6, 8, 5. On Winifred Rauschenbusch's rebellion, see Blake, "Private Life and Public Commitment," 91–99.

his upbringing naturally took the form of embracing the sort of philosophical authoritarianism that they abhorred and he would later indict. Initially, he found his way to the neomedieval absolutism proffered at Robert Hutchins's University of Chicago, where he was an undergraduate in the late 1940s. There he learned contempt for the Deweyan pragmatism that had guided the politics of his parents and their anti-Stalinist friends such as Sidney Hook. He was taught that pragmatism offered no moral resources for resistance to fascism, resources that only "something eternal, absolute, and good" could provide. "Since Dewey was a hero to all the people among whom I had grown up," he says, "scorning Dewey was a convenient form of adolescent revolt." He became a Platonist, since it "seemed clear that Platonism had all the advantages of religion, without requiring the humility which Christianity demanded, and of which I was apparently incapable." Plato offered the prospect of becoming "one with the One," of ascent to a place "where the full sunshine of Truth irradiates the purified soul of the wise and good," and to Rorty it then seemed obvious that "getting to such a place was what everybody with any brains really wanted."[12]

Embarking on a professional career in philosophy in the 1950s, Rorty eventually recognized that professional advancement required a turn—a linguistic turn—from Plato and Aristotle to the reigning methods of Carnap and Quine, but he nonetheless held out the hope, common to all hardnosed philosophers in the years following World War II, that the analysis of language pioneered by émigré logical positivists would secure the place Plato had promised philosophers as the arbiters of genuine knowledge. Landing a job at Princeton, a citadel of this hegemonic "analytical" view, Rorty seemed destined in the early 1960s for a distinguished, orthodox career. In the unsurprisingly jaundiced words of his ex-wife, "as a young man, my husband was a person of high and austere ideals, rather rigid, very reserved, a brilliant philosopher. He was dedicated to the greater glory of God through philosophy, and to developing his self-respect."[13]

But doubts that analytical philosophy could deliver the goods it promised grew over the course of Rorty's early career, to the point where he decided that philosophy as a discipline with a legitimate claim to "be foundational with respect to the rest of culture" by virtue of "knowing something about knowing which nobody else knows so well" was dead. As Jonathan Rée has said, "Rorty found his distinctive voice in the shock of a kind of bereave-

12. Rorty, "Trotsky and the Wild Orchids," 8–9; Derek Nystrom and Kent Puckett, *Against Bosses, Against Oligarchies: A Conversation with Richard Rorty* (Charlottesville: Prickley Pear Pamphlets, 1998), 50.

13. Amelie Oksenberg Rorty, "Dependency, Individuality, and Work," in Sara Ruddick and Pamela Daniels, eds., *Working It Out* (New York: Pantheon, 1977), 40. See also Nystrom and Puckett, *Against Bosses,* 50–56.

ment," the death of the Platonic primal father.[14] With the publication of *Philosophy and the Mirror of Nature* (1979), the proverbial ninety-five theses that he nailed to the door of the analytic establishment announcing the end of philosophy's pretensions to underwrite knowledge, Rorty launched a new career as a deflationary antiphilosopher, hitching his views to those of therapeutic, "edifying" thinkers such as Wittgenstein, Heidegger, and Dewey who had broken with the discipline's foundational ambitions.[15] Beginning in the late 1970s, Rorty attached a "pragmatist" label to his "reaction formation" against a philosophical quest for underlying first principles, thereby returning to the antiauthoritarian fold in which he was raised, with a newfound appreciation for the days when Sidney Hook bounced him on his knee.[16]

Rorty was drawn to the classical pragmatists, and Dewey in particular, because he saw them as fellow antiauthoritarians. Dewey's philosophical stories—those he told in the books that Rorty likes best, such as *Reconstruction in Philosophy* and *The Quest for Certainty*—were "always stories of the progress from the need of human communities to rely on non-human power to their realization that all they need is faith in themselves."[17] As John McDowell has said, Rorty has cast his own antiauthoritarianism as a "Deweyan narrative of Western culture's coming to maturity":

14. Richard Rorty, *Philosophy and the Mirror of Nature* (Princeton: Princeton University Press, 1979), 3, 392; Jonathan Rée, "Strenuous Unbelief," *London Review of Books* (15 October 1998), 9. The course of Rorty's bereavement can be traced in the introduction and the two successive retrospective essays appended to the second edition of the important anthology he edited and first published in 1967, *The Linguistic Turn* (Chicago: University of Chicago Press, 1992), 1–39, 361–74. See also Jürgen Habermas, "Richard Rorty's Pragmatic Turn," in Robert Brandom, ed., *Rorty and His Critics* (London: Blackwell, 2000), 31–55.

15. Rorty, *Philosophy and the Mirror of Nature*, 5. Ironically, *Philosophy and the Mirror of Nature* was published the same year that Rorty ascended to the pinnacle of the American philosophical profession, the presidency of the Eastern Division of the American Philosophical Association. But that year's divisional convention was not only the occasion for Rorty's coming out as an undoubted pragmatist in his presidential address, but also for a typically antiauthoritarian refusal to join the "analytic thugs" who dominated the professional affairs of the organization in an attempt to crush a democratic revolt by nonanalytic "pluralists" determined to elect a few of their number to leadership positions. Nystrom and Puckett, *Against Bosses*, 52–53. See the account of Rorty's response to the pluralist revolt in Neil Gross, "Richard Rorty's Pragmatism: A Case Study in the Sociology of Ideas," *Theory and Society* 32 (2003): 117–19. The presidential address, "Pragmatism, Relativism, and Irrationalism" (1980), was reprinted in Richard Rorty, *The Consequences of Pragmatism* (Minneapolis: University of Minnesota Press, 1982), 160–75.

16. *Against Bosses*, 50.

17. Rorty, "Pragmatism as Anti-Authoritarianism," 14. Since announcing his "pragmatist turn," Rorty has been embroiled in ongoing disputes with those who contest some of his readings of the classical pragmatists and aspects of his appropriation of their legacy. Although I have myself contributed to this criticism, I think it is important to stress that Rorty's pragmatist lineage, particularly from Dewey, is in important respects uncontestable. Like Rorty, Dewey devoted considerable energy to an antitrust suit against the same "epistemology industry" Rorty has been battling, and though their idioms are different, the two philosophers are in this regard part of the same firm.

In simple outline, the story goes like this. The sense of sin from which Dewey freed himself was a reflection of a religious outlook according to which human beings were called on to humble themselves before a non-human authority. Such a posture is infantile in its submissiveness to something other than ourselves. If human beings are to achieve maturity, they need to follow Dewey in liberating themselves from this sort of religion, a religion of abasement before the divine Other. But a humanism that goes no further than that is still incomplete. We need a counterpart secular emancipation as well. In the period in the development of Western culture during which the God who figures in that sort of religion was stricken, so to speak, with his moral illness, the illness that was going to lead to the demise famously announced by Nietzsche, some European intellectuals found themselves conceiving the secular world, the putative object of everyday and scientific knowledge, in ways that paralleled that humanly immature conception of the divine. This is a secular analogue to a religion of abasement, and human maturity requires that we liberate ourselves from it as well as from its religious counterpart.[18]

Rorty's philosophical project is to demolish this "secular analogue to a religion of abasement" by making any and every appeal to the authority of "things in themselves" look bad. He has devoted the last quarter century to the task of persuading his readers to "grow up" as he has, drawing on resources from both within the "analytic" tradition in which he was trained (especially the work of the later Wittgenstein, Quine, Wilfrid Sellars, and Donald Davidson) and the "Continental" tradition he was trained to despise (the sons of Nietzsche: Heidegger, Derrida, and Foucault), to undermine the philosophical superego. There can be, he attempts to show, no "way the world is in itself," no ahistorical "human nature" to which we can or should appeal in our quest for knowledge or virtue. We have only the descriptions of particular, human, historical language-games to work with; we cannot find a place outside of any such description—a "God's-eye view"—from which to compare it with the world as it is apart from any such description. For Rorty, as McDowell says,

> Full human maturity would require us to acknowledge authority only if the acknowledgement does not involve abasing ourselves before something non-human [or ahistorical]. The only authority that meets this requirement is that of human consensus. If we conceive inquiry and judgment in terms of making

18. John McDowell, "Towards Rehabilitating Objectivity," in *Rorty and His Critics*, 109. As McDowell notes, Dewey did not believe that liberating us from a self-abasing worship of a divine Other need amount to a liberation from religious belief as such. Rorty is more the militant secularist. Rorty's most overt characterization of his pragmatism as antiauthoritarianism was in a series of lectures entitled "Anti-Authoritarianism in Epistemology and Ethics," delivered in Catalonia in 1996, which have not been published in full. But for a summary statement, see Rorty, "Pragmatism as Anti-Authoritarianism." The essays on the work of McDowell and Robert Brandom in Richard Rorty, *Truth and Progress* (New York: Cambridge University Press, 1998) also draw on these lectures.

ourselves answerable to the world, as opposed to being answerable to our fellows, we are merely postponing the completion of the humanism whose achievement begins with discarding authoritarian religion.

If we are to grow up, we must abandon the epistemological and moral "discourse of objectivity," for "as Rorty sees things, participating in the discourse of objectivity merely prolongs a cultural and intellectual infantilism, and persuading people to renounce the vocabulary of objectivity should facilitate the achievement of full human maturity."[19] As Rorty himself says, he is urging us to "try to get to the point where we no longer worship *anything*, where we treat *nothing* as a quasi divinity, where we treat *everything*—our language, our conscience, our community—as a product of time and chance."[20]

It is also worth noting Rorty's oft-made response to another common criticism: that his pragmatism is a form of "linguistic idealism" that not only denies that language can *represent* the world as it is but also holds that language entirely *constructs* the world. That is, since Rorty contends that our knowledge of the world is always under a description, always embedded in one "language game" or another, he is said to believe that such descriptions wholly constitute the world. If this charge could be made to stick, it would be particularly wounding to Rorty's indictment of others for "immaturity," for one could say that nothing better defines infantile narcissism than an inability to admit that human beings are embedded in and decidedly constrained by a nonhuman world that is often beyond our control, a world, as Dewey said, to which the mature thing to do is to accommodate ourselves. But Rorty has readily acknowledged the existence of an independent, nonhuman world to which human beings stand in a *causal* relationship, a world that can occasion us to have beliefs about it if not "in itself" justify beliefs that purport to "represent" it. Leaning on Donald Davidson, he has said, "We can never be more arbitrary than the world lets us be. So even if there is no Way the World Is, even if there is no such thing as 'the intrinsic nature of reality,' there are still causal pressures. These pressures will be described in different ways at different times and for different purposes, but they are pressures none the less."[21] Pragmatists like James and Dewey held "that you

---

19. McDowell, "Towards Rehabilitating Objectivity," 110. In my bracketed addition, I have fiddled with McDowell's description a bit in order to make it clear that Rorty has not only set himself against an epistemological discourse of objectivity (McDowell's concern) but also against a moral discourse of objectivity grounded in some notion of the way human beings ahistorically are in themselves. Rorty is a thoroughgoing "historicist" who insists that "socialization, and thus historical circumstance, goes all the way down—that there is nothing 'beneath' socialization or prior to history which is definatory of the human." Richard Rorty, *Contingency, Irony, and Solidarity* (New York: Cambridge University Press, 1989), xiii.

20. Rorty, *Contingency, Irony, and Solidarity*, 22.

21. Richard Rorty, "Truth Without Correspondence to Reality" (1994), in Rorty, *Philosophy and Social Hope*, 33.

can't compare your beliefs with something that isn't a belief to see if they correspond. But they sensibly pointed out that that doesn't mean that there is nothing out there to have beliefs *about*. The *causal* independence of the gold or the text from the inquiring chemist or critic does not mean that she either can or should perform the impossible feat of stripping her chosen object bare of human concerns, seeing it as it is in itself, and then seeing how our beliefs measure up to it." Pragmatists grant "a wholehearted acceptance of the brute, inhuman, causal stubbornness of the gold or the text. But they think this should not be confused with, so to speak, an *intentional* stubbornness, an insistence on being *described in a certain way*, its *own* way. The object can, given a prior agreement on a language game, cause us to hold beliefs, but it cannot suggest beliefs for us to hold."[22] A causal encounter with a mind-independent object can cause us to believe "H_2O," "water," "trout stream," or "reflection of the glory of God," but it cannot determine which of these beliefs we hold. Beliefs rest not only on such encounters but on our purposes (chemistry, drinking, fishing, worship) and the vocabularies (scientific, everyday, sporting, religious) we use in their pursuit. This is not to say there is not a strong helping of Promethean hubris in Rorty's thinking and little of what Dewey termed "natural piety" in the face of our embeddedness in a world of causes we often cannot control. Rorty's concession to the causal force of a world outside of discourse might provide the opening wedge for a bit of natural (at least) piety on his part, but he has not pursued it.[23]

These arguments have been met with a storm of protest, and even some of Rorty's fellow neopragmatists such as Hilary Putnam find themselves "appalled" by some of his views.[24] I do not intend to canvass these disputes, let alone try to adjudicate them, because my interest here is in connecting Rorty's antiauthoritarian pragmatism to his patriotism and pointing up some of the difficulties—theoretical and practical—of the peculiar sort of Americanism this connection establishes. But to do so, I must at least attend to Rorty's response to perhaps the most common charge leveled against his pragmatism: that it is a form of epistemological, moral, and cultural relativism.

This charge, Rorty admits, has been "hard to shake off," and the reasons for this are perhaps obvious.[25] If we are denied a "God's-eye view" of the world as it is apart from the language games of particular, contingent, historically different communities of discourse pursuing particular, contin-

---

22. Richard Rorty, "Texts and Lumps" (1985), in Rorty, *Objectivity, Relativism and Truth* (New York: Cambridge University Press, 1991), 83.

23. See also Richard Rorty, "Inquiry as Recontextualization: An Anti-Dualist Account of Interpretation" (1988), in Rorty, *Objectivity, Relativism, and Truth*, esp. 101–2.

24. Hilary Putnam, "A Politics of Hope," *Times Literary Supplement* (22 May 1998): 10.

25. Rorty, "Introduction" to *Truth and Progress*, 2.

gent, and historically different purposes, then it would seem to be the case that our judgments about what is true, good, or rational are relative to the beliefs and justificatory practices of those communities. When two such communities come up with different, conflicting beliefs, there is no way to adjudicate the dispute by appeal to a neutral, context-free "skyhook" that stands apart from any and all language games. To use the example of the Nazi interlocutor that figures so prominently in such disputes, if a Nazi describes Jews as "subhuman vermin best exterminated" as his language game provides, then we have no recourse to a transcendent conception of human nature with which to challenge this description. All we have available to us for purposes of argument is the description authorized by our language game of Jews as human beings like ourselves. We can try to convince the Nazi to convert to our language game, but failing this, we will remain at loggerheads.

Rorty readily points out himself that these conclusions are entailed by his attack on the discourse of objectivity. But he refuses to admit to relativism. Relativism, he says, is "the view that every belief on a certain topic, or perhaps about *any* topic, is as good as every other." This view is what is sometimes termed "sophomoric relativism," and it is difficult even to find many sophomores who hold to it. Certainly, it is not Rorty's view. As he says, he is charged with relativism not because he believes one belief is as good as another but because he believes that the grounds for choosing between two incompatible beliefs are "less algorithmic" than his "objectivist" critics would like:

> Thus one may be attacked as a relativist for holding that familiarity of terminology is a criterion of theory-choice in physical science, or that coherence with the institutions of the surviving parliamentary democracies is a criterion in social philosophy. When such criteria are invoked, critics say that the resulting philosophical position assumes an unjustified primacy for "our conceptual framework," or our purposes, or our institutions. The position in question is criticized for not having done what philosophers are employed to do: explain why our framework, or culture, or interests, or language, or whatever, is at last on the right track—in touch with physical reality, or the moral law, or the real numbers, or some other sort of object patiently waiting about to be occupied.[26]

Rorty is perfectly willing to say one belief (his) is better than that of another (the Nazi's), but his critics insist that to avoid "relativism" he must ground this judgment in something that transcends both him and the Nazi, something that comes to his assistance and delivers an argumentative knock-

26. Rorty, "Pragmatism, Relativism, and Irrationalism," 166–67.

out blow to the Nazi. Rorty does not think any such aid and comfort can ever be forthcoming. The charge of relativism presumes a position—a language game above all other language games—from which to evaluate them. But Rorty argues that such a neutral standpoint or language-game is unavailable to us. Hence

> there will be no such activity as scrutinizing competing values in order to see which are morally privileged. For there will be no way to rise above the language, culture, institutions, and practices one has adopted and view all these as on a par with all the others. As Davidson puts it, "speaking a language . . . is not a trait a man can lose while retaining the power of thought. So there is no chance that someone can take up a vantage point for comparing conceptual schemes by temporarily shedding his own."

There are no "unwobbling pivots that determine the answer to the question: Which moral or political alternative is *objectively* valid?"[27]

Rorty also denies that his views are subject to the familiar charge of self-contradiction made against relativism, since this charge relies on objectivist premises about the nature of truth that he rejects. Relativists claim that it is *true* that all belief is relative to particular language games and thereby find themselves caught in a self-refuting contradiction. By claiming that relativism is true for all concerned, the relativist is advancing a context-independent claim about all belief (that it is relative) that his relativism forbids. He is paradoxically assuming a God's-eye view in venturing the claim that there can be no God's-eye view. Rorty argues that his claim that all belief is relative to particular language games is not a claim to context-independent "truth" because he denies that there is much one can say about context-independent truth, least of all that one has grasped it. "True," Rorty acknowledges, is an absolute, context-independent term; it makes no sense to say "true for me but not for you." But pragmatists do not believe that we can ever know whether or not a belief—including the belief that all beliefs are relative to particular language games—is true in this absolute sense. The best we can hope for, they say, is not absolute, context-independent truth but relative, context-dependent *justification*. We must admit, to be sure, that a belief we now believe to be well-justified may turn out not to be true. But as Rorty sees it, "true" in this sense is just a "cautionary" word, warning us that, however well-justified we think a belief may be, it may turn out to be unjustified at some future date to some future community. So when Rorty says that all belief is under a description and hence context-dependent, he takes himself to be making nothing more than a belief claim that he thinks

27. Rorty, *Contingency, Irony, and Solidarity*, 50; Rorty, "Trotsky and the Wild Orchids," 15.

he can (with a lot of help from philosophers like Davidson) demonstrate to be, for the moment, well-justified.

Rorty does not shy away from acknowledging that his antifoundationalism leaves us to our own cultural resources when confronted with oppression. "When the secret police come, when the torturers violate the innocent, there is nothing to be said to them of the form 'There is something within you which you are betraying. Though you embody the practices of a totalitarian society which will endure forever, there is something beyond those practices which condemns you.'"[28] Rortyan pragmatists must grant the force of the "hard saying" of Jean-Paul Sartre:

> Tomorrow, after my death, certain people may decide to establish fascism and the others may be cowardly or miserable enough to let them get away with it. At that moment, fascism will be the truth of man, and so much the worse for us. In reality, things will be as much as man has decided they are.[29]

This hard saying brings out Rorty's conviction that "there is nothing deep down inside us except what we have put there ourselves, no criterion that we have not created in the course of creating a practice, no standard of rationality that is not an appeal to such a criterion, no rigorous argumentation that is not obedience to our own conventions."[30] On this view,

> we can only hope to transcend our acculturation if our culture contains (or, thanks to disruptions from outside or internal revolt, comes to contain) splits which supply toeholds for new initiatives. Without such splits—without tensions that make people listen to unfamiliar ideas in the hope of finding means of overcoming those tensions—there is no such hope. The systematic elimination of such tensions, or of awareness of them, is what is so frightening about *Brave New World* and *1984*.[31]

---

28. Richard Rorty, "Introduction: Pragmatism and Philosophy" (1982) in *Consequences of Pragmatism*, xlii.

29. Jean-Paul Sartre, *L'Existenialisme est un Humanisme* (1946), as quoted in Rorty, "Introduction: Pragmatism and Philosophy," xlii. Conceding the force of Jeffrey Stout's remark that a favorable reference to Sartre by Rorty is "a sign of backsliding or an invitation to misreading," Rorty has since qualified his embrace of this hard saying. He now says: "Sartre should not have said that Fascism will be 'the truth of man.' There is no such thing. What he should have said is that the truth (about certain very important matters, like whom one can kill when) might be forgotten, become invisible, get lost—and so much the worse for *us*. 'Us' here does not mean 'us humans' (for Nazis are humans too). It means something like 'us tolerant wet liberals.'" "Hilary Putnam and the Relativist Menace" (1993), in Rorty, *Truth and Progress*, 53.

30. Rorty, "Introduction: Pragmatism and Philosophy," xlii.

31. Richard Rorty, "Introduction: Antirepresentationalism, Ethnocentrism, and Liberalism" (1991), in *Objectivity, Relativism, and Truth*, 14. See Rorty's reading of *1984* in these terms in *Contingency, Irony, and Solidarity*, 169–88. James Conant has contested this reading, arguing that Orwell's novel is a cautionary tale about the dangers of abandoning realist intuitions. Conant, "Freedom, Cruelty, and Truth: Rorty versus Orwell" in *Rorty and His Critics*, 268–342.

We cannot argue with a Nazi who will not grant us a toehold.[32] We may well have to treat him as we would a rattlesnake, that is, as a candidate for a literal knockout blow.

Rorty suggests, rightly I think, that the principal reason that his pragmatism has provoked outrage is that it denies us metaphysical aid and comfort in the face of Nazis and other enemies of our way of life. "That is why," he says,

> philosophers like myself find ourselves denounced in magazines and newspapers which one might have thought oblivious of our existence. These denunciations claim that unless the youth is raised to believe in moral absolutes, and in objective truth, civilization is doomed. Unless the younger generation has the same attachment to firm moral principles as we have, these magazine and newspaper articles say, the struggle for human freedom and human decency will be over.[33]

But Rorty's intention is not to lead us to despair, and he takes issue with Nietzsche and other downbeat European antifoundationalists who think that widespread circulation of the news that we are on our own, without backup from either God or Enlightenment rationalism, will lead to nihilism. Although pragmatists and Nietzscheans are both trying to deprive us of metaphysical comfort, pragmatists do not believe that only supermen can live without it. Dewey and Foucault are both attempting to free us from "the notion that outside the haphazard and perilous experiments we perform there lies something (God, Science, Knowledge, Rationality, or Truth) which will, if only we perform the correct rituals, step in and save us." But Dewey, unlike Foucault, is the antifoundationalist of choice because "his vocabulary allows room for unjustifiable hope, and an ungroundable but vital sense of human solidarity."[34]

Rorty's pragmatism thus leads him to a regulative ideal of a "postphilosophical" culture in which everyone is a pragmatist and no one "believes that we have, deep down inside us, a criterion for telling when we are in touch with reality or not, when we are in the Truth."[35] Such a culture would be

32. "It is one thing to say, falsely, that there is nothing to choose between us and the Nazis. It is another thing to say, correctly, that there is no neutral, common ground to which an experienced Nazi philosopher and I can repair in order to argue out our differences. That Nazi and I will always strike one another as begging all the crucial questions, arguing in circles." Rorty, "Trotsky and the Wild Orchids," 15.

33. Richard Rorty, "Introduction: Relativism: Making and Finding" (1999), in Rorty, *Philosophy and Social Hope*, xxviii.

34. Richard Rorty, "Method, Social Science, and Social Hope" (1981), in Rorty, *Consequences of Pragmatism*, 208.

35. Rorty, "Introduction: Pragmatism and Philosophy," xxxviii. I have for the moment bracketed Rorty's uncertainty in this quoted passage about whether or not postphilosophical culture need be confined only to intellectuals. He periodically pulls back from the hope for

one "in which men and women felt themselves alone, merely finite, with no links to something Beyond," yet also one in which men and women would take responsibility for their own fate, rather than despair over their aloneness. They would, he predicts, find an enhanced sense of community since "our identification with our community—our society, our political tradition, our intellectual heritage—is heightened when we see this community as *ours* rather than *nature's, shaped* rather than *found,* one among many which men have made."[36] They would find themselves in a new kind of culture, one that would be aware of its own contingency and hence open to free encounters with other cultures in the interest of weaving the richest, most rewarding web of beliefs and practices it could.

> In such a culture we would be more sensitive to the marvelous diversity of human languages, and of the social practices associated with those languages, because we shall have ceased asking whether they "correspond to" some nonhuman eternal entity. Instead of asking, "Are there truths out there that we shall never discover?" we would ask "Are there ways of talking and acting that we have not yet explored?" Instead of asking whether the intrinsic nature of reality is yet in sight . . . we should ask whether each of the various descriptions of reality employed in our various cultural activities is the best we can imagine—the best means to the ends served by those activities.[37]

Objectivists, the party of the superego, find the prospect of such a culture decadent because they want a culture that is "*guided,* constrained" by something outside itself, not one "left to its own devices." They complain that Rorty leaves us with beliefs and practices that are *merely* ours. But Rorty urges us to join him in becoming the sort of people who will accept the challenge of beliefs and practices that are merely *ours,* the sort of people who believe that a properly human life is one free of guides and external constraints and who will find strength not in God or Reason but in the solidarity and shared responsibility for weaving and reweaving a way of life. The sort of people, in short, who substitute hope for knowledge.[38]

There are, Rorty admits, no knockdown arguments on either side of this debate. He thinks he has made his opponents look bad, and they certainly think he looks awful. But "there is no way in which the issue between the pragmatist and his opponent can be tightened up and resolved according

---

culture-wide pragmatism, confining it sometimes only to intellectuals. As I will suggest, his waffling on this matter creates difficulties for his hopes for America.

36. Rorty, "Pragmatism, Relativism, and Irrationalism," 166.

37. Rorty, "Introduction" to *Truth and Progress,* 6.

38. Rorty, "Introduction: Pragmatism and Philosophy," xxxix. "Hope in Place of Knowledge" was the title of a short book Rorty published in German (*Hoffnung statt Erkentniss,* 1994) and French (*L'espoir au lieu de savoir,* 1995), which is incorporated into *Philosophy and Social Hope,* 21–90.

to criteria agreed to by both sides." This does not diminish the importance of what is at stake, for as Rorty sees it, "the issue about the truth of pragmatism is the issue which all the most important cultural developments since Hegel have conspired to put before us." But it is an issue that will be decided "only by a slow and painful choice between alternative self-images."[39]

Benign Ethnocentrism

Rorty says that the best term for his views is not "relativism" but "ethnocentrism." This may not sound like an improvement, but as he sees it, it is. While Rorty resists any reading of his arguments against the discourse of objectivity that burdens him with the claim that one belief is as good as another, he is happy to concede that even though he thinks his own beliefs are the best thing going, he can offer no noncircular justification for that judgment outside of the premises of those beliefs. Such ethnocentrism, "accepting the contingent character of starting points," is for a pragmatist unavoidable.[40]

Rorty's own ethos is liberal. Liberals, he says, are "people who think that cruelty is the worst thing we do," and who "hope that suffering will be diminished, that the humiliation of human beings by other human beings may cease." More positively, liberals believe in the primacy of free discussion, which means "the sort which goes on when the press, the judiciary, the elections, and the universities are free, social mobility is frequent and rapid, literacy is universal, higher education is common, and peace and wealth have made possible the leisure necessary to listen to lots of different people and think about what they say." Rorty's ideal liberal society would be held together by "a consensus that the point of social organization is to let everybody have a chance of self-creation to the best of his or her abilities, and that that goal requires, besides peace and wealth, the standard 'bourgeois freedoms.'" In such an ideal society, "discussion of public affairs will revolve around (1) how to balance the needs for peace, wealth, and freedom when conditions require that one of these goals be sacrificed to one of the others and (2) how to equalize opportunities for self-creation and then leave people alone to use, or neglect, their opportunities." In sum, as Rorty sees it, there is "nothing wrong with the hopes of the Enlightenment, the hopes which created the Western democracies." Indeed, he thinks "Western social and political thought may have had the last *conceptual* revolution it needs," and he does not hesitate to "defend the institutions and practices of the rich North Atlantic democracies."[41]

---

39. Rorty, "Introduction: Pragmatism and Philosophy," xliii–xliv.
40. Rorty, "Pragmatism, Relativism, and Irrationalism," 166.
41. Rorty, *Contingency, Irony, and Solidarity,* xv, 85, 63; Richard Rorty, "Solidarity or Objec-

It is not Rorty's liberalism that distinguishes him from Thomas Jefferson and John Stuart Mill, but his repudiation of the project of "grounding" his liberalism in anything deeper, more objective, more transcendent than the hopes he shares with other liberals. He would defend, "on the basis of solidarity alone, a society which has traditionally asked to be based on something more than mere solidarity."[42] The only sort of justification for their beliefs that liberals can hope for is "a circular justification of our practices, a justification which makes one feature of our culture look good by citing still another, or comparing our culture invidiously with others by reference to our own standards." Liberals, on Rorty's account, have no noncircular argument to make to the Nietzschean Nazi who would ask "Why not be cruel?"[43]

Rorty's liberalism is Enlightenment politics without Enlightenment philosophy. And it is this refusal of philosophical foundations, his pragmatism, that makes his bourgeois liberalism, *postmodernist* bourgeois liberalism. Pragmatism is the philosophy of "a mature (de-scientized, de-philosophized) Enlightenment liberalism."[44]

Postmodernist, pragmatist liberals are "liberal ironists." That is, liberalism is their political language game, the "final vocabulary" to which they have nothing but circular argumentative recourse when nonliberals say things like "What's so bad about humiliating another human being?" But they are well aware that there is nothing necessary about their final vocabulary, and hence they regard it ironically. The liberal ironist doubts her liberalism "because she has been impressed by other vocabularies, vocabularies taken as final by people or books she has encountered." Moreover, "she realizes that argument phrased in her present vocabulary can neither underwrite nor dissolve these doubts," and "insofar as she philosophizes about her situation, she does not think that her vocabulary is closer to reality than others, that it is in touch with a power not herself."[45]

Here, then, is the full measure of Rorty's "world-historical" vision: a liberal polity embedded in a postphilosophical culture. "The citizens of my liberal utopia," he says, "would be people who had a sense of the contingency of their language of moral deliberation, and thus of their consciences, and

---

tivity?" (1985), in Rorty, *Objectivity, Relativism, and Truth,* 34; Richard Rorty, "Postmodernist Bourgeois Liberalism" (1983), in Rorty, *Objectivity, Relativism, and Truth,* 198.

42. Rorty, "Postmodernist Bourgeois Liberalism," 198.

43. Rorty, *Contingency, Irony, and Solidarity,* 57.

44. Ibid., 57. See also Richard Rorty, "The Continuity Between the Enlightenment and 'Postmodernism,'" Unpublished paper (1997). Rorty has become disenchanted with the term *postmodernism,* which, as he says, "has been rendered almost meaningless by being used to mean so many things." Richard Rorty, "Afterword: Pragmatism, Pluralism, and Postmodernism" (1998), in Rorty, *Philosophy and Social Hope,* 262.

45. Rorty, *Contingency, Irony, and Solidarity,* 73.

thus of their community. They would be liberal ironists . . . people who combined commitment with a sense of the contingency of their own commitment."[46]

One attractive thing about this combination of commitment and contingency, Rorty points out, is that it makes for an ethnocentric liberalism that is not, in the troubling sense of the word, ethnocentric, yet does not have the defects of an anti-ethnocentrism that is so tolerant that it makes one think twice about criticizing Nazis. Ethnocentrism is bad when it leads to intolerant cultures that are like "windowless monads" cut off from other cultures or, worse, windowless monads that impose their will—sometimes even an exterminating will—on other cultures. Anti-ethnocentrism is bad when it leads to a "relativism" that advises tolerance of such oppressive cultures on the grounds that one culture is as good as another, and we have no way of judging which is best. This relativism is what Claude Lévi-Strauss called "the desperate toleration of UNESCO cosmopolitanism" in which, as Rorty says, "we have become so open-minded that our brains have fallen out."[47]

Liberal ironist culture avoids both these unhappy alternatives by forging an anti-anti-ethnocentric self-conception. It is ethnocentrically liberal and hence not tolerant of Nazis because Nazis are not liberals and violate the principles of a liberal people, a liberal *ethnos*. But because those principles are self-consciously acknowledged to be historically contingent and subject to doubt, liberal ironists are prepared, indeed eager, to know more about how other people do things in the hopes that doing so might enrich their own ethos. Tolerance, though not absolute tolerance, is one of the principles of liberal ethnocentrism. Liberal ironist culture is not a windowless monad but a monad prepared to fling open its doors and windows (if not to let just anyone inside):

> It is a culture which prides itself on constantly adding more windows, constantly enlarging its sympathies. It is a form of life which is constantly extending pseudopods and adapting itself to what it encounters. Its sense of moral worth is founded on its tolerance of diversity. The heroes it apotheosizes include those who have enlarged its capacity for sympathy and tolerance. Among the enemies it diabolizes are the people who attempt to diminish this capacity, the vicious ethnocentrists.[48]

Liberal ironism, in short, is ethnocentric without being relativist. Rorty's rejection of the latter and embrace of the former makes all the more sense.

46. Ibid., 61.

47. Richard Rorty, "On Ethnocentrism: A Reply to Clifford Geertz" (1986), in Rorty, *Objectivity, Relativism, and Truth*, 203–4. See also Rorty, "Philosophy and the Future" (1995), in Saatkamp, *Rorty and Pragmatism*, 203–4.

48. Rorty, "On Ethnocentrism," 204.

There is, that is, one *ethnos* whose ethnocentrism need not trouble us, and that is the *ethnos* to which Rorty belongs.

America the Contingent

Rorty admits that most liberals are not postmodernist ironists and most postmodernist ironists are not liberals. Hence his ethos is confined to a tiny *ethnos.* Nonetheless, his dream is for its globalization. Liberalism has fought the good fight with great successes. He is loyal to it, and he hopes it will extend its sway. But he thinks liberalism would be even better if it threw away the Enlightenment philosophical ladders and skyhooks with which it has ascended since the eighteenth century and continue to climb unaided by any such props. He sees pragmatism—philosophy without ladders and sky-hooks—"not just as clearing up little messes left behind by the great dead philosophers, but as contributing to a world-historical change in humanity's self-image."[49] He knows the globalization of postmodernist bourgeois liberalism is, to put it mildly, a long-term goal that, should it come to pass, will do so in a future he will not himself experience.

But one has to begin sometime. And somewhere. Pragmatism insists that we must start from where we are, from within the web of beliefs, the language game, of a particular culture. We may reweave that web, even radically, but we must begin within it, and depart it, if we do, only for the web of another community. For Rorty, connected criticism is the only conceivable kind of criticism.[50]

If a critic must begin within the circle of a particular "we," then "to imagine great things is to imagine a great future *for a particular community,* a community one knows well, identifies with, can make plausible predictions about." Such a community need not be a national community; it might exceed or lie within national boundaries. Yet for the foreseeable future, Rorty is convinced that projects such as his will be national projects, "psalms of *national* futures rather than of the future of 'mankind.'"[51] Fortunately for himself, Rorty thinks his own national culture is a particularly good place—if

49. Richard Rorty, "Robert Brandom on Social Practices and Representations" (1998), in Rorty, *Truth and Progress,* 132.

50. Rorty suggests that the discourse of objectivity may have begun in an effort to find an alternative to "merely" connected social criticism. He attributes the deceptive discourse to Plato and other Greeks gripped by a "fear of parochialism, of being confined within the horizons of the group into which one happens to be born, a need to see it with the eyes of a stranger." This gave rise to the misguided, unrealizable ambition of the intellectual to be "someone who is in touch with the nature of things, not by way of the opinions of his community, but in a more immediate way." Rorty, "Solidarity or Objectivity?" 21.

51. Richard Rorty, "Unger, Castoriadis, and the Romance of a National Future" (1988), in Rorty, *Essays on Heidegger and Others* (New York: Cambridge University Press, 1991), 184.

not the only place—to begin the world-historical transformation of humanity's self-image that pragmatism promises. "I see America pretty much as Whitman and Dewey did," Rorty says, "as opening a prospect on illimitable democratic vistas. I think our country—despite its past and present atrocities and vices, and despite its continuing eagerness to elect fools and knaves to high office—is a good example of the best kind of society so far invented."[52] And like many an American past and present, Rorty believes America can prefigure the future of the world.

Rorty, it should be said, has not always embraced America in this fashion. In the mid-1970s, he applauded George Santayana for avoiding the conviction that "it is up to American philosophy to express the American genius, to describe a virtue as uniquely ours as our redwoods and rattlesnakes." And it is important to emphasize that while Rorty has argued that America is a good place for a postphilosophical liberalism to flower, he still does not claim that it need be the only place it may do so. In this sense, he is not an "American exceptionalist." Indeed, in the late 1980s, he seemed to think the prospects were better in places like Brazil than among "we rich, fat, tired North Americans," immobilized by "bleak defensiveness and resignation." By the late 1990s, however, he was unironically quoting Whitman's *Democratic Vistas* to his countrymen without defensiveness and in the name of hope.[53]

Rorty's reasons for investing his liberal hopes in the United States are perhaps obvious. If historians no longer take liberalism to be the only American political tradition, it remains the preeminent one. And as Rorty sees it, "American democracy is the embodiment of all the best features of the West." His politics is simply a matter of fully realizing the ambitions of liberalism as he sees them, and he sees little need for a fundamental reconstruction of American institutions to do so.[54]

Rorty's reasons are fuzzier for thinking that America might be a site for the emergence of a postphilosophical culture, "the first nation-state to have the courage to renounce hope of justification on high—a source which is immovable and eternal." At times, it almost seems as if he believes this might be the case simply because Dewey and Whitman thought it might be so. As he reads these two American prophets, they "viewed the United States as an opportunity to see ultimate significance in a finite, human, historical project, rather than in something eternal and nonhuman." For both, "America" was "shorthand for a new conception of what it is to be human—a conception which has no room for obedience to a nonhuman authority, and in

---

52. Rorty, "Trotsky and the Wild Orchids," 4.

53. Richard Rorty, "Professionalized Philosophy and Transcendentalist Discourse" (1976), in Rorty, *Consequences of Pragmatism*, 70; Rorty, "Unger, Castoriadis, and a National Future," 178–79.

54. Rorty, "Cosmopolitanism Without Emancipation: A Response to Jean-François Lyotard" (1985), in Rorty, *Objectivism, Relativism, and Truth*, 211.

which nothing save freely achieved consensus among human beings has any authority at all." And like responsible pragmatists, neither Dewey nor Whitman believed in the *inevitable* promise of American life. They knew that "the price of temporalization is contingency," and hence "had to grant the possibility that the vanguard of humanity may lose its way, and perhaps lead our species over a cliff."[55]

Dewey and Whitman might, of course, have misjudged America, and so when estimating the prospects of a change of cultural self-image, one would like to have more than their word to go on. Why might we think Americans are incipient pragmatists of a Rortyan sort? Here Rorty says he can offer little more than the conviction that pragmatism and Americanism share a common orientation toward the future. Americans are pragmatists in the sense that they are inclined to judge an idea or action not by its pedigree but by its consequences. America, Whitman said, reckons justification and success "almost entirely on the future," and Rorty says, "if there is anything distinctive about pragmatism it is that it substitutes the notion of a better human future for the notions of 'reality,' 'reason,' and 'nature.'" Pragmatism and America alike "are expressions of a hopeful, melioristic, experimental frame of mind." Both look not to foundational truth for authority but to "the substance of things hoped for." This is not much to work with.[56]

One might, I suppose, try to thicken up the connection a bit more than Rorty does. For example, American nationalism is, in theory, a subscriptive, *creedal* nationalism, a matter of consenting to a set of abstract principles articulated in such sacred texts as the Declaration of Independence, the Constitution, and the Gettysburg Address, rather than an ascriptive racial or ethnic identity. Thus, in important respects to be an American is to have a particular web of beliefs, a shared language game. This peculiar sort of nationalism might make Americans more plausible candidates for liberal ironism, since this post-Philosophical view calls for a pragmatic understanding of "vocabularies." The United States does, of course, have a constitutional "foundation," but it is one that has invited reinterpretation and revision over the last two centuries.[57] Yet here as well, there are grounds for skepticism.

55. Rorty, *Achieving Our Country*, 16, 17, 18, 28. I will not contest these readings of Dewey and Whitman. But I do think Rorty overlooks the idealist metaphysics that undergirds Whitman's hopes. See *Democratic Vistas* (1868), in *Walt Whitman: Complete Poetry and Prose* (New York: Library of America, 1982), 984–86. Rorty is, with Dewey, on firmer ground. Dewey thought of America as a contingent "experiment" that had "not yet played out." Like Rorty, Dewey believed that "the United States are not yet made; they are not a finished fact to be categorically assessed." Dewey, "Pragmatic America," 309.

56. Rorty, "Truth Without Correspondence to Reality," 24, 27. An earlier version of this essay was titled "Americanism and Pragmatism."

57. For a provocative reading of constitutional change that argues for a process of often dramatic reweaving, see Bruce Ackerman, *We the People: Foundations* (Cambridge: Harvard University Press, 1991), and *We the People: Transformations* (Cambridge: Harvard University Press,

Trouble in Paradise

Rorty has no illusions about the difficulties that face the project of "pragmatizing" the American self-conception. In Rorty's maturation narrative of progress from religious to rationalist to pragmatist outlooks, most Americans remain in infancy, as does the culture generally. Americans are the most religious people in the Western world, and the national story to this day is inconceivable without a central place for its religious dimension. The American variant of the Enlightenment was among the most accommodating to religious, even evangelical, belief, and it is in God, not themselves, that Americans officially place their trust. In the millennium year 2000, Americans elected a president whose favorite philosopher is Jesus Christ, and his dubiously defeated opponent offered a concession speech echoing Lincoln's view of the nation as one guided by the majesty and mystery of God's purposes. Rorty himself has noted that "more than a century after Friedrich Nietzsche pronounced the death of God, approximately 90 percent of Americans say they still believe in Him, and about 35 percent of those people—some 70 million of us—say they believe that the Christian Scriptures are the inerrant word of God."[58]

Insofar as Americans look to the future for justification, it remains for most a promised future, not a contingent one. Far more Americans attempt to discern the fate of the nation by means of the Book of Revelation than subscribe to ungrounded Deweyan hope.[59] And insofar as Americans ascribe a secular identity to the nation, it is, for most, as the agent of necessary, universal, self-evident truths about human nature. Rorty is up against it if he is to rewrite the Declaration of Independence to read: "We ethnocentrically hold these warranted assertions to be the product of the justificatory practices of our community, that all men are born equal, endowed by our community, at least for the moment, with unalienable rights, that among these are life, liberty, and the pursuit of happiness."

1998). This is not to say that ascriptive, racial and ethnic identities have not also been an important part of American nationalism. See Rogers Smith, *Civic Ideals: Conflicting Visions of Citizenship in U.S. History* (New Haven: Yale University Press, 1997).

58. See Gustav Niebuhr, "Political Expressions of Personal Piety Increase, as Bush and Gore Showed," *New York Times*, 16 December 2000, B6. Al Gore, in his speech, described the "ruling principle of American freedom, the source of our democratic liberties," to be the motto: "Not under man, but under God and law." Nothing could be less Rortyan. Richard Rorty, "Fundamentally Flawed," *Civilization* (February/March 2000): 79. Recent surveys indicate that the world's "nonreligious and atheist" population has declined from 18.9 to 15.2 percent since 1970. Richard N. Ostling, "A Counter of Religions Books Them All," Rochester (NY) *Democrat and Chronicle*, 25 March 2001, 22A. On the moderate rationalism of the American Enlightenment see Henry May, *The Enlightenment in America* (New York: Oxford, 1976); and Mark Noll, *America's God* (New York: Oxford University Press, 2002).

59. See Paul Boyer, *When Time Shall Be No More: Prophecy Belief in Modern America* (Cambridge: Harvard University Press, 1992).

Rorty knows that he is cutting against the grain of the culture. When he says that pragmatists are "in the same situation as are atheists in an overwhelmingly religious culture," he is, in the American case, offering more than an analogy. Pragmatists must, as he all too gently puts it, "see themselves as involved in a long-term attempt to change the rhetoric, the common sense, and the self-image of their community."[60]

If these practical obstacles were not enough, Rorty's project for a pragmatist American culture is made all the more daunting by theoretical difficulties of his own making. Chief among these are the doubts that he raises about how committed to it he is himself. Having joined his liberalism and his pragmatism in his hopes for America, he sometimes sets them at odds, suggesting that pragmatist ironism might threaten more than enhance liberal prospects.[61]

In perhaps his most widely read book, *Contingency, Irony, and Solidarity* (1989), Rorty cannot seem to make up his mind whether the liberal utopia— that which he forecasts for America—will be one in which all of its citizens will indeed be ironists as well as liberals, or only some of its citizens will be ironists—and they only when they are not acting as citizens. Having asserted the first ideal in one chapter, he backs away from it in the next.[62] In the ideal liberal society, he says while backpedaling, intellectuals will be ironists, but nonintellectuals will not. Moreover, these intellectuals will be asked to confine their ironism to the solitude of their own private acts of self-creation in order to keep the public sphere free of corrosive doubt about the final vocabulary of liberalism.

What, one might well ask, has happened here to the postmodernist bourgeois liberal utopia? Why has Rorty torn it asunder? The answer, I would suggest, is that he fears that liberalism might not survive in a postphilosophical culture in which everyone is, by his lights, fully mature. Since his own pragmatism forbids a resort to philosophical shields against the agents of this culture, Rorty has to resort to other, principally political, measures to protect liberalism from people philosophically like himself.

Rorty tries to put these fears at ease by imagining a popular culture that is just "sort of" postphilosophical. If the masses in this utopia will not be fully mature pragmatists, they will nonetheless no longer be immature objectivists. Rather, they will be "commonsensically nominalist and historicist. So they would see themselves as contingent through and through, without feeling any particular doubts about the contingencies they happened to be." But it is hard to imagine that one could see oneself as contingent through

---

60. Richard Rorty, "Is Truth a Goal of Inquiry?" (1995), in Rorty, *Truth and Progress*, 41.

61. Nancy Fraser has offered a telling, fuller account of this two-mindedness than I do here in "Solidarity or Singularity?: Richard Rorty Between Romanticism and Technocracy," in Fraser, *Unruly Practices: Power, Discourse, and Gender in Contemporary Social Theory* (Minneapolis: University of Minnesota Press, 1989), 93–110.

62. Rorty, *Contingency, Irony, and Solidarity*, 61, 87.

and through without wondering whether one might be otherwise, without doubting the finality of one's current final vocabulary. Unless, that is, one is not only nominalist and historicist but also dim-witted, uncurious, and complacent. But, although there is an occasional whiff of Nietzschean contempt for the herd in Rorty's thinking, if he thought he could count on non-intellectuals to be halfway pragmatists, self-satisfied and deaf to doubt, it is not clear why he feels compelled to cordon them off from the irony of intellectuals by asking the latter to keep their mouths shut in public.[63]

Rorty must resort to this jerry-rigged and precarious sort of arrangement to protect liberalism from pragmatism because of one of the distinctive features of his pragmatism. Rorty is one of the few pragmatists who believes that "there is no reason why a fascist could not be a pragmatist, in the sense of agreeing with pretty much everything Dewey said about the nature of truth, knowledge, rationality, and morality."[64] But one of the most insistent things that Dewey said about truth, knowledge, rationality, and morality was that some justificatory practices are better than others, not just better for us but better as such. His model of a community with superior justificatory practices was the scientific community, and he thought that moral and political deliberation should emulate, if not mimic, these practices. Emulating these practices, he argued, would require that communities of inquiry of all sorts—including political communities—organize themselves democratically since procedural democracy was a crucial feature of scientific practice. This emphasis on "scientific method" and its democratic implications is what has led Deweyan pragmatists, including neopragmatists such as Hilary Putnam, to deny that a pragmatist could be a fascist since pragmatism incorporates an "epistemological justification of democracy."[65] But this is one of the crucial respects in which Rorty is not a Deweyan pragmatist; he wants a pragmatism stripped of any claim of superior "method."[66]

---

63. Earlier in *Contingency, Irony, and Solidarity,* Rorty attempts to universalize ironism by using Freud to argue against Nietzsche, suggesting that Freud gave everyone a creative unconscious, capable of metaphorical redescription. "What makes Freud more useful and more plausible than Nietzsche is that he does not relegate the vast majority of humanity to the status of dying animals. Freud's account of unconscious fantasy shows us how to see every human life as a poem" (35). But having said here that intellectuals are "just a special case" (37), Rorty then goes on in the passage I have quoted in the text to suggest that nonintellectuals would be incapable of the ironism of strong poets because they "would not be bookish, nor would they look to literary critics as moral advisors" (87). Rorty himself is decidedly "bookish," writing warmly and well about the role that novels can play in unsettling a reader's final vocabulary, but nothing about how movies, popular music, and even television can do the same for both intellectuals and nonintellectuals.

64. Rorty, "Truth Without Correspondence to Reality," 23.

65. Hilary Putnam, "A Reconsideration of Deweyan Democracy" (1990), in Putnam, *Renewing Philosophy* (Cambridge: Harvard University Press, 1992). 180. See also chapter 7.

66. Richard Rorty, "Pragmatism Without Method" (1983), in Rorty, *Objectivity, Relativism, and Truth,* 63–77. Deweyan pragmatism is, in this respect, closer to the thinking of Jürgen

Sometimes Rorty suggests that his pragmatism does include a modest, context-independent notion of rationality as "reasonable," committed to "free and open encounters" and an ideal of "unforced agreement." For the pragmatist, he says, "the desire for 'objectivity' boils down to a desire to acquire beliefs which will eventually receive unforced agreement in the course of a free and open encounter with people holding other beliefs."[67] One might call this an epistemological justification of democracy insofar as procedural democracy is the best guarantee of "free and open encounters." At the same time, a "fascist" committed to "free and open encounters" would be a contradiction in terms. But if Rorty is here advancing a context-independent notion of rationality, then he has qualified his ethnocentrism. Hence, a Rortyan pragmatist, unlike a Deweyan pragmatist, must entertain the possibility of a fascist brother and of a pragmatized culture that would be a very nasty and illiberal affair.[68]

A better resolution to Rorty's difficulties is to be found, as he at other times recognizes, in the "political liberalism" of the greatest of late-twentieth-century liberal political philosophers, John Rawls. Rawls's "political liberalism" might be seen as an abstract and elaborated version of Rorty's liberal anti-anti-ethnocentrism, that is, toleration with its brains intact. Designed for a society (and in the end, for a world) in which people hold a diversity of fundamental ethical and religious worldviews, Rawls's ideal liberal society is one in which no particular worldview is allowed to dominate public life. Instead, a plurality of such worldviews is permitted to exist in the private sphere as long as they are "reasonable" worldviews that subscribe to an "overlapping consensus" on principles of justice that are to guide the society. These principles, chosen from behind Rawls's famous "veil of ignorance" that insures impartiality, include the equal allocation of what Rorty calls "bourgeois freedoms," personal and civil liberties, and basic political rights; the equal opportunity to compete for offices and occupations; and the controversial "difference principle" that provides that inequalities are justifiable only if they work to "the greatest benefit of the least advantaged members of society."[69]

Habermas than to that of Rorty, and Habermas, as Rorty says, is "a liberal who is unwilling to be an ironist." Rorty, *Contingency, Irony, and Solidarity*, 61.

67. Richard Rorty, "Science as Solidarity" (1987), in Rorty, *Objectivity, Relativism, and Truth*, 39, 41.

68. For more on the difference made by Rorty's differences with Dewey and other pragmatists on the matter of "method," see the Introduction and chapter 7.

69. John Rawls, *Political Liberalism* (New York: Columbia University Press, 1993). This volume is a companion to Rawls's monumental *A Theory of Justice* (Cambridge: Harvard University Press, 1971) and builds on its arguments. Rawls extended his arguments to international politics in *The Law of Peoples* (Cambridge: Harvard University Press, 1999). For a brief, lucid summary (and criticism) of Rawls's political liberalism, see Stephen Holmes, "The Gatekeeper," *New Republic* (11 October 1993): 39–47. For Rorty's embrace of Rawls's theory, see Richard

In a Rawlsian liberal order, those with "unreasonable," nonliberal views who find themselves unable to subscribe to the overlapping consensus, need not shut up or be shut up, but they are not allowed to attempt to impose those views on other citizens. Thus, in a Rawlsian/Rortyan utopia in which everyone was a pragmatist, Martin Heidegger would not be sent to his room, but neither would he be allowed to threaten the liberal public order by organizing storm troopers to wage war on liberal institutions. Liberal pragmatists, such as Rorty, would have the power of the state at their disposal to insure that ironism did not threaten practices justified by the consensual principles of justice, couched in the liberal final vocabulary.

A Rawlsian polity would, then, provide a greater measure of protection for liberalism from corrosive, ironic doubt than an expectation that nonintellectuals will be complacent and intellectuals will be silent. But it would afford no impregnable shield. Doubt could wear away at the liberal final vocabulary, and one can reasonably wonder whether citizens who took this vocabulary to be contingent, historical, and thus conceivably "the wrong language" would go to the wall to defend it, as we know those who have regarded it as the vocabulary of God or human nature—a vocabulary bearing "metaphysical comfort"—have done.[70] Reinhold Niebuhr may well have been right when he argued that:

> There must always be a religious element in the hope of a just society. Without the ultrarational hopes and passions of religion no society will ever have the courage to conquer despair and attempt the impossible; for the vision of a just society is an impossible one, which can be approximated only by those who do not regard it as impossible. The truest visions of religion are illusions, which may be partially realised by being resolutely believed. For what religion believes to be true is not wholly true but ought to be true; and may become true if its truth is not doubted.[71]

One might still worry then that liberalism would not be as secure in an American culture informed by Rortyan pragmatism as it would be in a

---

Rorty, "The Priority of Democracy to Philosophy" (1988), in Rorty, *Objectivity, Relativism, and Truth*, 175–96; and Rorty, "Justice as a Larger Loyalty."

70. Rorty, *Contingency, Irony, and Solidarity*, 75. Richard Neuhaus has astutely noted that Rorty's distinction between hope and knowledge is "usually described in religious terms as walking by faith and not by sight." Neuhaus complains that Rorty falsely assumes a "necessary connection between religion and mindless certitude" and thus caricatures religious belief as a matter of certain knowledge of God's will (sight) rather than faith (hope) that God will see us through. Neuhaus, "Joshing Richard Rorty," *First Things* (December 1990): 17, 20. The classical pragmatists, particularly James, were more alert to this distinction, and critical though they were of religious knowledge claims, they were sympathetic to religious faith claims and tried to provide a few of their own. See Robert Westbrook, "An Uncommon Faith: Pragmatism and Religious Experience," in Stuart Rosenbaum, ed., *Pragmatism and Religion* (Urbana: University of Illinois Press, 2003), 190–205.

71. Niebuhr, *Moral Man and Immoral Society* (New York: Scribners, 1932), 81.

culture wedded to a social gospel, Jeffersonian rationalism, or Deweyan pragmatism.

Toward a New Old Left

Rawls's theory is sometimes criticized for its implicit Americanism, for working up the traditions and intuitions guiding American politics into an abstract theory that pretends to broader application. Rorty, of course, has no problem with this sort of ethnocentrism. But one of Rawls's principles, his "difference principle," is decidedly at odds with American intuitions about social equality since it is decidedly more egalitarian than the prevailing wisdom. Rorty has suggested that the "difference principle" is the common wisdom of American politics, and that disagreements between left and right amount only to disputes over the means to pursue it.[72] I do not think so. Rawls's principle requires more than "trickle-down economics," what Stephen Holmes labels "the classical liberal idea that differences in income or wealth between the rich and the poor are justified only if they are causally connected to an increase of productivity that is beneficial to the indigent."[73] While the American right has dubiously argued that the substantial upward redistribution of wealth it has fostered since the early 1980s has benefited all social classes, it is difficult to argue that conservative tax policies have been made with an eye to insuring the greatest possible benefits to the poor whatever their effects on the rich (which is what Rawls requires). Moreover, Rawls's principle rests on a radical conception of equality of opportunity that regards most of the differences between individuals that generate inequality as arbitrary, something that American conservatives and liberals alike would find hard to swallow. My sense is that Rorty's own egalitarian demand is for something like a decent social minimum for the poor, which is different from Rawls's principle but also unorthodox. Hence, though Rorty has never explicitly embraced Rawls's "difference principle," his liberalism is also more egalitarian than the American norm.

So despite his sometimes self-satisfied applause for bourgeois values and his undisguised contempt for Marxism, Rorty is a man of the left, and his political hopes for America rest on a revitalization of the American left and on progress toward a dramatically more egalitarian society. He hopes that by the end of the twenty-first century Americans will believe that "the first duty of the state is to prevent gross economic and social inequality, as opposed to our ancestors' assumption that the government's only *moral* duty

72. Richard Rorty, "First Projects, Then Principles," *Nation* (22 December 1997), 18.
73. Holmes, "Gatekeeper," 41. Whenever I teach Rawls's work and ask my students which of his views might be said to be "un-American," they always point to the difference principle.

was to ensure 'equal protection of the laws'—laws that, in their majesty impartiality, allowed the rich and the poor to receive the same hospital bills."[74] Rorty can best be regarded as part of a long line of liberal thinkers—John Stuart Mill, T. H. Green, John Dewey, C. B. Macpherson, John Rawls himself, and others—who believe that one can argue from liberal premises (such as Rorty's principle of equalizing opportunities for self-creation) to social-democratic conclusions.

Rorty hopes to revivify pride in American citizenship by renewing the civic ideals of prophets like Dewey and Whitman, which substituted "social justice for individual freedom as our country's principal goal." The agent of this revival would be a reborn American left, a "reformist left" heir to the legacy of Irving Howe and A. Philip Randolph. Given that "nations rely on artists and intellectuals to create images of, and to tell stories about, the national past," Rorty tells a story about the American left designed to foster pride in the alternative, social-democratic self-understanding he hopes Americans will embrace.[75]

This narrative, which is a declension narrative, goes like this: beginning in the early years of the twentieth century a broad "reformist left" comprised of American liberals and socialists "struggled within the framework of constitutional democracy to protect the weak from the strong." This coalition included everyone from Woodrow Wilson, Franklin Roosevelt, and Lyndon Johnson to Eugene Debs, W. E. B. DuBois, and Michael Harrington. The differences within this coalition were much less important than the convictions that divided it from the right, above all the belief that the American state should be engaged in a downward redistribution of wealth. In the era of this reformist left, which stretched from 1900 to 1964, left-wing intellectuals forged the American university into a socialist "church" and secured alliances with labor unions. This was a patriotic left that believed that "disgust with American hypocrisy and self-deception was pointless unless accompanied by an effort to give America reason to be proud of itself in the future." It was convinced that the "vast inequalities within American society could be corrected by using the institutions of a constitutional democracy—that a cooperative commonwealth could be created by electing the right politicians and passing the right laws." For the reformist left, support for the Cold War was consistent with this project, for it sought to turn that conflict into one in which America would "become both the leader of an international movement to replace oligarchy with social democracy around the world, and the nuclear superpower which halted the spread of an evil empire ruled by a mad tyrant."[76]

---

74. Richard Rorty, "Looking Backwards from the Year 2096" (1996), in Rorty, *Philosophy and Social Hope*, 246.
75. Rorty, *Achieving Our Country*, 4.
76. Ibid., 43, 48, 9, 54–55, 63.

But the Cold War and, above all, the war in Vietnam splintered the reformist left, and 1964 marked the emergence of a revolutionary New Left
that gave up on America. This New Left took the war as a clue that there
"was something deeply wrong with their country, and not just mistakes cor-
rectable by reforms. They wanted to hear that America was a very different
sort of place, a much worse place, than their parents and teachers had told
them it was." So they responded enthusiastically to arguments such as those
of Christopher Lasch that "the structure of American society makes it almost
impossible for criticism of existing policies to become part of political discourse." Believing that there was "nothing in America on which they could
rely," the young activists turned to a romantic embrace of third-world revolutionaries. The New Left "ended the Vietnam War" and "may have saved
our country from becoming a garrison state," yet its anti-Americanism and
its bitter resentment of liberals dramatically weakened the left. The war produced "a generation of Americans who suspected that our country was un-
achievable—that that war not only could never be forgiven, but had shown
us to be a nation conceived in sin, and irredeemable."[77]

Things got even worse for the American left in the last third of the century
as it replaced the politics of distributive justice with the identity politics of
race, gender, and sexual difference. The left increasingly became a "cultural
Left" that "thinks more about stigma than about money, more about deep
and hidden psychosexual motivations than about shallow and evident greed."
If left-wing intellectuals had once made universities into temples of social
democracy, they now formed an "academic left" embalmed in abstruse theory. Such self-styled radicals "have permitted cultural politics to supplant real
politics, and have collaborated with the Right in making cultural issues central to public debate." Although this cultural left can be credited with helping to make America "a far more civilized society than it was thirty years ago"
by fostering diversity and fighting racial and gender discrimination, it has left
the American left mute in the face of persistent economic inequality. Moreover, the cultural left has sustained the New Left's anti-Americanism, centered
now on "unmasking" a nefarious "mind-set," labeled things like "Cold War
ideology," "technocratic rationality," or "phallogocentrism." This is a mind-
set "nurtured by the patriarchal and capitalist institutions of the industrial
West, and its bad effects are most clearly visible in the United States."[78]

77. Ibid., 66, 67, 38. Rorty's use of Lasch as his New Left whipping boy is ironic in that Lasch
was among the severest critics of the New Left. And at the end of his life, he, like Rorty, embraced
the role of a "connected critic," though the populist narrative to which Lasch attached his criticism was decidedly different from Rorty's liberal story. See Lasch, *The Agony of the American Left*
(New York: Knopf, 1969), 115–212, and *The True and Only Heaven: Progress and Its Critics* (New
York: Norton, 1991). See also Robert B. Westbrook, "In Retrospect: Christopher Lasch, *The New
Radicalism*, and the Vocation of Intellectuals," *Reviews in American History* 23 (1995): 176–91.
78. Rorty, *Achieving Our Country*, 14, 81, 79.

If the American left is to reverse its decline, Rorty argues in the sort of exhortation that inevitably concludes a declension narrative, it must recover the goals and practices of the old reformist left. To do so, the cultural left will have to forge an alliance with the remnants of the reformist left and "have to talk much more about money, even at the cost of talking less about stigma."[79] The left should, in addition, "put a moratorium on theory":

> A political left needs agreement on projects much more than it needs to think through its principles. In a constitutional democracy like ours, leftist projects typically take the form of laws that need to be passed: laws that will increase socioeconomic equality. We need a list of First Projects—of laws that will remedy gaping inequalities—much more than we need agreement on First Principles.[80]

Rorty has urged the left to "banalize" its vocabulary. He suggests "we start talking about greed and selfishness rather than about bourgeois ideology, about starvation wages and layoffs rather than about the commodification of labor, and about differential per-pupil expenditure on schools and differential access to health care rather than about the division of society into classes."[81] Finally, and most importantly, Rorty insists that "the Left should try to mobilize what remains of our pride in being Americans"; it should again take up the mantle of connected criticism. "Unless the Left wraps itself in the flag," he contends, "it hasn't got a chance of practicing a majoritarian politics."[82]

There is much to quarrel with in Rorty's history of the American left. He greatly exaggerates the role of the university as a reform church in the first half of the century, perhaps generalizing unduly from the case of the University of Wisconsin. He overestimates the importance of an egalitarian redistribution of wealth to a program of the liberal wing of his "reformist left," and hence underplays the conflicts between liberals and socialists in that broad "coalition," conflicts that one need not be a Marxist to discern. After all, Woodrow Wilson threw Eugene Debs in jail for sedition—which, Rorty says, demotes Wilson to a "part-time leftist."[83] But most of the liberals Rorty places within the "reformist left" have been, at best, "part-time leftists," which is one principal reason why the United States has only a part-time welfare state.

Rorty vigorously defends the Cold War as a simple struggle against

---

79. Ibid., 91.
80. Ibid., 91; Rorty, "First Projects," 18.
81. Richard Rorty, "The End of Leninism, Havel, and Social Hope" (1995), in Rorty, *Truth and Progress*, 229.
82. Rorty, *Achieving Our Country*, 91–92; *Against Bosses*, 17.
83. Rorty, *Achieving Our Country*, 43.

tyranny, blinking the evidence that it shaped up as a battle between two imperial regimes—albeit one obviously less tyrannical than the other. He hyperbolically commends the New Left for ending the Vietnam war and forestalling an American "garrison state" and then condemns it for its resentment of those liberals who waged that war and built the national security state that prosecuted it. He attacks "identity politics" as an inferior politics at best, but proposes a social-democratic politics that, one critic has charged, "reinstates the priority of class as the irreplaceable principle of social organization, intellectual inquiry, and political struggle," thereby returning matters to "the vulgar Marxism Rorty wants us to forget."[84] He forcefully charges the "academic left" with a navel-gazing pseudo-politics of theoretical obscurantism, but in the process he crudely distinguishes cultural politics from "real" politics and seems to forget the importance of cultural politics to his own hopes for a postphilosophical culture—a cultural politics in which, as he himself has said, the university is a key site.[85]

Rorty says that "stories about what a nation has been and should try to be are not attempts at accurate representation, but rather attempts to forge a moral identity."[86] But a moral identity built around a story as easily contested as his is hard to embrace.

The practical difficulties confronting Rorty's political hopes for America are no less daunting than those facing his dream of a pragmatist cultural revolution. The constituency for a social-democratic America is small and shows no signs of growing. To suggest the obstacles to Rorty's hope, one need only turn to his own little utopian scenario, which calls on the deus ex machina of an economic collapse in 2014 that turns the nation into an armed camp and precipitates a military dictatorship. This regime is overthrown in 2044 by the Democratic Vistas Party, a coalition of trade unions and churches, which successfully brands its opponents as the "parties of self-

84. James Livingston, "Narrative Politics: Richard Rorty at the 'End of Reform,'" in Pettegrew, *A Pragmatist's Progress*, 188.

85. Richard Rorty, "Education as Socialization and as Individualization" (1989), in Rorty, *Philosophy and Social Hope*, 114–26 (higher education "is not a matter of inculcating or educing truth. It is, instead, a matter of inciting doubt and stimulating imagination, thereby challenging the prevailing consensus"); Richard Rorty, "The Humanistic Intellectual: Eleven Theses" (1989), in *Philosophy and Social Hope*, 127–30 ("the real social function of the humanistic intellectuals is to instill doubts in the students about the students' own self-images," 127); Richard Rorty, "John Searle on Realism and Relativism" (1994), in Rorty, *Truth and Progress*, 63–83; Rorty, "The Moral Purposes of the University," *Hedgehog Review* 2 (fall 2000): 106–16. James Livingston accuses me of offering, in an exchange with Giles Gunn, the same faulty distinction between "real" and "cultural" politics. But my target was not cultural politics but academic politics, one of its modest subsets that too many academics confuse with the whole. See James Livingston, *Pragmatism, Feminism, and Democracy: Rethinking the Politics of American History* (New York: Routledge, 2001), 197–98n19; and Robert Westbrook, "A New Pragmatism," *American Quarterly* 45 (1993): 438–44.

86. Rorty, *Achieving Our Country*, 13.

ishness," institutes an expansive welfare state, and establishes "fraternity" as "the name of our most cherished ideal."[87]

One of the surprising things about this scenario is the central role that Rorty grants to churches in building his cooperative commonwealth. Elsewhere, he says that "I find the rise of church attendance in the United States depressing. This rise makes me fear for the republic. If it continues, if more and more people seek solace in the world beyond, I fear that there will be less social reform, less pressure for social justice." He hopes instead for "the gradual replacement of the churches by the universities as the conscience of the nation."[88] By these lights, the Democratic Vistas Party should be a coalition of unions and university professors, much like that which putatively led the old reformist left. But that would perhaps be even more improbable. It would be tempting to suggest that Rorty is conceding the power of religious hope in forging a better world, but that too is improbable. If the future of the left depends on all the improbabilities packed into this brief scenario, then hope will be hard to sustain.

Not the least of the barriers to the future Rorty imagines is his underestimation of its opponents. He says that "the Left, by definition, is the party of hope. It insists that our nation remains unachieved."[89] The right is the party of stand-patters or even of memory of a better past. But much of the American right is as much a party of hope as the American left. It has tied its hope to a narrative of ever-expanding freedom and material well-being for all Americans under the sign of the creative destruction of capitalism. As George Will notes, the American right, "by coupling itself to unregulated capitalism, has become the party of permanent revolution"—the party of the forces that, as Marx said, melt all that is solid into air.[90]

Rorty's social-democratic vision is up against that of "market populism"—the belief, as Thomas Frank says, that "markets expressed the popular will more articulately and more meaningfully than did mere elections. Markets conferred democratic legitimacy; markets were the friend of the little guy; markets brought down the pompous and the snooty; markets gave us what we wanted; markets looked out for our interests."[91] Such market populism underwrites a political culture in which questioning the inequitable rewards that markets provide to a tiny class of citizens can be effectively denounced as demagogic "class warfare," while further fostering the upward redistribution of wealth passes as sound public policy. One of the great triumphs of

87. Rorty, "Looking Backwards," 247–49.

88. Richard Rorty, Julie A. Reuben, and George Marsden, "The Moral Purposes of the University: An Exchange," *Hedgehog Review* 2 (fall 2000): 107–8.

89. Rorty, *Achieving Our Country*, 14.

90. George Will, "Still Waiting for Lefty," *Newsweek* (25 May 1998): 86.

91. Thomas Frank, *One Market Under God: Extreme Capitalism, Market Populism, and the End of Economic Democracy* (New York: Random House, 2000), xiv.

American conservatives in the last generation has been to persuade a good part of the American working class to think of themselves in the first instance not as workers in need of the security that an expansive welfare state such as that Rorty envisions might provide but as taxpayers excessively burdened by the bill for the security of a minority of other, less-deserving Americans. As Casey Blake has said, if all America was Madison, Wisconsin, in the first part of this century, "with its secular Scandinavian farmers, its socialist German union members, and its progressive experts [such as Rorty's uncle, Paul Rauschenbusch, and his wife Elizabeth Brandeis], then we could well imagine an American left capable of transforming this country into something resembling Denmark."[92] But Madison was hardly the typical American community, and Denmark remains a distant goal.

I also believe Rorty does his hope no service by insisting that the American left adopt a wholly banal vocabulary. "Greed" and "selfishness" are explanatory variables of limited usefulness in explaining the inequality that besets American society. As Avishai Margalit—who shares Rorty's ambition to build a "decent society" that does not humiliate its members—has said, a decent society is one in which "*institutions* do not humiliate people," and moving toward such a society requires that one consider "the setup of the society as a whole."[93] For these purposes, a vocabulary of intentional terms such as "selfishness" will not do; a left without social theory is disarmed. Some of Rorty's critics have been fond of quoting to him John Dewey's remark in 1935 that "liberalism must now become radical, meaning by 'radical' perception of the necessity of thorough-going changes in the set-up of institutions and corresponding activity to bring the changes to pass." Rorty thinks that Dewey was wrong about this, but he interprets Dewey to have been calling for a wholesale replacement of a market economy with some alternative. But this was not Dewey's desire; his ideal had much in common with Rorty's vision of a semisocialist market economy regulated in the interests of the least well-off. Yet he did not see how mere appeals against greed could insure progress toward it.[94]

92. Casey Blake, "If All the World Were Madison, Wisconsin," *culturefront* (fall 1998): 88.

93. Avishai Margalit, *The Decent Society* (Cambridge: Harvard University Press, 1996), 2–3. Rorty quotes Margalit accurately (*Achieving Our Country*, 25), but does not point up the contrast between Margalit's theory of institutional humiliation and his "banal" analysis.

94. John Dewey, *Liberalism and Social Action* (1935), *Later Works*, 11:45. See Richard Bernstein, "One Step Forward, Two Steps Backward: Richard Rorty on Liberal Democracy and Philosophy," *Political Theory* 15 (1987): 540; and Thomas McCarthy, "Postscript: Ironist Theory as a Vocation," in McCarthy, *Ideals and Illusions: On Reconstruction and Deconstruction in Contemporary Critical Theory* (Cambridge: MIT Press, 1991), 42. Rorty's response to Dewey is in Rorty, "End of Leninism," 239n15. For Dewey's radical liberalism in the 1930s, see Robert B. Westbrook, *John Dewey and American Democracy* (Ithaca: Cornell University Press, 1991), 429–62; and Alan Ryan, *John Dewey and the High Tide of American Liberalism* (New York: Norton, 1995), 284–327.

Rorty's social-democratic hope cannot make do without greater conceptual resources than the American left now has at its disposal in public debate. He is undoubtedly right that novels, ethnographies, and other narratives that sensitize us to the pain and humiliation suffered by those too often out of sight and mind have a critical role to play in liberal politics. But the sentiments aroused by such stories must be coupled to moral and political principles if they are to be mobilized on behalf of a cooperative commonwealth. Rorty's vision, like that of other liberals who have tried to push liberalism in a social-democratic direction, requires something like the notion of "social citizenship" that British liberal T. H. Marshall advanced in 1949. That is, a conception of citizenship that went beyond the provision to all citizens of civil and political rights to the provision of "social rights," a guarantee of economic security, and the right to "a share in the full social heritage and to live the life of a civilized being according to the standards prevailing in the society." This notion, which had a profound effect on the making of the postwar British welfare state, is not one that has had much impact on the construction of the more anemic American welfare state. Even though we speak of Social Security benefits and Medicare as "entitlements," neither has ever been conceived of as a social "right." Rorty's "projects," such as universal health care and an equalization of school funding, are the right projects for his goals, but absent a principled and widely shared rationale for these projects, such as that provided by a conception of social citizenship, they are unlikely to be realized.[95]

Many American liberals who are trying to push a concept of "social citizenship" into debates over social policy in the United States argue that inclusive, even universal, programs for social citizenship that address the needs of both middle and low-income Americans are more likely to win wide public favor than those that target the needs of the poor alone.[96] Rorty ran afoul of those in the "reformist left" who hold this view with his proposal for means-testing Social Security benefits.[97] Commenting on an earlier version of this chapter, Rorty said

I am less sure about the difference you see between Britain and America on the matter of social citizenship. I should have thought that we had as deep a tradi-

95. T. H. Marshall, "Citizenship and Social Class" in Marshall, *Class, Citizenship, and Social Development* (Chicago: University of Chicago Press, 1964), 78. I draw in these final paragraphs on my contribution to a symposium on "Liberalism and the Left," *Radical History Review* 71 (1998): 46–51.

96. See Margaret Weir, Ann Shola Orloff, and Theda Skocpol, "The Future of Social Policy in the United States: Political Constraints and Possibilities," in Weir, Orloff, and Skocpol, eds., *The Politics of Social Policy in the United States* (Princeton: Princeton University Press, 1988), 421–45.

97. Rorty, "Making the Rich Richer," *New York Times* (6 March 2000). See Robert Kuttner, "Socially Inept," *American Prospect* (27 March 2000): 5.

tion of that sort as the Brits, and that the only difference is that they elected a Labor Government at about the time we were electing the goddamned 80th Congress, for incidental and transitory reasons. The post-war Labor Government produced irreversible changes, just as the New Deal did in America, but was able to go further than the New Deal did. I don't see that the intellectual/spiritual/moral traditions on which Attlee and Roosevelt drew were so different. It's just that Robert Taft was cleverer than Eden and Churchill.[98]

I beg to differ. The tradition of "social citizenship" was more deeply seated in Britain by the end of World War II, though one can find occasional important American expressions of the idea (such as FDRs 1944 State of the Union Address). The Labor party was the vehicle for giving this idea expansive expression in policy as the Democratic party in America was not and World War II in Britain was fought as a "people's war" in which the expectation was that sacrifice would be rewarded with a robust welfare state, which was not the case in the United States. The victory of the Labor party in postwar elections reflected this commitment and the triumph of the Republican party in the Congressional elections of 1946 manifested the steady erosion of support for such a state in America during the war. Hence I would argue the decidedly different politics of the two nations in the postwar years reflected substantial ideological differences between American liberals and British social democrats, not "incidental and transitory reasons."[99]

Even if the social citizenship principle could be established in the United States, "reform leftism" might well require further conceptual resources that liberalism, with its focus on individual rights, cannot best provide. Social citizenship might require solidarities that a strictly liberal political culture cannot sustain. Although one can argue that every citizen requires what John Dewey called "effective liberty," it is not evident that liberalism alone can provide the ethic of mutual obligation—the "fraternity"—that would move those who can fend for themselves to guarantee such freedom to their fellow citizens who cannot, especially since doing so is likely to be very expensive. Liberalism, that is, however necessary it is to the social-democratic future Rorty imagines, may not be sufficient.

Rorty has conceded that "communitarian" critics of liberalism have a point in their criticism of its individualism and that liberal democracy would be better served if it depended less on "a less individualistic conception of what it is to be properly human—one that makes less of autonomy and more of interdependence."[100] Rorty's concession to communitarianism seems

98. Rorty to Robert Westbrook, 10 July 2001.

99. For an astute illumination of these differences see James T. Kloppenberg, "Deliberative Democracy and the Problem of Poverty in America," in Kloppenberg, *The Virtues of Liberalism* (New York: Oxford, 1998), 100–123.

100. Rorty, "Priority of Democracy," 179. Historically liberals have poached on other tradi-

to me to sit uneasily with his assertion that J. S. Mill provided all the conceptual resources that liberalism requires.[101] Some have found greater resources for solidarity in liberalism than I suggest here, though the defense of "liberalism" that emerges from such accounts often seems to me better described as a plea for the sort of theoretical eclecticism I recommend here.[102]

Daunting as it will be to change the character of American political discourse, this is but part of the battle Rortyan liberals confront. A new old left must not only speak of obligation, reciprocity, community, and responsibility, but also figure out ways to sustain them in the practices of everyday life in the civil society of the United States. That civil society is not in particularly good shape and is especially depleted in its supply of what Robert Putnam has called "bridging social capital"—"norms, networks, and trust" that span social cleavages.[103] Only a democratic majority rich in such social capital, and only a left committed to such capital accumulation, can hope to move toward Rorty's ideals.

But however thoroughly one might want to take issue with the particulars of Rorty's connected criticism, I think he is correct in believing that connected criticism is what American culture and politics require, as a matter both of principle and strategy. We must, as the pragmatists say, begin from where we are—and where most American intellectuals are is America. As one of Rorty's sharpest critics, James Livingston, says, "a radical without a country—without some attachment to a political tradition that acknowledges but also transcends ethnic and class divisions—will inevitably sound like a tourist or a terrorist." Other critics may well tell stories about America and the American left different from Rorty's, but unless they do as he has done and connect their criticism and their vision of a better future to "the historical circumstances we call the American experience, we have no good reasons to hope for that future."[104] Our hope, that is, may differ from Rorty's, and we may fund it differently and invest it elsewhere. But it must begin as American hope.

---

tions—Christianity, civic republicanism, romanticism—to lend their thinking a communitarian cast. But such syncretism is rarer in postwar liberal political theory. For a critical narrative of the triumph of "rights talk" in American political thought and legal practice, see Michael Sandel, *Democracy's Discontent: American in Search of a Public Philosophy* (Cambridge: Harvard University Press, 1996).

101. *Contingency, Irony, and Solidarity*, 63.

102. See, for example, Kloppenberg, *Virtues of Liberalism*, esp. 3–20, 155–78.

103. Robert Putnam, "Tuning In, Tuning Out: The Strange Disappearance of Social Capital in America," *PS: Political Science and Politics* 27 (1995): 665.

104. Livingston, "Narrative Politics," 202n10. A subsequent, somewhat different, version of Livingston's essay includes an appendix entitled "Memo to the Cultural Left, or, How to Be 'Critical of the System' and Crazy about the Country." See Livingston, *Pragmatism, Feminism, and Democracy*, 108–14.

CHAPTER 7

Democratic Logic

✳

CONTEMPORARY American pragmatism is not of one mind; indeed, one might well say, with John Diggins, that it has a "split personality." Few would deny that the revival of interest in pragmatism among American intellectuals—and in the work of John Dewey, in particular—has turned on the influence of Richard Rorty. Yet Rorty has attracted sharp criticism from philosophers such as Richard Bernstein, Cheryl Misak, Richard Posner, Hilary Putnam, and Richard Shusterman who think of themselves as pragmatists no less than he does.[1]

American intellectual historians of a pragmatist bent have been among Rorty's severest critics. Having labored hard to figure out what Dewey had to say, we strenuously object when Rorty tries to get him to say things he did not say and that we cannot imagine him saying. Thus, over the last several years historians such as James Kloppenberg and I have found ourselves participating with Rorty in conferences in which our role is to say to him, often repeatedly, "Gee, that argument that you say that you and Dewey make is very provocative, but Dewey never made it and I do not believe he ever would make it since it is at odds with arguments he did make." Rorty then shrugs his shoulders and acknowledges genially that the Dewey he is talking about is one of his "imaginary playmates," a "hypothetical Dewey" who says the sort of things Dewey would have said had he made the "linguistic turn"

---

1. John Patrick Diggins, *The Promise of Pragmatism: Modernism and the Crisis of Knowledge and Authority* (Chicago: University of Chicago Press, 1994), 455.

and stops saying the things he in fact did say because he had not made that turn. We then grant Rorty every right to play with whomever he wishes, asking only that he stop saying things such as "those who share Dewey's pragmatism will say that although [democracy] may need philosophical articulation, it does not need philosophical backup."[2]

But what of Rorty's neopragmatist critics? Are they any less guilty of fashioning a hypothetical Dewey to serve their purposes? Here I want to consider in greater detail than I did in the introduction Hilary Putnam's argument that he has found an "epistemological justification of democracy" in Dewey's philosophy, perhaps the strongest claim by a neopragmatist for an inherent political valence to pragmatism.[3]

On the face of it, Putnam's contention is jarring. We may be sure, I think, that Dewey never offered anything that he *called* "an epistemological justification of democracy," for "epistemology" was a dirty word in Dewey's vocabulary. He blamed what he termed the "epistemology industry" of modern philosophy since Descartes for creating all the unsolvable problems that he wanted philosophers to stop trying to solve and simply get over. But, on inspection, what Putnam is offering is principally an argument that he ties not to conventional epistemological concerns but to Dewey's theory of inquiry, that is, his "experimental" logic. His central claim, which he also attributes to Dewey, is that "democracy is not just one form of social life among other workable forms of social life; it is the precondition for the full application of intelligence to the solution of social problems." Putnam says that for him (and Dewey) democracy is a "cognitive value" insofar as it is "a requirement for experimental inquiry in any area. To reject democracy is to reject the idea of being experimental."[4]

If Dewey did indeed offer this argument, he probably would have called it a "logical argument for democracy," insofar as logic was where he lodged his constructive efforts to write about knowledge, meaning, and truth after

2. Richard Rorty, "Philosophy of the Oddball," *New Republic* (19 June 1989): 38; Richard Rorty, "Dewey between Hegel and Darwin," in Dorothy Ross, ed. *Modernist Impulses in the Human Sciences, 1870–1930* (Baltimore: Johns Hopkins University Press, 1994), 56; "The Priority of Democracy to Philosophy" (1988), in Rorty, *Objectivity, Relativism, and Truth* (Cambridge: Cambridge University Press, 1991), 178. For a good example of an intellectual historian saying to Rorty the sort of things I describe, see James T. Kloppenberg, "Democracy and Disenchantment: From Weber and Dewey to Habermas and Rorty" in Ross, *Modernist Impulses*, 188–90.

3. For Putnam's own intellectual biography, see Lance P. Hickey, "Hilary Putnam" in *Dictionary of Literary Biography: American Philosophers, 1950–2000* (Detroit: Gale, 2003), 279:226–36.

4. Hilary Putnam, "A Reconsideration of Deweyan Democracy" (1990), in Putnam, *Renewing Philosophy* (Cambridge: Harvard University Press, 1992), 180; and "Between the New Left and Judaism," in Giovanna Borradori, *The American Philosopher: Conversations with Quine, Davidson, Putnam, Nozick, Danto, Rorty, Cavell, MacIntyre, and Kuhn* (Chicago: University of Chicago Press, 1994), 64.

he himself got over the traditional problems of epistemology. Nonetheless, as far as I know, for all his efforts to link democracy and experimental inquiry Dewey never referred to a "logical argument for democracy." Putnam never directs us to Dewey's use of anything like such a phrase. Of course, the fact that Dewey never made an argument that he called a "logical argument for democracy" does not mean he did not make the argument Putnam describes. But it does leave one wondering at the outset whether we are again being invited to entertain an imaginary playmate.

One might well ask why this matters. Is not the important matter whether Putnam's argument is convincing, not whether it is also, as he says, Dewey's argument as well? Well, I think it matters a great deal, if only to intellectual historians. We intellectual historians read philosophers and other nonhistorians who write about the figures who interest us not only because we are eager to find out if and how these figures will prove useful in addressing contemporary concerns but also because we are even more eager to see whether our contemporaries will have something to say about these figures that will help us to do our job, which is to make sense of the life and work of people such as Dewey who are no longer around to interrogate directly. As Dewey said, historians go to the past with questions formulated in the context of problems that vex us in the present, and we are always on the lookout for fresh questions.

In this particular case, Putnam's notion that Dewey had a logical argument for democracy intrigues me because I believe that in my own efforts to discern, as I put it elsewhere, "the implications for democracy of every aspect of [Dewey's] thinking," I have given his logic short shrift.[5] There are, to be sure, historians who have done a better job of tying Dewey's logic to his democratic faith. Kloppenberg, for example, has said that Dewey was taking on the challenge of "constructing a democratic political culture on the quicksand of instrumentalist logic." He met this challenge, Kloppenberg suggests, by deflecting the view of Max Weber who contended that "the logic of instrumental rationality contradicts the logic of democracy" and by arguing instead that "democracy is uniquely suited to the twentieth century" precisely "because the democratic community replicates the community of broadly conceived scientific enquiry that serves as the prototype of instrumental reasoning." This is because "free and creative individuals, in democratic as in scientific communities, collectively test hypotheses to find out what works best. These communities set their own goals, determine their own tests, and evaluate their results in a spirit of constructive cooperation."[6]

I think Kloppenberg is absolutely right to say that Dewey asserted this

5. Robert B. Westbrook, *John Dewey and American Democracy* (Ithaca: Cornell University Press, 1991), x–xi.
6. Kloppenberg, "Democracy and Disenchantment," 71, 79.

analogy between democratic community and scientific communities of inquiry guided by instrumental logic. But the analogy is not self-evident (as Weber would say), and we need to know more about the *argument* Dewey offered for it. Here is where Putnam promises to help us out.

Dewey's "Argument"

Before I proceed to Putnam's argument, it should be said that there is every reason to believe that Dewey might have made a logical argument for democracy. Trying to find "philosophical backup" for democracy, which Rorty is always saying "we Deweyans" do not need to do to sustain our democratic convictions, was the sort of thing that Rorty's "bad" Dewey—the real one—did all the time. Thus Dewey believed, as he put it in 1940, that "any theory of activity in social and moral matters, liberal or otherwise, which is not grounded in a comprehensive philosophy seems to me to be only a projection of arbitrary personal preference." Nearly forty years before, he declared that "American philosophy must be born out of and must respond to the demands of democracy, as democracy strives to voice and achieve itself on a vaster scale, and in a more thorough and final way than history has previously witnessed."[7]

In an essay entitled "Philosophy and Democracy" (1918), which I have come to regard as especially pivotal to understanding Dewey's philosophical project, he outlined the crucial questions confronting a philosopher of democratic convictions:

> Is democracy a comparatively superficial human expedient, a device of petty manipulation, or does nature itself, as that is uncovered and understood by our best contemporaneous knowledge, sustain and support our democratic hopes and aspirations? Or, if we choose to begin arbitrarily at the other end, if to construct democratic institutions is our aim, how then shall we construe and interpret the natural environment and natural history of humanity in order to get an intellectual warrant for our endeavors, a reasonable persuasion that our undertaking is not contradicted by what science authorizes us to say about the structure of the world?[8]

Although in this essay Dewey evoked a democratic *metaphysics,* his search for an "intellectual warrant" for democracy might well have extended to logic as well. In the conclusions to both *Studies in Logical Theory* (1903) at the beginning of his career as a pragmatist and *Logic: The Theory of Inquiry* (1938)

---

7. John Dewey, "Nature in Experience" (1940), *Later Works,* 14:150; John Dewey, "Philosophy and American National Life" (1904), *Middle Works,* 3:74.
8. John Dewey, "Philosophy and Democracy" (1919), *Middle Works,* 11:48.

near its end, Dewey made expansive claims for the social significance of logical theory. In the latter volume, for example, he wrote:

> Failure to institute a logic based inclusively and exclusively upon the operations of inquiry has enormous cultural consequences. It encourages obscurantism; it promotes acceptance of beliefs formed before methods of inquiry had reached their present estate; and it tends to relegate scientific (that is competent) methods of inquiry to a specialized technical field. Since scientific methods simply exhibit free intelligence operating in the best manner available at a given time, the cultural waste, confusion and distortion that results from failure to use these methods, in all fields in connection with all problems, is incalculable. These considerations reinforce the claim of logical theory, as the theory of inquiry, to assume and to hold a position of primary human importance.[9]

Finally, Dewey did, on occasion, explicitly link his own logical theory and democracy. "Democracy," he remarked in 1908, "is estimable only through the changed conception of intelligence, that forms modern science."[10] But remarks such as these constituted less a logical argument for democracy than promissory notes that such an argument would be forthcoming.

I do not believe that, strictly speaking, Dewey ever delivered on these promises. That is, one cannot find in Dewey's considerable logical writings (or elsewhere) an *argument* that one could call a logical argument for democracy, which, in Dewey's case, I take to mean an argument that demonstrates that democracy is entailed by Dewey's logical theory because, as Kloppenberg says, "the democratic community replicates the community of broadly conceived scientific enquiry that serves as the prototype of instrumental reasoning." In the midst of the Great Depression, Dewey certainly articulated his hope that such a replication would take place. "Consideration of the full application of science," he declared in 1930, must be "prophetic," looking forward to "a time when all individuals may share in the discoveries and thoughts of others, to the liberation and enrichment of their own experience":

> No scientific inquirer can keep what he finds to himself or turn it to merely private account without losing his scientific standing. Everything discovered belongs to the community of workers. Every new idea and theory has to be submitted to this community for confirmation and test. There is an expanding community of cooperative effort and of truth. It is true enough that these traits are now limited to small groups having a somewhat technical activity. But the existence of such groups reveals a possibility of the present—one of the

9. John Dewey, *Logic: The Theory of Inquiry* (1938), *Later Works*, 12:527.
10. John Dewey, "Intelligence and Morals" (1908), *Middle Works*, 4:39.

many possibilities that are a challenge to expansion, and not a ground for retreat and contraction.[11]

Given this clear formulation of the analogy between the scientific community and the democratic community, it is perhaps particularly noteworthy
that Dewey did not reintroduce and argue for it eight years later in the chapter on "Social Inquiry" in his *Logic*.

So when Putnam says "one can find" an "epistemological argument for
democracy" in Dewey's work, what he means is that one can piece together
such an argument, an argument for which Dewey provided the elements but
which he never put together himself. Putnam is thus not making an argument, like many of Rorty's, that he knows Dewey would not have made, but
he is making an argument that Dewey did not make. Yet Putnam is in effect
saying that Dewey could have made this argument.[12]

Putnam's Argument

Putnam's account of Dewey's logical argument has three elements, each
of which builds on that preceding it in the course of the argument. First,
Dewey, following Peirce, held that the best way that human beings had
found to fix beliefs—or, as Dewey preferred to call them, "warranted assertions"—was by means of the methods, practices, and values of a community
of competent inquirers, the best exemplification of which was the community of modern science. Such communities began their investigations under
the stimulus of particular doubts within the context of a body of warranted
assertions that they had no good reason to doubt, and they settled such particular doubts with warranted assertions that, like all warranted assertions,
were not certain but fallible and subject to revision should fresh doubts
about their warrant arise. Putnam says the recognition that "one can be both
fallibilistic *and* antiskeptical is perhaps *the* unique insight of American pragmatism."[13] Dewey's logic was an inquiry into inquiry, that is, an examination
of the methods, practices, and values of communities of inquiry that had
best served to generate warranted assertions.

Second, Dewey extended the range of inquiry to include judgments of
practice and moral judgments. This move is of particular significance for

11. John Dewey, *Individualism Old and New* (1930), *Later Works*, 5:115.
12. I think this poses an important yet neglected issue for intellectual historians. Too often
in summarizing the work of our subjects we fail to distinguish between arguments they did in
fact make and arguments that we have cobbled together from disparate sources that they could
conceivably have made.
13. Hilary Putnam, "Pragmatism and Moral Objectivity" (1991), in Putnam, *Words and Life*
(Cambridge: Harvard University Press, 1994), 152.

the argument, since it is the application of inquiry to value-laden "problematic situations" that makes inquiry available for the sort of issues most likely to confront social and political communities. As Putnam says, Dewey believed that "we have learned something about how to conduct inquiry in general, and that what applies to intelligently conducted inquiry in general applies to ethical inquiry in particular."[14]

Finally, Dewey argued that a community of inquiry should be democratic, not (in this case) on ethical grounds, but on what Putnam terms "cognitive" grounds. That is, the quality of inquiry is affected by the degree to which that community is inclusive or exclusive of all the potential, competent participants in that inquiry and by the democratic or undemocratic character of the norms that guide its practice. Here, Putnam draws on Dewey's argument in *The Public and Its Problems* (1927) against resting content with elite inquiry into social problems and for including the wider public in the making of public policy. Dewey argued that without the participation of the public in the formulation of such policy, it could not reflect the common needs and interests of the society because these needs and interests were known only to the public. And these needs and interests could not be made known without democratic "consultation and discussion which uncover social needs and troubles." Hence, Dewey said, "A class of experts is inevitably so removed from common interests as to become a class with private interests and private knowledge, which in social matters is not knowledge at all."[15] Elite rule was thus cognitively debilitating.

Effective inquiry required not only that the community of inquiry be inclusive but also that its practices be democratic. For Dewey, Putnam says, "the need for fundamental democratic institutions as freedom of thought and speech follows . . . from requirements of scientific procedure in general: the unimpeded flow of information and the freedom to offer and to criticize hypotheses."[16] Successful inquiry in all fields, including science, rested in part on a democratic "discourse ethics" that shaped the cooperation of the community of inquirers. As Putnam puts it:

> Where there is no opportunity to challenge accepted hypotheses by criticizing the evidence upon which their acceptance was based, or by criticizing the application of the norms of scientific inquiry to that evidence, or by offering rival hypotheses, and where questions and suggestions are systematically ignored, the scientific enterprise always suffers. When relations among scientists become relations of hierarchy and dependence, or when scientists instrumentalize other scientists, again the scientific enterprise suffers.[17]

14. Putnam, "Reconsideration of Deweyan Democracy," 186.
15. Ibid., 188–89; John Dewey, *The Public and Its Problems* (1927), *Later Works*, 2:365.
16. Putnam, "Reconsideration of Deweyan Democracy," 188.
17. Putnam, "Pragmatism and Moral Objectivity," 172.

Dewey well recognized that the democratic values embedded in inquiry were a "regulative ideal," and he was not blind to the corruptions that afflicted inquiry, even in science. Moreover, unlike Peirce, he was eager to stress the affinities rather than the differences between science and everyday knowing. This continuity cut both ways. Dewey took science off the apolitical pedestal on which Peirce tried to place it, recognizing in proto-Kuhnian fashion that scientific inquiry had its own necessary politics of which tenacity, arguments from authority, and consensual taste were an inextricable part. At the same time, he saw scientific inquiry as providing a much fuller reign to the democratic politics of knowledge evident, but all too often suppressed, in ordinary knowing. Dewey saw scientific communities as a model, not because they were or even could be perfectly democratic, but because in them democratic norms of inquiry more than held their own. And without such democratic norms, he held, inquiry was grievously injured.

Assessing the Argument

I think Putnam has indeed "found" a logical argument for democracy in Dewey's work and structured it in a fashion that I can well imagine Dewey emulating. It should be said, however, that not all of the elements of this argument were well-developed by Dewey. The most elaborated aspect of the argument was the second, the claim that one could, as he put it in the title of an early and damnably obscure article, elaborate the "logical conditions of a scientific treatment of morality." This is one of Dewey's best known, and most controversial, claims, and he worked it out in many of his logical writings over the course of his career. It is also the part of the argument to which Putnam devotes most of his attention, not only by way of sympathetically considering Dewey's efforts to develop a logic for moral inquiry but also by contributing arguments of his own to the cause.

Putnam's attentiveness to the second stage in his reconstruction of Dewey's logical argument for democracy is not surprising, for it is here that we begin to feel underfoot what Kloppenberg nicely terms "the quicksand of instrumentalist logic." As Putnam says, Dewey made two claims that leave many readers unsure that he is on solid ground. First, he complained (repeatedly) that many of the ills of modern society derive from a failure to bring scientific reasoning to bear on ethical problems. Although we are perfectly willing to allow such reasoning to enter into our consideration of the means to our valued ends, we refuse to apply it to an evaluation of those ends themselves. Dewey tells us, Putnam observes, that we have "to see every problem as an invitation to inquiry, to understand all inquiry as of one pattern, and to abandon the demands for ends that are beyond all evaluation." But having told us that scientific inquiry can do something that many do not believe it can do, Dewey then goes on to ratify our conception of scientific rationality as "an affair of the relations of means and consequences."[18] In other words, having got our hopes up that science could do something we did not think it could do, which we presumed meant that Dewey was going to offer us a new conception of scientific reasoning, he confirms our view of scientific reasoning and seems simply to be saying that we have decidedly underestimated what it—that is, instrumental reasoning—can do. Not surprisingly, many have remained skeptical of this claim.

As Putnam says, Dewey's argument essentially took the form of showing how moral judgments, like all judgments, are made in the context of particular problematic situations. In such situations our ends are transformed into what Dewey called ends-in-view. As such, they take shape as means to the resolution of the particular problem at hand. And as such, they are subject to inquiry, for we are now asking the question "Will this end-in-view solve this problem?" Dewey is trying to show us, as Putnam says, that "ends are neither laid up in a Platonic heaven nor the whims of individuals; they are, rather, ends-in-view, they guide conduct; in that capacity they are themselves means to solving a problem and as such rationality is competent to pronounce judgment on them."[19]

If one is willing to go this far with Dewey, a nagging question remains, that is, what *criteria* do we use to evaluate the success of our ends-in-view? When do we know that an evaluative problem has been successfully resolved? Here Putnam says several things that he says Dewey says, but that I myself believe Dewey did not say as clearly as Putnam does—and often left all too implicit. First, in the spirit of Peirce's critique of wholesale doubt, Putnam observes that communities of moral inquiry do not start from the position of doubting all of their values and prior evaluations. As he says,

> As long as discussion is still possible, as long as one is not facing coercion or violence or total refusal to discuss, the participants in an actual discussion always share a large number of both factual assumptions and value assumptions that are not in question in the specific dispute. Very often, parties to a disagreement can agree that the disagreement has, in fact, been resolved, not by appeal to a universal set of 'criteria' but by appeal to values which are not in question in *that* dispute.[20]

Putnam acknowledges that a persistent critic might still claim that "there is no reason to think that people who follow Dewey's method will come to

18. Hilary Putnam, with Ruth Anna Putnam, "Dewey's *Logic:* Epistemology as Hypothesis" (1990), in Putnam, *Words and Life,* 199–200.
19. Putnam, "Dewey's *Logic,*" 200.
20. Putnam, "Pragmatism and Moral Objectivity," 175–76.

agreement on values, even if each person separately leads what we might regard as a rational life." Dewey, Putnam says, responds that he is not in the business of making a priori claims one way or the other. As an antiskeptical fallibilist, he claims only that we should not presume that no such agreement is possible in advance of inquiry. There is no good reason to believe that moral inquiry "must lead to *unresolvable* problems, even if there is no *a priori* guarantee that the problems it leads to are resolvable."[21]

Putnam's Dewey would also have us be aware that the resolution of a moral problem need not be agreement on values:

> If you and I disagree in our 'values' a resolution need not take the form of a universalistic principle that you and I and all other persons can accept as valid. If the value disagreement concerns only our separate lives, then the apparent disagreement may be resolvable by simply relativizing the judgments in question; it may be the case that it is well for you to live your life in one way and for me to live mine in another. . . . The idea of ethical objectivity is not the same as and does not presuppose the idea of *a universal way of life*. Dewey supports the former and consistently opposes the latter. Not only individuals but also communities and nations may have different but satisfactory ways of life.[22]

Finally, Putnam says Dewey would readily admit that there are problems that moral inquiry cannot solve. "Believing that ethical objectivity is possible is not the same thing as believing that there are no undecidable cases or no problems which, alas, cannot be solved."[23] This possibility of unresolvable problems does not distinguish moral inquiry from other inquiry: "not all problems in physics or mathematics or geology or history can be settled either, but that does not support the idea that warranted assertibility and truth exist in one domain but not in another."[24]

When it comes to the resolution of moral problems through inquiry, Putnam admits that "Dewey can sound unreasonably optimistic if one does not keep in mind the range of different things that can count as the resolution of a problem."[25] My own view is that it is less Dewey than Putnam who brings this "range of resolution" to light.

One reason I think Putnam's version of Dewey's conception of moral inquiry is more satisfying than Dewey's own is that Putnam is more attentive than Dewey to its intersubjective context. Perhaps surprisingly, Dewey had much less to say about the communitarian context of inquiry generally—the first stage of the logical argument for democracy—than one might

21. Putnam, "Dewey's *Logic*," 214.
22. Ibid., 214–15.
23. Putnam, "Pragmatism and Moral Objectivity," 176.
24. Putnam, "Dewey's *Logic*," 215.
25. Ibid., 214.

think. Although Dewey endorsed Peirce's conception of the community of inquiry in his *Logic,* it was not until the 1930s that he really made much use of Peirce. And in his earlier work, he treated inquiry largely from the point of view of the individual and did not really say much about what difference the communitarian context of scientific investigation made to its practices.[26] This neglect of the social context of inquiry points, I think, to a curious feature of Dewey's philosophy generally, which I am hard-pressed to explain. Although he was always insisting on the primacy of the social, Dewey really did not have a whole lot to say that could in any strict sense be termed social theory. For example, although he claimed that psychology had to be a social psychology, he did not give us much social psychology, even in *Human Nature and Conduct* (1922), which was subtitled *An Introduction to Social Psychology.* For a well-developed, pragmatist social psychology, one has to turn to his friend, George Herbert Mead.

As I say, I think the neglect of social context in moral inquiry is a particularly noteworthy (and troubling) feature of Dewey's logical argument for democracy. Putnam is much too generous when he says that Dewey dealt capably with the problem of "moral disagreement."[27] As Kloppenberg and I have both observed, Dewey had too little to say even about intractable moral conflicts within individuals. Although he acknowledged that often the most an agent could do in any moral conflict was to "make the best adjustment he can among forces which are genuinely disparate," he was forever implying that such forces could be "unified" without ever, as William James put it, "butchering the ideal."[28]

About moral disagreements between individuals, Dewey had even less to say. He argued that in the final analysis moral decisions were shaped by character, by the sort of person one was or desired to be. But significant moral disagreements within a community of inquiry might well involve conflicts between individuals with quite different conceptions of the good life. Putnam to the contrary, Dewey does not seem to me to have ever addressed this problem head on. Putnam is giving Dewey too much credit when he says, in a Rawlsian or Habermasian vein, that Dewey

> anticipated an idea that has become a commonplace in contemporary moral
> philosophy, the idea that disagreement in individual conceptions of the good

26. The most notable exception, I would say, is a long, illuminating, and relatively neglected essay on "The Problem of Truth" (1911), *Middle Works,* 6:12–79.

27. Putnam, "Pragmatism and Moral Objectivity," 155.

28. John Dewey, "Three Independent Factors in Morals" (1930), *Later Works,* 5:288. See James T. Kloppenberg, *Uncertain Victory: Social Democracy and Progressivism in European and American Thought, 1870–1920* (New York: Oxford, 1986), 132–44; and Westbrook, *John Dewey and American Democracy,* 163, 416–17. Putnam is himself alert to this weakness of Dewey's ethics. See the comparison with James in Putnam, "Reconsideration of Deweyan Democracy," 190–99.

need not make it impossible to approximate (even if we never finally arrive at) agreement on just procedures and even agreement on such abstract and formal values as respect for one another's autonomy, non-instrumentalization of other persons, and such regulative ideas as the idea that in all our institutions we should strive to replace relations of hierarchy and dependence by relations of "symmetric reciprocity."[29]

Or, to put it another way, it is very difficult to discern a "theory of justice" for a pluralistic society in Dewey's logic of moral inquiry.

By far the sketchiest part of the logical argument for democracy in Dewey's work is its contention that communities of inquiry must be democratic if inquiry was to be effective. But here Putnam's recapitulation of the argument is so brief as to leave out an important consideration that Dewey did address forthrightly in contending that the community of inquiry engaged in the making of public policy should be inclusively democratic. That is, one might contend that because participation in communities of inquiry is limited to the *competent,* and since most members of the public are not competent, there is no need to include them and, indeed, including them would damage rather than enhance the relevant inquiries.

Dewey did not dispute the provision that inquiry should be left in the hands of the competent; it was an essential provision of the regulative ideal of inquiry that he shared with Peirce. But he contested the claim that most members of the public were not capable of competent participation in the inquiry necessary for the making of public policy. Most of the inquiries tributary to making public policy were, he agreed, best left to experts. One did not want a garage mechanic making economic predictions, any more than one wanted an economist working on one's car. But when it came to judging "the bearing of the knowledge supplied by others upon common concerns," he believed that most people possessed this capacity, and he charged that advocates of the rule of experts greatly exaggerated the intelligence and ability it took to render these kinds of judgments.[30]

This is not to say that Dewey did not believe that the quality of public opinion could be improved. Indeed, for this purpose, he advocated a kind of public education that would reconstruct a common schooling for American children to provide them with the skills and knowledge necessary to effective citizenship. He envisioned schools that would "cultivate the habit of suspended judgment, of skepticism, of desire for evidence, of appeal to observation rather than sentiment, discussion rather than bias, inquiry rather than conventional idealizations."[31] Dewey also called for the revital-

29. Putnam, "Pragmatism and Moral Objectivity," 155.
30. Dewey, *Public and Its Problems* (1927), *Later Works,* 2:364.
31. John Dewey, "Education as Politics" (1922), *Middle Works,* 13:334.

ization of local "publics" in which adults could also learn by doing. The education that participating in such local, face-to-face publics provided would, he predicted, "render nugatory the indictment of democracy drawn on the basis of the ignorance, bias and levity of the masses."[32] In sum, as Putnam concludes, Dewey's logical argument for democracy was a logical argument for a radical democracy, one "which develops the capacities of all its men and women to think for themselves, to participate in the design and testing of social policies, and to judge results."[33]

Deliberative Democracy

Perhaps the best way to fit the logical argument for democracy that Putnam reconstructs within the larger context of Dewey's democratic thought is to see it as the elements of an argument for *procedural* democracy. Dewey was often impatient with procedural arguments for democracy, believing that too often they *reduced* democracy to its procedures and slighted its wider meaning as a "way of life." But democracy is, among other things, a set of procedures, and in the elements of the logical argument Putnam pieces together, Dewey was, I think, reaching for a normative ideal for procedural democracy rooted in an expansive conception of the community of inquiry.

Seen in this light, I think we might say that Dewey was anticipating an ideal that contemporary democratic theorists have dubbed "deliberative democracy." The flavor of what deliberative democracy means can be conveyed by its features as stipulated by political theorist Joshua Cohen. A deliberative democracy, Cohen says, is an ongoing, independent association whose members share "a commitment to co-ordinating their activities within institutions that make deliberation possible and according to norms that they arrive at through their deliberation." It is a pluralistic association in which members "have diverse preferences, convictions and ideals concerning the conduct of their own lives." The members also "recognize one another as having deliberative capacities, i.e. the capacities required for entering into a public exchange of reasons and for acting on the result of such public reasoning." In a deliberative democracy, deliberation will ideally be free and reasoned and will take place among parties who are formally and substantively equal. Deliberation aims, Cohen says, at a "rationally motivated *consensus*"—though there is no guarantee that such a consensus will emerge.[34]

32. Dewey, *Public and Its Problems*, 371.
33. Putnam, "Reconsideration of Deweyan Democracy," 199.
34. Joshua Cohen, "Deliberation and Democratic Legitimacy," in Alan Hamlin and Philip Pettit, eds., *The Good Polity: Normative Analysis of the State* (London: Blackwell, 1989), 21–23. The literature of deliberative democratic theory is enormous and ever-growing. Perhaps the most

The family resemblances between Dewey's conception of democracy as a community of inquiry and this conception of deliberative democracy are perhaps obvious. To use Dewey's language, one might say that a deliberative democracy is an association in which individual members seek by means of deliberation to transform their individual "desires" into a collective consensus about what is "desirable." Thus, though Dewey does not, as I have said, have as fully elaborated a logical argument for democracy as one might hope, his logic—and Putnam's—might still prove of greater interest to theorists of deliberative democracy than it thus far has.[35]

Dissin' Deliberation

But a logical argument for deliberative democracy is not necessarily a convincing logical argument for deliberative democracy, and the train of logic in Putnam's Deweyan argument is vulnerable to criticism at each of the three steps of contention that guide its progress. One must begin with a pragmatist conception of truth as the work of communities of inquiry; then one must contend that political and moral questions are "truth-apt"; and finally one must demonstrate that democratic communities of inquiry are epistemically superior to nondemocratic ones.

Even pragmatists cannot be presumed to consent to this train of logic. Rorty, who wants a "pragmatism without method" and has done his best to read Peirce out of the pragmatist canon, gets off the boat before it sets sail by trying to dispense with the classical pragmatists' conception of truth.[36]

---

widely discussed version of the theory is that offered in Amy Gutmann and Dennis Thompson, *Democracy and Disagreement* (Cambridge: Harvard University Press, 1996). See also the volume of critical essays on this book, Stephen Macedo, ed., *Deliberative Politics: Essays on "Democracy and Disagreement"* (New York: Oxford University Press, 1999). Two other important and influential collections are James Bohman and William Rehg, eds., *Deliberative Democracy: Essays on Reason and Politics* (Cambridge: MIT Press, 1997), and Jon Elster, ed., *Deliberative Democracy* (Cambridge: Cambridge University Press, 1998). A useful guide to much of this literature is James Bohman, "The Coming of Age of Deliberative Democracy," *Journal of Political Philosophy* 6 (1998): 400–425.

35. Pragmatist contributions to the literature of deliberative democracy have been modest. The leading figures here are James Johnson and Jack Knight. See their "Aggregation and Deliberation: On the Possibility of Democratic Legitimacy," *Political Theory* 22 (1994): 277–96; "Political Consequences of Pragmatism," *Political Theory* 24 (1996): 68–96; "What Sort of Equality Does Deliberative Democracy Require?" in Bohman and Rehg, *Deliberative Democracy*, 279–319; "Inquiry into Democracy: What Might a Pragmatist Make of Rational Choice Theories?," *American Journal of Political Science* 43 (1999): 566–89; and Johnson, "Arguing for Deliberation: Some Skeptical Considerations," in Elster, *Deliberative Democracy*, 161–84. See also Eric MacGilvray, "Experience as Experiment: Some Consequences of Pragmatism for Democratic Theory," *American Journal of Political Science* 43 (1999): 542–65.

36. Richard Rorty, "Pragmatism without Method" (1983), in Rorty, *Objectivity, Relativism, and Truth*, 63–77.

As we have seen, Peirce himself did not think inquiry could be extended to matters of moral judgment and, hence, departs at the second stop. And Walter Lippmann, who thought in the 1920s that public policy could and should be submitted to expert communities of inquiry, called for excluding the public from that inquiry on the grounds of its incompetence, thereby denying the epistemic superiority of democracy. But no pragmatist has worked harder to break the link between pragmatism and deliberative democracy than Richard Posner.

Posner is the closest thing among American neopragmatists to a "philosopher king."[37] The most distinguished of contemporary "legal pragmatists," he has not only had an academic career at the University of Chicago and published an impressive array of books on legal theory, law and economics, law and literature, sex and the law, and moral philosophy, but he has done so while serving as a federal judge on the United States Court of Appeals for the Seventh Circuit.[38] Among the many debates in which Posner has been an important voice is that over the political implications of pragmatism.

What makes Posner a particularly intriguing participant in this debate is that, like Rorty, he claims that pragmatism has "no political valence," yet unlike Rorty, he is drawn to pragmatism by its commitment to methods of inquiry modeled on modern science ("in an important sense," Posner has said, "pragmatism is the ethics of scientific inquiry").[39] Since it is this commitment from which other pragmatists—classical pragmatists such as Dewey and neopragmatists such as Putnam—have derived a "political valence" for pragmatism, either Posner is wrong about the political implications of this commitment or the other pragmatists who have argued that it brings a lot of democratic baggage with it are mistaken.

37. "Antiphilosopher" king would perhaps be better, given Posner's insistence that judges and other political elites need not bother to know much philosophy.

38. Two recent profiles of Posner are James Ryerson, "The Outrageous Pragmatism of Judge Richard Posner," *Lingua Franca* (May/June 2000): 26–34, and Larissa MacFarquhar, "The Bench Burner," *New Yorker* (10 December 2001): 78–89. Posner's books include *Economic Analysis of Law* (Boston: Little Brown, 1972); *The Economics of Justice* (Cambridge: Harvard University Press, 1981); *Law and Literature: A Misunderstood Relation* (Cambridge: Harvard University Press, 1988); *The Problems of Jurisprudence* (Cambridge: Harvard University Press, 1991); *Sex and Reason* (Cambridge: Harvard University Press, 1992); *Overcoming Law* (Cambridge: Harvard University Press, 1995); *The Problematics of Moral and Legal Theory* (Cambridge: Harvard University Press, 1999); *An Affair of State: The Investigation, Impeachment, and Trial of President Bill Clinton* (Cambridge: Harvard University Press, 1999); *Public Intellectuals* (Cambridge: Harvard University Press, 2001); and *Breaking the Deadlock: The 2000 Election, the Constitution and the Courts* (Princeton: Princeton University Press, 2001). Among other things, Posner is a leading expert on antitrust law, and he attempted (unsuccessfully) to mediate the extraordinarily significant antitrust case against computer software giant Microsoft. See Ken Auletta, "Final Offer," *New Yorker* (15 January 2001): 40–46.

39. Posner, "What Has Pragmatism to Offer Law?" in Michael Brint and William Weaver, eds., *Pragmatism in Law and Society* (Boulder: Westview Press, 1991), 34; Posner, *Problems of Jurisprudence*, 465. No legal scholar has insisted more vigorously than Posner on the value of social science, especially economics, to legal practice.

Posner initially argued strenuously that the latter is the case. This determination is not surprising. Posner is perhaps the most conservative of neo-pragmatists, an intellectual of the libertarian right, and he has gone to some pains to deny any left-leaning tropism to pragmatism.[40] He claims that "not only has pragmatism no inherent political valence, but those pragmatists who attack pieties of the right while exhibiting a wholly uncritical devotion to the pieties of the left (such as racial and sexual equality, the desirability of a more equal distribution of income and wealth, and the pervasiveness of oppression and injustice in Western society) are not genuine pragmatists; they are dogmatists in pragmatists' clothing."[41]

Posner thus endorses in toto William James's claim that pragmatism is a strictly methodological doctrine. As James said, it "stands for no particular results." Like a hallway, "innumerable chambers open out of it."[42] In an early formulation of his pragmatism, Posner contended that the pragmatic method has three essential elements: a rejection of absolute certainties in epistemology, ethics, and politics; consequentialism—"the insistence that propositions be tested by their consequences"; and "an insistence on judging our projects, whether scientific, ethical, political, or legal, by their conformity to social or other human needs rather than to 'objective,' 'impersonal' criteria."[43]

It is this last element of Posner's pragmatism, his left-wing critics among pragmatists have argued, that is, whatever he may say, particularly democratic in its implications.[44] How, they ask, is a judge (or anyone else) to determine the social and human needs that are to serve as the criteria against which to measure our projects? Here Posner in good pragmatist fashion contends that we have no certain and indubitable conception of these needs to which to appeal. Instead, he argues for a "weak" objectivity grounded in social consensus about these needs and the best means to serve them.[45] But how, then, to judge the legitimacy of such a consensus? Clearly a consensus

40. And it is important to distinguish Posner's libertarianism—the nineteenth-century liberalism of John Stuart Mill that has come to form (at the cost of considerable confusion) a branch of contemporary American conservatism—from the often authoritarian moralism of traditionalist conservatives such as Posner's onetime colleague on the federal bench, Robert Bork. Bork and other such conservatives usually regard pragmatism as a species of relativism posing no less a threat to the moral fabric of society than other varieties of antifoundationalist philosophy. See Bork, *Slouching Toward Gomorrah* (New York: HarperCollins, 1996). For an example of Posner's distance from this sort of conservatism, see Posner, "The Moral Minority," *New York Times Book Review* (19 December 1999): 14.

41. Posner, "What Has Pragmatism to Offer Law?" 34.

42. William James, *Pragmatism* (1907; Cambridge: Harvard University Press, 1975), 32.

43. Posner, "What Has Pragmatism to Offer Law?," 35–36.

44. Here I follow the argument in Knight and Johnson, "Political Consequences of Pragmatism."

45. And in the absence of such a consensus, particularly in the face of widespread and divisive conflict, he urges judges to proceed as cautiously as possible.

that is the product of the power of some to impose their will on others lacks legitimacy as grounds for judging law or policy. Posner's argument would seem to require some strictures on the formation of a consensus that would lend legitimacy to it as a criterion of judgment.

Appropriately for a pragmatist, Posner's strictures are methodological; the legitimacy of a consensus rests not on its substance but on the procedures by which it has developed. The closer the formation of a consensus approximates the practices of free inquiry, the more legitimate (and "weakly objective") that consensus is, since "pragmatists believe that truth is what free inquiry—unforced, undistorted, and uninterrupted—would eventually discover about the objects of inquiry."[46]

But Posner's pragmatist critics have asked that he take this commitment to unforced, undistorted, and uninterrupted inquiry fully to heart and recognize its democratic implications. As two such critics put it, "Unforced inquiry entails reasoned deliberation. If we are to avoid 'premature closure,' however, it also seemingly entails free and equal access for relevant actors to all relevant arenas of deliberation, debate, and decision." Posner has been reluctant to accept this conclusion, for it seems to open the door to a pragmatist argument for the "pieties of the left" he has scorned. And he is correct about this. As his critics say, a pragmatist conception of reasoned political deliberation "demands that the pragmatist challenge social and economic barriers that distort or subvert the sort of unforced inquiry that reasoned deliberation requires"—such as racial, sexual, and class inequalities. Pragmatism has decidedly egalitarian implications, and Posner hazards contradiction in resisting them.[47]

But resist them he has. In *Law, Pragmatism, and Democracy* (2003), Posner offers his most extended effort yet to disentangle pragmatism from its apparent tropism for egalitarian, deliberative democracy and (implicitly) to answer his critics. Reiterating his commitment to free inquiry and other elements of philosophical pragmatism (Darwinism, fallibilism, and emphasis on the consequences of belief), he now contends that this philosophical commitment is irrelevant to the formulation of ideals for democratic politics, not because philosophical pragmatism does not have a political valence but because this valence is an unhappily utopian one.

Posner, in short, now admits that a conception of democratic politics as

46. Posner, *Problems of Jurisprudence*, 114–15.

47. Knight and Johnson, "Consequences of Pragmatism," 87, 89. For the sort of robustly egalitarian conclusions that the marriage of pragmatism and political theory invites, see Elizabeth Anderson, "What Is the Point of Equality?" *Ethics* 109 (1999): 287–337; and Knight and Johnson, "What Sort of Political Equality Does Deliberative Democracy Require?" In hazarding a contradiction between his epistemology and the politics for which it has an elective affinity, Posner is not alone and joins a host of first-rate thinkers. For some other prominent examples, see Ellen M. Wood, *Mind and Politics* (Berkeley: University of California Press, 1972).

unforced inquiry does point to the sort of deliberative democracy that Dewey, Putnam, and other pragmatist radicals advocate. Deliberative democracy "adapts Dewey's notion of epistemic democracy to the political realm" and is "epistemically the most robust form of democracy":

> Dewey's philosophical project of overturning Platonic epistemology provides support for making democracy the default rule of political governance in the same way that Platonic epistemology provides support for the authoritarian political system described in the *Republic*. In short, Dewey turned Plato on his head by accepting the linkage between knowledge and politics but arguing that knowledge is democratic and so should politics be.[48]

Posner finds Dewey's argument for the epistemic superiority of democratic inquiry convincing, and indeed he argues for its limited relevance for judicial decision-making and other elite communities of inquiry. It is the argument that therefore democratic politics—the politics of ordinary citizens—can be, need be, or should be epistemically robust that he attacks. That is, he accepts the justification for epistemic democracy, but denies that it carries as a consequence a convincing epistemological argument for deliberative political democracy. Democratic politics has little to do with unforced inquiry, he asserts. Dewey and other radical pragmatists misconceive politics as, in important respects, a quest for truth—"the pooling of different ideas and approaches and the selection of the best through debate and discussion"—but it is not in any important respect a quest for truth, nor could it be or should it be. "The problem with the suggested linkage between epistemic and political democracy, the problem that gave rise to Dewey's pessimism about our actual existing democracy, is that deliberative democracy, at least as conceived of by Dewey, is as purely aspirational and unrealistic as rule by Platonic guardians" (107). In other words, philosophical pragmatism does have a tropism for deliberative democracy, but so much the worse for philosophical pragmatism since "the bridge [Dewey] tried to build between epistemic and political democracy is too flimsy to carry heavy traffic" (113).

Philosophically, the flimsiness of the bridge, as Posner sees it, lies principally in the second element of Dewey and Putnam's epistemological argument, the claim that moral and political inquiry is truth-apt. Deliberative democracy, he rightly says, centers on "reasoning about ends," and he questions "the very possibility of such reasoning." Moral and political debates, he believes, are "indeterminate and interminable" (132–33). Hence, politics is not a matter of providing a venue for such debates, but simply the pur-

---

48. Richard Posner, *Law, Pragmatism, and Democracy* (Cambridge: Harvard University Press, 2003), 11, 17. Subsequent page citations to this book are in the text.

suit of power to protect and advance "existing, unreflective, presumably selfish preferences" (133). Since moral argument, let alone political dispute, is not truth-apt, epistemic arguments have no purchase in these realms of experience.[49]

Hence, Posner distinguishes between philosophical pragmatists such as Dewey who insist on building a bridge between epistemic and political democracy and "everyday pragmatists" such as himself who dynamite any attempt to do so. Everyday pragmatists, he happily admits, are the sort of "unedifying," even vulgar, pragmatists who are "practical and business-like, 'no nonsense,' disdainful of abstract theory and intellectual pretension, contemptuous of moralizers and utopian dreamers" (50). His pragmatism "has no moral compass," certainly not one with an epistemic needle. Despite his own regard for some elements of philosophical pragmatism, if the price of such regard is, as it apparently is for many, an affinity for deliberative democracy, Posner would just as soon join another club (55).[50]

Everyday pragmatists like himself may be democrats, Posner says, but not of the deliberative sort. More interested in what is "pragmatic" in the sense of realistic and "workable" in current circumstances than in what is true to philosophical pragmatism and conceivable in an imagined future, they see democracy in unabashedly frank terms as a kind of constrained aristocratic rule. For them, "democracy is conceived of as a method by which members of a self-interested political elite compete for the votes of a basically ignorant and apathetic, as well as determinedly self-interested electorate" (16), or as he more colorfully puts it:

> There is in every society a class of (mostly) men who are far above average in ambition, courage, energy, toughness, personal magnetism, and intelligence (or cunning). In other words, society is composed of wolves and sheep. The wolves are the natural leaders. They rise to the top in every society. The challenge to politics is to provide routes to the top that deflect the wolves from resorting to violence, usurpation, conquest, and oppression to obtain their place in the sun. . . . Democratic politics, by giving these natural leaders a competitive arena in which to strive for political power and attain it in a chastened, socially unthreatening, in fact socially responsible, form, performs an indispensable social function unacknowledged in the conventional pieties of democratic discourse. (183–84)

49. Posner develops this skeptical attack on moral reasoning most fully in *Problematics of Moral and Legal Theory*, esp. 3–90.

50. Though he is obviously averse to ceding "pragmatism" entirely to the Deweyans he opposes. At one point, Posner says that to say that pragmatists have an affinity for deliberative democracy is the same thing as saying that because Charles Lindbergh was both a first-rate pilot and an isolationist, therefore "there is something in flying a plane well that makes a person an isolationist" (47). This curiously bizarre analogy is belied by his own clear and convincing account of exactly what it is in philosophical pragmatists' epistemology that draws them to deliberative democracy.

Perhaps the most misleading of these conventional pieties (fully embraced by deliberative democrats such as Dewey) is that democracy is "self-government" rather than a measure of control of the governing wolves by the governed sheep (164).

Posner's notion of "realistic" democracy is heavily indebted to Joseph Schumpeter, who, despite an occasional lapse into Nazi sympathies, articulated the essentials of the most sensible democratic theory for "everyday pragmatists" in his *Capitalism, Socialism, and Democracy* (1942). Neither Schumpeter's role as a founder of the conservative thrust of postwar "democratic elitism" nor his decidedly inegalitarian, un-Deweyan political theory bothers Posner in the least, quite the contrary. Nor is he perturbed by the virtual eclipse of any distance between the norms of Schumpeterian theory and the actually existing character of American politics. Indeed, Posner calls upon "everyday pragmatists" to rise to the defense of American politics as it is, and dispense with ideals at odds with this politics that only serve to engender pessimism and alienation.[51]

Despite his disavowal of any "moral compass," Posner is guided by an overriding conviction of the virtues of political and social stability; expansive, if not unconstrained, elite power; and the protection of property rights. He easily acknowledges the many undemocratic features of the U.S. Constitution, but says we should be grateful that ours is a "mixed republic" in which aristocratic and democratic institutions hold one another in check. Contemptuous of the intelligence of ordinary people, he is alarmed at the prospect of investing significant power in their hands and grateful that it is unlikely. He argues imaginatively both against the impeachment of Bill Clinton and for the hotly disputed outcome of the 2000 presidential election (in which he apparently did not bother to vote) on grounds of stability (213–26, 317–56).[52] Alert to the charge of complacency, he nonetheless courts it with impunity.

A Better Bridge

From where a conservative, "everyday pragmatist" such as Posner sits, philosophical pragmatist arguments for deliberative democracy are the worst sort of utopianism, "a pipe dream hardly worth the attention of a serious person" (163). This is a charge that pragmatists must take seriously,

---

51. On Schumpeter's role in postwar democratic theory, see David M. Ricci, "Democracy Attenuated: Schumpeter, the Process Theory, and American Democratic Thought," *Journal of Politics* 32 (1970): 239–67.

52. Posner has offered a fuller treatment of the Clinton impeachment in *Affairs of State* and of the 2000 election debacle in *Breaking the Deadlock*.

for it is not only "everyday pragmatists" that set themselves firmly against pipe dreams. As Dewey himself said, "Not all who say *Ideals, Ideals* shall enter the kingdom of the ideal, but only those shall enter who know and respect the roads that conduct to the kingdom."[53]

Is the bridge Dewey attempted to build on the road between deliberative epistemic democracy and deliberative political democracy as philosophically and practically flimsy as Posner suggests? Is a truth-apt politics not only difficult to establish, but inconceivable, as he asserts in his claims for the futility of "reasoning about ends"? Does the apparent intractability of many moral and political disagreements pose intractable obstacles for deliberative democracy? Must we rest content with a democratic politics that merely aggregates existing preferences, requires little deliberation, and serves principally to keep the wolves at bay?

I have already suggested that Putnam builds a better bridge between epistemic democracy and political democracy than Dewey did, one which is responsive to skepticism such as Posner's about "reasoning about ends" (though Posner has little to say about Putnam). And another neopragmatist, Cheryl Misak, as I have said, builds better still in this regard, offering an extended version of Putnam's argument that stands as the best epistemological justification for democracy offered by a pragmatist.[54]

As we have seen, Misak's neo-Peircean pragmatism rests on what she nicely terms a "low-profile" (deflationary, anticorrespondence) conception of truth nested firmly in human inquiry, which is the means for resolving doubt and sorting out true from false beliefs. "A minimal characterization of good inquiry" is that it "takes experience seriously," and hence beliefs to be adequately tested must be subject to the widest possible range of experience. Therefore, effective inquiry must be communal and democratically inclusive. "Truth and objectivity are matters of what is best for the community of inquirers to believe, 'best' here amounting to that which best fits with the evidence and argument." To assert a belief is to make a truth claim and thereby to undertake a commitment to subject that belief to a community of inquiry.[55]

For the pragmatist, as Misak says, "a true belief is one that would withstand doubt, were we to inquire as far as we fruitfully could on the matter. A true belief is such that, no matter how much further we were to investigate and debate, that belief would not be overturned by recalcitrant experience and argument" (49). But since no inquiry can be exhaustive, we can never know for sure that any of our beliefs are true, however indubitable they may seem

---

53. John Dewey, "The Pragmatic Acquiescence" (1927), *Later Works*, 3:151.
54. See chapter 1, a bit of which I repeat here.
55. Cheryl Misak, *Truth, Politics, Morality: Pragmatism and Deliberation* (London: Routledge, 2000), 78, 1. Subsequent page citations to this book are in the text.

at present. Truth is thus a "regulative ideal," an ideal that is unrealizable and yet serves a valuable function, in this case that of keeping the road of inquiry open (98). Truth is "what inquirers must *hope* for if they are to make sense of their practices of inquiry" (69). Truth is the aim of inquiry, but the best that can be secured at any moment in its course is well-justified belief, which is not necessarily true. It is *rational* to adopt currently well-justified beliefs, even if these beliefs later prove to be false (53).

Pragmatism's low-profile conception of truth thus opens the door to "moral cognitivism," a door closed by correspondence theories of truth that insist that a proposition is true "if and only if it corresponds to something like a fact in the believer-independent world" (2). Pragmatism insists not on such correspondence—a criterion that moral belief cannot meet—but only that in morals and politics we have "genuine beliefs with truth as their aim," and that these beliefs answer to experience and to inquiry (88). Moral and political beliefs meet this relatively low threshold and are thus truth-apt for pragmatists. Though its conception of truth may be low-profile, pragmatism is a good deal more strongly antiskeptical and antirelativist than even pragmatists such as Rorty and Posner would allow.[56]

Pragmatism's low-profile conception of truth also leaves its conviction of the truth-apt character of moral and political beliefs unthreatened by disagreement—even the seemingly "indeterminate and interminable" debates that Posner believes undermine deliberative inquiry in these realms. The pragmatist conception of truth makes agreement a regulative ideal as the goal of inquiry. Yet, unlike some deliberative democrats, pragmatists need not make a fetish of actual agreement (though, as I say, Dewey tended to do so). Adding heft to Putnam's similar arguments on this point, Misak demonstrates that although pragmatists respect "bivalence" (the notion that a statement must be false if not true) and "stability" (the notion that true statements must remain true from person to person), their conception of truth does not require the unrestricted application of these principles (as cognitivism grounded in a correspondence theory would). Echoing Putnam, she urges a view that

> is not one which insists that all moral and political questions must have right answers, whether or not we can ever know them. That would be a strenuous cognitivism. Neither is it a view that infers from the fact that morals and politics are rife with unanswerable questions that the notion of a right answer [is] inappropriate. That would be a strenuous non-cognitivism. I have advocated a cognitivism which is modest, in that it holds that our moral judgments aspire to truth and have varying chances of attaining it. (144)

56. For Posner's weaker antiskepticism and antirelativism, see *Problematics of Moral and Legal Theory*, 8–17.

This modest cognitivism asserts that moral and political beliefs are (pragmatically) truth-apt—they answer to experience and they are subject to inquiry—yet does not falter in the face of a measure of nonbivalence or instability. Again echoing Putnam, Misak observes that beliefs may, for example, prove disjunctive, if not entirely so: "We need not think of agreement as being a case of which one way of life is best or which goods are good for all. Rather we might agree that a number of (but not all) incompatible ways of life or a number of (but not all) incompatible things are reasonable, permissible, or acceptable" (137). The qualifications are important; not everything goes. Pragmatist epistemology alone is enough to provide grounds for criticism of those who refuse to open their beliefs to the widest possible range of experience and inquiry. Misak's pragmatist, unlike Rorty's, would have something modestly adversarial and context-independent to say to a Nazi or any other antidemocrat (something along the lines of: "Your 'belief' is not really a belief since you refuse to respect the experience of others and thereby open your belief to the sort of inquiry that the very act of asserting a belief implies").[57] But within these limits, pragmatism not only tolerates but invites a plurality of values and ways of life: "Because there are different ways in which a human life can go well, we can have a plurality of right answers to our questions" (138).

Not only disjunctive judgments, but regretful and tragic judgments are conceivable outcomes of pragmatist inquiry. We may be confident that we have reached the right answer to a difficult moral question and yet still "feel the pull of the defeated reasons." Hence, we regret the need to act in circumstances that force us to choose between compelling, if not equally compelling, alternatives. Or even more painfully, we may confront a situation in which the incompatible alternatives are equally compelling (or distressing), and we are thus faced with a tragic choice. The pragmatist readily admits that moral inquiry faces a continuum,

> which ranges from 'right answer with no regret' to 'no acceptable answer at all.' We ought to be prepared for a range of responsiveness to experience and reasons—a range of objectivity, if you like. We expect that some questions would indeed have right or best answers for all and that some questions would have right or best answers for an individual. But others may not. (142)

Moral and political disagreement, then, need not bring pragmatist bridge-building between epistemic democracy and political democracy to a halt. Pragmatists want to foster deliberative inquiry rather than agreement, which may or may not be its consequence. Misak, like Putnam, points to the

---

57. Misak's book is constructed in large measure around the question of how to respond to the arguments of a particular Nazi, Carl Schmitt.

obvious political inference. Pragmatism leads to the conclusion that, as she says, "deliberation must be encouraged and political institutions and mechanisms for decision-making must be as inclusive as is reasonably possible. The pragmatist voices the requirement that we try, at least until such attempts fail, to include rather than exclude others" (96). Many of the liberal principles—autonomy, equal moral worth, tolerance, cultural pluralism, free speech—that Posner worries about sacrificing to democracy are embedded in pragmatist democracy as crucial features of its deliberative practices. But since inequality can pose an obstacle to entry into these practices, Posner's conservative concern about the left-leaning egalitarianism of pragmatist deliberative democracy remains well-placed.

Because pragmatists have a relatively modest notion of what deliberation requires—openness to the widest possible range of experience bearing on our beliefs—Misak insists that they should not attempt to specify methodological standards of inquiry too precisely. Here the understandable respect that pragmatists have for the methods of the scientific community of inquiry can be misleading if it results in an inflexibility in the conception of what "inquiry" and "deliberation" might amount to in any given case. As Misak says, the pragmatist "must remain agnostic about the details as to how inquiry (of any kind) should go. She will say that inquirers must expose themselves to new evidence, argument, and perspectives. For if truth is that which would best fit with the evidence and argument, were inquiry to have proceeded as far as it could fruitfully go, then the best way to inquire about the truth is to take in as much and as varied evidence and argument as one can" (96).

Posner rightly complains that some deliberative democrats conceive of moral and political deliberation on the model of a faculty seminar. Caring more for deliberation of this sort than for democracy and distressed that ordinary people do not think or talk like academics, they then pull back from expansive democratic hopes and vest their politics in elite, undemocratic institutions such as courts. Deliberative democracy then ends up being more elite and even less democratic than Posner's expressly "elite democracy" (155–57). Populist critics have advanced similar complaints. Pragmatist deliberative democracy, as Misak conceives it, would cast its lot with these populists, willing to take the people as they are. As she says, "moral judgment is inextricably bound up with our relations to others and anyone who stands in such relationships has plenty of engagement in moral deliberation. Truth requires us to listen to others, and anyone might be an expert" (96). Pragmatists must allow for different modes of expression and argument, and guard against the condescension of intellectuals.[58]

58. Populist complaints about the theory of deliberative democracy include J. M. Balkin,

Of course, a strong philosophical bridge between epistemic democracy and deliberative political democracy, such as that which Misak builds, will not necessarily bear much practical traffic in our political culture if Americans do not embrace the ideals of this sort of expansive democratic politics, build the institutions necessary for its practice, and then sustain it with their active citizenship. As Dewey was often painfully aware, even a good argument for deliberative democracy is a purely academic exercise without a politics designed to push reality closer to its ideals. Posner is without doubt correct that the exceptionally limited democracy of his "everyday pragmatism" is much closer to the current nature of American democracy than that prescribed by philosophical pragmatists such as Putnam and Misak—though I think by focusing on national electoral politics, he slights promising pockets of deliberative democracy that have existed and continue to exist in the cultures of social movements, in local political settings, and in civil society generally.[59]

But Posner is more right than wrong about the anemic state of American democracy. He is correct to say that, on the whole, the prospects for a more expansive American democracy are gloomier today than they were in the early nineteenth century. The American state grows ever more detached from popular control, and democrats find themselves struggling less to expand the power of ordinary citizens than to prevent its further erosion.[60] And even in civil society, where the picture is somewhat brighter, the resources necessary for building democratic publics have dwindled (150–54). Self-rule is imperiled.[61]

"Populism and Progressivism as Constitutional Categories," *Yale Law Journal* 104 (1995): 1935–90; Emily Hauptmann, "Can Less Be More? Leftist Deliberative Democrats' Critique of Participatory Democracy," *Polity* 33 (2001): 398–421; Meira Levinson, "Challenging Deliberation," *Theory and Research in Education* 1 (2003): 23–49; Richard Parker, *"Here the People Rule": A Constitutional Populist Manifesto* (Cambridge: Harvard University Press, 1994); Parker, "Taking Politics Personally," *Cardozo Studies in Law and Literature* 12 (2000): 103–27; and Lynn Sanders, "Against Deliberation," *Political Theory* 25 (1997): 347–76. Posner says populist democracy "has almost no support among political theorists" (*Law, Pragmatism, and Democracy,* 155). If so, so much the worse for political theory.

59. Recent explorations of some of these pockets include Frank M. Bryan, *Real Democracy: The New England Town Meeting and How It Works* (Chicago: University of Chicago Press, 2004); Paul Osterman, *Gathering Power: The Future of Progressive Politics in America* (Boston: Beacon Press, 2002); Francesca Polletta, *Freedom Is an Endless Meeting: Democracy in American Social Movements* (Chicago: University of Chicago Press, 2002); and Mark Warren, *Dry Bones Rattling: Community Building to Revitalize American Democracy* (Princeton: Princeton University Press, 2001).

60. See Jonathan Chait, "Power from the People," *New Republic* (16 July 2004): 15–19, which argues persuasively that the administration of George W. Bush is "the least democratic in the modern history of the presidency" (15).

61. See Robert Wiebe, *Self-Rule: A Cultural History of American Democracy* (Chicago: University of Chicago Press, 1995). Concern about the well-being of American civil society has centered on the research of Robert Putnam, especially *Bowling Alone: The Collapse and Revival of American Community* (New York: Simon and Schuster, 2000). But see also Theda Skocpol, *Diminished Democracy: From Membership to Management in American Civic Life* (Norman: University

The practical task for deliberative democrats is, then, daunting, even though, for pragmatists, deliberative democracy is, like truth, not a utopian but a regulative ideal. "Its role," as Misak says, "is to set a direction and provide a focus of criticism for actual arrangements" (98). It sets horizons and invites piecemeal reform, ever alert to not only the possibilities for, but also the constraints on a more expansive democracy. Indeed, at this moment in our history, a good measure of "everyday pragmatism" might well serve deliberative democrats and make for a chastened, modest politics.[62]

But this is not to say that pragmatist democrats should, as Posner would have them do, adopt a democratic ideal so chastened, modest, and everyday that it closes the gap between "is" and "ought" and dispenses with the will to believe in self-government. To do so would not be pragmatic in any sense of the term. For one might reasonably suppose that only the demand for more democracy will insure that we do not get less democracy or even no democracy at all.

---

of Oklahoma Press, 2003), which departs from Putnam and many others concerned about the weakness of American civil society in insisting—valuably, I would say—that a revitalization of local civic activity must be tied to wider state, regional, and national centers of political power and be unafraid of overt political conflict. The crucial need is for a rejuvenation of "membership-based associational life" on every scale.

62. Jeffrey Issac offers a forceful argument for a chastened, modest politics indebted to both philosophical and everyday pragmatism in *The Poverty of Progressivism: The Future of American Democracy in a Time of Liberal Decline* (Lanham, Md.: Rowman and Littlefield, 2003). See also Mark Button and Kevin Mattson, "Deliberative Democracy in Practice: Challenges and Prospects for Civic Deliberation," *Polity* 31 (1999): 610–37; and James Johnson, "Arguing for Deliberation: Some Skeptical Considerations" in Elster, *Deliberative Democracy*, 161–84. Perhaps the most widely publicized practical proposal for more deliberative democracy is James Fishkin's call for "deliberative polling." See Fishkin, *Democracy and Deliberation: New Directions for Democratic Reform* (New Haven: Yale University Press, 1991), and *The Voice of the People: Public Opinion and Democracy* (New Haven: Yale University Press, 1995). See also Ethan Leib's imaginative proposal for a truly popular "fourth branch" of American government, *Deliberative Democracy in America: A Proposal for a Popular Branch of Government* (State College: Pennsylvania State University Press, 2004).

CHAPTER 8

Democratic Evasions

★

I<small>F</small> the disagreements between Richard Rorty and Hilary Putnam about what a "neo-Deweyan" ethics and politics might mean have pitted two of the distinguished elders of contemporary American philosophy against one another, those that divide Rorty and Cornel West have a decidedly intergenerational cast. West's quarrel with Rorty is very much a friendly oedipal contest: West was once Rorty's student, and the disputes between these two philosophers are suffused with mutual respect and obvious affection. Indeed, one looking for a good example of the sort of "conversation" that Rorty idealizes would be hard pressed to find a better one than the dialogue he and West have conducted. Nonetheless, the differences between Rorty and West are substantial and of considerable moment, for, unlike many such controversies nowadays, this one is more than academic. At stake is nothing less than the "social hope" we Americans, and we American intellectuals in particular, might reasonably nourish.[1]

Geistesgeschichte

West's work has from the early 1980s been marked by an effort to integrate American pragmatism with the variety of other traditions shaping

---

1. See Richard Rorty, "Postmodernist Bourgeois Liberalism" (1983), in Rorty, *Objectivity, Relativism, and Truth* (Cambridge: Cambridge University Press, 1991), 197–202; and "Method, Social Science, and Social Hope" (1981), in Rorty, *Consequences of Pragmatism* (Minneapolis: University of Minnesota Press, 1982), 190–210.

his thinking, especially evangelical Christianity, African-American social thought, and Marxism.[2] And his disagreements with Rorty were apparent for some time as well. All this came to a head in *The American Evasion of Philosophy* (1989), and it is here that West most clearly stakes out his claim to offer a reappropriation of the pragmatic tradition, and of Dewey's philosophy in particular, more satisfying than that of Rorty and other rivals. "Rorty's neopragmatism," he complains, "only kicks the philosophical props from under liberal bourgeois capitalist societies; it requires no change in our cultural and political practices." Rorty kicks out these props in order to demonstrate that our conviction that they provide essential support for the "liberal bourgeois" society he favors is an unnecessary illusion. West wants a pragmatism that will not only kick out these props but also recommend some major structural renovations in that same society, renovations that go well beyond what he regards as Rorty's tepid liberalism. He calls for "a reconception of philosophy as a form of cultural criticism that attempts to transform linguistic, social, cultural, and political traditions for the purposes of increasing the scope of individual development and democratic operations."[3]

West's reappropriation of pragmatism takes the form of the sort of "dramatic narrative" of the history of philosophy that pragmatists—Dewey and Rorty in particular—have often deployed effectively. Such narratives comprise a Whiggish variety of history which Rorty, following Hegel, has termed *Geistesgeschichte*. This is history, he observes, that "wants to justify the historian and his friends in having the sort of philosophical concerns they have—in taking philosophy to be what they take it to be. . . . It wants to give plausibility to a certain image of philosophy." At the heart of this history is an effort at canon reformation. The *Geisteshistoriker* assembles a pantheon of heroes who serve as the main characters in a drama that "shows how we have come to ask the questions we now think inescapable and profound. Where

---

2. Recent surveys of West's thought and politics capture this eclecticism. See Rosemary Cowan, *Cornel West: The Politics of Redemption* (Cambridge: Polity Press, 2003); Clarence Sholé Johnson, *Cornel West and Philosophy* (New York: Routledge, 2003); Mark David Wood, *Cornel West and the Politics of Prophetic Pragmatism* (Urbana: University of Illinois Press, 2000); and George Yancy, ed., *Cornel West: A Critical Reader* (Oxford: Blackwell, 2001). The best introduction to the full dimension of West's work is Cornel West, *The Cornel West Reader* (New York: Basic Books, 1999).

3. Cornel West, *The American Evasion of Philosophy: A Genealogy of Pragmatism* (Madison: University of Wisconsin Press, 1989), 206, 230. Subsequent page citations to this book are in the text. West outlines his intellectual autobiography in *Prophesy Deliverance!: An Afro-American Revolutionary Christianity* (Philadelphia: Westminster Press, 1982), 13–24; *The Ethical Dimensions of Marxist Thought* (New York: Monthly Review Press, 1991), xi–xxxiv; and *Cornel West Reader*, 3–47. His criticisms of Rorty are anticipated in "The Politics of American Neo-Pragmatism" in John Rajchman and Cornel West, eds., *Post-Analytic Philosophy* (New York: Columbia University Press, 1985), 259–75. For thoughtful recent considerations of West's pragmatism, see the essays by Hilary Putnam, Lewis Gordon, Clevis Headley, and Eduardo Mendieta in Yancy, *Cornel West*.

these characters left writings behind, those writings then form a canon, a reading-list which one must have gone through in order to justify being what one is." We require such heroes and such canons, Rorty concludes, because "we need to tell ourselves detailed stories about the mighty dead in order to make our hopes of surpassing them concrete."[4]

The common claim of every neopragmatist *Geisteshistoriker* is that one or more of the major American pragmatists must be rescued from the limbo in which they have resided for two generations and assume a prominent place in the current canon. Thus, one might well date the origins of neopragmatic narratives to Rorty's surprising assertion at the beginning of *Philosophy and the Mirror of Nature* that Wittgenstein, Heidegger, and *Dewey* were "the three most important philosophers of our century." Lately another common feature of these stories has become established as well, for several neopragmatists (though not Rorty) have joined in arguing that their tale must begin with Ralph Waldo Emerson. West advances one of the most vigorous and compelling versions of this argument.[5]

In Emerson, West argues, we find the origins of two valuable strains of thought as well as a debilitating limitation that subsequently shaped the thinking of most of the great and near-great among American philosophers. First, Emerson initiated the healthy "evasion" of the "epistemology-centered problematic of modern philosophy" with its quest for incorrigible foundations for knowledge in favor of a view of knowledge "not as a set of representations to be justified, grounded, or privileged but rather as instrumental effects of human will as it is guided by human interests, which are in turn produced by transactions with other humans and nature" (36). Second, Emerson launched a "theodicy" of "power, provocation, and personality" that stressed the "dynamic character of selves and structures, the malleability of tradition and the transformative potential in human history"

4. Richard Rorty, "The Historiography of Philosophy: Four Genres," in Richard Rorty, J. B. Schneewind, and Quentin Skinner, eds., *Philosophy in History* (New York: Cambridge University Press, 1984), 57, 61, 73. Rorty usefully contrasts *Geistesgeschichte* with the equally Whiggish "historical reconstructions" performed by many analytical philosophers that seek to justify the philosopher/historian and his friends in "giving the particular solutions to philosophical problems they give" and to lend "plausibility to a particular solution of a given philosophical problem by pointing out how a great dead philosopher anticipated, or interestingly failed to anticipate, this solution" (57).

5. Richard Rorty, *Philosophy and the Mirror of Nature* (Princeton: Princeton University Press, 1979), 5. Besides West, others arguing for the central place of Emerson in the pragmatic tradition include Russell B. Goodman, *American Philosophy and the Romantic Tradition* (Cambridge: Cambridge University Press, 1990); David Jacobson, *Emerson's Pragmatic Vision* (University Park: Pennsylvania State University Press, 1993); David Marr, *American Worlds Since Emerson* (Amherst: University of Massachusetts Press, 1988); and Richard Poirier, *The Renewal of Literature: Emersonian Reflections* (New York: Random House, 1987) and *Poetry and Pragmatism* (Cambridge: Harvard University Press, 1992). This new interest in Emerson and his legacy owes much to the work of Stanley Cavell. See especially *Conditions Handsome and Unhandsome: The Constitution of Emersonian Perfectionism* (Chicago: University of Chicago Press, 1990).

(10).[6] Third (and less happily), West finds in Emerson an irrepressibly bourgeois individualism and elitism. Despite the disruptive features of his philosophy and the democratic cast of his rhetoric, Emerson's politics rested on "a refined perspective that highlights individual conscience along with political impotence, moral transgression devoid of fundamental social transformation, power without empowering the lower classes, provocation and stimulation bereft of regulated markets, and human personality disjoined from communal action" (40).

Emerson's salutary evasion of the quest for certainty, his romantic vision of human agency and possibility, and his bourgeois blindnesses echoed in the thought of Peirce, James, and Dewey, whether or not they acknowledged the reverberations: "Dewey plays Joshua to Emerson's Moses, with Peirce as a ground-breaking yet forgotten Aaron and James a brilliant and iconoclastic Eleazar" (76). Though West scrutinizes the work of Peirce and James at length, his long chapter on Dewey is the centerpiece of the story he tells, and rightly so. For as West says (pulling yet another analogy out of the same bag), "if Emerson is the inventor of the American religion, Dewey is its Luther—that is, he must seriously think through the implications of the notions of power, provocation, and personality, the themes of voluntarism, optimism, individualism, and meliorism in relation to the plethora of intervening intellectual breakthroughs and in light of the prevailing conditions in order to give direction as well as vitality to the American religion" (85). It is Dewey who gave the philosophical evasion its most powerful formulation, who provided Emerson's romanticism with a more social and democratic complexion, and who stretched middle-class reform to its limits (while remaining, West complains, woefully indifferent to the virtues of Marxism).

Heroic though Dewey's efforts to reconstruct and extend this tradition were, it was, West tells us, in deep trouble at mid-century: "meretricious Stalinism, pernicious fascism, obstinate imperialism, and myopic Americanism were formidable foes that left American pragmatism with little room to maneuver" (113). In this context, W. V. Quine, Wilfred Sellars, and Nelson Goodman kept the evasion alive among professional philosophers; Sidney Hook, Reinhold Niebuhr, and Lionel Trilling gave the theodicy a more realistic cast by providing it with something of a tragic sensibility; and

6. West is a professor of religion and I am not, but I am puzzled by his use of the term *theodicy*, which as I understand it refers to the problem of explaining evil in the face of God's omnipotence and goodness. I do not see how one can call Emerson's views on "power, provocation, and personality" a theodicy. They seem to me to be more of an American version of what, to borrow a term from Isaiah Berlin and Charles Taylor, might be called romantic "expressivism," more a philosophical anthropology than a theodicy. When I think of Emerson's theodicy, I think of his essay on "Compensation" with its view of a long-run, cosmic balancing of the accounts of good and evil—a view from which James and Dewey vigorously dissented.

C. Wright Mills and W. E. B. DuBois tried to supply pragmatists with a social theory that would take better account of the constraints of class and elite power and racial oppression. But no one was able or willing to bring it all together and reinfuse the mixture with Dewey's radically democratic meliorism. Instead, postwar pragmatism gave way to "an Augustinian pessimism regarding the human lot coupled with a fervent privatism and careerism in an expanding economy" (114).

There things more or less remained for pragmatism until Rorty shook things up by giving a new paint job to the pragmatic evasion of the foundational obsessions of modern philosophy in the early 1980s. But Rorty's neopragmatism couples philosophical audacity with weak liberalism, "a fervent vigilance to preserve the prevailing bourgeois way of life" (206). So what we really need, West concludes, is a new "prophetic pragmatism" that is epistemologically evasive, romantically hopeful in an Emersonian vein yet alert to the tragic constraints on human will, open to the lessons of Marxism and postmodernism, and dedicated to the interests of the "wretched of the earth" (212). So like the dramatic narratives of every *Geisteshistoriker,* West's history ends with himself.[7]

Prophetic Pragmatism

Despite his title, West is far less interested in the American evasion of philosophy than in the fate of the Emersonian theodicy and the "culture of creative democracy" it promises. He gives no close account of Emerson's own evasion of epistemology, and it is not until his lengthy (and accomplished) analysis midway through the book of Dewey's signal essay on "The Need for a Recovery of Philosophy" that he provides a full treatment of the pragmatic attack on what Dewey called the "epistemology industry."[8] Moreover, epistemological issues fall out of the story altogether in the discussion of the mid-century pragmatic intellectuals.

On the other hand, an engagement with Emersonian romanticism is sustained throughout the narrative (except when, as in the case of Quine, there is only evasion and no Emerson), and West's most original and effective moments as a historian or critic—his discussions of Emerson's racial views, of

---

7. With none of the thin efforts at self-effacement that usually mark such narratives—a risky bit of exposure rendered doubly risky by West's assertion of his own "prophetic" credentials, the sort of thing one usually leaves it to others to say. These sorts of advertisements for himself have generated a great deal of mockery and resentment. See, for example, Leon Wieseltier, "All and Nothing at All," *New Republic* (6 March 1995): 31–36.

8. West does refer his readers to the best recent account of Emerson's engagement with modern philosophy: David Van Leer, *Emerson's Epistemology* (Cambridge: Cambridge University Press, 1986).

the limits of James's anti-imperialism, of Dewey's creative misreading of Emerson, or of the importance of tragedy—are centered there. What animates West's story, above all, are his contention that, until Dewey came along, the Emersonian commitment to democracy was a limited one and his distress that the Deweyan moment was so short-lived and practically impotent. One can, on West's own evidence, be a pragmatist in the narrow sense (an "evader") and not subscribe to the Emersonian theodicy. And one can be an Emersonian romantic (or one of its immanent critics) without giving much thought to epistemological questions. Strictly speaking, West has two narratives at work here, which come together whenever one of his Emersonian romantics—James, Dewey, himself—is also a pragmatist.

Thus, despite the impression West sometimes leaves, the connections between the pragmatic evasion of philosophy and Emersonian democracy are on his account contingent, not necessary. He does not advance the "epistemological justification for democracy" upon which Putnam and others have relied to tie the two together.[9] He thereby opens himself up to Rorty's objection that pragmatism "is neutral between alternative prophecies, and thus neutral between democrats and fascists." One should not, Rorty says, look to "professorial pragmatism" for prophecy, and he ruefully accepts West's contention that his own work as a professional philosopher is "barren" of political implication. The anti-epistemological evasion "is socially useful only if teamed up with prophecies—fairly concrete prophecies of a utopian social future. Pragmatist philosophy professors like Quine, Putnam, Davidson, Bernstein, and myself can play a social role only if they can find some prophet to whom to attach themselves." To Rorty, the term *prophetic pragmatism* sounds as odd as "charismatic trash-disposal."[10]

Rorty acknowledges that in an earlier era there might have been some relation between pragmatic philosophical doctrines and social reform because conservatives were "still trying to justify repressive institutions in either religious or rationalist terms. So bringing pragmatist arguments to bear against religious or rationalist arguments for political conservatism was a useful thing for James and Dewey to do." I still think this kind of dismantling of absolutisms (of the left as well as the right) is something that needs to be done, and Rorty's sense that this is no longer necessary suggests a certain blindness to the character of American politics. But, as I have said, if one eschews a connection between pragmatist epistemology and democratic politics, then pragmatic antifoundationalism can be tied without effective objection to some pretty nasty social prophecies. This contingency helps explain why so many of West's evaders prove disappointing democrats.[11]

9. See chapter 7.
10. Richard Rorty, "The Professor and the Prophet," *Transition* 52 (1991): 75–77.
11. Rorty, "Professor and the Prophet," 76.

Rorty admits that James and Dewey managed to be both pragmatists and prophets. But he thinks in our time a division of labor should prevail, which West—by force of his own example—disputes (though, to be sure, he has yet to make much of a mark as a professional philosopher).[12] What Rorty wants to contest, above all, is Dewey's contention that philosophers have something special—what he called general "ground maps"—for social and cultural criticism. West would, I believe, dispute this as well, although he (like Dewey) wants a cultural criticism that breaks down disciplinary barriers.

But as long as foundationalism remains a powerful force in our culture, there is, even on Rortyan terms, something perfectly sound about assigning a measure of epistemological trash-disposal to "prophetic pragmatists." And, as we have seen, some neopragmatists, if not Rorty, are eager also to distinguish their thinking about matters of knowledge and truth from postmodern skepticism—for political as well as philosophical reasons.

But if neopragmatists had no epistemological disagreements among themselves, this would not guarantee they would not have much to argue about among themselves, if not at the level of "ground maps" then at the level of prophecy. Among philosophical friends, one can often cut to the ethical/political chase and, as Dewey said, ask who has the greater wisdom, that is, "a sense for the better kind of life to be led."[13]

What Rorty and West are arguing about is less Dewey's pragmatism than his prophecy and his wisdom. What West and others have shown is that Dewey transformed Emersonian romanticism into a vision of an inclusive and fully-participatory democratic culture. This is not an aspect of Dewey's thought that Rorty has sought to appropriate (though I would say it is at the heart of Dewey's philosophy). His own lightly sketched political philosophy owes more to John Rawls than to Dewey. For Rorty, liberal-democratic poli-

12. To which I say, so what? Pragmatists, as Dewey said, should be measured by the manner in which they address not the "problems of philosophy" but the "problems of men." By this measure, much of West's work is exemplary. Nonetheless, his relative inattentiveness to the problems of philosophers, as well as the celebrity he has courted in engaging the problems of men, has left West open to the charge of Wieseltier and others that "he is not a philosopher but a cobbler of philosophies" ("All or Nothing at All," 34). And also occasioned a recent, bitter public dispute with Harvard president Lawrence Summers over West's scholarly accomplishments, among other things. For what it is worth, my view is that American higher education would be much the richer if every faculty made room for the likes of West. Though I should say, I found his "rap" CD, *Sketches of My Culture* (2001), which was at the center of the dispute with Summers, to be an unintentionally stunning comic performance. See Sam Tanenhaus, "The Ivy League's Angry Star," *Vanity Fair* (June 2002): 200–203. For a sharp indictment of West less inflammatory than Wieseltier's but nonetheless cast along similar lines, see David Steigerwald, *Culture's Vanities: The Paradox of Cultural Diversity in a Globalized World* (Lanham, MD: Rowman and Littlefield, 2004), 183–92.

13. See John Dewey, *Experience and Nature* (1929), *Later Works,* 1:309; and "Philosophy and Democracy" (1918), *Middle Works,* 11:143–44. Rorty denies any need for even Deweyan "ground maps" in "Dewey's Metaphysics" (1977) in Rorty, *Consequences of Pragmatism,* 72–89.

tics sometimes seems to involve little more than making sure that individuals hurt one another as little as possible and interfere minimally in the private life of others. There is little in his social or political vision of the communitarian side of Dewey's thinking, nothing of Dewey's veneration of the *shared* experience of citizens. He argues for the importance of solidarity in public life, but his is an extremely thin solidarity, amounting to little more than a common aversion to pain and humiliation and explicitly not "a common possession or a shared power." Rorty's is a politics centered on negative liberty, "our ability to leave people alone."[14]

West's democratic vision is much closer to Dewey's own. Though he repeats the charge of Niebuhr and Mills that Dewey was blind to the realities of power—a charge belied by Dewey's activism in the 1930s—and gives Dewey insufficient credit for the alliances he forged with "working people," West clearly shares Dewey's hope for a more participatory democracy. "To speak of an Emersonian culture of creative democracy," he declares,

> is to speak of a society and culture where politically adjudicated forms of knowledge are produced in which human participation is encouraged and for which human personalities are enhanced. Social experimentation is the basic norm, yet it is operative only when those who must suffer the consequences have effective control over the institutions that yield the consequences, i.e., access to decision-making processes. (213)[15]

It is unfair to Rorty to picture him as altogether complacent about the ills of our social order. He is in most respects a good old-fashioned New Deal liberal, and one might even extend to him the label of social democrat. He cares deeply about the plight of the wretched of the earth, and of late he has written movingly about the need to institute a more adequate program of technocratic social engineering to care for their needs (and of the irrelevance of the politics of the academic left to these needs). Moreover, he does not deny that he has failed to appropriate Dewey's radical democratic vision, nor does he fail to understand how others could find it appealing. He just thinks it has exhausted its relevance for "rich North Atlantic democracies" and for "downbeat Alexandrian" intellectuals like himself—though he is willing to admit it might have some relevance in such places as Brazil.[16]

14. Richard Rorty, *Contingency, Irony, and Solidarity* (Cambridge: Cambridge University Press, 1989), 91, and "The Priority of Democracy to Philosophy" (1988), in Rorty, *Objectivity, Relativism, and Truth,* 175–96.

15. Here West articulates some of the rudiments of the "epistemological justification for democracy," though he does not develop the point.

16. See Richard Rorty, "Intellectuals in Politics," *Dissent* (fall 1991): 483–90; "On Intellectuals in Politics" (an exchange with Andrew Ross), *Dissent* (spring 1992): 263–67; "The Intellectuals at the End of Socialism," *Yale Review* 80 (1992): 1–16; and "Unger, Castoriadis, and the Romance of a National Future" (1990), in Rorty, *Essays on Heidegger and Others* (Cambridge:

The contrast between Rorty and West reminds me a great deal of that between Walter Lippmann and Dewey in the 1920s. Against Dewey's insistence that participatory democracy must be the central regulative ideal of American life, Lippmann contended that it had lost its relevance to modern industrial societies and polities. Most people, he argued, regard self-government as a secondary, purely instrumental good, and if they can be assured of welfare and security without it, they will settle for a minimal and relatively insignificant role for themselves as citizens. The criterion that should be used to assess a government, Lippmann said, was not the extent to which citizens were self-governing but "whether it is producing a certain minimum of health, of decent housing, of material necessities, of education, of freedom, of pleasures, of beauty." Without denying the need for such things, Dewey contended that one might still hope that the American people could have a significant say as citizens and workers about how and in what form they were to provide them to one another. Roberto Unger has said that "the great political question of our day has become: Is social democracy the best that we can reasonably hope for?" If so, then Rorty's answer to this question is (with Lippmann) "Yes, if that," while West has responded (with Dewey and Unger) "No, not by a longshot."[17]

Postmodernist, Christian Marxism

If West's prophetic pragmatism is more Deweyan than Rorty's deflationary liberalism, it is not without its own difficulties. Chief among these is the difficulty it encounters—as much a practical as a theoretical difficulty—in responding to the Lippmanns and the Rortys of the world with much more than imagination and a hope that some would say borders on the fanciful. As we have seen, this is a concern, call it the "utopia problem," that those much more conservative than Rorty (such as Posner) have pointed up in an effort to discredit radically democratic pragmatism. But before I turn (again) to this issue, I would like to take note of a few of the more evasive theoretical features of West's prophetic pragmatism.

First, West never adequately explains why he thinks it is so important to hang onto Marxism or, to put it better, never describes what it is that he be-

---

Cambridge University Press, 1991), 177–92. As I suggest in chapter 6, Rorty's politics has become even more clearly social democratic since the early 1990s. For a sketch of West's social political vision, see Roberto Unger and Cornel West, *The Future of American Progressivism: An Initiative for Political and Economic Reform* (Boston: Beacon Press, 1998).

17. Walter Lippmann, *Public Opinion* (1922; New York: Free Press, 1965), 196–97; Roberto M. Unger, *Social Theory: Its Situation and Its Task* (Cambridge: Cambridge University Press, 1987), 14. For a full account of the Lippmann-Dewey debate, see Westbrook, *John Dewey and American Democracy*, 293–318.

lieves remains valuable in Marxism. This, of course, has become an even more difficult rhetorical task since the collapse of state socialism in the Soviet Union and Eastern Europe, which has, rightly or not, also discredited Marxism in the public mind. West chides Dewey for failing to come to terms with Marxism, but later he says that

> the significant difference between [Antonio] Gramsci and Dewey is not that the former accepts Marxist theory and the latter rejects it, but rather that Gramsci tenaciously holds onto Marxist theory in those areas where it fails, e.g. politics and culture. Dewey accepted much of the validity of Marxist theory and simply limited its explanatory scope and rejected its imperial, monistic, and dogmatic versions. (107, 221)

In the 1930s, Dewey picked up a good deal of Marxist class analysis and threw it in the pot with Henry George, Thomas Jefferson, Thorstein Veblen, and other influences to produce just the sort of theoretical eclecticism West himself recommends. What more does he want?[18]

One thing West should seriously consider jettisoning, for both strategic and theoretical reasons, is the polemical language of Marxism (something Dewey advised his left-wing colleagues during the Depression to do). West uses terms such as *bourgeois* and *petty bourgeois* and *middle class* not only to place American pragmatists but to put them in their place, less to explain them than to warn us to wipe their clay off our feet. But, as I have said, the best of American radicalism has always marched under a "petty bourgeois" banner, and American petty bourgeois social thought is a rich and valuable tradition. And as socialists scramble in the wake of the destruction of the Soviet empire to remodel their ideals, they might give that tradition another look, not in spite of the fact that it is petty bourgeois but because it is so.[19]

In a response to the original version of this essay, West says that

> my defense of Marxist theory rests upon its insights regarding the operations of power in capitalist society—operations that highlight the role of corporate, financial and political elites that impede a more egalitarian distribution of wealth and power; i.e. obstruct the flowering of democratic individuality among the citizenry. Forms of American radicalism that overlook, ignore or

---

18. For a more adequate critical account of Dewey's encounter with Marxism, see Peter Manicas, "Dewey and the Class Struggle" in Murray G. Murphey and Ivan Berg, eds., *Values and Value Theory in Twentieth-Century America* (Philadelphia: Temple University Press, 1988), 67–81. See also chapter 5.

19. Christopher Lasch got this project off to a good start in *The True and Only Heaven: Progress and Its Critics* (New York: Norton, 1991). Interestingly enough, Lasch's dramatic narrative includes many of the same characters—Emerson, James, Niebuhr, Martin Luther King, Jr.—as West's, though his reading of these figures is decidedly different. Robert Johnston extends the project brilliantly in *The Radical Middle Class: Populist Democracy and the Question of Capitalism in Progressive Era Portland, Oregon* (Princeton: Princeton University Press, 2003).

downplay these operations of power are not worthless, they simply *miss* something crucial about what limits the flowering of democratic individuality in capitalist America.

Agreed. But Marxism is not the only tradition to have these "operations of power" in its sights; the same is true of the petty-bourgeois populist tradition.[20]

Second, I wish West had said more about the manner in which he combines his Christianity and his pragmatism. The old pragmatists were all religious men, if not conventionally so, but neopragmatists have been largely inattentive to religious experience. One of the most attractive features of West's work is his firm defense of religious faith to intellectuals who are too often its cultured despisers. Yet West usually defends his faith in largely personal, therapeutic terms—as "a rich source of existential empowerment and political engagement" (233).

What West fails to confront as squarely and attentively as he might is the question to which he says Niebuhr responded with little more than "philosophical mush," that is, how is religious belief compatible with pragmatic truth (156–57)? How, that is, can one be a faithful Christian who believes, among other things that Christ was the Son of God, and at the same time, be faithful to pragmatism, which cannot authorize the truth of this proposition? I suppose that West would agree that James's effort to buttress religious belief with his pragmatism on grounds of the worthwhile consequences of belief for the believer was a failure. For a pragmatist, as Dewey pointed out, the therapeutic comforts of faith are not compelling evidence for religious truth claims, as James sometimes implied they were. But I also suppose that West would agree with Dewey that there is more to experience than a quest for persuasive truth claims. Pragmatism, while skeptical of the truth claims of religion, does not deny the reality of religious experience or the imaginative power of the faiths such experience generates. As Dewey said, "The realm of meanings is wider than that of true-and-false meanings; it is more urgent and more fertile. . . . A large part of our life is carried on in a realm of meanings in which truth and falsity as such are irrelevant." Because, unlike Rorty, I think religious absolutism remains a threat to a democratic public life, I believe we need more Christian pragmatists like Niebuhr who can explain to people how it is that one can subscribe to a faith in Christ and yet opt for a public life grounded in the humility and uncertainty of a common, fallible, pragmatic search for nothing better than warranted assertions about matters of fact and value.[21]

---

20. West, "A Reply to Westbrook, Brodsky, and Simpson," *Praxis International* 13 (1993): 46.

21. John Dewey, *Experience and Nature* (1929), *Later Works* 1:307. For an elaboration on my characterization of the relationship between pragmatism and faith, see Robert Westbrook, "An

I do not mean to say that West has not wrestled with these questions. He has said that he stands in the Christian tradition of "Montaigne, Pascal, and Kierkegaard—figures in touch with (and often tortured by) an inescapable demon of doubt inscribed within their humble faith." This, it seems to me, is the wing of the Christian tradition in which Christian pragmatists must stand if they are to remain both Christians and pragmatists. But the challenge of doing so is a difficult one, and no neopragmatist is better placed than West to confront it in the extended fashion it merits. We could use his version of Dewey's *A Common Faith*, a version no doubt far more sympathetic to particularistic communities of belief than Dewey was, yet equal to Dewey's concern for a conception of the "religious" that would foster rather than fracture democratic community.[22]

Finally, I wish West was more wary than he is about the marriage of pragmatism and postmodernism. As we have seen, one of the most important divides among neopragmatists is that between many social theorists and philosophers who have turned to pragmatism in order to work their way out of the skeptical implications of much postmodernist thinking and other philosophers and literary theorists who have embraced pragmatism because they see it as a homespun, American version of such skepticism. Rorty said some years ago that James and Dewey "are waiting at the end of the road which Foucault and Deleuze are currently traveling," but as Thomas Grey has observed, many neopragmatists "can be seen as still working within the scientific empiricist tradition broadly conceived," and they are attracted to pragmatism precisely because it enables them to do so and to weave their way between the Scylla of positivism and the Charybdis of postmodernist nihilism.[23] West is well aware that pragmatism does not authorize the latter. As he notes, "Dewey champions doubt—it is the very motor for provocation—yet he sidesteps modern skepticism" (89). Yet the final chapter of *The American Evasion of Philosophy* is filled with praise for the "significant breakthroughs" of critics who see this as a distinction without a difference (237).

Uncommon Faith: Pragmatism and Religious Experience," in Stuart Rosenbaum, ed., *Pragmatism and Religion* (Urbana: University of Illinois Press, 2003), 190–205.

22. Cornel West, "Introduction" (1999), *Cornel West Reader*, xvi. For a good, if very brief, example of the sort of thing I have in mind, see West's "Philosophical View of Easter" (1988), *Cornel West Reader*, 415–20. In this essay he struggles to explain how he can insist on the "truth-value" of the Christian resurrection claim, without subjecting that claim to the tests that pragmatism requires. My own view, admittedly that of an outsider, is that Christian pragmatists might do better to give up claims to warranted religious truth and rest content with hopeful faith claims, though these would include faith in (as yet) unwarranted truth claims. See Westbrook, "Uncommon Faith," 197–98.

23. Rorty, *Consequences of Pragmatism*, xviii; Thomas C. Grey, "Holmes and Legal Pragmatism," *Stanford Law Review* 41 (1989): 790. For an exemplary, generous, but nonetheless critical engagement of postmodernist thinking by a contemporary pragmatist, see Richard J. Bernstein, *The New Constellation: The Ethical-Political Horizons of Modernity/Postmodernity* (Cambridge: MIT Press, 1992).

Pragmatists, to my mind, need to position themselves more centrally than West does between the epistemological, moral, and cultural relativisms of the academic left and the reactionary rationalisms of the intellectual right.[24]

The Politics of Truth

His book, West tells us, "is, among other things, a political act" (8). "Prophetic pragmatism," he concludes, "rests upon the conviction that the American evasion of philosophy is not an evasion of serious thought and moral action. Rather such evasion is a rich and revisable tradition that serves as the occasion for cultural criticism and political engagement in the service of an Emersonian culture of creative democracy" (239).

This rhetorically buoyant conclusion brings to mind an exchange of letters John Dewey had with his friend and fellow philosopher, Max Otto, in early 1941. Otto wrote to Dewey to tell him he had been reading Dewey's 1903 essay on Emerson with his students at the University of Wisconsin, and that he was troubled by Dewey's "contention that Emerson is the philosopher of democracy." No one, Otto ventured to say, who had as little to say as Emerson did about the practice of democracy could lay claim to that title. "Emerson's negative attitude toward the means and organizations which are necessary to make democratic ideals function seems to me a serious weakness. Emerson was transported by the spirit of reform; but from every device of reform he turned resolutely away."[25]

Dewey responded that he had forgotten he had ever said Emerson was the philosopher of democracy, and this was certainly not something he would say in 1941. Whatever he had said nearly forty years ago had to be put into its context, "before the World War, before lots of things, that have changed the meaning of things, democracy and philosophers included." Dewey still thought Emerson was "a great representative of democratic ideas," as long as he was properly "translated." Otto was right about his neglect of means, but unlike most commentators, Dewey thought this neglect could not be attributed to a naive optimism on Emerson's part. "Instead of being over optimistic," Dewey concluded, "he was, it seems to me, unduly pessimistic about actualities, his optimism being for (rather abstract) possibilities."[26]

Like Emerson, West is transported by the spirit of democratic reform, yet decidedly vague about, if not, like Emerson, resolutely averse to, its devices.

24. As I have said, Cheryl Misak, *Truth, Politics, Morality: Pragmatism and Deliberation* (London: Routledge, 2000) is a fine example of this positioning.

25. Max Otto to John Dewey, 4 January 1941, Max Otto Papers, State Historical Society of Wisconsin, Madison.

26. John Dewey to Max Otto, 23 January 1941, Otto Papers.

And, if West cannot be said to be unduly pessimistic about "actualities," his plea for a prophetic pragmatism is marked by an almost feverish optimism for rather abstract possibilities. Prophetic pragmatism, he says, can be "a material force for individuality and democracy . . . a practice that has some potency and effect or makes a difference in the world" (232). Not one to underestimate the power of the word—even when its distribution is in the hands of a small university press—West tells us that, while revisiting American pragmatism with him will not provide a "panacea for our ills," it will help us to "reinvigorate our moribund academic life, our lethargic political life, our decadent cultural life, and our chaotic personal lives for the flowering of many-sided personalities and the flourishing of more democracy and freedom" (4).

Although I wish all this was true, I find myself incapable of working up such abstract aspirations, at least not now. West seems to me to take too little account of what his fellow pragmatist Richard Bernstein has described as the difficult dilemma of those who would venture today beyond Rorty's modest call for a greater measure of social democracy to West's immodest prophecy of a flowering of expansive deliberative democracy. As Bernstein says, "The coming into being of a type of public life that can strengthen solidarity, public freedom, a willingness to talk and to listen, mutual debate, and a commitment to rational persuasion presupposes the incipient forms of such communal life." But what can one do in a situation such as our own "in which there is a breakdown of such communities, and where the very conditions of social life have the consequences of furthering such a breakdown?" Nothing grand, if not nothing, Bernstein concludes, and I find myself agreeing with him. This eclipse of democratic publics was a difficulty that began to plague Dewey in the 1920s when he tried to deflect Lippmann's realism, and since that time things have only gotten worse. For now, as Bernstein says, Deweyan democrats can only "seize upon those experiences and struggles in which there are still the glimmerings of solidarity and the promise of dialogical communities in which there can be genuine participation and where reciprocal wooing and persuasion can prevail."[27] Let us then, by all means, be hopeful, but let us not be optimistic.[28]

Perhaps West's optimism about the potential potency of his neopragma-

---

27. Richard J. Bernstein, *Beyond Objectivism and Relativism: Science, Hermeneutics, and Praxis* (Philadelphia: University of Pennsylvania Press, 1983), 226, 228. More recently, West has himself eloquently stated Bernstein's point. "We have," he writes in a 1992 postmortem on the Los Angeles riots, "created a rootless, dangling people with little link to the supportive networks—family, friends, school—that sustain some sense of purpose in life. We have witnessed the collapse of the spiritual communities that help us face despair, disease and death and that transmit through the generations dignity and decency, excellence, and elegance" ("Learning to Talk of Race," *New York Times Magazine* [2 August 1992]: 26).

28. West responds that "my alternative is not simply an exhortative prophecy of the word, but rather a discerning of those embryonic or feeble forms of communal life . . . that keep alive

tism grows in part out of his entrenchment as an "organic intellectual" in the "prophetic wing of the black church," one of the few incipient dialogical communities that continues to afford some resistance to the constriction of democratic life. This after all, as West says, was the community that produced Martin Luther King Jr., "the best of what the political dimension of prophetic pragmatism is all about" (234). Yet even here there is cause for concern, as West well knows. Few have equaled his unsparing portrait of the afflictions of African-American communities, afflictions against which black Christians (and others) are bravely waging a losing battle. Moreover, it seems to me a sign of deep trouble that again and again we find ourselves having to reach back a generation or two to the civil rights movement for a model of the sort of democratic politics we hope to cultivate.[29]

One can, however, easily quote West against himself when he slips into the sort of bouts of ebullient optimism that mark *The American Evasion of Philosophy*. His Christianity, he says, is less that of the resurrection and its promise of "a new heaven and earth" than that of Christ on the cross. "The centrality of Good Friday—and especially Holy Saturday, when God is as dead for Christians as God was for Nietzsche—for me prevents me from embracing Easter too quickly."[30] No one than he has more relentlessly pressed on fellow neopragmatists the need for an appreciation of the tragic dimensions of human experience. Warning that the legacy of Jefferson and Emerson must be joined with that of Lincoln, whose grasp of the constraints of human finitude has too often been absent from pragmatist thinking, West urges neopragmatists to hold at bay both "facile optimisms and paralyzing pessimisms."[31] There are stones in the passway to democracy, he warns, and not all are stones of hope. "Despair and hope are inseparable. One can never understand what hope is really about unless one wrestles with despair," and hence "when you talk about hope, you have to be a long-distance runner."[32]

But the tragic sensibility, the chastened hope, which West at his best commends, invites intellectuals to assume not the heroic, self-dramatizing stance

---

some semblance of democratic communities requisite for a participatory democratic project. To put it bluntly, I am as realistic as Westbrook in regard to where we are now—but I still glimpse possibilities that he puts little credence in. This small disagreement may be more temperamental than empirical." Perhaps it may. West, "Reply," 47.

29. See Cornel West, "Nihilism in Black America," in West, *Race Matters* (Boston: Beacon Press, 1993), 9–20. I do not, of course, mean to suggest that study of the civil rights movement does not continue to yield valuable and fresh insights into the conditions and character of effective democratic politics. See, for example, David Chappell, *A Stone of Hope: Prophetic Religion and the Death of Jim Crow* (Chapel Hill: University of North Carolina Press, 2004).

30. West, "Philosophical View of Easter," 420, 415.

31. Cornel West, "Pragmatism and the Sense of the Tragic" (1993), *Cornel West Reader*, 175.

32. Cornel West, "Chekov, Coltrane, and Democracy" (1998), and West, "The World of Ideas" (1993) in West, *Cornel West Reader*, 554, 298–99.

to which he is sometimes given ("I am a prophetic Christian freedom fighter") but a more modest conception of their roles and capacities, even though modesty is not a virtue that intellectuals are ordinarily inclined to cultivate.[33] Yet humble roles boldly and fearlessly performed are nothing to be ashamed of. As Dewey said, "A combination of such modesty and courage affords the only way I know of in which the philosopher can look his fellow man in the face with frankness and with humanity."[34]

So when neopragmatists consider the role that they might play, as neo-pragmatists, in contemporary American political culture, they might begin, at least, with tasks more limited that those West lays out for them. Consider the aptness for our time of the somber recommendations to intellectuals offered by C. Wright Mills in 1959 in an essay tellingly titled "The Decline of the Left," which West quotes at length but without comment:

> In summary, what we must do is to define the reality of the human condition and to make our definitions public; to confront the new facts of history-making in our time, and their meanings for the problem of political responsibility; to release the human imagination by transcending the mere exhortation of grand principle and opportunist reaction in order to explore all the alternatives now open to the human community.
>
> If this—the politics of truth—is merely a holding action, so be it. If it is also a politics of desperation, so be it. But in this time and in America, it is the only realistic politics of possible consequence that is readily open to intellectuals. It is the guide line and the next step. It is an affirmation of one's self as a moral and intellectual center of responsible decision, the act of a free man who rejects "fate"; for it reveals his resolution to take his *own* fate, at least, into his own hands.[35]

This sort of "politics of truth" would address but half of West's ambitious agenda. It would help reinvigorate "a sane, sober, and sophisticated intellectual life in America," but it would not—at least directly or in the short run—promise much by way of regenerating "the social forces empowering the disadvantaged, degraded, and dejected" (239). But this half a loaf is not to be discounted too steeply. If American intellectuals could speak once again without embarrassment or apology of a politics of truth, we might at least begin to recover the integrity of our own dialogical community and put

33. Cornel West, "The Making of an American Radical Democrat of African Descent" (1991), in West, *Cornel West Reader*, 13. Ordinarily "readers" of this sort, of which there are many, are put together by admiring others not by their principal, as this one is. Doing so bespeaks a certain immodesty, and tends to lend credence to the unfair and unhappy charge of Wieseltier and others that West's work is little more than an exercise in self-promotion. See "West Wind," *New Republic* (13 and 20 September 1999): 10.

34. John Dewey, "Philosophy and Civilization" (1927), *Later Works*, 3:10.

35. C. Wright Mills, "The Decline of the Left," in Mills, *Power, Politics, and People* (New York: Oxford, 1963), 235. West quotes this passage on page 138 of *American Evasion*.

ourselves in a better position to contribute something to the reconstruction of the larger society when the opportunities to do so present themselves.

A politics of *truth*, of course, necessarily raises epistemological questions. What, its practitioners are pressed to say by their adversaries, do they mean by truth? Here, in what one might call the politics of truth about truth, even Rorty, for all the self-deprecating talk of his philosophical labors as "trash-disposal," must grudgingly confess to a role. He, no less than any pragmatist, has been ill-disposed to leave the terrain of epistemological politics to warring tribes of dogmatists and skeptics. West has put it well:

> To be modern is to live dangerously and courageously in the face of relentless self-criticism and inescapable fallibilism; it is to give up the all-too-human quest for certainty and indubitability owing to the historicity of our claims. Yet to give in to sophomoric relativism ("Anything goes" or "All views are equally valid") is a failure of nerve, and to succumb to wholesale skepticism ("There is no truth") is a weakness of the will and imagination. Instead, the distinctive mark of modernity is to pursue the treacherous trek of dialogue, to wager on the fecund yet potentially poisonous fruit of fallible inquiry, which require communicative action, risk-ridden conversation, even intimate relation.[36]

Pragmatism thus bears the special promise to establish a well-fortified third party in the inescapable epistemological debates that a modern politics of truth entails and to contest there both the forces of certainty and those of bottomless doubt. And these epistemological debates *are* themselves political and of wide consequence because, as I have argued repeatedly, Deweyan pragmatism is a defense of the discourse ethics of democracy and, for all their sharp differences, dogmatism and skepticism alike threaten democracy. And for this reason, those committed to a democratic faith will, in turn, be drawn to pragmatism as the epistemology of choice. Rorty to the contrary, pragmatism and democratic prophecy are joined at the hip. Should pragmatists defeat their adversaries and establish an unskeptical fallibilism at the heart of our intellectual life, however unlikely this seems at the moment, theirs would be no mean achievement—for pragmatism and for democracy. Trash disposal is, indeed, a modest, humble vocation, but few complain and many are glad when the trashman cometh.

36. West, "Introduction," *Cornel West Reader*, xvii.

CHAPTER 9

Educating Citizens

★

Oₙₑ need not be a Deweyan pragmatist to recognize that the relationship between public schooling and democracy is a conceptually tight one. Schools have become one of the principal institutions by which modern states reproduce themselves, and insofar as those states are democratic, they will make use of schools to prepare children for democratic citizenship. The very notion of democratic "public" education reflects this fact: democratic public schools are ostensibly not only schools supported by public finance but also schools that educate every student for the responsibilities and benefits of participating in public life. One reasonable measure of the strength and prospects of a democracy is the degree to which its public schools successfully devote themselves to this task.

By this measure, American democracy is now weak and its prospects dim. The anemia of public life in the United States—a polity in which even such minimal practices of citizenship as voting do not engage many Americans—is reflected in public schooling that, despite lip service to education for democratic citizenship, has devoted few resources or even much thought to its requirements. We suffer, as Benjamin Barber has said, from a dearth of "civic literacy," which he characterizes as "the competence to participate in democratic communities, the ability to think critically and act with deliberation in a pluralistic world, and the empathy to identify sufficiently with others to live with them despite conflicts of interest and differences in character." In the mid-1970s, a study of Pennsylvania high school seniors who had just completed a high school civics course found that they had characteristically little understanding of democracy and its traditions. Most of them believed that "the main characteristic of democracy was that it leaves the citizen alone." But democracy does not leave citizens alone; it brings them together to deliberate on and act in their common interests.[1]

One finds little inclination among educators or the public at large to address this erosion of the understanding and practice of democratic citizenship among young Americans and those who instruct them, or even to see in it a gravely troubling development. As Barber observes,

> The logic of democracy begins with public education, proceeds to informed citizenship, and comes to fruition in the securing of rights and liberties. We have been nominally democratic for so long that we presume it is our natural condition rather than the product of persistent effort and tenacious responsibility. We have decoupled rights from civic responsibilities and severed citizenship from education on the false assumption that citizens just happen.[2]

Many have decried the shortcomings of American public schools, but few have attributed their difficulties to a weakness of democratic imagination, will, and purpose. Few of the many reports on the dire condition of schooling in the United States that have filled bookshelves recently have anything to say about the education of citizens. When our leaders speak of the failures of public education, they find its purposes and deficiencies quite elsewhere. "We measure every school by one high standard: Are our children learning what they need to know to compete and win in the global economy?" President Bill Clinton declared in his State of the Union Message of 1994 (to enthusiastic congressional applause). This is, indeed, a high standard, but it could conceivably be met without revitalizing democratic education; indeed, the educational purposes of American democracy and those of American capitalism have often conflicted and might be expected to continue to do so. Some have argued that Clinton's standard is more likely to be met by "privatizing" American schools. If our aim is to educate our children for the market, the argument goes, why not use the market to do so if we are more likely to succeed in that fashion? Citizens would hesitate to entrust the education of future citizens to private corporations, but we seldom address the education of our children with their prospective citizenship in mind. We want, above all, for them to have good jobs that will enable them to be full participants in an "American Way of Life" that we have for decades defined as a rich and rewarding private life of material abundance.

1. Benjamin Barber, "America Skips School," *Harper's* (November 1993): 44; Pennsylvania study cited in Richard M. Battistoni, *Public Schooling and the Education of Democratic Citizens* (Jackson: University Press of Mississippi, 1985), 4–5.

2. Barber, "America Skips School," 44.

This is the principal promise to which we have come to hold our schools accountable.[3]

For this reason, the schools cannot and should not be indicted too harshly for failing to educate our children for democratic citizenship. Too often, bashing the public schools has served as an easy substitute for exploring the larger contexts in which their shortcomings can be explained. Why should schools provide an education for public life when American public life, as Walter Lippmann long ago observed, has become a phantom? The practices of the public schools mirror a wider constriction of democratic life in the United States, the near erasure of citizenship as a significant element of the lives of most Americans. Most adult Americans no longer live to any significant degree as citizens, and hence it is not surprising that few feel a compelling need to educate American children for public life. The shortcomings of the schools in this respect reflect, as Barber says, a more general "absence of democratic will and a consequent refusal to take our children, our schools, and our future seriously." If one shares Barber's concern, as I do, and believes that freedom as well as democracy is at stake, then it is worth trying to figure out why it is that our public schools do not educate for democratic citizenship and how we might reconstruct them so that they could do so. Here, a little history is helpful.[4]

The Collapse of Common Schooling

The history of American public schooling reflects a more general two-mindedness about democracy that has been a feature of American political culture since the nation's founding. Few among the nation's founders had much good to say for democracy, which in the late eighteenth century remained synonymous for many with mob rule, and insofar as they used the term it was usually as an abusive epithet directed at their political oppo-

3. "Excerpts from President Clinton's State of the Union Message," *New York Times,* 26 January 1994, A15. For an astute analysis of Clinton's educational program by a critic concerned about its implications for democratic citizenship, see B. Todd Sullivan, "Economic Ends and Educational Means at the White House: A Case for Citizenship and Casuistry," *Educational Theory* 43 (1993): 161–79. We may perhaps take some comfort in the minority views of one leading Clinton advisor on domestic policy, William Galston, that "a wealthy community that determines the worth of all activities by the extent to which they add to its wealth has forgotten what wealth is for. A system of training, education, and culture wholly subservient to the system of production denies the fuller humanity of its participants" (*Liberal Purposes* [Cambridge: Cambridge University Press, 1991], 202). Such an adversarial view had little effect on Clinton education policy and is, as far I can discern, nowhere in evidence in the thinking of George W. Bush and his advisors, including their vaunted but as yet far from effective effort to "leave no child behind."

4. Walter Lippmann, *The Phantom Public* (New York: Macmillan, 1925); Barber, "America Skips School," 45.

nents. "The ancient democracies, in which the people themselves deliberated," Alexander Hamilton declared, "never possessed one feature of good government. Their very character was tyranny; their figure deformity: When they assembled, the field of debate presented an ungovernable mob, not only incapable of deliberation, but prepared for every enormity." Democracies, James Madison observed, "have ever been spectacles of turbulence and contention; have ever been found incompatible with personal security or the rights of property; and have in general been as short in their lives as they have been violent in their deaths."[5]

Finding themselves faced with an excessively democratic republic bereft of the balancing influences of a monarchy and hereditary aristocracy, the framers of the federal Constitution proclaimed the doctrine of popular sovereignty and then designed a machinery for governing that provided for no institutions or public spaces for popular government beyond a limited franchise. Representative government, they hoped, would limit the dangers of democracy and sustain rule by the best men. Representation, Madison argued, might act as a kind of filter to "refine and enlarge the public views, by passing them through the medium of a chosen body of citizens, whose wisdom may best discern the true interests of their country, and whose patriotism and love of justice, will be least likely to sacrifice it to temporary or partial considerations."[6]

Yet if the architects of the Constitution were skeptical of the civic virtue of most Americans, they were unwilling to abandon the extra insurance against the threat of democracy that public education for civic virtue might provide. "A well-instructed people alone can be permanently a free people," President Madison told Congress in 1810, seconding the view of his predecessor, George Washington, who had reminded the audience for his "Farewell Address" that "virtue or morality is a necessary spring of popular government" and "in proportion as the structure of a government gives force to public opinion, it is essential that public opinion should be enlightened."[7]

Yet those American founders with a greater enthusiasm for democracy were not—as their opponents often portrayed them—advocates of rule by

5. Alexander Hamilton, "New York Ratifying Convention First Speech" (1788), in Harold Syrett, ed., *The Papers of Alexander Hamilton* (New York: Columbia University Press, 1962), 5:39; James Madison, "Federalist X" (1787), in Bernard Bailyn, ed., *The Debate on the Constitution* (New York: Library of America, 1993), 1:408.

6. Madison, "Federalist X," 409.

7. James Madison, "Second Annual Message" (1810), and George Washington, "Farewell Address" (1796), in James D. Richardson, ed., *Messages and Papers of the Presidents* (New York: Bureau of National Literature, 1897), 2:470, 1:212. For a full account of the views of the founders on education, see Lorraine Smith Pangle and Thomas L. Pangle, *The Learning of Liberty: The Educational Ideas of the American Founders* (Lawrence: University Press of Kansas, 1993).

an uneducated people. Thomas Jefferson, for example, took issue with the antidemocratic republicanism of the Constitution and argued that the more democratic a republic was, the more it measured up to republican ideals. A republic, for Jefferson, meant "a government by its citizens in mass, acting directly and personally, according to rules established by the majority; and that every other government is more or less republican, in proportion as it has in its composition more or less of this ingredient of the direct action of the citizens." But Jefferson intended that these citizens would be well educated for their responsibilities, and in 1784 he developed an elaborate plan for "the More General Diffusion of Knowledge" by means of a system of state-supported public schooling. "I know no safe depository of the ultimate powers of the society but the people themselves," Jefferson wrote, "and if we think them not enlightened enough to exercise their control with a wholesome discretion, the remedy is not to take it from them, but to inform their discretion by education."[8]

By the second quarter of the nineteenth century, in the wake of the enfranchisement of most of the white male citizenry and their incorporation into the extraconstitutional institution of the mass political party, few American political leaders spoke ill of democracy, though many continued to worry over its practices. A general consensus on the necessity of public education for democratic citizenship persisted throughout the nineteenth century, holding within its confines those fearful of the consequences of democracy and those eager to expand its reach. Generally speaking, it was the former who took the initiative in consolidating a system of tax-supported, public schools. Such conservative Whigs as Horace Mann and Henry Bernard led a "common school" movement designed to provide the sort of education for these active, enfranchised farmers and artisans that would contain this democratic impulse and forestall any threat it might pose to private property and social order. "It may be an easy thing to make a Republic," Mann remarked, "but it is a very laborious thing to make Republicans; and woe to the republic that rests upon no better foundations than ignorance, selfishness, and passion." For Americans, he argued, "the qualification of voters is as important as the qualification of governors, and even comes first, in the natural order":

> The theory of our government is, not that all men, however unfit, shall be voters,—but that every man, by the power of reason and the sense of duty, shall become fit to be a voter. Education must bring the practice as nearly as possi-

---

8. Thomas Jefferson to John Taylor, 28 May 1816; and Jefferson, "A Bill for the More General Diffusion of Knowledge" (1784), in Thomas Jefferson, *Writings* (New York: Library of America, 1984), 1392, 365–73; Thomas Jefferson to William C. Jarvis, 28 September 1820, in Paul L. Ford, ed., *The Writings of Thomas Jefferson* (New York: G.P. Putnam, 1899), 10:161.

ble to the theory. As the children now are, so will the sovereigns soon be. How can we expect the fabric of the government to stand, if vicious materials are daily wrought into its frame-work? Education must prepare our citizens to become municipal officers, intelligent jurors, honest witnesses, legislators, or competent judges of legislation—in fine, to fill all the manifold relations of life. For this end, it must be universal. The whole land must be watered with the streams of knowledge.

The common school, reformers argued, was the best defense against the common man. As one put it, "The best police for our cities, the lowest insurance of our houses, the firmest security for our banks, the most effective means of preventing pauperism, vice and crime, and the only sure defense of our country, are our common schools; and woe to us, if their means of education be not commensurate with the wants and powers of the people." As Ralph Waldo Emerson observed, such conservatives urged the cause of public education on the grounds that "the people have the power, and if they are not instructed to sympathize with the intelligent, reading, trading, and governing class, inspired with a taste for the same competitions and prizes, they will upset the fair pageant of Judicature, and perhaps lay a hand on the sacred muniments of wealth itself, and new distribute the land."[9]

The working people whom Mann and other reformers feared may not have appreciated the portrait of themselves offered in the literature of common school reform, but they shared with reformers a desire for universal education for citizens (that is, white males). No less than Mann did they wish to be citizens ruled by ignorance, selfishness, and passion, and they proved eager to educate their children for responsible democratic citizenship. Fierce critics of all forms of monopoly power and often wary of state authority, antebellum spokesmen for American "workingmen" were firm supporters of public education. Rush Welter exaggerates only a little when he characterizes their view of democratic public policy as that of "anarchy with a schoolmaster." Hence, the United States was unique among industrializing nations in that support for public education cut across class lines, a peculiarity that can be attributed to the fact that American workers were enfranchised before bourgeois reformers attempted to deploy the power of the state to educate them. As two historians of social class and schooling in America have said, "the dominant classes feared disorder, articulated their concerns in terms of civic virtue, and pursued educational reform as an in-

9. Horace Mann, "Twelfth Annual Report" (1848), in Lawrence Cremin, ed., *The Republic and the School: Horace Mann on the Education of Free Men* (New York: Teachers College Press, 1957), 92; Mann, *Lectures on Education* (Boston: William B. Fowle, 1848), 57–58; Alonzo Potter of Utica, New York, as quoted in Jonathan Messerli, *Horace Mann: A Biography* (New York: Knopf, 1972), 373; Ralph Waldo Emerson, "The Conservative" (1841), in Emerson, *Essays and Lectures* (New York: Library of America, 1983), 186.

strument of order. The working classes, like working classes elsewhere, strongly desired schooling for their children. But, unlike some other working classes, they were prepared to join in political coalitions favoring public schooling because they had already been mobilized by political parties into the state as voting citizens."[10]

This is not to say that there was not significant political conflict over the shape of common schooling in the nineteenth century, nor to ignore the exclusive character of nineteenth-century American citizenship and common schooling, which was largely schooling for white, northern students. Nor is it to offer a brief for the sort of education for democratic citizenship that the common schools offered their pupils, an education grounded in rote learning from texts such as Noah Webster's spellers and William McGuffey's readers, texts that extolled the virtues of obedience and an unthinking patriotism.[11] But it is to point up the "common-ness" of common schooling, the fact that it was schooling for the role that the children it reached would come to share whatever their social class. Whatever the limitations and shortcomings of the civic education these schools provided, they did—as schools putatively dedicated to education for citizenship—furnish a setting in which a struggle for a more genuinely democratic civic education might be waged.

My assessment of nineteenth-century common schools parallels the view I have offered elsewhere of the partisan politics that helped occasion them. We do ourselves a disservice, I have argued, if we "weave a democratic romance" around the nineteenth-century American political parties, as scholars such as Walter Dean Burnham have been prone to do. Nonetheless, this is not to say that "the possibilities of democracy in America have not been adversely affected by the decline of the party" over the course of the twentieth century. The political party was the one broadly participatory institution in American political life, and, for this reason, it was the one institution that held within it the promise of a more expansive democracy. It was the genius of the Populists to see this and to attempt to reconstruct and radicalize the participatory practices of the party system in order to democratize control of the political economy. Their defeat and the subsequent decay of these practices and the partisan culture that fostered them cut most

10. Rush Welter, *Popular Education and Democratic Thought in America* (New York: Columbia University Press, 1962), 50; Ira Katznelson and Margaret Weir, *Schooling for All: Class, Race, and the Decline of the Democratic Ideal* (New York: Basic Books, 1985), 45.

11. For a good account of common school practice, see Jean H. Baker, *Affairs of Party: The Political Culture of Northern Democrats in the Mid-Nineteenth Century* (Ithaca: Cornell University Press, 1983), 71–107. As studies such as Baker's of nineteenth-century American political culture make clear, the schools were not the only nor the most important agencies of civic education. Children learned as much if not more from the rich, expressive rituals and popular culture of the public and partisan life they encountered outside the classroom as they did from the pieties conveyed by their schoolteachers.

Americans off from the active role in organized public life that might have been theirs.[12]

The struggle for democratic civic education was cut short by the dramatic transformation of American public schools in the early twentieth century. Nineteenth-century common schooling had been rooted, like much of American culture, in the hope for a "one-class" society of petty proprietors. Wage labor was perceived as a temporary stage for American workers on their way to independent ownership of productive property; schooling was designed to educate workers who would eventually achieve such a "competence." By the late nineteenth century it was clear to many that the development of industrial capitalism meant that wage labor would be the permanent condition of most Americans. A new wave of reformers, many of them as fearful of the nation's plain people as their antebellum predecessors, launched a series of "progressive" reforms designed to wrest political power from partisan machines tied to working class voters and invest it in the hands of a new middle class of managerial experts. At the same time, they moved to create a system of public schools that aimed less at common schooling for democratic citizenship than at differentiated schooling devised to accommodate the needs of an economy believed to be divided permanently along class lines. "Increasing specialization in all fields of labor has divided the people into dozens of more or less clearly defined classes," observed reformer Ellwood P. Cubberley. "The employee tends to remain an employee; the wage earner tends to remain a wage earner." Public schools, especially urban ones, had to accommodate this reality, he declared. "Our city schools will soon be forced to give up the exceedingly democratic idea that all are equal, and that our society is devoid of classes, as a few cities have already in large part done, and to begin a specialization of educational effort along many new lines in an attempt better to adapt the school to the needs of these many classes in the city life."[13]

In the first two decades of the twentieth century, reformers in alliance with business interests launched a campaign for "industrial education" that focused on the transformation of the American high school, seeking to change this elite, college-preparatory bastion of the upper-middle class into a socially diverse institution designed to prepare boys and girls for jobs in the higher reaches of blue collar labor and the lower echelons of white col-

12. See Robert B. Westbrook, "Politics as Consumption: Managing the Modern American Election," in Richard W. Fox and T. J. Jackson Lears, eds., *The Culture of Consumption* (New York: Pantheon, 1983), 151–52. The most comprehensive and effective effort to offer a clear-eyed view of nineteenth-century popular politics is Glenn C. Altschuler and Stuart M. Blumin, *Rude Republic: Americans and Their Politics in the Nineteenth Century* (Princeton: Princeton University Press, 2000).

13. Ellwood P. Cubberley, *Changing Conceptions of Education* (Boston: Houghton Mifflin, 1909), 10, 56–57.

lar work. In this, they were quite successful. Between 1890 and 1920 enrollment in high schools grew from 200,000 to almost 2 million students, and the percentage of those fourteen to seventeen years of age in high school grew from 6.7 percent to 32.3 percent. The high school curriculum in 1890 was centered on instruction in classical and modern languages, mathematics, and science, but by the 1920s students were also studying such things as mechanical drawing, woodworking, ironworking, pattern making, cooking, bookkeeping, stenography, typing, and commercial law. "For a long time all boys were trained to be President," the president of the Muncie, Indiana school board told sociologists Robert and Helen Lynd. "Then for a while we trained them all to be professional men. Now we are training boys to get jobs."[14]

An even more radical effort by the advocates of industrial education to create a dual school system with separate vocational schools controlled by businessmen was, however, a failure. It met with stiff opposition from a coalition of labor unions, teachers, parents, and critics anxious to hang on to the common school tradition. At the 1915 convention of the National Education Association, industrial education supporter J. Stanley Brown accurately (and somewhat ruefully) described this debate as one that pitted parents and various "social, ethical, and religious organizations" who wanted the student "to develop his own life in the way which seemed best to his parent and himself and that his duties as a citizen demand" against "manufacturers, the commercialists, or the industrialists" who were less concerned with schooling the boy to be "the best citizen, the most honest and careful man" than with making "every individual employee subordinate to the production of his particular institution." The defenders of "unitary" schooling managed to defeat the proponents of a separate system for vocational education, but their victory was a Pyrrhic one. For the upshot of this conflict was the creation of the comprehensive high school in which students were "tracked" into separate vocational and liberal arts curricula—in sum, a dual system under one roof.[15]

The leading advocates of industrial education insisted that their reform program was a democratic one since it provided schooling adapted to the particular needs of each student. Because students of different classes faced very different work lives after they left school, reformers argued, they were best served by a differentiated education that took account of this fact. On this rendering, as historian David Nasaw has said, "democracy meant offer-

14. Robert L. Church and Michael Sedlak, *Education in the United States: An Interpretive History* (New York: Free Press, 1976), 289; Lawrence A. Cremin, *American Education: The Metropolitan Experience, 1876–1980* (New York: Harper and Row, 1988), 544–47; Robert and Helen Lynd, *Middletown* (New York: Harcourt, Brace, and World, 1929), 194.

15. J. Stanley Brown, as quoted in David Nasaw, *Schooled to Order: A Social History of Public Schooling in the United States* (New York: Oxford, 1979), 150.

ing every student the opportunity for an education equally adjusted to what school officials assumed would be his or her future vocation." If schools were to be a functional component of a society permanently divided along class lines, these proponents of "social efficiency" argued, they had not only to educate all social classes but also educate them differently.[16]

In a sense, this transformation of the high school did make for a more democratic, or at least a more egalitarian, system of public education. For it meant more hours and days of schooling for more children, and greater access to the higher reaches of secondary education for children of the white working class—access that was eventually extended to racial and ethnic minorities as well.[17] But this was an access to schooling that now served, above all, to reproduce the inegalitarian social order of the larger society, schooling that no longer offered much common schooling for democratic citizenship, the one role that lay in the future of children of all classes.

Civic education did not disappear from American public schools with the triumph of vocationalism, and in the midst of concern about such matters as the "Americanization" of immigrants and the challenge of international communism, periodic calls have gone out for its invigoration. Generally speaking, however, education for democratic citizenship has been increasingly marginalized in public schools, a status perhaps best indicated by its consignment to a narrow range of courses in "social studies."

What arguments have been advanced for the importance of civic education have defined citizenship in terribly banal and generally nonpolitical terms. In the *Cardinal Principles of Secondary Education* (1918) citizenship was characterized as "a many-sided interest in the welfare of the communities to which one belongs; loyalty to ideals of civic righteousness; practical knowledge of social agencies and institutions; good judgment as to means and methods that will promote one social end without defeating others; and as putting all these into effect, habits of cordial cooperation in social undertakings." This sort of bland mush, with its understanding of citizenship as a set of essentially *social* attitudes and practices, has persisted to this day. Core courses in citizenship have passed from history to civics to various ventures in social science, including courses in "values clarification" in which a host of values are "clarified" but few values in particular are defended as essential to democracy and thereby exemplary.[18]

Even educational reformers who are apparently alert to and concerned about the thinness of American citizenship are unable to muster much of a

16. Nasaw, *Schooled to Order,* 132.

17. See Patricia Albjerg Graham, "What America Has Expected of Its Schools over the Past Century," *American Journal of Education* 101 (1993): 83–98.

18. *Cardinal Principles of Secondary Education* (Washington: Government Printing Office, 1918), 13. On values clarification and democratic values, see Battistoni, *Public Schooling,* 92–93.

response. For example, Ernest L. Boyer, reporting on American secondary education in 1983 for the Carnegie Foundation for the Advancement of Teaching, noted that "the Jeffersonian vision of grassroots democracy" had come to seem "increasingly utopian" and "civic illiteracy" was spreading. "Unless we find better ways to educate ourselves as citizens," he said, "we run the risk of drifting unwittingly into a new kind of Dark Age—a time when, increasingly, specialists will control knowledge and the decision-making process." But Boyer, like many others, defines this crisis as one of citizens' "ignorance about government and how it functions," and he recommends little more than a few courses in civics. But if students knew more about how American government functioned, they would only then be aware of how fully "the decision-making process" had in fact drifted into the hands of specialists, and the question would remain how they might be educated to stem this drift. Few critics have been so bold as to suggest that democratic civic education is a matter not only of knowing about politics but of acquiring the knowledge, the skills, and the moral dispositions one needs to engage in a full measure of self-government. To conceive of civic education as a matter of accruing data about politics rather than political "know-how" is characteristic of the modern fetish of "information." Information, no matter how equitably distributed, is less important for democracy than deliberation. As Christopher Lasch remarked,

> What democracy requires is public debate, not information. Of course it needs information, too, but the kind of information it needs can be generated only by vigorous popular debate. We do not know what we need to know until we ask the right questions, and we can identify the right questions only by subjecting our own ideas about the world to the test of public controversy. Information, usually seen as the precondition of debate, is better understood as its by-product. When we get into arguments that focus and fully engage our attention, we become avid seekers of relevant information. Otherwise we take in information passively—if we take it in at all.[19]

Few have had the temerity to point out that this larger task of cultivating political know-how would require democrats to put civic education at the heart of public schooling and to figure out how not only courses in civics but the entire public school curriculum might serve this purpose.[20]

On the whole, then, the twentieth century has witnessed the rapid rise to preeminence of schooling for what one report termed "occupational com-

19. "The Lost Art of Argument" in Lasch, *The Revolt of the Elites and the Betrayal of Democracy* (New York: Norton, 1994), 162–63).

20. Ernest L. Boyer, *High School: A Report on Secondary Education in America* (New York: Harper and Row, 1983), 105–6. An exception is Battistoni, *Public Schooling*, to which I shall return.

petence" and the relegation of civic education to, at best, an afterthought. Once the principal institution for vocational training, the high school has now become for many students a way station on their path to enrollment in a new layer of "differentiated" schooling that emerged with the explosive growth of institutions of mass higher education in the last sixty years. One is far more likely to hear one's child spoken of as "human capital" than as a citizen in waiting. American public schools have become, above all, a vast, variegated system funneling this human capital into its final destination in the hierarchies of the undemocratic world of modern work.[21]

Reconstructing Civic Education

What one makes of this history depends on the democratic theory to which one subscribes. Few Americans openly admit to being antidemocratic; instead, we argue about what democracy should mean. Since the 1920s, American democratic theory has been dominated by thinkers who have advanced views under the banner of "democratic realism," a view similar to that which founders such as Hamilton had no qualms about proudly declaring undemocratic realism. Such "neo-Hamiltonians," as Barber has termed them,

> insist that the public mind must be filtered and refined through the cortex of its betters. Give everyone the franchise, but don't let them do anything much with it. Protect them from the government with a sturdy barrier of rights, but protect government from them with a representative system that guarantees they will not themselves be legislators. In short, let them vote the governors in and out, but don't let them govern themselves. Let them enjoy freedom from government, but don't let them govern themselves freely.

Such democrats can regard the collapse of common schooling and the marginalization of civic education with equanimity, for by their lights democratic citizenship is not terribly ill-served by prevailing practice. Since citizenship need not amount to much, there is no need to devote much of our educational resources to training our children for its practice.[22]

The triumph of this neo-Hamiltonian democratic theory has accompa-

---

21. National Commission on the Reform of Secondary Education, *The Reform of Secondary Education* (New York: McGraw-Hill, 1973), 32–33, 49–61. On the explosion of vocationally oriented higher education, see Daniel O. Levine, *The American College and the Culture of Aspiration, 1915–1940* (Ithaca: Cornell University Press, 1986); and Steven Brint and Jerome Karabel, *The Diverted Dream: Community Colleges and the Promise of Educational Opportunity in America, 1900–1985* (New York: Oxford, 1989).

22. Benjamin Barber, *An Aristocracy of Everyone: The Politics of Education and the Future of America* (New York: Ballantine, 1992), 244. For a brief history of the development of the neo-Hamiltonian theory, see Robert B. Westbrook, *John Dewey and American Democracy* (Ithaca: Cornell University Press, 1991), 280–86, 543–46.

nied the steady desiccation of American citizenship since the turn of the twentieth century and served to legitimate it. Since the 1890s electoral participation by American citizens has declined dramatically, political parties have decomposed, and public life has become a sideshow for most Americans, if that. Periodically, we are reminded of our citizenship by election campaigns in which candidates are packaged by professional consultants for sale to television audiences whose opinions are packaged by pollsters for sale to candidates. It does not require much education to participate in this sort of spectatorial, consumer politics, and not surprisingly, elections are a market in which many alienated, preoccupied, or uninterested citizens fail to shop.[23] If this be sufficient democracy, then there is little need for a reconstruction of civic education. Neo-Hamiltonians are, to be sure, no less fearful of an ignorant democratic public than their Hamiltonian ancestors, but unlike those ancestors, they do not confront a public widely organized into participatory political institutions. There is little to fear from the uneducated nonvoter, and the "party" of nonvoters is our largest. Hence, neo-Hamiltonians look not to education but to indifference for the protection of social order from the unruly mob; apathy, they argue, has its virtues.

But American two-mindedness about democracy has remained very much in evidence in the twentieth century and beyond, and neo-Hamiltonian theory has not gone unopposed. For modern democrats of a more Jeffersonian turn of mind, the neglect of civic education in American public schools is deeply troubling. Among those concerned about democracy and public schooling, perhaps no thinker is more significant than John Dewey. Dewey was not only the most important advocate among modern liberal intellectuals of an expansive participatory democracy, but throughout his career he addressed himself to the pivotal role of the school in fostering such a democracy.

At the heart of Dewey's work as both a philosopher and an activist was a belief that democracy as an ethical ideal called on men and women to build communities in which the necessary opportunities and resources were available for every individual to realize fully his or her particular capacities and powers through participation in political, social, and cultural life. This ideal, he said, rested on a "faith in the capacity of human beings for intelligent judgment and action if proper conditions are furnished"—a faith, he argued, "so deeply embedded in the methods which are intrinsic to democracy that when a professed democrat denies the faith he convicts himself of treachery to his profession." Education in a democracy, as Dewey saw it, had to be guided by this ideal and sustained by this faith.[24]

23. Westbrook, "Politics as Consumption," 152–73.
24. John Dewey, "Creative Democracy: The Task Before Us" (1939), *Later Works,* 14:227.

One might reasonably view Dewey's work in the philosophy and practice of education as an effort to reconstruct "common schooling" so that it might remain pertinent to modern industrial democracies. He was a bitter critic of the industrial education movement in the early twentieth century, and he struggled to envision an education for the world's work that would not foster class divisions or preclude schooling for the shared tasks that democratic citizens had to undertake together. All members of a democratic society, he believed, were entitled to an education that would enable them to make the best of themselves as active and equal participants in the life of their community.[25]

For a child to become an effective member of a democratic community, Dewey argued, he must have "training in science, in art, in history; command of the fundamental methods of inquiry and the fundamental tools of intercourse and communication," as well as "a trained and sound body, skillful eye and hand; habits of industry, perseverance, and, above all, of serviceableness." In a democratic community children had to learn to be leaders as well as followers, possessed of "power of self-direction and power of directing others, powers of administration, ability to assume positions of responsibility" as citizens and workers. Because the world was a rapidly changing one, children could not, moreover, be educated for any "fixed station in life," but schools had to provide each child with training that would "give him such possession of himself that he may take charge of himself; may not only adapt himself to the changes which are going on, but have power to shape and direct those changes."[26]

The critical task of Deweyan or neo-Jeffersonian democratic educators, of course, is to figure out what civic education in the public schools for a more expansive citizenship would look like. Dewey himself, alas, had relatively little to say about the particulars of civic education, though most of what he had to say about "democracy and education" is at least indirectly relevant. But since Deweyan democrats are not a particularly noteworthy presence among those few critics who have devoted much attention to civic education in the schools, guidance is hard to come by. The most satisfying extended treatment of this issue I have found is in Richard Battistoni's *Public Schooling and the Education of Democratic Citizens*, though here I can only sketch the bare outline of the proposals he advances.[27]

Beyond providing students with literacy and other basic skills in mathe-

25. On Dewey's criticisms of industrial education, see Westbrook, *John Dewey and American Democracy*, 173–82.

26. John Dewey, "The School as a Social Centre" (1902), *Middle Works*, 2:93; Dewey, "Ethical Principles Underlying Education" (1897), *Early Works*, 5:59–60.

27. Even Battistoni confines himself largely to the high school, and he says nothing about the internal and external structures of authority and power in the school, structures that Dewey contended had to be made more democratic than they were in his time and ours.

matics, Battistoni argues that the goal of education for democratic citizenship should be that of "developing in students skills and attitudes necessary to direct participation in political affairs, as well as a set of substantive values which underlie our political institutions and procedures." This task, as he sees it, calls for a number of reforms. The civics curriculum must be rethought, and history must be returned to a central place in its offerings—not history as a "parade of institutional and historical facts," not history as the bland pieties of most school textbooks, but history as the story of the conflict-ridden formation of the complex tradition within which all American citizens must exercise their practical judgment.[28] Moreover, civics instruction should openly and unapologetically teach the values that must underlie democratic politics. As Battistoni says:

> Fundamental to democratic citizenship are principles such as democratic equality and justice; a belief in every person's ability and responsibility to participate in public affairs; a concern for the dignity of each individual and her or his personal choices, combined with a dedication to cooperating and sharing experiences; a commitment to resolve public disputes through a process of reasoned debate and conflict *transformation;* and an attachment to public affairs and one's fellow citizens.

Unlike most others who have called for a revitalized civics curriculum, Battistoni contends that it should include more than courses offered under the rubric of "civics" or "social studies." As he says, "if we want students to be knowledgeable and capable of making decisions about the wide range of issues which constitute contemporary American politics, we should provide them with a broad-based secondary school education which includes the sciences, literature, and the arts as well as history and government. This means that teachers in all high school disciplines must be aware of the connections between their particular lessons and desirable civic skills and attitudes." Teachers of literature have as much to teach future citizens as teachers of history, and for democrats "compartmentalized learning in secondary schools must come to an end."[29]

Civic education, Battistoni cogently argues, must not only educate students for participatory politics but also that education itself must be participatory. By this he means not only that learning in the classroom should take the form of joint deliberation but also that students should be encouraged to move beyond the walls of the school and explore the civic life of adults in

28. For an even more compelling argument for the importance of history to civic education, see Eamonn Callan, "Beyond Sentimental Civic Education," *American Journal of Education* 102 (1994): 190–221.

29. Battistoni, *Public Schooling,* 187–90. For a powerful example of the use of literature—in this case, Eudora Welty's story, "Where Is the Voice Coming From?"—to teach civic values, see Callan, "Beyond Sentimental Civic Education," 212–14.

class assignments and internships. Finally, Battistoni argues that "to provide a more complete civic education for future citizens, we must integrate not only courses and activities but also *students* from different backgrounds and interests"—schools must once again be common, and the comprehensive high school must be defended from its critics and "untracked." As Battistoni is well aware, his proposals—particularly this last one—reach deep into the heart of the most bitter conflicts embroiling American society. As he concludes, "Many of the factors mitigating against a renewal of the public high school are part of larger problems in American society as a whole (racial and ethnic conflicts, 'white flight' from urban areas, privatization of interests, economic instabilities, the decline in local and urban communities), and major changes in society may be necessary" before the public schools can provide the sort of education he recommends.[30]

I would imagine that to those given to what Battistoni calls "participatory-republicanism" his proposals will be attractive or at least of the sort with which a productive argument about civic education might begin. But participatory-republicanism is a minority and adversarial view to which few Americans are committed, or of which many are even aware. Civic education of the sort Battistoni recommends would be a hard sell, especially to those who have invested so heavily in "differentiated" schooling for "occupational competence." In some respects, to be sure, there need be no necessary conflict between preparing children for a more active citizenship and girding them for competition in "the global marketplace." Education for public life and education for work are not inherently at cross purposes. In the nineteenth century, for example, American democrats believed that petty proprietorship was an essential foundation for democratic citizenship because it cultivated the skills and virtues (above all, the independence) requisite to good democrats. As Abraham Lincoln told an audience of Wisconsin farmers in 1859, "In these Free States, a large majority are neither *hirers* nor *hired*. Men, with their families—wives, sons and daughters—work for themselves, on their farms, in their houses, and in their shops, taking the whole product to themselves, and asking no favors of capital on the one hand, nor of hirelings or slaves on the other." Such citizens, he declared, "can never be the victim of oppression in any of its forms. Such community will be alike independent of crowned-kings, money-kings, and land-kings."[31]

It is much more difficult—some would say impossible—to make the case for wage labor as a reinforcing influence on democratic citizenship.[32] Yet

30. Battistoni, *Public Schooling*, 190–94.

31. Abraham Lincoln, "Address to the Wisconsin State Agricultural Society" (1859), in Lincoln, *Speeches and Writings, 1859–1865* (New York: Library of America, 1989), 97, 100.

32. For a forceful argument for the incompatibility between wage labor and democratic citizenship, see Herbert Croly, *Progressive Democracy* (New York: Macmillan, 1914), 378–405.

insofar as American employers have become disenchanted with a merely docile workforce suited to the unskilled jobs that are becoming in increasingly short supply and are calling for workers in full command of basic skills and possessed of a disposition for lifelong learning, the purposes of citizenship and capitalism might coincide, at least in part. As Deborah Meier has said, if schools take their task to be that of teaching children "to become learners (not learn*ed* but a learn*er*)," they will cultivate such habits as "being reliable, someone you can count on, resilient, capable of dealing with frustration, not expecting certainties and absolutes" that are essential to all "decent worthy human vocations. Including the vocation of citizen." But whether American employers would appreciate employees armed not only with technical skills and these admirable habits but also with the capacity and desire to deliberate on the ends of the enterprise and the economy is another question. Here one is entitled to greater skepticism about any simple, unproblematic grafting of education for participatory citizenship onto the prevailing aims and purposes of American schools. Dewey, at least, argued that schooling for democracy would only be fully functional when democracy had been extended to the workplace.[33]

Revitalizing Democratic Publics

Even if one could make American public schools more effective vehicles of civic education, it would not be worth doing as long as American public life remains as anemic as it is today. As the neo-Hamiltonians contend, there is no point to educating children for a citizenship that will not be there to practice when they become adults. One could argue, I suppose, that students educated for a more participatory democracy might lead the struggle to create it. In this fashion, the schools would serve as the principal agency of democratic social change; it would be the schools, as George Counts once put it, that would dare to build a new social order.[34] But one might just as easily imagine such students drifting into cynicism when confronted with the thoroughly dysfunctional character of their education. And, in any case, one cannot expect adults to commit their tax dollars to schools whose purposes they fail to understand or appreciate. Nor can democrats expect ready assent to their project from those who have turned the schools to their current, often contrary, purposes. The schools simply are not an independent locomotive of social transformation sitting idly on a siding, readily available for democratic engineers who would take the controls.

33. Deborah Meier, "A Talk to Teachers," *Dissent* (winter 1994): 82, 84.
34. George S. Counts, *Dare the School Build a New Social Order?* (New York: John Day, 1932).

Thus neo-Jeffersonians must commit themselves not only to a reconstruction of civic education but also to a much broader revitalization of American public life—an even taller order. Jefferson himself recognized this task. He called not only for the civic education of all citizens, but also for the creation of the public spaces for the exercise of the popular sovereignty that the Constitution had neglected to mandate. He proposed that the state of Virginia be divided "into wards of such size as that every citizen can attend, when called on, and act in person." Such a ward system, he argued, "by making every citizen an acting member of the government, and in the offices nearest and most interesting to him, will attach him by his strongest feelings to the independence of his country, and its republican constitution." Dewey shared Jefferson's conviction about both the necessity and the insufficiency of democratic schooling for the making of a more democratic public life. "It is unrealistic, in my opinion," he wrote in 1937, "to suppose that the schools can be a *main* agency in producing the intellectual and moral changes, the changes in attitudes and disposition of thought and purpose, which are necessary for the creation of a new social order." The defects of schools mirrored and sustained the defects of the larger society, and these defects could not be remedied apart from a struggle for democracy throughout that larger society. Schools would take part in democratic social change only "as they ally themselves with this or that movement of existing social forces." Like Jefferson, Dewey believed democracy must rest ultimately on active, face-to-face, local publics. "Democracy must begin at home," he said, "and its home is the neighborly community."[35]

Apart from the civic education it provides to children, the school—that is, the school building—might play a role in this larger project. The idea of "community schools" has been revived in recent years. These schools would serve not only to educate children in a neighborhood but also function as wider social centers for adults as well as children, remaining open in the late afternoon and early evening to serve this larger community. For the most part, recent community school initiatives have been conceived as contributing to a more humane, efficient, and democratic means of meeting the social welfare needs of the American poor. Community schools, their advocates have argued, might serve as centers for job training, recreation, health care, adult education, and other social services. In the most imaginative programs, the school curriculum is integrated with provision of these services, as in a school in West Philadelphia in which the studies of

35. Thomas Jefferson to Samuel Kercheval, 12 July 1816, in Jefferson, *Writings,* 1399; John Dewey, "Education and Social Change" (1937), *Later Works,* 11:414; Dewey, "Can Education Share in Social Reconstruction?" (1934), *Later Works,* 9:207; Dewey, *The Public and Its Problems* (1927), *Later Works,* 2:368. See also Dewey's appreciative account of Jefferson's ward system in "Presenting Thomas Jefferson" (1940), *Later Works,* 14:213–18.

middle school students have been folded into their active participation in neighborhood health care services. In their most radical formulations, community school programs foresee what Michael Walzer has termed a "socialization of the welfare state," which would thoroughly decentralize the distribution of social welfare services and solicit the participation of those who receive these services in their management.[36]

This sort of community school project is an important democratic initiative. But community schools might also well serve efforts to revitalize local, democratic publics, for in many neighborhoods the school is the one remaining public space of any significance, and it might conceivably serve as a site for citizens to gather and deliberate. And, as such, it might serve not only the poor but all American citizens. Anemic citizenship is not only a problem in the inner city. Indeed, few developments have been more damaging to participatory democracy than the mass exodus of American citizens to the suburbs—the preeminent landscape of the overweening claims of private life in this country.

During the early twentieth century, when the rich possibilities of community schools were first broached, some of their proponents grasped the opportunities they might afford deliberative democracy. In Rochester, New York, Edward Ward led a "social centers" movement that for a brief time (1907–1911) established local, democratic publics in many of that city's neighborhood schools, and then spread to a number of other cities in the years immediately preceding World War I. Like other neo-Jeffersonian democrats, Ward was distressed that American citizenship had been reduced for most to little more than voting, and that voting had been detached from the joint deliberation with other citizens that would render public opinion informed and reflective. "The people," he said, "is a great vegetable." If the public was to regain its animal spirits, it had to be organized in small, deliberative bodies. As he said, "When the members of the electorate add to their common function of participating in the decision upon public questions, the function of consciously organizing to deliberate upon public questions, then the people become a reasoning, a self-knowing being."[37]

Civic education for children, Ward argued, must be connected with active citizenship for adults. Children who went to schools by day that served adult

---

36. Michael Walzer, "Socializing the Welfare State" in Amy Gutmann, ed., *Democracy and the Welfare State* (Princeton: Princeton University Press, 1988), 13–26. On the Philadelphia community schools project, see Ira Harkavy and John L. Puckett, "Toward Effective University-Public School Partnerships: An Analysis of a Contemporary Model," *Teachers College Record* 92 (1991): 556–81; and Lee Benson and Ira Harkavy, "Progressing Beyond the Welfare State," *Universities and Community Schools* 2 (spring–summer 1991): 2–28.

37. Edward J. Ward, *The Social Center* (New York: Appleton, 1913), 69. For introducing me to Ward and the social centers movement, I am indebted to Kevin Mattson. See his *Creating a Democratic Public: The Struggle for Urban Participatory Democracy During the Progressive Era* (University Park: Pennsylvania State University Press, 1998), 48–67, 105–29.

citizens in the evening could gain a palpable sense of the public life for which they were preparing themselves. "The great central object of the training of youth is the development of good citizenship; the great difficulty is in the visualizing of the business of democracy," Ward observed. Schools that were used for deliberation and voting gave students a "point of contact from which they may go on to the understanding of the civic process as a reality." Young people would be welcomed into the common rooms of their schools to hear their parents deliberate, and here they could make concrete sense of the purposes of their schooling. As Ward put it, "Where the man is, there is the boy's heart, also. When the adults of the community are using the neighborhood building for actual political expression in common council then the idea of citizenship is visualized" and schooling becomes a "civic apprenticeship." If, as Deborah Meier says, the shortcomings of American schooling can be linked to the fact that "what we do in schools bears little resemblance to anything that we can convince kids powerful adults do later on in their lives," then maybe there is something to be learned from this lamentably short-lived social centers movement.[38]

There is some evidence that Americans might well take to a more participatory public life. For example, recounting his efforts to initiate a "national conversation" about American pluralism, Sheldon Hackney, the former chairman of the National Endowment for the Humanities, reported that he was met with an enthusiastic response from citizens who gathered in local communities throughout the country to discuss such questions as "what holds our diverse society together, what values we need to share if we are to succeed as a democratic society, what it means to be American as we approach the 21st century." Not only were these conversations, as Hackney described them, exemplary of the discussions one might expect to find in local, democratic publics, they seemed to whet the appetite for further debate. At the end of the discussions, Hackney says, the question generally asked was "How can we continue to meet and pursue this subject?" One might well have taken this question as an invitation to help organize more permanent publics, though unfortunately Hackney proposed to move in another direction. The NEH, he said, was to make a film on American pluralism for broadcast on television, using "mass communications to broaden the conversational circle." But mass communications do not broaden conversational circles; they preclude them.[39]

Even though one might take this example as a hopeful glimmering of "dialogical community," any effort in the present to extend American democracy and shape public schooling for that purpose will encounter enormous

38. Ward, *Social Center,* 17, 128; Meier, "Talk to Teachers," 83.
39. Sheldon Hackney, "Organizing a National Conversation," *Chronicle of Higher Education* (20 April 1994): A56.

obstacles—most of them far more daunting than the myopia of such men of good will as Sheldon Hackney. As one friend of mine has astutely asked, "Would the boy (or girl) today really rather listen to his father (or her mother) deliberating at school, or would both prefer to be home playing video games, watching tv, or instant messaging their friends? Would the fathers and mothers prefer to be doing the same thing?"[40] And whatever lessons we might take from Ward and his Rochester experiment, one must be the lesson of its defeat within a few years at the hands of powerful interests—in this case, machine politicians—threatened by a more democratic politics.[41] In an inegalitarian society, those with much to lose are right to be wary of deliberative gatherings of those with much to gain from its reconstruction. If democracy was in the interest of those who hold the reins of power in the United States, we would have more of it.

So what is to be done, or, at least, where might democrats begin? I have little doubt that sociologist Theda Skocpol is right to suggest that an important step that Americans could take to reinvigorate democracy would be to stem the tide toward professionally managed advocacy groups and return to a system of interest-advocacy by federated "membership-based associations" (of whatever ideological persuasion, tree-hugging environmentalists and Bible-quoting Christian conservatives alike). Such associations, in which the rank-and-file do not merely pay dues but themselves undertake much of the work of the association, provide "opportunities for the many to participate in organized endeavors alongside the elite few." And Skocpol is right, as well, to worry over the recent calls for civic engagement that have been marked by an obsessive localism detached from politics. "Classic American voluntary groups were built by and for the citizens of a nation on the move," she observes. "These associations expressed broadly shared identities and values, engaged in raucous conflict with one another, and linked local people to state, regional, and national centers of power."[42]

Yet it seems to me that Jefferson, Dewey, and Ward were nonetheless correct to contend that we must also make more of a space in local, face-to-face settings in which citizens can come together regularly less to advocate settled views than to deliberate face-to-face about matters of shared concern, be it the prospect of a new Wal-Mart Superstore in their community or a for-

40. James Kloppenberg to Robert Westbrook, 9 June 2004.

41. Community schools—and the deliberative publics that might gather in them—require money to keep them going. And if the activities of citizens are to be the activities of *citizens*, they must be publicly funded. This places a powerful weapon in the hands of those like the politicians who killed the Rochester movement in its infancy. No American opponent of a more democratic politics is likely to attack it as too democratic, but many lie in wait to contend that it is too expensive.

42. Theda Skopol, *Diminished Democracy: From Membership to Management in American Civic Life* (Norman: University of Oklahoma Press, 2003), 254, 256.

eign war in which their sons and daughters are dying. To be sure, if such fo-rums are little more than "talking shops," few citizens will likely attend to them, preferring to stick to their TV and video screens. But in my experi-ence, if something of moment is at stake and if such forums are sites at which power, direct or indirect, is exercised, the people—or, at least, many of them—will come. And where better to locate this space than in the nation's elementary schools, existing buildings underutilized for hours each day and serving relatively small neighborhoods of tax-paying citizens?[43]

It was Dewey's hope, as it is the hope of neopragmatists including Hilary Putnam, Cheryl Misak, and Cornel West, that Americans would deliberate in such spaces not only as citizens but as pragmatists (whether they called themselves such or not). They would come to meetings believing that their debates were "truth-apt" in a "low-profile" sort of way, and hence they would delight in any consensus they might reach but be undeterred or undis-couraged by persistent disagreement and willing to revisit what had once seemed settled conviction. They would conduct their debates within the strictures of a "discourse ethics" that would invite a wide range of views and modes of argument. But those strictures would also preclude an open-mind-ededness through which their brains might fall out—Nazis might well be shown the door. And they would make sure the schools in which they met were doing all they could to provide the children of their community with the capacity to join the forum when they came of age. These Deweyan schools would be "supremely interesting places" that had become "the dangerous outposts of a humane civilization."[44] Here too, we have a long way to go.

It may be, as Michael Walzer once gloomily suggested, that in modern so-cieties citizenship will further wither in favor of more passionate identities of class, ethnicity, religion, and family that "do not draw people together but rather separate and divide them" and hence "make for the primacy of the private realm."[45] But to believe this is to guarantee the permanent eclipse of an expansive democratic citizenship—the will to disbelieve works in much the same self-fulfilling fashion as the will to believe. To imagine that American democracy can be reconstructed and revitalized requires, as John Dewey said, an abiding faith in the ability of ordinary men and women to educate themselves and their children for self-government and in their will to use the power at their disposal to wage the long struggle necessary to se-

43. In suggesting the need for more formal public space for democratic deliberation, I do not mean to ignore the important role that informal spaces—lunchrooms, coffeehouses, beauty shops, church basements, park benches, and so forth—continue to play in the Ameri-can public sphere.

44. John Dewey, "Education as Politics" (1922), *Middle Works,* 13:334.

45. Michael Walzer, "Citizenship," in Terence Ball, James Farr, and Russell L. Hanson, eds., *Political Innovation and Conceptual Change* (Cambridge: Cambridge University Press, 1989), 218.

cure the means of self-government.[46] Democrats of this neo-Jeffersonian sort must expect a torrent of criticism from neo-Hamiltonians who will charge that such a faith is utopian, unreasonable, and even reckless, and they must be prepared for frustrations, setbacks, and self-doubt.

But such is the fate of the hopeful, who here must be distinguished from the pessimistic. It is worth reminding ourselves that the emphasis of Christopher Lasch's splendid formulation of the meaning of hope, which I quoted at the outset of this tour of pragmatism and neopragmatism, can be reversed.[47] Recall that Lasch, inclined to worry more about blind sanguinity than myopic gloominess, sought above all to distinguish hope from optimism. But hope, as he well knew, must too be contrasted with pessimism. And so: Hope implies a deep-seated trust in life that appears absurd to those who lack it. The best is always what the hopeful are aiming for. Their trust in life would not be worth much if it had not enjoyed successes in the past, while the knowledge that the future holds further successes demonstrates the continuing need for hope. A dark despair that things will somehow only get worse, furnishes a poor substitute for the disposition to see things through even when they do.

46. Or, as Cornel West has said, echoing Dewey, "Democratic faith consists of a Pascalian wager (hence underdetermined by the evidence) on the abilities and capacities of ordinary people to participate in decision-making procedures and institutions that fundamentally regulate their lives." West, "The Limits of Neopragmatism" (1990), in West, *The Cornel West Reader* (New York: Basic Books, 1999), 186.

47. See the last paragraph of the Introduction of this book.

Index